AF519413

AIDS, NGOs and GLOBALISATION

AIDS, NGOs and GLOBALISATION

Tarun Bikash Sukai

AKANSHA PUBLISHING HOUSE
NEW DELHI • GUWAHATI • VISAKHAPATNAM

AKANSHA PUBLISHING HOUSE
4649-B/21, Ansari Road
Darya Ganj, New Delhi - 110 002
Ph.: 23263193 / 9811582579 / 09435116718
Fax: 011-23263193
Email: ektabooks@yahoo.com
www.akanshapublishinghouse.com

AIDS, NGOs and Globalisation

© Author

First Published 2010

ISBN 978-81-8370-240-9

All rights reserved. No part of this publication may be reproduced or transmitted, in any form or by any means, without prior permission of the author. Any person who does any unauthorized act in relation to this publication may be liable to criminal prosecution and civil claims for damages.

[The responsibility for the facts stated, conclusions reached etc., is entirely that of the author. The publisher is not responsible for them, whatsoever.]

PRINTED IN INDIA

Published by Akansha Publishing House, New Delhi and Printed at Harmain Offset Press, Delhi.

DEDICATED TO MY FAMILY

AND

ALL THOSE WHO ARE FIGHTING WITH

AND

AGAINST HIV / AIDS

Contents

III: AIDS, NGOs AND GLOBALISATION

IV: CONCLUSION

Preface

The human immunodeficiency virus (HIV), which causes acquired immunodeficiency syndrome (AIDS) is the leading infectious cause of adult deaths in the world. Since 1981, when AIDS was first reported in USA, it has spread widely affecting all countries including India. Given the scale of epidemic, AIDS is now considered not only a health problem, but also a developmental and security threat. Moreover, the epidemic is affecting developed and developing countries differently. Up to 95 percent of new infections now occur in developing countries, which are least equipped to respond the challenge effectively. Poverty, economic disparities, illiteracy , and culture and gender-related issues all contribute to India's vulnerability to HIV/AIDS and the enormous potential for the epidemic to spin out of control unless the problem is addressed properly. The valuable lessons learnt in different countries show that HIV/AIDS can be prevented with high political commitment, adequate financial and human resources, and sustained interventions. It is also clear that HIV/AIDS can't be tackled by the government alone, it requires a broad multi-sectoral response. Within this partnership, NGOs are also making significant contribution in HIV/AIDS prevention and care. So far India is concerned, NGOs like other countries, were first to respond especially in the initial years when response to HIV/AIDS from government was slow. Since its inception, National AIDS

Control Organisation (NACO) recognizes the importance of NGO participation and sought cooperation in all activities for the implementation of National AIDS Control Programme (NACP). A comprehensive guideline for the involvement of NGOs was drawn up in consultation with the representatives of NGOs and State AIDS Control Societies. However, is an exclusive reliance on NGOs a viable solution? Will NGOs be able to discharge their duties properly with limited finance? Are the beneficiaries happy with the services of NGOs? This book is a modest attempt to discuss all these issues. It intends to focus on NGOs in HIV/AIDS prevention and care in West Bengal. The book highlights the significant role that NGOs can perform and a critical appraisal of their ability in the context of globalisation.

In an explicit manner, the book is an outcome of my long drawn research in NGO sector. The data provided in this book have been collected and interpreted on the basis of a scientific methodology. The reason for selecting West Bengal is that it is placed in moderate prevalence states category by NACO where HIV infection rate has crossed 5 percent or more among the high-risk behaviour groups. With logical research framework and based on primary and secondary data, the book is divided into eleven chapters. Chapter-1 is an introductory part, which depicts global and national HIV/AIDS scenario and response to the epidemic in India. Chapter-2 gives an overview of relevant literature, while Chapter-3 marks the details of methodology. Chapter-4 draws a socio-economic picture of West Bengal and its HIV/AIDS scenario. Chapter-5 gives a state level overview of NGOs in HIV/AIDS care. The subsequent four Chapters (6, 7, 8, 9) have made a portrayal on contribution of NGOs in HIV/AIDS prevention and care in West Bengal. Chapter-10 is devoted to understand the role of NGOs in the context of globalisation. The last chapter stands to make a critical analysis. I wish that this book will be worth and useful for the government, NGOs, funding agencies, academicians and researchers in designing, implementing, monitoring and evaluating HIV/AIDS programmes.

At the end, I would like to acknowledge the active support and cooperation of many individuals and institutions. I am grateful to Prof. Asok Kumar Sarkar, my research guide, without whose constant support it would not have been possible to complete the entire work. Any acknowledgement of gratitude to him in words will not suffice here. I am equally grateful to Prof. N. B. Biswas, my research co-guide, for his valuable advice and encouragement throughout the research.

I extend my deep sense of gratitude to the key informants who provided primary data and to the higher level authorities of various NGOs who replied to the mailed questionnaires. I also gratefully acknowledge the cooperation and support of six NGOs such as Society for Community Intervention and Research, Durbar Mahila Samanwaya Committee, Bhoruka Public Welfare Trust, MANAS Bangla, Human Development Research Institute and Society for Positive Atmosphere and Related Support to HIV/AIDS, who have been the main source of information in case studies. In absence of their help, this work would not have been materialized. I would like to place on record my sincere thanks to Dr. K. Mishra and Dr. (Mrs.) I. Mazumdar (BPWT), Dr. D. P. Mallick (HDRI), Prof. R. Chakraborty and Mr. Sanjib Chakraborty (MB), Dr. P. Roy (DMSC), Mr. Simon (SCIR), Dr. S. Panda and Mr. Subhajit Banerjee (SPARSHA), Mr. Suresh Kumar, Dr. R. Shukla and Ms. Sohini Banerjee (WBSAP&CS), and Mr. Mahesh Nathan (WBPSU), without their support data collection of the study would not have been possible.

I am obliged to the librarians and their helping staff of Indira Gandhi National Open University, Voluntary Health Association of India, Jawaharlal Nehru University, Visva-Bharati University, Assam University, NIT (Silchar),

SAATHII (Kolkata) and American Library (Kolkata) for allowing me to consult the necessary documents and resource materials.

I shall remain ever grateful to Prof. Tapodhir Bhattacharjee, Hon'ble Vice Chancellor, Assam University for his encouragement and granting me the study leave to complete the present work. I extend my sincere thanks to Prof. G. Mishra, Dr. B. S. Gunjal, Dr. Subhabrata Dutta, Dr. M. Tineshowri Devi, Dr. Sanjoy Roy, Dr. M. Gangabhusan, Dr. Amalendu Chakraborty, Dr. Prajit Palit, Dr. Niranjan Roy, Dr. B. R. Choudhury and Dr. Bela Das for their continuous encouragement. I am also thankful to Mr. Alok Chakraborty, and Mr. Pulak Dhar for their active cooperation.

Without the support and encouragement from friends, colleagues and family members this work would not have been possible. My heartfelt gratitude goes to my parents and other family members, without their support and inspiration, this work would have never seen light of the day. I find no appropriate words to express my warm appreciation to my wife Rina who is the main source of my motivation and strength. I consider myself fortunate to have had such a loving family support.

Lastly, I am indebted to Akansha Publishing House, New Delhi for finalizing the manuscript and bringing out this book within a short period of time. The strength of this work belongs to the efforts of all these people, while the weaknesses are of mine alone.

Silchar

Tarun Bikash Sukai

List of Tables

List of Figures

List of Charts

Abbreviations

AAI	Accelerating Access Initiative
ACT UP	AIDS Coalition to Unleash Power
AIDS	Acquired Immuno Deficiency Syndrome
AIDSCAP	AIDS Control and Prevention Project
AIIH&PH	All India Institute of Hygiene & Public Health
APN+	Asia Pacific Network of People Living with HIV/AIDS
APCASO	Asia Pacific Council of AIDS Service Organisations
ANC	Antenatal Clinic
ART	Anti Retroviral Therapy
ARV	Anti-retroviral Drugs
ASO	AIDS Service Organisation
AusAID	Australian Agency for International Development
BCC	Behaviour Change Communication

BDO	Block Development Officer
BNP+	Bengal Network of People with HIV Positive
BPWT	Bhoruka Public Welfare Trust
BSS	Behavioural Surveillance Survey
CBO	Community Based Organisation
CBPC	Community Based Peer Counsellor
CCC	Community Care Centre
CCM	Country Coordinating Mechanism
CDMU	Community Development Medical Unit
CHV	Community Health Volunteer
CINI	Child In Need Institute
CMOH	Chief Medical Officer (Health)
CPT	Calcutta Port Trust
CRC	Convention on the Rights of the Child
CREA	Creating Resources for Empowerment in Action
CSO	Civil Society Organisation
CSW	Commercial Sex Worker
DACC	Darjeeling AIDS Control Centre
DFID	Department for International Department
DGHC	Darjeeling Gorkha Hill Council
DGHS	Director General of Health Services

DIC	Drop-in-centre
DMSC	Durbar Mahila Samannaya Commitee
DOTS	Directly Observed Treatment, Short courses
ELISA	Enzyme-Linked Immunosorbent Assay
FGD	Focussed Group Discussion
FHI	Family Health International
FSW	Female Sex Worker
GAVI	Global Alliance for Vaccines and Immunization
GD	Group Discussion
GFATM	Global Fund for AIDS, TB and Malaria
GIPA	Greater Involvement of People with AIDS
GOs	Government Organisations
GOI	Government of India
GPA	Global Programme on AIDS
GRP	Government Railway Police
HAART	Highly Active Antiretroviral Therapy
HDRI	Human Development Research Institute
Health GAP	Health Global Access Project
HIPC	Heavily Indebted Poor Countries
HIV	Human immunodeficiency virus
ICDS	Integrated Child Development Services

ICESCR	International Covenant on Economic, Social & Cultural Rights
ICMR	Indian Council of Medical Research
ICRW	International Commission on Research on Women
ICTC	Integrated Counselling and Testing Centres
IDU	Injecting Drug User
IEC	Information, education, communication
ILO	International Labour Organization
IMF	International Monetary Fund
INGO	International Non-Governmental Organisation
IPC	Indian Penal Code
ITPA	Immoral Traffic Prevention Act
KABP	Knowledge, Attitude, Behaviour and Practice
KNP+	Kolkata Network of HIV Positive People
LLO	Life Link Organisation (Nigeria)
MASUM	Mahila Sarvangeen Utkarsh Mandal
MANET	Malawi Network of People Living with HIV/AIDS
MB	MANAS Bangla
MDG	Millennium Development Goal
MIS	Management Information System

MSF	Medecins Sans Frontieres
MSM	Men having Sex with men
MTCT	Mother-to-Child-Transmission
MTP	Medium Term Plan
NACA	National Action Committee on AIDS
NACOSA	The National AIDS Convention of South Africa
NACO	National AIDS Control Organization
NACP	National AIDS Control Programme
NCERT	National Council of Education, Research and Training
NECTOI	The National Employment Council for the Operating Transport Industry (Zimbabwe)
NGO	Non-Governmental Organisation
NICED	National Institute of Cholera and Enteric Diseases
NORAD	Norwegian Agency for Development Cooperation
NRHM	National Rural Health Mission
NSEP	Needle Syringe Exchange Programme
OCAFI	Olongapo City AIDS Foundation Inc. (Philippines)
OI	Opportunistic Infections
OPD	Out Patient Department
ORW	Out Reach Worker
OST	Oral Substitution Therapy

PAHO	People Affected by HIV/AIDS Organisation (Congo)
PC	Project Coordinator
PCA	Participatory community assessments
PCP	Pneumocystis carini pneumonia
PCR	Polymerase Chain Reaction
PE	Peer Educator
PEPFAR	President's Emergency Plan For AIDS Relief
PHC	Primary Health Centre
PIL	Public Interest Litigation
PLWHA/PLHA	People living with HIV/AIDS
PLWHAF	People living with HIV/AIDS and Friends
PNAC	Philippine National AIDS Council
PPTCT	Prevention of Parent to child Transmission
PRI	Panchayati Raj Institute
PSC	Public Service Contractors
RAIDS	Rural HIV/AIDS Initiatives by WB in Sub-Saharan Africa
RCH	Reproductive Child Health
RCSHA	Resource Centre for Sexual Health and AIDS
RNTCP	Revised National TB Control Programme
RTI	Reproductive Tract Infection

SAARC	South Asian Association for Regional Cooperation
SAATHII	Solidarity and Action Against The HIV Infection in India
SACA	State Action Committee on AIDS
SACS	State AIDS Control Society (SACS)
SAEP	School AIDS Education Program
SCD	Society for Community Development
SCIR	Society for Community Intervention and Research
SEARO	South East Asia Regional Office
SGSY	Swarnajayanti Gram Swarojgar Yojana
SHG	Self Help Group
SHIP	STD/HIV Intervention Programme
SLARTC	Socio-Legal Aid Research and Training Centre
SPARSHA	Society for Positive Atmosphere & Related Support to HIV/AIDS
STD/STI	Sexually transmitted disease/infection
STM	School of Tropical Medicine
SUDA	Single Use Diagnostic Screening
SWAA	Society of Women and AIDS in Africa
TAAH	Theory and Action Against Health
TAC	Treatment Action Campaign (South Africa)

TB	Tuberculosis
TIP	Targeted Intervention Programme
TRIPS	Trade Related Aspects of Intellectual Property Rights
UNAIDS	United Nations Joint Programme on HIV/AIDS
UNCTAD	United Nations Commission on Trade and Development
UNDP	United Nations Development Programme
UNESCO	United Nations Educational, Scientific & Cultural Organisation
UNFPA	United Nations Population Fund
UNGASS	United Nations General Assembly Special Session on HIV/AIDS
UNICEF	United Nations Children's Emergency Fund
UNIFEM	United Nations Development Fund for Women
UNHCR	United Nations High Commissioner for Refugees
UN-NGLS	United Nations Non-Governmental Liaison Service
UNODC	United Nations Office on Drugs and Crime
USAID	United States Agency for International Development
UTA	University Talk AIDS

VCTC	Voluntary Counselling and Testing Centre
VDRL	Venereal Disease Research Laboratory Test
VHAI	Voluntary Health Association of India
VO	Voluntary Organization
WB	World Bank
W.B.	West Bengal
WBSAP&CS	West Bengal State AIDS Prevention & Control Society
WBPSU	West Bengal Programme Support Unit
WFP	World Food Programme
WHO	World Health Organization
WTO	World Trade Organisation

SECTION-I
CONCEPTUAL FRAMEWORK

1
Introduction

The Acquired Immuno Deficiency Syndrome (AIDS) is the fourth leading infectious cause of adult deaths in the world. As an epidemic, it has affected almost every country on the globe. AIDS is a fatal transmissible disease of the immune system caused by the human immunodeficiency virus (HIV). HIV slowly attacks and destroys the immune system, the body's defense against infection, leaving an individual vulnerable to a variety of other infections. AIDS is the final stage of HIV infection (*Encyclopedia Britannica* 2003; Barnett and Whiteside 2002; Unnikrishna et al. 1993). The pathology of HIV involves three stages (1) primary HIV infection, (2) the asymptomatic phase, and (3) AIDS. Primary HIV infection is first stage during which transmitted HIV replicates rapidly. The second phase – asymptomatic period, lasts an average of 10 years. During this period the virus continues to replicate concurrent to a gradual decrease in the CD4 count (the number of T-cells). When the CD4 count falls to about 200 cells per micro-litre of blood (in an uninfected adult it is about 1000 cells per micro-litre), patients begin to experience opportunistic infections (OIs). This is AIDS. Full blown AIDS is the final stage of HIV infection. The most common OIs include *Pneumocystis carini pneumonia (PCP),*

Mycobacterium tuberculosis, herpes simplex infection, Kaposi's sarcoma, lymphomas and toxoplasmosis. Death results from the unremitting growth of opportunistic pathogens or from the body's inability to fight off malignancies.

HIV is transmitted by the direct transfer of bodily fluids, such as blood and blood products, semen and other genital secretions, or breast milk from an infected person to an uninfected person. HIV is not spread by coughing, sneezing or casual contact. The primary means of HIV transmission worldwide is heterosexual intercourse with an infected individual. HIV is fragile and cannot survive long outside of the body. Therefore, direct transfer of bodily fluids is required for transmission. Sexually transmitted diseases, such as syphilis, genital herpes, gonorrhoea, and chlamydia, increase the risk of contracting HIV through sexual contact, probably due to the genital lesions that they cause (Encyclopedia Britannica 2003; Barnett and Whiteside 2002; Unnikrishna et al. 1993). Tests for the disease are done through the identification of HIV antibodies, which accumulate after four weeks to six months after the exposure. The most common test for HIV is the enzyme-linked immunosorbent assay (ELISA). Other tests are Western blot, Polymerase Chain Reaction (PCR) and Single Use Diagnostic Screening (SUDA). There is no cure or effective vaccine for HIV infection. Efforts at prevention have focused primarily on changing sexual behaviour, promoting use of condoms, discouraging needle reuse, etc. To treat HIV infection, antiretroviral drugs (ART) are available. Since HIV rapidly rebuilds resistance to any single antiretroviral treatment, combination treatment is necessary for effective viral suppression. Highly active antiretroviral therapy (HAART), a combination of three or more drugs, has resulted in a marked drop in the mortality rate from HIV infection. Though HAART largely halts viral replication and thereby allowing the immune system to reconstitute itself, but it does not appear to eradicate HIV. Viral replication resumes if HAART is discontinued. Each drug has unique side effects and, in addition, treatment with combinations of these drugs leads to additional side effects.

AIDS is now considered not only as a health problem, but also as a developmental and security threat. Although the epidemic began in USA more than 29 years ago, over 96% of new infections now occur in low and middle income countries, which are unfortunately least equipped to respond effectively to the challenge (UNAIDS 2008). It is now well recognized that AIDS is affecting developed and developing countries differently. In developed countries, AIDS is now a chronic disease and a manageable health problem largely due to the availability of anti-retroviral medication. However, in developing countries, AIDS is now destroying societies, nations and communities. Even now less than 25% of those at risk of HIV infection have access to basic prevention services (Jha et al. 2002). The antiretroviral treatments (ART) that have increased the longevity of patients in the industrialized countries are unfortunately beyond the reach of those in the developing world. The disease is therefore, widening the gap between thc haves and have-nots, between rich and poor nations, thereby presenting a new ethical and human rights dilemma (Narain 2004).

Global HIV/AIDS Scenario

At the end of 2007, UNAIDS estimated 33.2 million (30.6–36.1 million) people living with HIV/AIDS worldwide (see Table-1.1). While 30.8 million (28.2 – 33.6 million) of these were adults, 15.4 million (13.9 – 16.6 million) were women and 2.1 million (1.9 – 2.4 million) were children under the age of 15 years. Total number of people newly infected with HIV in 2007 was 2.5 million (1.8 – 4.1 million). Total AIDS deaths in 2007 was 2.1 million (1.9 – 2.4 million), out of which adults 1.7 million (1.6 – 2.1 million), children under 15 years were 290 000 (270 000 – 320 000). More than 25 million already died since the beginning of the epidemic, bringing the number of infected more than 65 million worldwide (UNAIDS 2008). Over 6800 new HIV infections a day in 2007 and over 5700 persons die from AIDS, mostly because of inadequate access to HIV prevention and treatment services. More than 96% of new infections are occurring in low and middle-income countries. Out of these new infections, about 1200 are in children under 15 years of age and about 5800 are in adults aged 15 years and older of whom: — almost 50% are among women. Young people aged 15–24 account for an estimated 45% of new HIV infections worldwide (UNAIDS 2008).

Today, AIDS is the leading cause of death in Sub-Saharan Africa which has highest number of HIV positive people (22.5 million), followed by South and South-East Asia with 4.0 million infected individuals. In seven Sub-Saharan African nations, more than 22% of the population aged 15 to 49 is infected with HIV. Africa accounts for 83% of all AIDS deaths worldwide. The epidemic has an adverse effect on life expectancy in Sub-Saharan Africa. Gains made in life expectancy before 1980 have been lost and it is estimated that life expectancies affected by HIV infection and AIDS may be less than 40 years (UN Population Division 2001). The epidemic is growing fastest in South Africa where it is estimated that over 1500 new infections occur daily (UNAIDS 2002). In South Africa, AIDS deaths are widespread that small children now play a new game called "Funerals". In Zimbabwe, the AIDS epidemic has shortened life expectancy by 22 years. Two out of every three Zimbabweans aged 15 to 39 are HIV positive. Sub-Saharan Africa remains the region most heavily affected by HIV, accounting for 67% of all people living with HIV and for 75% of AIDS deaths in 2007. More than 90% HIV infected children are living in Sub-Saharan Africa. In sub-Saharan Africa alone, the epidemic has orphaned nearly 12 million children aged less than 18 years (UNAIDS 2008). However, some of the most worrisome increases in new infections are now occurring in populous countries in other regions, such as Indonesia, the Russian Federation, and various high-income countries.

Table-1.1
Global HIV/AIDS Estimation, 2007 (Region-wise)

Region	*A & C living with HIV/AIDS (Range)*	*Newly infected (A & C) in 2007*	*Adult Prevalence Rate * (%)*	*Main mode of trans-mission for Adults*
1	*2*	*3*	*4*	*5*
Sub-Saharan Africa	22.5 million *(20.9 - 24.3 million)*	1.7 million *(1.4 - 2.4 million)*	5.0 % *(4.6-5.5%)*	Heterosexual
Middle East & North Africa	3,80,000 *(2.7 - 5.0 lakh)*	35,000 *(16,000-65,000)*	0.3 % *(0.2-0.4%)*	Heterosexual, IDU
South & South East Asia	4.0 million *(3.3 - 5.1 million)*	3,40,000 *(1.8 - 7.4 lakh)*	0.3 % *(0.2- 0.4%)*	Heterosexual, IDU
East Asia	8,00,000 *(6.2 - 9.6 lakh)*	92,000 *(0.21 – 2.2 lakh)*	0.1% *(< 0.2 %)*	Heterosexual, IDU, MSM
Latin America	1.6 million *(1.4 - 1.9 million)*	1,00,000 *(0.47 – 2.2 lakh)*	0.5% *(0.4- 0.6%)*	Heterosexual, IDU, MSM
Caribbean	2,30,000 *(2.1 - 2.7 lakh)*	17,000 *(15-23 thousand)*	1.0% *(0.9- 1.2%)*	Heterosexual, MSM

(Contd...)

1	2	3	4	5
Eastern Europe & Central Asia	1.6 million *(1.2 - 2.1 million)*	1,50,000 *(0.70 – 2.9 lakh)*	0.9% *(0.7- 1.2%)*	IDU
Western & Central Europe	7,60,000 *(0.6 - 1.1 million)*	31,000 *(19-86 thousand)*	0.3% *(0.2- 0.4%)*	MSM, IDU
North America	1.3 million *(0.48 - 1.9 million)*	46,000 *(38-68 thousand)*	0.6% *(0.5- 0.9%)*	Heterosexual, IDU, MSM
Oceania	75,000 *(53,000 - 1,20,000)*	14,000 *(11-26 thousand)*	0.4 % *(0.3- 0.7%)*	MSM
TOTAL	33.2 million *(30.6 - 36.1 million)*	2.5 million *(1.8- 4.1 million)*	0.8% *(0.7- 0.9%)*	

Source: UNAIDS Report on the Global AIDS Epidemic 2008.
* The proportion of adults (15-49 years of age) living with HIV/AIDS in 2001, using population numbers.
A & C = Adult and Children

AIDS was relatively slow in coming to Asia and until the late 1980s; no Asian country had experienced a major epidemic. But now it is spreading rapidly and the epidemic is in a fairly advanced stage in many countries (WHO 1997; Phoolcharoen 1998). According to surveillance data, the rapid spread of HIV in Asia began when high HIV prevalence (up to 30% or more) among female sex workers (FSWs) in Thailand, Combodia and Myanmar reported. Thailand is the first country to report HIV in Asia. Both in Thailand and Myanmar, the epidemic has been shown to occur in waves beginning with the reported increase in HIV infection among injecting drug users (IDUs) and sex workers, followed by their partners, and then ultimately from mother to children during child birth or through breast-feeding (WHO 2003). In Asia, an estimated 5.0 million (4.1 million–6.2 million) people were living with HIV in 2007 and approximately 380000 (270000–490000) died from AIDS-related illnesses.

Table-1.2

HIV/AIDS Epidemic in Selected Asian Countries

Country	*Adult HIV (15-49yrs) Prevalence (%)*	*PLWH in 2007 (numbers)*	*Heterosexual*	*Injecting drug use*
Bangladesh	< 0.1	12,000	+	+
Bhutan	0.1	<500	+	—
DPR Korea	< 0.1	n/a	—	—
Indonesia	0.2	2,70,000	+	+ +
India	0.3	24,00,000	+ + +	+
Maldives	< 0.1	<100	+	—
Myanmar	0.7	2,40,000	+ + +	+ +
Nepal	0.5	70,000	+	+ +
Thailand	1.4	6,10,000	+ + +	+ +
Sri Lanka	< 0.1	3,800	+	—
Timor Leste	< 0.1	n/a	n/a	n/a

Source: UNAIDS (2008) and WHO (2003) for sources of HIV transmission.
Notes: (—) unknown or minimal HIV transmission;
(+) limited HIV transmission.
(+ +) moderate HIV transmission;
(+ + +) major HIV transmission.
PLWHA= People Living With HIV/AIDS.

Based on the HIV prevalence rates, Asian countries could be divided into three broad categories – (1) those with HIV prevalence rate more than one percent among general population, namely, Cambodia, Myanmar, Thailand and parts of India; (2) those with prevalence of less than one percent in general population, but more than five percent among population with high-risk behaviour, namely, Malaysia, Nepal Indonesia, Vietnam, China and Pakistan; and (3) the remaining countries with low prevalence of less than one percent among high- risk population (see Table-1.2).

Though the national HIV prevalence rates relatively low in most of the Asian countries, there is no cause for complacency. National HIV infection levels are highest in South-East Asia, where there are disparate epidemic trends. During 2007 alone, nearly 3.8 lakh (2.0-6.5 lakh) people acquired HIV in Asia. Many countries are experiencing serious localized epidemics. The epidemics in Cambodia, Myanmar and Thailand all show decline in HIV prevalence. However, epidemics in Indonesia (especially in its Papua province), Pakistan, and Viet Nam are growing rapidly. New HIV infections are also increasing steadily, in populous countries such as Bangladesh and China (UNAIDS 2008). In Asia, where infection rates are much lower than in Africa, HIV causes a greater loss of productivity than any other disease, and is likely to push an additional 6 million households into poverty by 2015 unless national responses are strengthened (Commission on AIDS in Asia 2008).

In Asia, therefore, the epidemic remains dynamic and is evolving rapidly. Nearly half of the world's population lives in Asia and it has the potential to significantly influence the course and over all impact of the global HIV/AIDS pandemic. The region's vulnerability to HIV can be attributed to various factors like men having multiple sex partners and patronizing sex workers, injecting drug use, high prevalence of sexually transmitted infections (STIs), low condom use, illiteracy, poverty and limited access to health and information services (Narain 2004). Poverty is one of the major contributors to societal vulnerability. While the infected poor tend to die soon after developing AIDS, poverty and other social factors force women to undertake prostitution for survival and thereby enhancing the risk of acquiring HIV. These risk behaviours and vulnerability that are responsible for promoting, facilitating and fuelling HIV transmission are present virtually in all countries, and therefore, the chances of further spread are significant.

The epidemic has effects on the agriculture, education, health, labour and transport sectors. AIDS pushes people deeper into poverty as households lose bread earners, livelihoods are compromised and savings are consumed by the cost of health care and funerals. Women are left bearing bigger burdens as caregivers, workers and mothers. Yet, their legal, social and political status leaves them more vulnerable to HIV/AIDS. The vast majority of people living with HIV/AIDS worldwide are in the prime of their working lives. The epidemic hits productivity through absenteeism, organizational disruption, adding costs, diverting resources and depleting skills. In all affected countries, the HIV/AIDS epidemic is putting the health sector under strain. Overall quality of health care dropped. There is a shortage of hospital beds. While demand for health services is expanding, more health care personnel are affected by HIV/AIDS. Development has ceased in many countries where struggling economies are no longer able to repay loans to strengthen the health and agricultural sector. AIDS has a profound impact on growth, income and poverty. For countries with HIV/AIDS prevalence rates of 20% or more, the GDP growth has been estimated to drop by an average of 2.6% annually (UNAIDS 2002). HIV has inflicted the "single greatest reversal in human development" in modern history (UNDP 2005).

AIDS Epidemic in India

The first HIV infection in India was detected in 1986 in a group of female sex workers from Chennai. Within a short period it has evolved as one of the most serious public heath problems across the whole country. The initial cases of HIV/AIDS were detected among the commercial sex workers in Chennai and Mumbai, and among the IDUs in north - eastern state of Manipur. In Mumbai, the prevalence rate of HIV among sex workers increased dramatically from one percent in 1986 to 18 percent in 1990 and to 51 percent in 1996 (Larson and Narain 2001). By 1996 Maharashtra, Tamilnadu and Manipur together constituted 77 percent of total AIDS cases in India (UNAIDS/WHO 2002).

HIV situation in the country is assessed and monitored through regular annual sentinel surveillance mechanism established since 1992. The sentinel surveillance started with 180 sentinel sites. Over the years, the numbers of sentinel sites were increased from 180 in 1998 to 703 in 2005. This was expanded greatly for 2006 surveillance round to a total of 1,122 sites, to cover all the districts of the country. Out of these, 628 sites are established at Antenatal clinics where blood is collected for HIV testing from the pregnant women attending these clinics. Other 494 sites are established among high-risk group populations such as STD clinic attendees, Female Sex Workers (FSWs), Injecting Drug Users (IDUs), Men who have Sex with Men (MSM), Migrants, Truckers and Transgender (NACO/HSS 2006).

The total number of people living with HIV/AIDS (PLWHA) in the country is estimated to be 2.47 million (2.0-3.1 million). Andhra Pradesh, Tamil Nadu, Karnataka and Kerala contribute 63% of total PLWHA in India. The highest number of PLWHA is in Andhra Pradesh and Maharashtra, with nearly 0.5 million each. Apart from these high prevalence states, Gujarat, Uttar Pradesh and West Bengal have higher burden of the epidemic with greater than 0.1 million PLWHA in each of these states (NACO/HSS 2006). Based on the revised estimates (NACO/HSS 2006), the adult HIV prevalence in 2006 is estimated to be 0.36% (0.27% - 0.47%)

Figure-1.1: State-wise Estimated Adult HIV Prevalence in India, 2006.

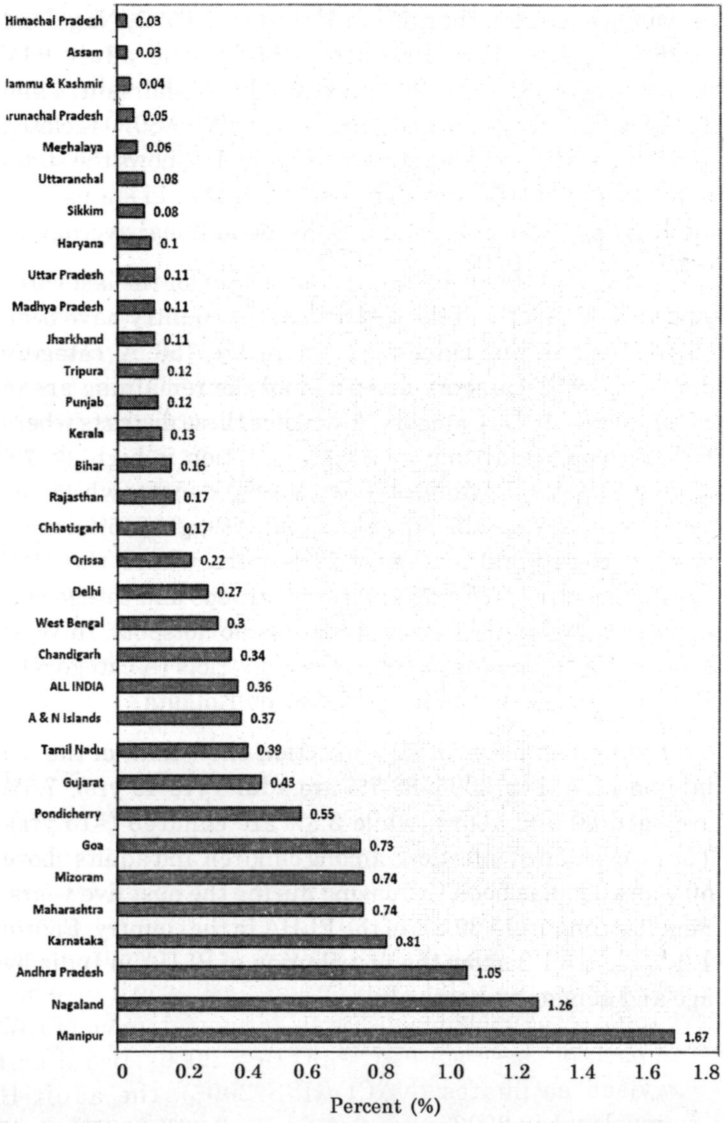

Source: NACO, 2006.

at the all India level. Estimated HIV prevalence is greater among males (0.43%) than females (0.29%). The adult HIV prevalence is more than 1% in Manipur (1.67%), Nagaland (1.26%) and Andhra Pradesh (1.05%). The adult HIV prevalence is less than 1% in Karnataka, Maharashtra and Tamil Nadu, while Mizoram and Goa (0.70%-0.80%) is closed to the high HIV prevalence states. Figure-1.1 shows the state-wise estimated HIV prevalence. It shows that 11 states have adult HIV prevalence greater than the national average.

Based on the sentinel surveillance data for the last three years (2004-2006), all the districts in the country have been classified into four categories. There are 156 'A' category districts, 39 'B' category districts and the remaining are in categories 'C' & 'D'. Category 'A' denotes those districts where HIV Prevalence among general population is high. (> 1% among ANC clinic attendees), category 'B' denotes where the HIV Prevalence among high-risk groups is high. (> 5% among High risk groups), category C denotes where the HIV Prevalence is < 5% among high-risk groups and category D denotes those districts where there is no hotspots. In West Bengal, there are 4 high prevalence districts (A category) – Purulia, Burdwan, Uttar Dinajpur and Kolkata.

Recent estimates of HIV infection show that, of the 2.5 million PLWH in 2006, 88.7% are adults (15-49 yrs), 7.5% are aged 50 and above, while 3.8% are children (<15 yrs). The proportion of infections among children and adults above 50 years age has been increasing during the past five years. Females constitute 39.3% of the PLHA in the country. Figure 1.2 & Figure 1.3 show the distribution of PLHA in India by age and gender respectively.

Figure-1.2: Percentage Distribution of PLWHA by Age in India, 2006.

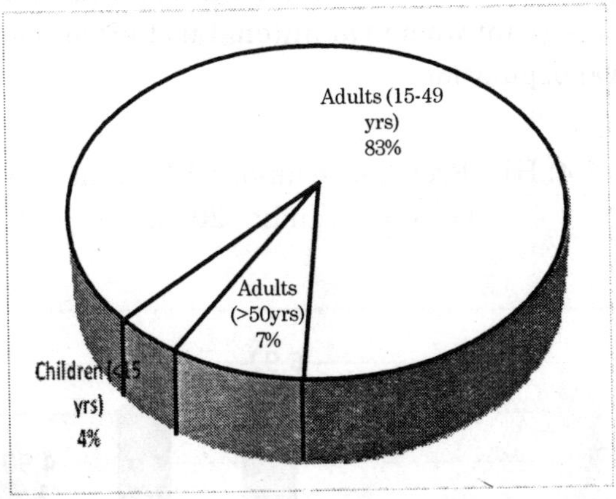

Source: NACO, 2006.

Figure-1.3: Percentage Distribution of PLWHA by Gender in India, 2006.

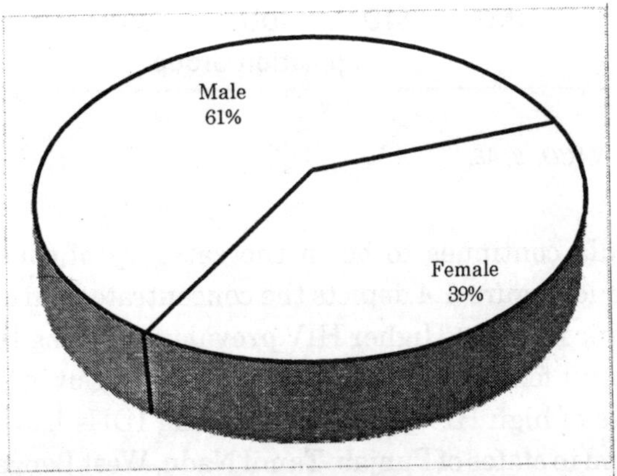

Source: NACO, 2006.

The HIV Prevalence among high-risk groups continues to be nearly six to eight times greater than that among general population. HIV Sentinel Surveillance utilizes data from the pregnant women at antenatal clinic as a surrogate for general population.

Figure-1.4: HIV Prevalence among Different Population Groups in India, 2006.

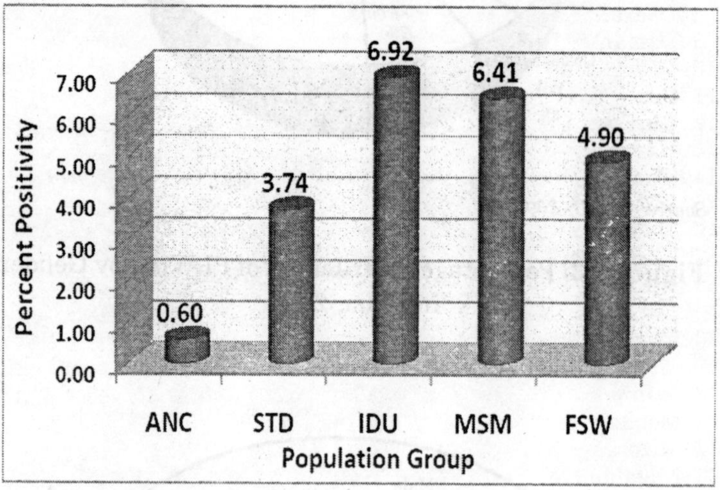

Source: NACO, 2006.

India continues to be in the category of concentrated epidemic. Figure-1.4 depicts the concentrated nature of HIV epidemic in India. Higher HIV prevalence among IDUs is an important feature of North Eastern States. But in 2006, new pockets of high HIV prevalence among IDUs has also been recorded in states of Punjab, Tamil Nadu, West Bengal, Kerala and Maharashtra indicating dual nature of the epidemic in the country (see Table-1.3).

Table-1.3
State-wise HIV Prevalence among Different Population Groups, 2006

Sl. No.	State/UT	STD	*ANC*	IDU	MSM	*FSW*
1	A & Nicobar Island	0.80	0.17	NS	NS	NS
2	Andhra Pradesh	24.40	1.26	NS	10.25	8.84
3	Arunachal Pradesh	0.42	0.00	0.00	NS	0.00
4	Assam	0.50	0.00	2.86	0.78	0.40
5	Bihar	0.40	0.50	0.20	0.30	0.60
6	Chandigarh	1.66	0.25	17.60	4.80	0.67
7	Chattisgarh	2.58	0.00	NS	NS	1.65
8	Dadra& Nagar Haveli	NS	0.00	NS	NS	NS
9	Daman & Diu	NS	0.00	NS	NS	NS
10	Delhi	2.00	0.00	10.00	12.27	1.40
11	Goa	8.6	0.50	NS	4.8	NS
12	Gujarat	3.31	0.50	NS	11.20	6.40
13	Haryana	0.81	0.13	0.00	0.00	0.40
14	Himachal Pradesh	0.60	0.00	NS	0.44	0.66
15	Jammu & Kashmir	0.00	0.00	2.50	NS	0.00
16	Jharkhand	0.40	0.00	0.40	NS	0.87
17	Karnataka	7.57	1.00	3.60	19.20	9.60
18	Kerala	1.23	0.13	9.57	0.40	0.00
19	Lakshadweep	0.00	0.00	NS	NS	NS
20	Madhya Pradesh	0.47	0.00	NS	NS	1.07
21	Maharashtra	10.00	0.75	20.40	15.60	12.80
22	Manipur	4.80	1.25	20.00	10.40	11.60
23	Meghalaya	1.18	0.00	3.30	NS	NS
24	Mizoram	3.07	1.00	1.60	NS	10.40
25	Nagaland	0.00	0.93	1.25	NS	16.40
26	Orissa	2.80	0.50	10.40	NS	1.00
27	Pondicherry	4.03	0.25	NS	2.47	1.44
28	Punjab	0.27	0.00	13.80	4.80	1.60
29	Rajasthan	1.60	0.00	NS	0.00	1.20
30	Sikkim	0.00	0.10	0.20	NS	NS
31	Tamil Nadu	8.00	0.25	24.20	5.60	3.60
32	Tripura	0.45	0.42	0.00	NS	NS
33	Uttar Pradesh	0.62	0.00	4.63	NS	1.00
34	Uttaranchal	0.00	0.00	NS	NS	NS
35	**West Bengal**	**1.01**	**0.00**	**4.00**	**6.60**	**7.58**

Source: NACO, 2006.
Note: NS–No sites

By the end of April 2005, a total of 1, 04,824 AIDS cases had been reported (NACO 2005). The estimated number of HIV infected people in the country calculated on the basis of sentinel surveillance data. However, the estimates mainly focused on people belonging to 15 to 49 years age group and did not take into account the unreported cases of AIDS. Epidemiological analysis of reported AIDS cases reveals that the disease is mainly affecting people in the sexually active age group. A majority of the patients (88.6%) are in the age group of 15 to 49 years, thereby making a considerable economic impact to the country (Anand et al. 1999). Trends indicate two distinct characteristics of the spread of HIV infection from groups practicing risk behaviours to general population and from urban to rural areas (NACO 2001b). The predominant modes of transmission of HIV infection in AIDS patients are heterosexual contact (87.4%), injecting drug use (1.8%), blood and blood products (1.7%), perinatal (4.7%), and others (4.4%). The analysis also reveals that males account for 74.88% of AIDS cases and females 25.12%. The ratio between male and female is 3:1 (see Table-1.4).

Table-1.4
Mode of HIV Transmission in India, 2007

Sl. No.	*Risk/Transmission Categories*	*Percentage*
1	Sexual	87.40
2	Perinatal Transmission	4.70
3	Blood/Blood products	1.70
4	Injectable Drug Users	1.80
5	Others (Not specified)	4.40
	TOTAL	100.00

Source: NACO, 2007.

The transmission of HIV to the children in India occurred in the early phase of the epidemic and mostly through the transfusion of infected blood and blood products (Bhushan et al. 1994; De et al. 1990; Sen. et al. 1993; Sengupta et al. 1992; Singh et al. 1991). A considerable number of thalassaemic and haemophilic children were infected through this route. Although the situation has improved since then, India is yet to achieve 100% safe blood transfusion through out the country. The situation is more difficult in peripheral places – in rural settings as well as in hilly areas.

Contaminated blood and blood products are still a matter of concern as sources of HIV infection (*Indian Express* 2001). Of the nearly 2 million bottles of blood transfused every year in the country, the professional blood donors were reportedly supplying more than half. Currently, only 60% of the demand is being met through official sources, and this has implications for HIV transmission (Salunka et al. 1998). The 'component therapy' rather than whole blood transfusion is yet to be exploited to its potential. Kumar and his colleagues documented mother - to – child transmission (MTCT) of HIV in 1995 (Kumar et al. 1995). The study recorded an overall vertical transmission rate of 48% in the tribal women of Uttar Pradesh. The problem of IDUs is limited to north-eastern states and the metropolitan cities. Needles sharing among IDUs are a high-risk activity that has fuelled the spread of HIV/AIDS. Since drug use is illegal and covert, these high-risk populations are particularly difficult to target for intervention.

In 2006, the Behavioural Surveillance Survey (BSS) conducted among the general population (15-49 years) as opposed to surveys earlier conducted in groups observing high-risk behaviour – is the biggest of its kind in the world. A total of 97,240 respondents were interviewed in which males and females participated in equal proportion; urban and rural representation was also equal in this survey (NACO/

BSS 2006). The BSS shows that awareness level varies widely from state to state. The percentage of respondents aware of HIV/AIDS has significantly increased over the years (BSS 2001 - 67%, BSS 2006 - 80%). The proportion of respondents aware of HIV/AIDS was significantly higher in urban (92%) areas and among male (87%) respondents. Except for Bihar (47%), in all other states more than 60 percent of the respondents had heard of HIV/AIDS. The awareness level was more than 90 percent in some states – Delhi, Andhra Pradesh, Tamil Nadu and Pondicherry, Kerala, Maharashtra, Goa and all North Eastern states, where the literacy level as well as the media exposure of the respondents was also quite high. The male as well as female respondents in both rural and urban areas were more familiar with the terminology "AIDS" (80%) than "HIV" (64%). Nearly three-fourths (62% in BSS 2001) of the respondents in BSS 2006 were aware that sexual contact could lead to HIV/AIDS. Nine out of ten respondents in urban areas as against seven out of ten in the rural areas were aware of this aspect. Four out of every five respondents (three out of five in BSS 2001) reported that HIV/AIDS could be transmitted by infected blood during transmission. Three-fourths (two-thirds in BSS 2001) of respondents were aware that HIV/AIDS could be transmitted through needle sharing. As in case of other issues, in this case also the awareness was observed to be significantly higher in urban areas (87%) and among male respondents (82%). Compared to the other routes of transmission, mother-to-child transmission was less known to the respondents across all states and union territories in the country. Only half (55% in BSS 2006 and 49% in BSS 2001) of the respondents in the country were aware that HIV/AIDS could be transmitted through breast-feeding. Nearly two-thirds of the respondents in BSS 2006 were aware that consistent condom use could prevent transmission of HIV/AIDS. There was a significant increase of 15 percent in this regard from BSS 2001. Four-fifths of respondents in BSS 2006, against three-fourths of respondents in BSS 2001, reported mass media as the source of information on STD/HIV/AIDS. The level of exposure to messages on HIV/AIDS is significantly higher in urban areas (urban 89%, rural 73%) and among males (males 84%, females 72%). Generally awareness levels are higher in high-prevalence states than the low-prevalence states. The rural women particularly are the most disadvantaged in terms of awareness especially in Bihar, Gujarat, Uttar Pradesh, Madhya Pradesh and West Bengal. Compared to the awareness of HIV/AIDS, the awareness regarding STDs was significantly lower among various respondent categories (31% in BSS 2001 to 38% in BSS 2006). Awareness of linkage between STDs and HIV/AIDS remains low although the awareness about this issue has increased significantly from 18% in BSS 2001 to 24% in BSS 2006. One of the key factors precipitating the spread of HIV is STI. It is now established that an individual with STI not only vulnerable to contracting HIV, but can also spread infection to others more rapidly. STI rates also indicate the extent of unprotected sex. Majority of such STI infected people do not turn up for timely treatment – especially the women due to social stigma. Fifty-six percent of the respondents in BSS 2006 felt that PLHA should be allowed to stay in village/community. Higher stigma levels were observed in rural areas and among female respondents in this regard. Acceptability of PLHA in the community was reported highest in Andhra Pradesh and Delhi (74%) and lowest in Bihar (30%). Only one-fifth of the respondents were aware of ICTC and the proportion was significantly higher in urban areas and males. The lowest awareness in this regard was observed in Bihar (6%), Jammu & Kashmir (8%), Madhya Pradesh, Punjab, Chandigarh and Uttarakhand (9%). The awareness about PPTCT is also low (overall 13%, urban 20%, and rural 10%).

In India, another feature of the epidemic is the existence of a dual epidemic of TB and HIV/AIDS. With about 14 million

TB cases prevalent in India, HIV/AIDS also poses a twin challenge of HIV/TB co-infection. Approximately 65% of the AIDS cases are reported to be opportunistic TB infection cases (NACO 2001). Other major opportunistic infections reported are Candidiasis (57.5%), Cryptococcus (36%), PCP (3.8%), Kaposi sarcoma (0.6%) and others (8%). Treatment of TB among the HIV infected people is a new threat to the National TB Control Programme. Some of the drugs, which are referred for TB treament, create complications in case of HIV infected persons. Simultaneously, looking for HIV among TB patients will also create the problem of scaring away of innumerable TB infected cases in India from seeking treatment under DOT strategy. HIV/AIDS is not a disease that spread randomly, but is transmitted as a result of a specific behavioural pattern and has strong socio-economic impact. It not only costs huge funds in terms controlling the opportunistic infections such as TB, pneumonia and Cryptococcal meningitis, but also seriously affects individuals in their prime productive years causing grave economic loss to them and their families. All these aspects provide an unusual task of HIV infection through many routes, which comes with its long period of invisibility and does not reveal the OIs till a few years.

The attributable reasons for such accelerated spread of the epidemic in the country at present is migration and mobility in search of employment from economically backward to more advanced regions, low literacy levels leading to low awareness among the potentially high-risk groups, gender disparity, RTIs/STIs both among men and women. The social stigma attached to STIs also holds good for HIV/AIDS in, even in much more serious way. This along with a large population and population density, HIV/AIDS is one of the most challenging health problem ever faced by the country.

The future of the epidemic in India is contingent upon the extent and effectiveness of current and future prevention efforts. Moreover, since it takes 7-10 years for people with

HIV to develop AIDS, the annual toll will continue to grow in future, requiring further efforts for the next several years. This will have a major impact on the already fragile health and economic infrastructure in terms of direct medical and patient care costs, indirect costs in the form of absenteeism and decreased productivity. In terms of economic impact studies during 1990s indicated that India might have lost up to US$ 11 billion due to HIV/AIDS by 2000 (Charles et al. 1993). The impact of epidemic has been documented at the family and community level, especially in the poor and marginalized groups. Poor families become poorer and lower-middle income group become poor. Significant but less quantifiable are the emotional psychological costs to the individual, family and community.

Response to HIV/AIDS in India

(A) Government Response

From the very beginning, the Government of India is fully committed to preventing HIV/AIDS before it emerges as a catastrophic epidemic. It looks at HIV/AIDS prevention and control as a development issues with deep socio-economic issues and not merely a public health issue. In 1985, the Indian Council of Medical Research (ICMR) established a task force on AIDS to screen sera from high-risk groups at National Institute of Virology, Pune and ICMR Centre for Advanced Research in Virology located in Christian Medical College, Vellore. The first detection of HIV in 1986 in Chennai led to the formation of National AIDS Committee. The members of the Committee were senior government officials from Health and other departments and administrator of Voluntary Health Association of India (VHAI) – a leading NGO. Discussions and deliberations at this forum led to the evolution of National AIDS Control Programme in 1987, which concentrated in surveillance, information, education and communication (IEC), blood safety in the areas perceived to be risk prone. As a part of this programme, a Central AIDS Cell and AIDS cell in each States were established. This programme of 1987 was reviewed in 1990 in consultation with WHO and a medium – term plan (MTP) for three years prepared with an estimated cost of US $20 million. The focus of MTP was on four identified high-risk metropolitan cities – Delhi, Mumbai, Chennai and Kolkata and the states of Maharashtra, Tamil Nadu, Manipur and West Bengal.

A comprehensive five-year strategic plan was launched during 1992-97 with World Bank credit as the National AIDS Control Programme Phase-I (NACP-I). The National AIDS Control Organisation (NACO) was established in 1992 to coordinate the nationwide programmes. The major component of NACP-I were: (1) strengthening the management capacity for AIDS control; (2) promoting public awareness and community support; (3) improving blood safety and promoting rational use of blood; (4) building surveillance and clinical management capacity; and controlling STDs. Project activities were to be implemented through the existing government health infrastructure, private sector, NGOs and mass media institutions. The coordination of the project, procurement and development of policies and technical guidelines – were the functions of Govt. of India. Implementation was the responsibility of State governments and NGOs funded by Govt. of India through NACO. A sub-committee was appointed to examine the social, ethical and legal issues related to HIV/AIDS and to make recommendation to the government. NACP-I was extended up to October 1999.

The Second phase of NACP (NACP-II) started from November 1999 for a period of five-years (1999-2004). The NACP-II has been started through a participatory process with GOI, State governments, UNAIDS and bilateral agencies working in collaboration with community members, PLWHA, industry and labour organizations, NGOs and civil societies.

Each States and Union Territories (UTs) has registered States AIDS Control Society, which will be accountable for the implementation of the programme at the state level. The NACP-II was formulated with two key objectives of reducing the spread of HIV infection in the country and to strengthen India's capacity to respond to HIV/AIDS on a long-term basis (NACO 1999a; 1999b). The specific objectives NACP-II include interventions to change behaviour, especially among high-risk groups through targeted interventions, decentralization of service delivery through State AIDS Control Societies (SACS), protection of human rights, operational research and management reform. Another feature of this phase is inter-sectoral collaboration with all government departments, elected representatives of the people, chambers of commerce and industry, community-based organizations (CBOs) and the civil society in general. The project cost was approximately US $229.8 million (Rs. 1155 crores). The World Bank assured $191 million with GOI's share of 38.8 million. Besides it, USAID assisted AVERT project in Maharashtra for Rs. 166 crores and DFID assisted projects for Orissa, Kerala, Gujarat, Andhra Pradesh and West Bengal for Rs. 104 crores. The World Bank and DFID assisted projects are for duration of 5 years (1999-2004), while USAID's AVERT project for 7 years (1999-2006).

During the last few years, NACP has witnessed rapid expansion and decentralization in the country. SACS have been set up in 35 States/UTs and three municipal corporations of Mumbai, Chennai and Ahmedabad. These 38 SACS have adequate financial and administrative powers to identify and respond to local needs. Each SACS developed a Project Implementation Plan (PIP) as part of preparation for addressing the second phase, which allows for addressing specific needs of the epidemic in the state. SACS operate through regular health infrastructure and have designated district nodal officers to carry out the programme activities with the help of NGOs. The government in 2002 adopted two landmark policies, the National Blood Policy and the National AIDS Prevention and Control Policy. Considerable progress has been made during past few years in implementing TI projects. Some of the specific areas of response are being discussed here.

Over 1000 blood banks were upgraded and 82 blood component separation facilities were set up to ensure blood safety in the country. Testing for all transfusion-transmitted infections has been mandatory for all blood banks and strict licensing system has been introduced under the Drug and Cosmetics Act. There are 1088 public sector and 2100 private blood banks collecting over 5 million units both in 2006, and 2007 (NACO 2007). The work of the Programme on blood safety has yielded good results with transmission of HIV through Blood Transfusion reduced from 6.07 percent (1999) to 1.7 percent (2006) and 1.1 percent (2007). Over 18,000 medical officers from government hospitals and 10,000 private physicians were trained in STI care management (Saukat and Panakadan 2004). The guideline for STI management and treatment were revised and a training manual prepared by NACO was widely disseminated. At the end of 2007, 845 STI treatment centres treating over 2.3 million patients and 5 regional STI centres were upgraded to conduct training, research, supervision and monitoring. By 2007, 4245 Integrated Counselling and Testing Centres (ICTCs) tested 5.5 million persons and provided counseling, social and psychological support to those infected and affected by HIV (NACO 2007). The Prevention of Parent to Child Transmission (PPTCT) programmes offers a combination of low-cost, short-term prevention drug treatment, safe delivery practices, counseling and support, and safe infant - feeding methods. In January 2003, GFATM assigned a grant of US $ 100 million for PPTCT programmes. In 2007, 8.3 percent of HIV infected pregnant women received Nevirapine

Prophylaxis to reduce the risk of transmission to child. HIV spending in India has seen a growth of 28 percent in 2006-07 i.e. from US$ 133 million in 2005-06 to US$ 171 million in 2006-07 (NACO 2007).

The school AIDS Programme of NACO is a crucial intervention which focuses on raising awareness level, helping young people in resisting peer pressure to participate in risky behaviour and helping to develop safe and responsible lifestyles. Life skills education provided in 114,345 government secondary schools (79 percent) are some key achievements in the prevention front during 2007 (NACO 2007). Another example of a successful programme for youth is Universities Talk AIDS (UTA) programme, which covered 3.5 million students in 4044 institutions in the country during 2003. This programme is implemented by NSS with assistance from the WHO and NACO. Besides this, the Family Health Awareness Campaigns another innovative initiative to create awareness and encourage health-seeking behaviour among rural population on STIs and RTIs, and also sensitize field level health functionaries. During this campaign in 2000, 126 million target beneficiaries (15 to 49 yrs) were covered, 3.5 million cases referred and 1.5 million cases were treated (Saukat and Panakadan 2004). Under IEC activities, multimedia campaigns are being taken up. All print media, electronic media, small and folk media are also being used. Special communication packages are developed for vulnerable groups like MSMs, IDUs, truckers and sex workers. AIDS hotline with 1097 toll-free number have established in major cities of the country. Recognizing the adequate information and understanding, NCERT developed an AIDS education training package for teachers (NACO 1995).

Since April 2004, free ART is being provided through selected government hospitals. On the care and support front, 137 ART centers provide free ART to 118,052 adults (19.6%) and 8347 (35.1%) children with advanced HIV infection.

National Paediatric ART Initiative was launched in late 2006. Positive People Networks have been established and/or strengthened in 22 states and 221 districts. (NACO 2007). Government has funded about 35 community care centers. Linkages have been made between HIV care services and revised National TB Control (RNTCP) to facilitate free TB treatment. Quality of condoms was improved and included in schedule R of the Drugs and Cosmetics Act. A combination of free distribution and social marketing strategies is being used to make quality condom available to the high-risk group and general population. The NACP-II has an inbuilt component for monitoring and evaluation to ensure that continuous central information on the course of epidemic and response is being supplied for taking quick remedial actions. This evaluation system includes a computerized MIS, training of programme management staff, conducting base line, mid-term and final evaluation, and conducting annual performance reviews (APER).

The success of NACP is dependent in the coverage and quality of targeted intervention projects (TIPs) that have been launched among the most vulnerable groups. About 790 TIPs are being implemented across the country and covering 43% of the most-at-risk population such as CSWs, MSMs, truckers, street children, IDUs, migrant workers and prison inmates in 2007. TIPs use innovative approaches based on best available practices in the counter, combining behaviour change communication (BCC), counseling and general health care including the treatment of STDs, promotion of condom use and creating an enabling environment that nurtures empowerment. These interventions are carried out by NGOs, as they are best suited to reach these populations, which often can be hard to access and may not trust the public establishments. NACO has also developed guidelines for the effective participation of NGOs in NACP. The government hopes that all participating agencies in the government and

NGO sector including international and bilateral agencies will also adopt policies and programmes in conformity with NACP in their efforts to prevent and control HIV/AIDS in India. Currently, NACP-III (2007-2011) is in operation from June 2007.

(B) NGO Response to HIV/AIDS in India

From the above discussion, it is found that NGOs play a key role in combating the AIDS epidemic. Voluntary organizations and NGOs have a long and rich history in India. During the 19th and early 20th century, on the one hand, mainly Christian churches came into existence to intervene in the social and religious life of the indigenous people through improvement of health, social welfare and social reform. On the other hand, as a part of anti-colonial resistance numerous indigenous organizations emerged to accelerate social and religious reform (Sheth and Sethi 1996). In fact, more involvement of initiatives of NGOs has been occurring since late 1970s. At present, NGOs have become very crucial in the process of decentralization of power and development (Mathew 1999). In India, in the process of development, NGOs play a key role in carrying out various programmes related to formal and non-formal education, social awareness, income generation training, rural entrepreneurship development, computer training, agro-based training, safe drinking water, low cost sanitation, family counseling, legal aid for women, child labour, welfare for the disables, aged and backward communities and so on (Sarkar 2005).

Especially in the field of health care, NGOs have acquired a considerable importance in India since 1978 (Pattanaik 1988). In the same year, the Alma-Ata Conference gave birth to a new approach in health care i.e. 'Primary Health Care Approach' and fixed a goal of "Health for All By 2000 A.D". The said conference was preceded by a joint study of WHO and UNICEF for finding out alternative approaches to meet the basic health needs of the Third World people. The study examined some of the isolated voluntary health projects in these countries like in Jamkhed of India. The conclusion drawn from the study went strongly in favour of NGOs (Sarkar 2005). In 1983, National Health Policy also recognized the need for greater reliance on the voluntary and private sector for achieving the goal of "Health For All By 2000 A.D" (Duggal 1988). In 1985, Ministry of Health and Family Welfare agreed with the Planning Commission on the issue of greater involvement of NGOs in health care (Duggal, Gupta & Jesani 1986). In 2000, National Population Policy also focused on the voluntary and non-profit sector for population control. During last two and half decades, NGOs have contributed remarkably in the health sector by their innovative genius in the field of health, family welfare and in preventing the spread of communicable diseases.

Similarly, NGOs also made significant contribution in HIV/AIDS control and prevention programme. The history of HIV/AIDS action in India began in the voluntary sector, with efforts towards awareness and control at a time when government responses were restricted to denial. Among the first, were the Indian Health Organisation in Mumbai (then Bombay), the Gujarat AIDS Awareness and Prevention unit in Ahmedabad, and the AIDS Research Foundation of India in Chennai (then Madras). It was some four years after the Indian Health Organisation (now Indian People's Organisation) began its pioneering efforts in the red light areas of Mumbai in 1982 that the ICMR and Directorate General of Health Services (DGHS) launched a national programme of serological surveillance (Chatterjee and Sehgal 2004). This was to be the important event toward a national approach to the epidemic – National AIDS Control Programme of 1987. In response to national and international pressure, two years later, a medium-term plan was worked out in collaboration with WHO. It was evident from these influences that the challenge of HIV/AIDS would require a level of mobilization well beyond the capacity of India's strained public health system. In 1992, National AIDS Control Organisation (NACO) was established to coordinate the National AIDS Control Programme (NACP). NACO identified the importance of NGO participation and sought cooperation in all activities taken up for the implementation of NACP. A comprehensive guideline for the involvement of NGOs was drawn up in consultation with the representatives of NGOs and State AIDS Control Societies (SACS). Some pilot studies and intervention projects were started with the help of NGOs in Delhi, Kolkata, Mumbai and Guwahati. NGOs are also associated with training activities, IEC assessment studies, risk behaviour studies and the preparation and distribution of IEC materials. In this context, it would be appropriate to discuss about the activities of NGOs engaged in HIV/AIDS prevention and care in India.

Shalom, an NGO in Manipur has received international recognition for its work on injecting drug use and HIV. In 1995, Shalom set up a needle and syringe pilot project, which was initially regarded, controversial by the authorities. The authorities perceived the project to be a blatant endorsement of drug use, but evidence showed that the intervention actually helped to reduce rampant practices of needles sharing among IDUs and subsequently helped to decrease HIV transmission. It now has evolved into a statewide programme involving twelve other NGOs under Manipur SACS and receives support from national and international agencies.

Mahila Sarvangeen Utkarsh Mandal (MASUM), Pune was set up in 1987 at the request of local women and engaged in identifying the various forms of exploitation and abuse faced by women and helped them to organize themselves to deal with these problems. A few kilometers outside the Pune city the draught zone starts. Many people migrated to urban cities like Mumbai for employment and returning home after contracting the HIV. MASUM set up Streewadi Arogya Kendra (the feminist health centre) as a part of an action research project of ICMR. The center was serving the women with STIs and RTIs. Despite many problems faced by them, members of MASUM started to have an influence on community attitudes. A group of local youth performs street plays about the problem of deserted women, violence against women, illiteracy and AIDS to sensitize the people. In 1994, the group won the first prize from the India health organization for an instructive play on HIV/AIDS. MASUM's activities are assisting to promote new attitudes and forms of behaviour leading to a social climate in which women are more assertive and less open to exploitation and abuse – thereby becoming less vulnerable to HIV infection.

Lawyers' Collective, Mumbai – a small group of practicing lawyers involved in Public Interest litigation (PIL) became famous with Dominic D'Souza case. D'Souza, a young man from Goa, was detected HIV positive in February 1989 after donating blood to a local hospital. Due to his HIV-positive status, he was arrested and placed in a separate cell under the Goa Public Health Act. Mr. Anand Grover on behalf of Lawyers' Collective filed a PIL and D'Souza was released after 64 days' detention when the court delivered the verdict of amending the Act. Thereafter, it was no longer mandatory to detain people with HIV. Later on, it felt that there was a dire necessity for a new comprehensive legislation to deal with the multi-faceted human rights issues arising from HIV/AIDS epidemic in the country. It started to train lawyers with a view to develop a countrywide network of lawyers to take up such individual cases. It also organizes workshops to frame policies for protecting human rights of PLWHA. The Collective works in collaboration with WHO and UNDP, and represents in National Legal and ethical Committee on HIV/AIDS of NACO. The Collective's lobbying of political leaders at the national level helped in persuading the government to leave its plan for mandatory testing and confinement of people with HIV. It also publishes a journal "The lawyers" and presently operating from two offices in Mumbai and in Delhi. They never charge any fees; the personal resources of its members finance all PIL activities.

Seva Mandir, Udaipur has been working over past 30 years with the local tribal people (the Bhil) in a wide variety of rural development activities. There were not known cases of HIV/AIDS in this zone, social, economic and geographical elements combine to make local the people vulnerable to STDs along with HIV. Everyday about 8000 trucks ply up and down NH-8 between Delhi and Mumbai. This highway like others across the country is therefore major route not only for goods, but also for the spread of STDs and HIV/AIDS. Roadside hotels (Dhaba) at the truck stops near Udaipur are very popular among the truckers. Because, near the highway, tribal women sell sex to the truckers in order to survive, exposing themselves at the risk of contracting HIV and then passing it to their husbands and sexual partners. Pre – marital and extra-marital sex are common and widely accepted among the Bhils. Seva Mandir's AIDS programme started in 1992. It formed 6 Highway Contact Teams to contact local women, dhaba workers and sex workers and 14 Village Contact Teams to visit communities for disseminating information on STDs and HIV/AIDS, distributing condoms and referring villagers to Seva Mandir's health clinics for STD treatment. Seva Mandir's AIDS programme now covers more than 200 villages and it has incorporated AIDS awareness in all of its other development projects. The formation of these teams helped to sharpen the focus on HIV/AIDS. The changing social climate brought about by Seva Mandir is helping to give individuals and communities the choice of breaking away from high-risk sexual behaviour and to choose other forms of safer sexual expression (Satpathy 2003).

NGO Response to HIV/AIDS in West Bengal

The present study has been conducted to understand the NGO response to HIV/AIDS in West Bengal. The main reason for selecting West Bengal is its unique and long history of NGOs started with the social reform movement of Brahmo Samaj. Subsequently, due to its unique socio-political background, numbers of movements were organized in West Bengal, such as freedom movement, Tebhaga movement, Naxalite movement, land reform movement, etc. (Sarkar 2005). These movements led to form a large number of NGOs. Besides it, first National AIDS Control Policy aided by WHO was also started in West Bengal in 1987. NACO has also classified West Bengal in the Group-B states where HIV infection rate among high-risk group crossed 5% or more. Nature of activities of a few NGOs engaged in HIV/AIDS prevention can be worthy to mention in this regard.

Durbar Mahila Samanaya Committee (DMSC), Kolkata is a network of women sex workers from Sonagachi, the largest red-light area in Kolkata existing for over a century. DMSC now mobilized around 60,000 sex workers in West Bengal. The peer education programme of early 1990s led to the empowerment of these sex workers. This peer-to-peer interaction elicited more open and accepting response from the sex workers. One of the DSMC's most documented successes is the dramatic increase in over all condom use from 2.7% in 1992 to over 90% in 1998 among female sex workers (FSWs). The Sonagachi project is now considered as an example of a 'best practice' intervention in the world, which clearly demonstrates that close involvement and ownership of the project by the community are essential for a sex worker (or any marginalized group) project to success. Presently DMSC is implementing numbers of TI projects in different districts of West Bengal. Besides HIV/AIDS project, DSMC developed a self-run cooperative called Usha Cooperative society to save the sex workers from pimps and moneylenders by extending loans to them. DMSC also took the leaderships in mobilizing all the sex workers of the country and protested with one voice against social injustice and demanded government attention particularly on police harassment, recognition of sex workers as workers, poor health care and forced HIV Testing. The DMSC is also now receiving funds from international agencies like WHO, USAID, UNAIDS and Bill and Melinda Gates Foundation. Recently DMSC organized international conference of sex workers in India.

Society for Positive Atmosphere and Related Support to HIV/AIDS (SPARSHA) is a unique organization of HIV positive and HIV negative people. In the late 1980s, a group of children and young persons with hemophilic contracted HIV through transfusion of contaminated blood and blood products. The care needs of these youth remained unaddressed for long. The HIV infected hemophiliacs, therefore, had no other way but to form a loose group with support, inspiration and active participation of a few health care providers. This was a pioneering effort which was initiated 1998 and paved the way for greater involvement of PLWHA. In 2001, Australian Agency for International Development (AusAID) funded a project entitled "Creation of a Support Network for People Living with HIV in West Bengal" which helped the group to consolidate into a registered body named SPARSHA. It is mainly run by a group of PLWHA and their friends and now implementing TI projects of WBSAP&CS. It has also undertaken and complemented numbers of research projects of DFID, UNDP, UNICEF and WBSAP&CS. It is also providing subsidized ART to children of impoverished family, reaching out to PLWHA in need of home-based care and running a residential community care center for PLWHA in Howrah district.

MANAS Bangla, Kolkata is a network having seven member organizations to coordinate and enhance their efforts in promoting health and general wellbeing of MSM. It is dealing with issues on homophobia, violence and stigma around sexual and gender identities. The focus is on empowerment and affirmation of the rights based on sexualities or gender of MSMs. HIV infected MSMs are doubly stigmatized because of their sexual behaviour and their HIV status. MANAS Bangla is currently implementing a TI project of WBSAP&CS, which is first in the state as well as in the whole northeastern India. It is a nodal intervention using rights based approach and is entirely community owned.

From the above discussion, it is evident that many NGOs in West Bengal are working among the different vulnerable groups infected and affected by HIV/AIDS epidemic. Hence, initiating an in-depth study to understand the role of NGOs in HIV/AIDS prevention and care in West Bengal is meaningful and realistic.

REFERENCES

Anand, K. et al (1999). "Impact of HIV/AIDS on the national economy of India", *Health Policy*, 47(3), 195-205.

Barnett, A. and Whiteside (2002), *AIDS in the Twenty-First Century: Disease and Globalization,* Palgrave-Macmillan: New York.

Bhusan, V., M. Chandy, P.G.Babu, D. Denison, A. Srivastava, N.K. Saraswati and T.J.John (1994), "Transfusion Associated HIV Infection in Patients with Hematologic Disorders in Southern India", *Indian Journal of Medical Research*, 99:57-70.

Brodhead, T. and J.O'Mally (1989), 'NGO and Third World Development: Opportunities and Constraints.' *Paper presented at the WHO's Global Programme on AIDS Management Committee Meeting*, 6-8.

Charles, M. et al. (1993), 'The economic impact of AIDS on Thailand'. In D.E. Bloom and J.V. Lyons (eds.), *Economic Implication of AIDS in Asia,* pp. 7-34, UNDP: New Delhi.

Chatterjee and Sehgal (2004), 'HIV/AIDS Awareness and Control: The Role of Non-Governmental Organisations in the Country'.

In S. Panda, A. Chatterjee and A. S. Abdul-Quader (eds) *Living with AIDS virus: The Epidemic and the Response in India*, Sage: Delhi.

De, M., D. Banerjee, S.Chandra and D.K. Bhattacharya (1990), "HBV and HIV seropositivity in Multi-Transfused Hemophiliacs and Thalassaemics in Eastern India", *IJMR*, 91: 63-66.

Duggal, R., Gupta, M. and Jesani, A. (1986), *NGOs in Rural Health Care*, FRCH: Mumbai.

Duggal, R. (1988), "NGOs, Government and Private Sector in Health", *Economic and Political Weekly*, March 26, pp. 633-636.

Encyclopedia Britannica (2003), "*AIDS*", Encyclopedia Britannica Online, 12 April 2003. http://search.cb.com/eb/article?en=4225

GFATM (2003), *Report of Global Fund to fight AIDS, TB and Malaria, 2003*. www.globalfundatm.org

Indian Express (2001), "This HIV Positive Women Got the Virus from Her own Blood, Awaits Destiny", *Indian Express*, 3rd June 2001, Pune.

Jha, P. et al. (2002), "Improving the health of global poor", *Science*, 295(5562), 2036-39.

Kumar, R.M., S.A. Udaman and A. Khurranna (1995), "A Prospective Study of Mother-to-Infant HIV Transmission in Tribal Women from India", *Acquired Immuno Deficiency Syndrome Human Retroviral*, 9: 238-242.

Larson, H.J. and J.P. Narain (2001), "Beyond 2000: Responding to HIV/AIDS in the New Millennium", *SEA/AIDS/122*, WHO/SEARO: New Delhi.

Mathew, G. (1999), "Decentralised Institution – Government and Voluntary sector", *Economic and Political Weekly*, Feb.27, p. 529.

NACO (1995), *AIDS Education in School: A Training Package*, Ministry of Health and Family Welfare, Govt. of India: New Delhi.

NACO (1999a), *The Scheme for Prevention and Control of AIDS (Phase-II)*, pp. 2-12, Ministry of Health and Family Welfare, Govt. of India: New Delhi.

NACO (1999b), *The Status of HIV/AIDS*, Ministry of Health and Family Welfare, Govt. of India: New Delhi.

NACO (2001b), *The Current Status and Trends of HIV/AIDS Epidemic in India*, pp. 1-18, Ministry of Health and Family Welfare, Govt. of India: New Delhi.

NACO (2005), *HIV/AIDS Updates*. (www.nacoonline.org)

NACO (2001a), *National Baseline General Population Behavioural Survey*, pp 52-54, Ministry of Health and Family Welfare, New Delhi.

Narain, J.P. (2004), *AIDS in Asia – The Challenge Ahead*, Sage: New Delhi.

Phoolcharoen, Wiput (1998), "HIV/AIDS Prevention in Thailand: Success and Challenges", *Science*, 280(5371), 1873-74.

Salamon, Lester M. (1995), *The International Guide to Non-profit Law*, Wiley: New York.

Salunka, S.R. et al. (1998), "HIV/AIDS in India: A Country Responds to a Challenge", *AIDS*, 12 (Suppl. B): S27-S31.

Sarkar, A. (2001), "Development Through NGOs in Barak Valley: A Critical Analysis", *Social Action*, Vol. 51, Jan-March, pp. 61-73.

Sarkar, A. (2005), *NGOs – The New Lexicon of Health Care*, Concept: New Delhi.

Satpathy, R.C. (2003), 'AIDS Control: Indian Perspective'. In Satpathy, R.C. (ed.), *Encyclopedia of AIDS*, Vol.-3, pp 247-284.

Shaukat, M. and Panakadan, S. (2004), 'HIV/AIDS in India: Problems and Response'. In J.P.Narain (ed.), *AIDS in ASIA – The Challenges Ahead*, Sage Publications: New Delhi, pp. 158-170.

Sheth, D.L. and Sethi, H. (1996), 'The NGO Sector in India: Historical Context and Current Discourse' in *Development Policy and Administration*, Sage: New Delhi, pp 281-301.

Sen, S. et al. (1993), "AIDS in Multi-Transfused Children with Thalassemia", *Indian Paediatry*, 30: 455-60.

Sengupta, B. et al. (1992), "Serosurveillance of Transmissible Hepatitis B and C Virus in Asymptomatic HIV Infection in Haemophilics", *IJMR*, 96: 256-58.

Singh, Y.N. et al. (1991), "HIV Infection in Asian Indian Patients with Haemophilia and those who had Multiple Transfusions", *IJMR* 93: 12-14.

UNAIDS/WHO (2002), *AIDS Epidemic Update*, December 2002. http://www.unaids.org

UNAIDS (2002), *Report on the Global HIV/AIDS epidemic.* http://www.unaids.org

UNAIDS (2002), *Report on the Global HIV/AIDS epidemic –July 2004*, Geneva. http://www.globalizationandhealth.com

UNAIDS (2008), *UNAIDS Report on the Global AIDS Epidemic 2008.*

UN Population Division (2001), *World Population Prospects: The 2000 Revision,* New York: UN Population Division.

Unnikrishna, S.S., K. Abhayambika, R. Verghese, M, Leghori, Sarojini (1993), "Clinical presentation of AIDS – a Kerala experience", *Journal of Associate Physicians of India*, 41 (1): 38-40.

WHO (1997), *AIDS: No time for complacency*, WHO Regional Office for South-East Asia: New Delhi. www.who.int/HIV_AIDS/first.html

WHO/SEARO (2003), *HIV/AIDS Programme Report*, WHO/SEARO, New Delhi. www.who.int/HIV_AIDS/first.html

WHO (2003), *HIV/AIDS in Asia and the Pacific Region*, WHO/SEARO: New Delhi. www.who.int/HIV_AIDS/first.html

2

Studies on NGOs

Voluntary organizations, now popularly known as non-governmental organizations (NGOs) embrace a wide array of agencies within and across different countries of the world. NGOs are simply agencies or groups, which are different from government bodies. However, NGOs are distinctive in containing a voluntary component and because they don't operate for profit. Most commonly, NGOs are defined as voluntary and non-profit organizations working towards the development and amelioration of suffering with non-self serving aims and free from state control in managing day to day affairs (D. Rajasekhhar 2000). NGOs are funded through individual and corporate donations, levies imposed on members or grants from international and government agencies. Hence, the following terms usually come up: NGOs, Voluntary Organizations (VOs), Community Based Organizations (CBOs), Peoples Organizations (POs), Public Service Contractors (PSCs), and Non-Profit Organizations (NPOs). The first term, NGO, is the most widely used as the umbrella organization within which other terms can be included depending on the scale of operations (Korten 1990).

The term 'NGO' applies to diverse organizations that work together outside of government to address a need, advance a cause or defend an interest (Brodhead and O'Mally 1989). NGO encompasses a whole range of organizations that differ in size, function and geographical location. Thus, the term can be used to describe small, locally based and loosely established voluntary and largely grass-roots types of associations, as well as large national and even transnational voluntary associations with formal constitutions employing hundreds of staff. However, World Bank defines NGO as "private organizations that pursue activities to relieve suffering, promote the interests of the poor, protect the environment or undertake community development" (World Bank 1987; Mercer et al. 1991). Based on a close scrutiny of goals, relationships among various organizations and operational methods, it was deduced that NGOs play two broad roles in society: (1) operational roles and (2) educational and advocacy roles. Operational NGOs are more central to international responses in the post-cold war world. They have the responsibility of fund raising. The rendering of services is central to most NGO budgets. While the target of operational NGOs is beneficiaries or victims in case of emergencies, the educational and advocacy NGOs seek to influence citizens, and through public opinion, bear fruit in the form of additional resources for their activities as well as new policies, better decisions and enhanced international regimes. These NGOs help to reinforce various norms promoted through public education campaigns. This heightened awareness among public audiences in turn helps hold the state accountable for their international commitments (Gordenkar and Weiss 1996).

In increasing numbers, NGOs have voiced their concerns in international discourse about numerous problems of international scope. NGOs assumed a central role in activities involving human rights, complex humanitarian emergencies, the UN relationship, the global environment, the international women's movement, operational coalitions and state relations, and AIDS. They also bring local experiences to bear on international decision making (Gordenkar and Weiss 1996). The NGO expansion, dubbed as "barefoot revolution" can be attributed to several external and internal factors. A declining faith in the capacities of governments to solve the interrelated problems of social welfare, development and environment, lead to the global upsurge of organized private activity through a non-profit sector. The non-profit sector has grown increasingly important in its efforts to provide alleviation of societal problems and injustices and the promotion of democratic values throughout the world in recent years. This sector has also become a major economic force with sizeable expenditures and multiple levels of paid and volunteer employment. NGOs make up the sub-set of non-profit sector involved in development work (Salamon 1995). In the beginning of 1980s, several developed and developing countries started thinking of privatization, liberalization and withdrawal of state from social sector programmes like education, health, nutrition, etc. Because these countries were facing the problem of BOP (Balance of payment), reduced their budgets in social sector and started taking loan from International Monetary Fund (IMF) and World Bank (WB) for the survival of country's economy. During the implementation of IMF and WB's programme, an understanding was developed that investment in public sector was wasteful and therefore, the emphasis on NGOs was better. It was assumed where government failed to reach out to the marginalised sections and created gap, NGOs could bridge the same (Sarkar 2005). The end of cold war was perhaps most important influence on NGO expansion. The end of cold war also brought it with the end of ideological and social orthodoxy. UN practitioners and diplomats became less reluctant to interact with NGOs, opening up new avenues of communication and cooperation within the decision making process. The UN became a forum of governments and NGOs. They also contribute advanced knowledge on issues such as gender, human rights, environments, AIDS, relief assistance and community development (Gordenkar and Weiss 1996).

In India, VOs or NGOs have a long history. It is clear that NGO is legacy of the colonial system and its growth in independent India is very steady to reinforce the development process. Health care and education were prominent among the initial concerns of many NGOs in the 1950s and 1960s. However, NGOs have increasingly moved into projects directly targeted at alleviating poverty and attempting to raise the incomes of the poor. Thus, projects aimed at increasing the farmers' incomes became fashionable in 1970s. A different trend was also emerged in the 1970s, where the emphasis was not so much on service delivery or development programmes, but on organising the poor with a view to enabling them to exercise greater influence over decisions affecting their lives. This 'empowerment' approach has its roots in the view that literacy can often become a means by which the poor can reflect on the causes of their poverty and find ways to tackling them (Chandra 2005). In 1980s, new concerns came to the fore such as gender and environment, with social forestry and soil conservation prominent among the environmental concerns. These reflect an increasing concern about how projects affect the wider setting in which the poor live. This extension of interests comes from 'innovation' – another characteristic that NGOs emphasize. The 1990s have witnessed yet more changes in the nature of NGO activities. Work in the areas of gender and environment has been widened, deepened and integrated under the umbrella of 'sustainable development'. There are two reasons for this. First reason stems from a concern with cost recovery and the desire among the NGOs (especially Northern NGOs) to transfer the recurrent costs of project management to the community following the withdrawal of the support agency. This is based on the belief that development interventions can be sustained over longer term only if community assumes ownership of the project or programme. A second reason for the interest in sustainability is bound up with the desire to avoid promoting dependence on an external agency. This is based in part on NGOs' not wishing to be perceived as benevolent patrons, especially when external dependence simply replaces the influence of locally dominant elites without addressing the structural reasons for such dominance.

Therefore, it is found that NGOs have been around us for a long time and involved in performing various developmental and welfare activities. At the same time, there was widespread skepticism outside NGO circles about the potential of NGOs in development. This has now diminished. However, there are many contradictory views about the comparative advantages and weaknesses of NGOs. These views range from quasi-denial of NGOs' effectiveness to hyperbolic exaggeration. One way of assessing the impact and effectiveness of NGO interventions is to attempt to isolate those features of NGOs, which place them in a comparatively advantageous position. But it is not an easy task to come to any firm overall conclusions about either the factors, which characterize the uniqueness of NGO interventions, or the degree to which NGOs have succeeded in their tasks. There are four main reasons for this. The first is simply a lack of data. For all the evidence provided, the extent of reliable evidence upon which judgments have been made and are made still remains minute in comparison with both the absolute numbers of NGO interventions and the very different types of project embarked upon. The second is that there still seems to be confusion in the eyes of both the general public and the agencies over claims and assertions about the comparative advantage of NGOs and the evidence, which is available. The third is the growing realization that a range of both complex and external factors plays a powerful role in influencing the outcome of NGO intervention in very different social, economic and political contexts. Finally, the lack of an agreed method of assessing the performance of NGO projects and programmes create a handicap in judging the impact (Chandra 2005).

Unfortunately, there is a meagre literature on the NGOs working in various issues and situations in India. The role of NGOs in HIV/AIDS care is one of such unexplored areas of social science discipline. In this regard, Baviskar writes, "Systematic studies are required to say anything with confidence about them. In absence of such studies, our understanding of NGOs will remain vague, superficial and hazy" (Baviskar 2001). It is found that there are only few NGOs who are exclusively working in the HIV/AIDS field. Most of the NGOs engaged in health sector are running HIV/AIDS programmes in India. Therefore, in order to understand and find out the trends of research in NGO sector, it is worthwhile to examine the existing literature on NGOs in health care as well. Considering the available literature, the review, in two parts, has focused studies on health care and NGOs response to HIV/AIDS.

Studies on NGOs in Health Care

Duggal, Gupta and Jesani (1986) conducted a study on "*NGOs in Rural Health Care*" at the behest of ICMR to gain a deeper insight into the role and functioning of many different types of NGOs in Maharashtra, a state having the largest number of such agencies. The study brought out the target variation between the aims and motivation of the various NGOs as well as their different approaches, which vary from the running rural hospitals to community participation and conscientisation. An interesting finding of the study was that NGOs had neglected the socially and economically backward districts as compared to their better concentration in the average and highly developed districts of Maharashtra. This highlighted the need to pay more attention to the deprived masses of backward districts.

Baru (1987) made a study on "*Factors influencing variations in health services*" in Andhra Pradesh. The study was limited in two well-developed districts (Krishna and Guntur) as well as two backward districts (Medak and Mehbub Nagar). It considered public, private and voluntary sector providing health care services. With regard to voluntary sector, study explored that growth and distribution of voluntary agencies were skewed in favour of well-developed districts.

The Ford Foundation has been engaged with NGO programmes in India since the 1970s. In order to systematically analyse documents and disseminate the experiences of NGOs implementing health and family planning programme in India, it initiated a project in 1986. Under the project, twelve case studies, entitled ANUBHAV were published. Each case study included details regarding the NGO i.e. genesis of the project and its evolution, its organizational structure, staffing pattern, funding and cost structures, the range and mode of service delivery, institutional relationships with the government and other institutions, community participation, information systems and programme impact. The lessons of these projects were shared with NGO policy planners, researchers and donors (Pachauri, 1994). Based on these documented case studies (published in ANUBHAV series) many scholars have given many interpretations. For instance, Peter Berman and Priti Dave (1994) point out that NGOs show a high degree of creativity and innovation in developing varied source of financing to reduce dependency and enable them to sustain their programmes. Their health programmes operate as efficiently as public services and provide supplementary support rather than substitute services. They suggest further development of voluntary sector financing, which may reinforce overall health care intervention. Rajesh Tandon (1994) studied the ANUBHAV projects in order to know the nature of community participation in health. He suggested a policy framework in promoting effective community participation for better health in India.

Bhattacharjee (1996) has completed a study on "*NGO Approaches to Health and Development in India: Strategies and Sustainability*". He observes in order to achieve appreciable and sustainable results; an NGO will have to make long-term commitments to the community. He observed that NGOs could overcome different of its problems through financial stability. But dependence on government or donors will affect their role as a pressure group. Therefore, they will have to generate their own funds. Increasing the number of pay clinics can do such generation of fund. The NGO then will become a channel to redistribute money from rich to poor.

Dr. Sunil Mishra (2000) analysed 14 action research projects of the Population Foundation of India. The Population Foundation of India was established in 1970. It had either supported or itself commissioned around 320 projects. The Foundation selected 14 action research projects carried out by voluntary organizations during 1995-96 for the case study and qualitative evaluation. Main purpose was to assess the effectives of the NGOs in brining about the desired changes in the individual and community value systems. Among the 14 projects, three were related to infant mortality and fertility, three were pertaining to integrated health, family planning and development; four to reproductive health and family planning in urban slums among industrial workers; another three to reproductive health and family planning and the remaining one to family planning; through rural medical practitioners. Mishra brought together all the 14 case studies (evaluation report) of action research projects in a volume and analyzed the dynamics of social change, the factors that led to success and the problems. He found that NGO could work as catalyst of change. A concern for community participation as well as a need for mass education, under an NGO was, very crucial to bringing about an attitudinal change in health behaviour.

Varma (2001) in his article on "*Reproductive and sexual health of adolescents: An NGO experience.*" describes a particularly successful initiative in the mobilization of target group. He provides background of an NGO operating in Delhi, and then sets out to describe the experience it had in implementing a reproductive and sexual health programme for adolescents. Varma concludes by describing briefly the lessons learnt, which cover the importance and applicability of research with intervention in developing an effective design; community development approach; addressing the environment along with the individual; and the role of adolescent development.

Gupta (2003) in his article on "*Contribution of NGOs in implementing population policy*" has analyzed the role played by NGOs in implementing the government's national population policy in Bangladesh. He has noted that the target oriented, heavy-handed approach to population control, with an element of coercion, created an adverse impact. Gupta has also discussed population and empowerment of women; contribution of NGOs, and IEC strategies adopted by NGOs in handling population policy. He has emphasized that in the ultimate analysis the challenge of the population explosion will be met only if it is understood in proper perspective, particularly by the political leadership. He has concluded by noting that NGOs' major contribution has been the sensitisation of various stakeholders, especially in bringing home the realisation that the family welfare programme needs to be linked with sustainable development, empowerment of women, and social and gender equity.

Vishnu and Sudarshan (2003) examine the case of Karuna Trust and Vivekananda Foundation a public sector–voluntary organisation partnership for primary health care services. They discuss the four key aspects of partnership between the public sector and NGOs: participation in health policy, effects of decentralisation; partnerships out of services; and quality assurance activities. They describe the case background profile and context followed by policy and political environment and the legal framework and go on to the work in the area of reproductive and child health. Their work highlights the constraints of the partnerships. Notable among them are: people with vested interest even attempted to withdraw control of the health centres from the NGOs through a resolution passed by the *zilla parishad*; there were huge financial implications, as the finance sharing between the government and the NGO was in the ratio of 75:25 as against the 90:10 agreed in the partnership terms; and unnecessary bureaucratic constraints interfered the smooth operations of these NGO run PHCs. The article also lists policy implications. There must be explicit, transparent and adequate policy mechanisms, which ensure the involvement of all stakeholders in the partnership process. There is also a need for coordination across various government departments and implementing agencies for the smooth transition of handing over, thereby preventing undue bureaucratic delays.

Gomez (2004) examines the feasibility of the government's partnership with NGOs in reproductive health in Mexico. In 1995 the Mexico government began to develop policies on establishing collaborative agreements with civil society organisations and currently working together. He analyses whether the conditions exist in Mexico for successful partnerships between the public sector and NGOs in reproductive health. In-depth interviews were carried out with key informants in the public sector of national and state level, and the NGO sector in six states in Mexico. Partnerships were found to be an option for the provision of reproductive health services in geographical areas where the population is under-served, and for services the government does not provide. While the contribution of NGOs to the reproductive health field is recognized at least at the federal level, there are still very few public agencies that collaborate with NGOs, and agreements are often limited to short-term financing of projects. Gomez-Jauregui concludes that the future of NGOs in Mexico will depend largely on their ability to obtain funding from within the country. More effective mechanisms are needed by the government to generate resources for health care. The government must recognize the specific contribution of NGOs, including inputs of social capital and creation of community networks, and must share decision-making more equitably with NGOs for partnerships to succeed.

Tikku (2004) has conducted a study with respect to NGOs in three north Indian states. The research examines the functioning of NGOs and their role in combating nutritional and health problems prevalent among children, adolescents and women in Delhi, Haryana and Rajasthan. The NGOs also dealt with other related areas to supplement and complement their main focus on health and nutrition. However, not many of them were involved in tackling endemic and emerging diseases like jaundice, TB, malaria, dengue and HIV/AIDS/ STD, which should be given more emphasis. It was found also that there is no proper mechanism for obtaining and analyzing information on health and nutritional services provided by voluntary organisations. Each state should have a district-wise database on nutritional and health services provided by NGOs. Lack of coordination/support from government departments, and inadequacy and or untimely release of budgets were among the other problems cited.

Mercer et al. (2004) through their article on "*Effectiveness of an NGO primary health care programme in rural Bangladesh: Evidence from the management information system*" looks at the effectiveness of an NGO primary health care programme in rural Bangladesh. It is based on data from the programme management information system reported by 27 partner NGOs from 1996 to 2002. On the basis of a crude indicator of socio-economic status, the programme is poverty-focused. The data indicate that relatively high coverage has been achieved for reproductive and child health services. There is good service coverage among the poorest one-third and others, and the infant and child mortality differential has been eliminated over recent years. A rapid decline in infant mortality among the poorest from 1999–2002 reflects a reduction in neonatal mortality of about 50 per cent. Allowing for some under-reporting and possible misclassification of deaths to the stillbirths category, neonatal mortality is relatively low in the areas covered by the NGOs. The lower child and maternal mortality for the areas covered by these NGOs combined, compared with estimates for Bangladesh in recent years, may at least in part be due to high coverage of reproductive and child health services. Other development programmes implemented by many of the NGOs could also have contributed. Despite the limited resources available, and the lower infant and child mortality already achieved, there appears to be scope for further prevention of deaths, particularly those due to birth asphyxia, acute respiratory infection, diarrhoeal disease and accidents. Maternal mortality in the NGO areas was lower in 2000–2002 than the most recent estimates for Bangladesh.

Sarkar (2005) made a study on "*NGOs in Health Care in West Bengal*". The study shows that there is plurality among NGOs in terms of their emergence, basis of initiating programme, approach, type of service, promoter's background, source of funding, organizational setup, nature of activity etc. In West Bengal NGOs prefer to work in socio-economically developed areas and can't continue work in the community for long time due to financial unsustainability. The study shows a high-degree of dependence on national and foreign funds that influences priorities of the NGOs. They focus primarily on preventive and promotive services with little emphasis on curative services. Thus NGOs generate 'demand' for care but there is little effort to provide services to address their needs. Ultimately people, having received the awareness from NGO, go to public and private sector for better curative services. This kind of trend proves that health services provided by the government and private sectors are complementary for NGOs of West Bengal. The study suggested that there is need to integrate the services of government, private and NGO sectors in providing better health care.

Mugisha et al. (2005) in the article on "*Are reproductive health NGOs in Uganda able to engage in the health SWAp?*" has tried to explore the ability of reproductive health (RH) NGOs in Uganda to survive in the context of SWAp (sector-wide approaches) and decentralisation. The authors argue that contrary to perceptions that this may increase NGOs' financial vulnerability, a SWAp and a decentralised system may actually provide an opportunity that should be embraced by NGOs to enhance their sustainability and effectiveness by reducing their current dependency on donors' funding. The article discusses the systemic weaknesses of many NGOs that currently make them vulnerable, and observes that unless these are addressed, such NGOs will lose their space in the SWAp and decentralisation arena. The authors suggest that NGOs need to recognize the opportunities that participating in public-private partnerships through a SWAp can offer them for long-term and significant funding. They need also to develop their capacity of proactive participation in a SWAp and decentralised context by becoming more entrepreneurial in nature, through reorienting their organisational philosophies, and strategic planning and budgeting so as to be able to partner effectively with the public sector in accessing funds made available through health sector reform.

Studies on NGOs response to HIV/AIDS

The review of the studies on NGOs response to HIV/AIDS is divided into two parts – namely (A) studies conducted in other countries and (B) in India.

(A) Studies conducted in other countries

Aldaba, Fernando T.; Josefa P. Petilla (1997) made a case study on "*Governance and HIV: Government - Civil Society Interface: An Aspect of Governance Critical to an Effective Response*" in Philippines. There exists a dynamic inter-relationship between good governance, a successful government organisation (GO) - civil society organisation (CSO) interface, and an appropriate response to the HIV/AIDS epidemic. This case study specifically examines three examples of interface: the Philippine National AIDS Council (PNAC) at the national level; and Olongapo City AIDS Foundation Inc. (OCAFI) and Inter-agency HIV/AIDS Network (IHAIN) in the province of Palawan at the local level. The study also looks into another interface which it considers crucial to the success of the HIV/AIDS response - the interface between Pinoy Plus, the sole organisation of people living with HIV/AIDS (PLWHA) in the Philippines, and GOs and NGOs. The conclusions from the three examples of interfaces reveal that the HIV/AIDS epidemic requires a multi-sectoral and collaborative response. There should be openness and humility, tolerance of other's ideas, and parties must be frank and comfortable enough to make and receive criticism. Finally the interface must extract commitment from members and must be inspirational, motivating others to emulate the successful partnership. A successful interface is able to strengthen and energize the active participants to the interface. Good governance is eventually strengthened by increasing examples and models of collaborative efforts between government and civil society and by expanding such responses to issues other than HIV-AIDS.

David Wilkinson and team (2000) made a study on "*An evaluation of the Ministry of Health/NGO Home care programme for people with HIV/AIDS in Cambodia*". Cambodia had one of the fastest growing epidemics in Asia, but has also had an active government and NGO response. In 1998, the Cambodian Ministry of Health established a partnership with a group of NGOs to develop and deliver home care in Phnom Penh and in Battambang Province. The findings clearly show that home care has an impact at a number of levels. This has reduced the suffering of people with HIV/AIDS, improved their quality of life and that of their caregivers' increased understanding of HIV/AIDS helped to empower the poorest by providing social and economic support. The findings have also shown that the cost of delivering home care compared favorably with outpatient services and with home cares services in other countries.

Chillag K. et al. (2000) made a study on "*Factors affecting the delivery of HIV/AIDS prevention programs by community-based organizations*". The Community based organizations (CBOs) play a frontline role in HIV/AIDS prevention activities. CBOs face formidable challenges to effective delivery of HIV prevention services including client characteristics such as homelessness and CBO characteristics such as limited resources and staff turnover. Despite these obstacles, CBOs are generally well positioned to deliver services to specific high-risk populations because they understand their local communities and are connected to the groups they serve. This qualitative study illustrates that structural, socio-cultural, organizational, and individual client factors both facilitate and act as barriers to delivery of HIV prevention services. These challenges and successes helped to identify critical technical assistance needs.

Roy, C.M. and Cain R. (2001) in their article on "*The involvement of people living with HIV/AIDS in community-*

based Organizations: contributions and constraints" paid attention on this neglected aspect. An important feature of the social and organizational response to the HIV epidemic has been that many people living with HIV/AIDS have demanded to have a say in the development of policies and the delivery of services. Surprisingly little attention has been paid in the literature to this involvement. This paper is based on a participatory action research project that involved 70 people with HIV/AIDS in 15 focus group discussions. Findings from the study show the complexities of translating organizational commitments to involve people with HIV/AIDS into practice. This paper outlines the organizational contributions of people with HIV, and examines the difficulties and obstacles to their meaningful involvement. The paper concludes with a discussion of the challenges of user empowerment and with recommendations for policy and practice.

UN-NGLS (United Nations - Non Governmental Liaison Service) has been publishing its "*Voices from Africa*" series for the best part of a decade now. Written entirely by African activists, practitioners and professionals, the series is designed to provide an opportunity for Africans to share their work, concerns, ideas and views with an international readership and help shape a more positive and balanced picture of African realities. The 10th series, focuses on the theme of "*NGO response to HIV/AIDS: Country Experiences*" and has been prepared for the Special Session of the UN General Assembly (UNGASS) on AIDS in New York in June 2001.This series included few country experiences from Africa, some of them are being discussed below.

1. Marie Rose Sawadogo (2001) has discussed about Burkina Faso in her article on "*Private and Community-based HIV/AIDS Approaches in Burkina Faso*". Burkina Faso is the third most affected country in West Africa with an adult prevalence rate of 6.5%, and there is no sign the

epidemic has stopped its spread. The country's population is vulnerable to HIV/AIDS because of poverty, high internal and external migration, weak health services, low levels of school enrolment, and certain traditional practices and beliefs regarding women. The impact of HIV/AIDS is increasingly visible in all sectors of society and in the daily life of each citizen. Initial response to HIV/AIDS in the country came essentially from the government, which set up a national control programme to tackle the epidemic in 1987, with development partners readily providing assistance. Civil society was slower in responding, and the first AIDS control associations came into being only in the early 1990s. One of these earlier groups is the Private and Community-based HIV/AIDS Control Initiative (IPC), set up in December 1994 under the legal responsibility of Plan International as a liaison agency for the London-based International Alliance Against HIV/AIDS. The IPC is now an autonomous NGO in Burkina Faso. A cornerstone of its work was a campaign in 1996 to raise public awareness about HIV/AIDS. Early awareness efforts in the country had centered on IEC campaigns, but this approach was considered inadequate in bringing about changes in attitudes and behaviour.

Although it is difficult to evaluate the actual impact of associations working on HIV/AIDS issues in Burkina Faso, a number of lessons have been learned. Sustained investment in associations and additional financial resources are needed to consolidate them and broaden responses to the disease. Other needs include developing "relay associations" to increase responses to HIV/AIDS; building the training capacity of NGOs; improving administrative procedures; instigating leadership training sessions; intensifying resource mobilization efforts; improving impact evaluations; increasing the profile of AIDS and of people living with the disease; and better sharing of experiences among community-based associations and organizations to improve skills and involve a community's leading actors. IPC believes that the close link between association members and the communities they target will increase their ability to identify needs and appropriate responses. The main hurdle to active participation by association members is the voluntary nature of the work. In addition, the failure of donors to provide institutional support to community-based organizations and the lack of access to funds, materials, and technical and human resources poses many other problems.

2. Leiliane M'Boa, Aristide Kacou, Mariette Wandandi, Samuel Lijalem Hassan, Victor Kamanga, Dora Ofobrukweta, Regina Clement Akpan, Anne Fiedler and Esther Guzha in their article on "*NGO and Community Responses to HIV/AIDS*" narrated the case studies of few NGOs in Congo, Malawi, Nigeria and some other countries. In the Democratic Republic of the Congo, about one million adults and children are infected with HIV/AIDS. In July 1994 a non-governmental group, the People Affected by HIV/AIDS Organization (PAHO), was launched to provide assistance to infected and affected persons, help them come to terms with the disease, and lead valued lives. The first stage of PAHO's work is to gain these people's confidence and help them understand that they are full human beings with rights and duties. Fieldworkers who visit beneficiaries in their homes tactfully perform this groundwork. The second stage involves the organization of information sessions at which people living with HIV/AIDS describe their experiences to groups of 30 to 50 people with whom they feel secure and accepted. This encourages them to speak frankly and openly about their seropositivity. This process of realization helps ensure that people living with HIV/AIDS will adopt more responsible behaviour and reduce the spread of AIDS. It also awakens caution in others by warning people about the AIDS epidemic through personal experience and example. In its work, PAHO

draws on the skills available in local institutions such as the Society for Women and AIDS in Africa (SWAA/Congo), National AIDS Control Programme (PNCS), National AIDS Coordination Office (BCC/SIDA) and the World Health Organization's then Global Programme on AIDS. PAHO has a total of 35 active members; with 250 beneficiaries including 75 women living with HIV, 20 HIV-positive men and 25 children, and 130 AIDS orphans.

Malawi is one of the world's poorest countries where the situation is grim with high rates of HIV infection. Although AIDS is under-reported, the National AIDS Control Programme (NACP) estimated a total of 265,000 cases in the country between 1985-1998 and some 400,000 AIDS orphans. One of the major concerns is access to treatment for the disease. Most citizens in Malawi, faced with low income and a hand-to-mouth existence, have no access to treatment. This must also be viewed against a background of inadequate health facilities, drug supplies and medical personnel in public hospitals. Growing demand for health services due to increased illness is also exerting further pressure on an overburdened infrastructure. Founded in 1997, the Malawi Network of People Living with HIV/AIDS (MANET+) is an umbrella group for people living with AIDS (PLWHA) and HIV/AIDS community-based organizations. It has 30 HIV and AIDS support groups across the country. The network is based on the principle of Greater Involvement of People Living with HIV/AIDS (GIPA) is a critical component to ethical and effective national responses to the epidemic. MANET+ has been working to improve access to treatment in Malawi by advocating for a stronger medical infrastructure, training of medical personnel and health care workers in the use of antiretroviral, negotiations for subsidies from suppliers or reduced prices of antiretroviral drugs, legislation enabling parallel importing and compulsory licensing, and a national drug policy and management programme.

In Nigeria, Life Link Organisation (LLO) is a non-governmental, non-profit group founded in May 1994. It works in selected prisons in five states of Lagos, Kano, Abuja, Edo and Oyo—on reproductive health issues related to the prevention of sexually transmitted infections (STIs) and HIV/AIDS. LLO's mission is to provide health and psychosocial services by disseminating information, and providing education and counselling by well-trained personnel. Its activities target four groups: prisoners, prison staff, their wives, and youth. So far LLO has reached more than 8,200 people with its HIV/AIDS education programmes. LLO is the only group in Nigeria that has targeted prison communities with HIV/AIDS prevention and control programmes. Initially, certain authorities could not understand why HIV/AIDS education was needed in prisons. Prison communities are vulnerable to HIV/AIDS for several reasons. Homosexual practices exist among certain inmates; blood-contaminated instruments such as razor blades can be shared; and some prison guards can be exposed to high-risk behaviours because they are regularly transferred from one post to another but are unable to take their wives. LLO had to be persuasive with cogent reasons and facts. It also had to be tolerant, persistent and patient in order to convince those who were antagonistic. Before the starting of education programme, knowledge of HIV/AIDS and STIs was low. Today a good number of prison community members are well informed about HIV/AIDS and STIs, and unsafe homosexual practices have been reduced in prisons where HIV/AIDS prevention activities have been carried out. The prisons now carry out HIV/AIDS prevention programmes in collaboration with the National Action Committee on AIDS (NACA) and the State Action Committee on AIDS (SACA). Trained peer health educators at each location have formed Anti-AIDS Clubs to ensure the continuation of the programme. There are now 16 clubs in the prison communities with whom LLO works, and each has a minimum of 25 members.

3. Brian Williams, Eleanor Gouws, Janet Frohlich, Catherine Campbell and Catherine MacPhail narrated the experiences of South Africa in the artlicle on "*Lessons From the Front: NGOs and the Fight Against HIV/AIDS in South Africa*" It is another article from "*Voices from Africa*", 10th Series' published by UN-NGLS. South Africa has experienced successive epidemic waves of HIV/AIDS. Today about five million people are infected in the country. As the epidemic matures, up to one million people a year may die and by 2010 one million children will probably be orphaned by AIDS. The National AIDS Convention of South Africa (NACOSA) was formed in 1990 to bring together government, the private sector, trade unions, political groups, AIDS activists and NGOs. They would work together to define principles and determine strategies for intervention. NACOSA was also given a mandate to develop a National AIDS Plan. The article examined two community-based projects: one is in Hlabisa, which is the largest rural district of South Africa's nine provinces and the other is in Carletonville, a major industrial centre in Gauteng. It is about 700 kilometers from Hlabisa, but linked to it by men who live in Hlabisa and migrate to Carletonville to work in the mines.

The Hlabisa Project covers about 3,000 square kilometres and is home to some 215,000 predominantly Zulu-speaking people. Homesteads are widely scattered and people depend on subsistence farming, migrant labour and pensions. Hlabisa has a well-developed health service including a 430-bed hospital, 13 fixed primary health care clinics and a mobile clinic service. The South African Medical Research Council (MRC) has conducted research in the area since the early 1990s, and this has led to substantial improvements in community health care. In 1991 community-based, directly observed therapy (DOTS) was introduced through volunteers and community health workers who now manage 90% of tuberculosis patients. Rural society is highly complex and involves a range of cultural norms including attitudes toward polygamy, the importance of traditional forms of governance, and low levels of education. As a result of this diversity, scientists working on HIV/AIDS and related health issues in Hlabisa have developed good communications with the community. The *Inkosi* (Chief) and his *Izinduna* (Counsellors) eventually hosted a community meeting in Hlabisa in 1997. A Community Advisory Board (CAB) was also elected by the community to promote partnership among researchers, research participants and community members. Community educators, appointed by the CAB, were employed to raise awareness of HIV/AIDS among young people, encourage appropriate STI treatment-seeking behaviour, provide support for people living with HIV, prepare the community for participation in vaccine trials, and inform the community of research findings. Programmes for home-based and paediatric AIDS care were also introduced. In this way it has been possible to bridge the gap between the community and research workers and ensure that the rights and dignity of the community are protected. The community of Hlabisa has benefited from research into community-based health care provision, but the epidemic continues unabated.

The Carletonville Project has been given the name Mothusimpilo, or "working-together-for-health." It was set up to develop a sustainable community-based intervention and evaluate the impact on behaviour, sexually transmitted diseases and HIV in Carletonville, the biggest gold mining complex in the world. About 70,000 migrant mine workers, drawn from rural areas in South Africa and neighbouring countries, live in single sex hostels without their wives or families. In addition about 200,000 people live in the historically white town of Carletonville, the historically black township of Khutsong, and several smaller settlements in the area. The intervention was initially targeted at sex workers and mine workers since it was felt that they were at highest risk. The intervention has two main aims: first, to ensure that all health services in the area—public, private and mine-based—provide syndromic management of STIs while working closely with traditional healers; second, to develop effective and sustainable community-based peer education and condom distribution. Periodic presumptive treatment for women at high risk was subsequently added. Efforts were also made to ensure that the main stakeholders were involved in the design, management and implementation of the project. In addition to the locally based Carletonville AIDS Committee, these included the national and provincial departments of health, mine management and unions, various research organizations, and the principal donors namely DFID (UK) and USAID. In many areas the project has been very successful. Women at high risk in what are locally known as hotspots (informal settlements close to mine shafts where alcohol and sex may be obtained) have developed an active and very effective programme of peer education. This has been extended to women at high risk living in Khutsong. Peer education among mine workers has been less successful, partly because the industry is unwilling to allow men time off work to be trained. Some of the schools in the area are developing their own AIDS programmes with the support of project staff. There is also an effective home-based care project running in Khutsong, but it remains short of funds and support.

4. Milly Katana in her article on "*NAP+, The People's Own Voice*" discussed about the role of NAP+. Since 1994, NAP+ has taken up the challenge of living in communities where people living with HIV/AIDS (PLWHA) face varying degrees of hostility. Its mission is to improve their quality of life by forming and strengthening networks and associations of PLWHA. NAP+ works through the four sub-regional groupings in Southern, Eastern, Western and Central Africa. These sub-regional groups support the central secretariat

based in Nairobi (Kenya) in coordinating efforts of the network. However the strongest links are still the country networks or associations, and individuals in countries where no networks or associations have yet been established. The country networks and associations maintain autonomy to implement activities that respond to the needs of the local membership and communities.

People living with HIV/AIDS across Africa have benefited from the efforts of NAP+ in different ways. First, through supporting the formation and strengthening of support groups and networks, PLWHA realize that there is still something they can control. When support groups or networks are created, members share their experiences of living with the disease, discuss their challenges and set priorities to enhance their survival. It is not until one finds a similar "species" that he or she can realize there is hope for tomorrow, and he or she needs to take some action concerning their life. In an effort to meaningfully involve PLWHA in all issues affecting their lives, NAP+ and its affiliate national networks and associations have encouraged their members to train as AIDS and family counsellors, clinical officers, organizational development experts, professional social workers, journalists, managers, teachers and nurses. NAP+ has encouraged its members to live as role models and to give HIV/AIDS a human face. This has a far-reaching impact on prevention. PLWHA not only preventing any further spread of HIV in communities through self-preservation, but also giving hope to other community members who may be infected with HIV but are not sure of steps to take in order to stay alive. Role modeling is done at both country and regional level. In countries where PLWHA have publicly been on the frontline of prevention, efforts are now paying off. For example, Uganda is registering a downward trend in new infections. This is particularly attributed to, among other factors, the efforts of PLWHA who have engaged in countrywide mobilization efforts. NAP+ through its networks and associations, have formed strong lobbying and advocacy groups to improve their quality of life. Such a movement is sweeping across sub-Saharan Africa, from South Africa to Mali, from Cameroon to Ethiopia. The issues under consideration range from family stigma and discrimination to access to care and treatment. There are considerable achievements in this area, although a lot of work still needs to be done.

5. Moses Chingono discussed about the transport sector on his article on "*AIDS Education and Prevention in Zimbabwe's Transport sector*". The National Employment Council for the Operating Transport Industry (NECTOI) is a non-profit statutory body in Zimbabwe established in 1985. NECTOI represents the interests of 2,500 employers through the Transport Operators Association and the Zimbabwe Rural Transport Organisation, and between 70,000-100,000 employees through the Transport and General Workers Union. The Council has equal representation from employers and employees. NECTOI incorporated an AIDS education and prevention programme in its activities in 1992 as a result of the heavy toll exerted upon the industry by the AIDS epidemic, which threatens to cripple the country's entire transportation workforce. The programme, designed to promote behaviour change and responsible behaviour, is divided into three phases. Phase-I began in 1992 to promote and design specific programmes for individual transport operators. During this phase, company-based awareness programmes were conducted for all employees including Senior Managers. NECTOI recruited, selected and trained company-based health facilitators whose task was to coordinate AIDS education activities in their workplaces. The employees themselves selected the peer educators. This phase was fully funded by NECTOI, with additional technical and material support from the Swedish International Development Authorities (SIDA). The outreach phase began

in Phase-II when it was realized that the more mobile employees of the transport industry were difficult to reach. This phase, funded by AIDSCAP through Family Health International (FHI), ran from 1995 to July1998. The project covered three major transport routes through Zimbabwe linking the capital city Harare to border posts leading to Mozambique, Zambia, South Africa and Botswana. Along these routes, 21 truck stop sites were identified for the outreach programme. Phase-III, funded by the Norwegian Agency for Development Cooperation (NORAD), has been running since January 1999 and has as its objectives to strengthen NECTOI's capacity to sustain workplace-based interventions throughout the transport sector.

NECTOI offers a range of services including peer education training in which workers' representatives learn to offer ongoing informal education to co-workers; condom distribution; short presentations of factual information about HIV/AIDS; development, production and distribution of literature and posters; STI diagnosis and treatment at existing company-based clinics; counselling services; and voluntary HIV testing. In addition to 70,000-100,000 transport company employees, the programme also benefits their spouses, family members and social contacts, as well as their communities. NECTOI develops, produces and distributes sector-specific information, education and communication (IEC) materials for use by transport companies. Materials include posters, charts, and booklets in three local languages, t-shirts, caps, bags, newsletters, license disk holders, peer education carrier bags, and weekly radio programmes on popular channels. NECTOI has managed to reach commercial sex workers and gain their confidence and trust. This has been very difficult given the reluctance of this group to provide information to outsiders. As a result of its activities, NECTOI has noted significant successes in terms of an increase in demand for condoms and IEC materials; significant sexual behaviour change and establishment of an open communication channel between commercial sex workers and health authorities. Good and effective planning, professional implementation, and strong networking with local health programmes have brought about the success in NECTOI's programme. The adult education principles employed by project staff also promoted community participation and yielded good results. At the same time, the programme faces significant constraints. There continues to be unmet demand for condoms and IEC materials, as well as a lack of incentives for peer educators, which results in low morale. It is also difficult to carry out regular follow-up visits because of the distance between project sites.

Horizons (2002) published a Research Summary on "*Greater involvement of PLHA in NGO service delivery: findings from a four-country study*" Seventeen NGOs in Burkina Faso, Zambia, India and Ecuador participated in this study, which examines the ways in which people with HIV/AIDS (PLHA) are involved in NGO programmes and service delivery. The study identified four distinct types of PLHA involvement. These are namely access to services, inclusion, participation and finally involvement, where PLHA take part in management, policy making and strategic planning. The study concluded that PLHA involvement strengthens NGOs as well as enhancing the lives of PLHA. But it is distinct from public disclosure and visibility, and requires a supportive environment. The study recommended ways in which NGOs can create a supportive environment in order to improve their own work and approaches.

Jocelyn DeJong (2002) in his book entitled "*A Question of Scale: Expanding NGO Impact in HIV/AIDS*" discussed about the specific challenge of deliberately increasing the scale of HIV/AIDS prevention, care and support programmes in developing countries. AIDS activities initiated by non-governmental organisations (NGOs) have been highly influential on thinking and strategies found within the HIV/AIDS sector. Yet despite their proliferation, NGOs often experience particular difficulties in increasing the scale of their activities to reach larger numbers of people, to have an impact at levels higher than the "community" and to address the broader social determinants of HIV/AIDS. Perceiving the urgent need for NGOs to expand the scale of their activities in the face of an escalating epidemic, Horizons and the International HIV/AIDS Alliance launched an initiative to examine the nature of the challenge to scale up in the context of HIV/AIDS internationally. This publication was prepared as part of this initiative. While the focus of the publication is on the activities of non-governmental organisations, it recognizes that increasingly NGOs are engaging in partnerships with governments, academic institutions and other organisations in their quest to widen the impact of their activities. The publication consists of three main sections. The first provides a background to and definitions of the term "scaling up" and describes contrasting perspectives to defining this term within the field of HIV/AIDS. In section two, drawing on the existing broader experience of scaling up development programmes, a typology of these processes relevant to HIV/AIDS is proposed. Substantial attention is paid to some of the risks inherent in the scaling up process, as cautionary tales for those interested in embarking on it. The publication also analyses the varied obstacles to scaling up programmes, both in general and how the sensitive nature of HIV/AIDS and diversity of contexts complicate the process. The third section examines the institutional implications of scaling up and the many internal dimensions that must be taken into consideration to prepare for scaling up. The publication concludes with some discussion of the relevance of the arguments made here for both donors and AIDS-support organisations.

The International HIV/AIDS Alliance (the Alliance) has published a Policy Briefing on "*Participation and empowerment in HIV/AIDS programming*" in July 2002, which provides an overview of the many lessons that the Alliance and its partners have learned about participation and empowerment in HIV/AIDS work. Meaningful participation and empowerment of affected populations in HIV/AIDS programming increases the impact of prevention and care interventions. Participation requires an investment in the development of appropriate skills, attitudes and behaviours of facilitators. NGOs and NGO support organizations are in a strong position to support participation of communities in responding to HIV/AIDS. The provision of technical and financial support for this is important. This briefing also discussed about different models of the continuum of participation and empowerment in HIV/AIDS programming. As an example of project level participation, participatory community assessments (PCA) are widely used jointly by Alliance partners and affected communities to develop effective project strategies. PCAs support community members in assessing the local context, identifying needs and resources, and making decisions collectively about how to achieve change. The process helps all concern to develop an understanding of behaviours, attitudes, services, and community norms and values that influence vulnerability to HIV infection. In order to carry out effective PCAs with those most marginalized, it is necessary to identify the relevant groups successfully and then create safe spaces where they feel empowered to participate without fear of discrimination from the wider community. In 2001, partners of the Alliance in Ukraine, along with community members and drug users themselves, carried out 20 participatory community assessments across the Ukraine. They looked mainly at HIV vulnerability and injecting drug-related harm. It has been found that the use of participatory tools increased understanding of the vulnerability among the community people, and specifically injecting drug users. Relationships between drug users, the wider community and NGOs improved, resulting in an increase in volunteers from such groups. The assessment process resulted in a high level of community mobilization, with self-help groups officially registering, securing premises and funding and establishing one of the first harm-reduction programmes in Kiev.

Helmut Kloos, Tadesse Wuhib, Damen Haile Mariam and Bernt Lindtjorn (2003) have reviewed the role of CBOs in their article on *"Community-based organizations in HIV/ AIDS prevention, patient care and control in Ethiopia"*. This review has provided a preliminary evaluation of the suitability of community-based organizations (CBOs) to contribute to HIV/AIDS prevention, care/support and control programs in Ethiopia. Findings show that the multi-sectoral HIV/AIDS Strategy, the current Health Policy, and plans to strengthen the *kebeles* (communities) facilitate the development of CBOs and programmes and infrastructure through the HIV/AIDS Council, the Ministry of Health and various other governmental organizations. CBOs studied are at different stages of planning and implementing preventive and care/ support programs but little is known about their progress, operations and effectiveness due to the lack of monitoring and evaluation mechanisms. Although most CBOs are either still in the formative stage or in process of carrying out HIV/ AIDS prevention programs on a limited scale, their self-initiative, their knowledge of and acceptance by the community, and their relative cost-effectiveness render them suitable as owners, advocates and participants in programs. Several organizations and health agents are operating in integrated primary health and HIV/AIDS prevention programs that have a multi-disease, multi-organizational and poverty-reduction focus and use appropriate and promising behavioral change communication methods that may contribute significantly to overcoming social stigma and reduce HIV exposure risk. Recommendations are made for further research towards identifying, promoting, strengthening and upscaling CBOs and programmes to the regional and national levels.

James Putzel (2004) in his paper on "*Governance and AIDS in Africa: Assessing the International Community's Multisectoral Approach*" analyses the international community's response to HIV/AIDS in Sub-Saharan Africa. The paper is based on fieldwork undertaken in Uganda, Senegal and Malawi, originally in the context of consultancy work for the Department for International Development (DFID) of the UK government. The paper begins with an exploration of the political and epidemiological dimensions of the crisis. It then outlines the main parameters of an "organizational template" elaborated and imposed on developing countries by the World Bank, UNAIDS and the Global Fund to fight AIDS, Tuberculosis and Malaria (GFATM). The template is evaluated based on an assessment of its implementation and focusing on key political issues, including the role of state leadership in organizing a multisectoral response and in mobilizing religious and associational/NGO sectors. The author argues that the organizational template misinterprets the experience of countries that have achieved some success in fighting the virus, and that it is overly influenced by the "post-Washington consensus", which brings together neoliberal prescriptions with prescriptions promoting popular participation and the defense of human rights. As with religious organisations, the associational sectors (NGOs, community based organisations, or CBOs, and professional associations) have been pivotal players in both Uganda and Senegal's HIV/AIDS campaigns, particularly in getting messages on behaviour change to communities and in providing counseling, and care and treatment to HIV positive people and people living with AIDS. However, the central state played the leading role, not only in creating the space for the NGO sector to act, but also in initially mobilizing the sector around HIV/AIDS. The AIDS crisis provides new opportunities for reviving public health sectors and creating an ethos of public service within the public sector and the medical profession, but also forces policy-makers to confront difficult trade offs between individual rights and the public good.

O'Gorman, Patrick & Paul Hardacre (2004) conducted a study on the practices of NGOs working with the injecting drug users (IDUs) in SAARC countries. Asian Harm Reduction Network (AHRN) in collaboration with the United Nations Office on Drugs and Crime, Regional Office for South Asia (UNODC, ROSA) published the report of the study as "*Documentation of Best Practices and Needs Assessment of Service Providers in South Asian Association for Regional Cooperation (SAARC) Countries*". This report consists of two main components. The first component outlines the threats of HIV transmission through injecting drug use in the SAARC countries including India. Many unreached groups of individuals injecting drugs are present in most countries in the region. The combination of high-risk drug taking practices, lack of relevant information and essential services, and mutual distrust between these high-risk population groups and mainstream health and social care services has led to a critical situation in the transmission of blood-borne viruses like HIV. Each country faces a different level of threat. A profile of the situation in each SAARC country is provided. NGOs currently working in drug treatment services are best placed to build bridges with people using and injecting drugs. This report recommends the scaling-up of capacity and services amongst NGOs in each country in the region through a three-part training strategy: (1) training in a holistic approach to street-based outreach, (2) workshops to develop model projects which respond to the needs of people injecting drugs and (3) ongoing training throughout subsequent phases through exchange visits to suggested demonstration sites.The second component of this report captures the current reported capacity of NGOs providing drug treatment and drug use related services in each country. The Directory of Service Providers in the SAARC Region included as Appendix in this report shows detailed information on the capacity and services provided by the listed NGOs. This directory can be used to determine the potential that currently exists. If this potential is harnessed through the strategy outlined in this report, it will become a force to arrest the epidemic of blood-borne viral transmission related to injecting drug use in the SAARC region.

UNAIDS (2005) in its report on "*A scaled-up response to AIDS in Asia and the Pacific*" summarises the AIDS challenge in Asian and Pacific countries. While some countries have already made their decision and begun to scale up effective AIDS programmes, in others there is still hesitation. Using the best available evidence, it discusses the reasons why critical services currently reach only a fraction of those in need. It also outlines the action needed that will allow the region to seize this key moment of opportunity. The report observed that growing political and financial support for AIDS efforts has been accompanied—and in some cases preceded—by stronger civil society engagement. Organizations of people living with HIV and AIDS (PLWHA) are advocating for increased access to treatment and care, and working to alleviate the stigma associated with the disease. In Cambodia, civil society organizations and people living with HIV joined with the national government and international donors to develop a national AIDS treatment plan. NGOs created by former drug users have initiated drug-substitution programmes in India and organized harm-reduction services in South-East Asia. Sex worker advocacy groups have created and expanded programmes in Bangladesh, India, Cambodia and Thailand, while programmes for men who have sex with men (MSM) have emerged in Pakistan, Nepal, the Philippines and Thailand. In some countries, lawyers' collectives have taken up legal battles to fight instances of discrimination against people living with HIV. Finally, the report makes recommendations for urgent implementation of strategies known to work, by global, regional and national political leaders, by international donors, the UN system, civil society and other key stakeholders in Asia and the Pacific. The report specifically recommended that countries should increase support to civil society organizations' involvement in national responses by identifying and implementing viable and effective mechanisms for financing, building capacity and promoting coordination of civil society organizations. These include, among others, legal recognition, tax incentives, streamlined contracting regulations, and financial support to build effective and accountable community-based organizations.

(B) Studies conducted in India

Creating Resources for Empowerment in Action (CREA), New Delhi published a series of annotated bibliographies on Reproductive Health Research in India carried out during 1990-2000. These bibliographies are part of the Gender and Reproductive Health Research Initiative' sponsored by the Ford Foundation. Six areas of concern in reproductive health were identified of which HIV/AIDS was one. The designated team searched on each of these research areas. Accordingly a team comprising Dr. Vimala Nadkarni, Anita Rego and Deeksha Vasundhra prepared annotated bibliography on HIV/AIDS along with a critical review paper, which looked at the content gaps, methodological issues and ethical concerns in the research. This has culminated into inviting proposals for future.

The annotated bibliography lists 126 studies carried out during 1990-2000 on HIV /AIDS. State-wise 33 studies were conducted in Maharashtra, 21 in Delhi, 13 in Tamil Nadu, 12 in Karnataka, 8 in West Bengal, and 5 each in Andhra Pradesh and Uttar Pradesh. It indicates 77% of the studies conducted in the above mentioned seven states only. Numbers of study conducted in the remaining states were below five and even no study was conducted in few states. Seven studies were conducted involving more than one state. City-wise 21 studies were conducted in Delhi, 17 in Mumbai, 11 in Chennai, 10 in Bangalore and 8 in Kolkata. It means most of the studies were conducted in urban areas. Surprisingly numbers of study conducted in Andhra Pradesh (5), Manipur (4) and Nagaland (1) are comparatively less in spite of their high HIV infection rate. There were six studies conducted in other countries.

Medical practitioners, social scientists, funding organizations, government organizations and individuals have researched the two-decade long epidemic widely. The existing research on HIV/AIDS in India has been grouped under the following categories and presented in Table-2.1.

K.S. Rao, R.D. Pillai and R.R. Rao conducted a study on "*Awareness of AIDS / HIV among voluntary organizations in Andhra Pradesh*" during 1988-91. The aim of the study was to assess the knowledge about transmission of AIDS, misconceptions and safe sexual behaviour among voluntary organizations. A structured questionnaire was administered to different voluntary organizations in Andhra Pradesh after conducting 27 AIDS/HIV health educational programmes for them. The majority of the participants were aware about AIDS/HIV and the associated aspects. Ignorance (61%) was reportedly higher among the rural youth even after the health education session. It is found that post-intervention had a significant impact on knowledge gain.

Table-2.1
Research on HIV/AIDS in India during 1990-2000

Sl. No.	*Themes of Research*	*No. of Studies (%)*
1.	Understanding and awareness of HIV/AIDS	42 (35.0%)
2.	Safer sexual practices and other modes of risk reduction	18 (15.0%)
3.	Biological and societal vulnerabilities to HIV/AIDS	15 (12.5%)
4.	Economic impact of HIV/AIDS	03 (02.5%)
5.	Disclosure, stigma and discrimination	06 (05.0%)
6.	Mental health issues including substance abuse	13 (10.8%)
7.	The rights of positive people	01 (00.8%)
8.	Prevention programmes and interventions	15 (12.5%)
9.	Mixed themes	07 (05.9%)
	Total	120 (100%)

Asthana S. and Oostvogels R. (1996) in an article on "*Community participation in HIV prevention: problems and prospects for community-based strategies among female sex workers in Madras*" examined problems and prospects for participation in HIV prevention strategies among commercial sex workers (CSWs) in Madras. Based upon the experiences of a pilot project established by the Tamil Nadu State Government AIDS Cell and WHO, they found that the organization of the commercial sex trade in Madras is not highly conducive to collective action. Identifying the factors that have frustrated attempts to promote community-based strategies in the city, the paper suggests that this approach is unlikely to succeed unless there are significant changes to the institutional arrangements that keep sex workers in a position of subordination and exploitation.

Paul and Gopalakrishnan (2003) investigated the *impact of training on knowledge of functionaries of NGOs* regarding mode of transmission and prevention of STIs including HIV/AIDS. This study began with the research mission of ascertaining the present level of knowledge of NGO functionaries dealing with MCH issues and their training requirements. They adopted a cross-sectional study design, using percentages and chi-square tests as the method of statistical analysis. They came up with the following results. Almost all representatives of NGOs were aware that HIV infection has emerged as a new threat. A majority of them were aware that use of condom during intercourse could prevent STDs, but could not relate this with HIV/AIDS prevention. They also were of the view that avoiding sex with multiple partners could prevent HIV/AIDS. The major sources of information on HIV/ AIDS were newspaper and TV. A major lacuna in knowledge, which needs to be substantiated, includes use of disposable/sterilised needles for preventing HIV/AIDS, mother-to-child transmission of HIV, complications of STDs, need for partner's treatment in STDs, and concept of window period for HIV detection.

From the above review, it is clear that NGOs/CBOs are at the forefront in the battle against HIV/AIDS and have so far played a significant role. AIDS activities initiated by NGOs have been highly influential on thinking and strategies found within HIV/AIDS sector. In this context, associations/networks of PLWHA are also crucial, as their involvements strengthen NGOs as well as improve the quality of PLWHA's lives. Yet despite their proliferation, NGOs experience particular difficulties in increasing the scale of their activities to reach large number of people, to have a greater impact at higher level than "community" and to address the broader social determinants of HIV/AIDS. Besides this, other issues that need to be considered include the difficulties of many NGOs to integrate their activities with those of other NGOs, the government and the communities; and the generally weak

IEC methodologies and instruments that were not often appropriate for local needs and realities. The review also indicates that the relative effectiveness of different NGOs/CBOs in different communities depends on many factors associated with individual organizations, their communities and collaborations with and support by other community or outside organizations. Strong government support and commitment will be crucial in scaling up the existing community-based prevention and patient care programs to a truly national multi-sectoral HIV/AIDS programme by building on available models, starting with existing capacities and building them through learning by doing, by giving the highest priority to prevention, by promoting accountability and improving fiscal sustainability, among others. Key components for the success of the HIV/AIDS programme include strong partnerships, selection of the right personnel, adequate and appropriate training, support from community leaders, a supportive supervisory system, participatory reviews and monitoring, consistent technical and financial support and an active Home Care Network.

However, such studies on NGOs response to HIV/AIDS are not found in India. The objective of a large percentage of studies in India is to assess the level of knowledge about HIV/AIDS. It is also seen from the above review of literature that few state level studies on the role of NGOs in health care were conducted (Duggal et.al 1986; Baru 1987; Sarkar 2005). There is no doubt on the fact that NGOs play a key role in combating HIV/AIDS. But no such state-level study on the contribution of NGOs in HIV/AIDS prevention and care was undertaken in India so far. Thus, it is pertinent to explore and examine the NGOs response to HIV/AIDS in detail.

REFERENCES

Aldaba, Fernando T. and Josefa P. Petilla (1997), "Governance and HIV: Government - Civil Society Interface: An Aspect of

Governance Critical to an Effective Response", *HIV POLICY.ORG* http://www.hivpolicy.org/bib/HPP000204.htm

Asthana S, Oostvogels R. (1996), "Community participation in HIV prevention: problems and prospects for community-based strategies among female sex workers in Madras", *Social Science Medicine* 1996 Jul; 43(2): 133-48.

Baru, R. (1987), 'Factors Influencing Variations in Health Services – A Study of Selected Districts of Andhra Pradesh', *M.Phil. Dissertation*, Centre for Social Medicine and Community Health, School of Social Sciences, Jawaharlal Nehru University, New Delhi.

Baviskar, B.S. (2001), "NGOs and Civil Society in India", *Sociological Bulletin*, March 2001, 50 (1).

Berman, P. and Dave, P. (1994), 'Experiences in paying for Health Care in India's Voluntary Sector'. In S. Pachauri (ed.) *Reaching India's Poor – Non-Governmental Approaches to Community Health*, Sage: New Delhi.

Bhattacharjee, S. (1996), 'NGO Approaches to Health and Development in India: Strategies and Sustainability', *M.A. Dissertation*, Prins Leopold Instuut Voor Tropische Geneeskunde: Belgium.

Brodhead, T. and J.O'Mally (1989), 'NGO and Third World Development: Opportunities and Constraints.' *Paper presented at the WHO's Global Programme on AIDS Management Committee Meeting*, 6-8.

Chandra, P. (2005), *NGOs in India: Role, Guidelines and Performance Appraisal*, Akansha Publishing House: New Delhi.

Chillag K. et al. (2000), "Factors affecting the delivery of HIV/AIDS prevention programs by community-based organizations", *AIDS Education and Prevention: An Interdisciplinary Journal*, Vol. 14, Issue-3.

David Wilkinson and Team (2000), "*An evaluation of the Ministry of Health/NGO Home care programme for people with HIV/AIDS in Cambodia*". http://www.aidsallaince.org

DeJong, Jocelyn (2002), *A Question of Scale: Expanding NGO Impact in HIV/AIDS,* ITDG Publishing: London, UK.

Duggal, R., Gupta, M. and Jesani, A. (1986), *NGOs in Rural Health Care,* FRCH: Mumbai.

Gomez, Jauregui (2004), "Feasibility of Government partnerships with NGOs in the Reproductive health field in Mexico", *Reproductive Health Matters,* 12(24), pp. 42– 55.

Gordenker, L and Weiss, T.G. (1996), 'Pluralizing Global Governance: Analytical Approaches and Dimensions'. In Gordenker and Weiss (eds.) *The UN and Global Governance,* Lynne Rienner: Boulder, p. 17.

Gupta, V.S. (2003), "Contribution of NGOs in implementing population policy", *Yojana,* 47(7), pp. 6–9.

Horizons (2002), "*Greater involvement of PLHA in NGO service delivery: findings from a four-country study*". http://popcouncil.org/horizons/ressum/plhabf/plhabf_impact.html

Katana, Milly (2001), "NAP+, The People's Own Voice" in *Voices from Africa,* No. 10, UN-NGLS: NY. http://www.unsystem.org/ngls/documents/publications.en/voices.africa/number10 / a15katana.htm

Kloos Helmut, Tadesse Wuhib, Damen Haile Mariam and Bernt Lindtjorn (2003), "Community-based organizations in HIV/AIDS prevention, patient care and control in Ethiopia", *Ethiopian Journal of Health Development,* 2003; 17(Spec No):3-31.
www.cih.uib.no/journals/EJHD/ejhdv17-special-issue/ejhd-v17-special-issue-review- article.pdf

Korten, David (1990), *Getting to the 21st Century: Voluntary Action and the Global Agenda,* Kumarian Press: West Hartford, CT.

M'Boa Leiliane, Aristide Kacou, Mariette Wandandi, Samuel Lijalem Hassan, Victor Kamanga, Dora Ofobrukweta, Regina Clement Akpan, Anne Fiedler and Esther Guzha (2001), "NGO and Community Responses to HIV/AIDS" in *Voices from Africa,* No. 10, UN-NGLS: NY.
http://www.unsystem.org/ngls/documents/publications.en/voices.africa/number10 /a13compil.htm

Mercer, Alec, Mobarak Hossain Khan, Muhammad Daulatuzzaman and Joanna Reid (2004), "Effectiveness of an NGO primary health care programme in rural Bangladesh: Evidence form the management information system", *Health Policy and Planning*, 19(4), pp. 187–98.

Mercer, M.A., L. Liskin and S.J. Scott (1991), "The role of non-government organization in the global response to AIDS", *AIDS Care*, 3(3): 265-270.

Mishra, S. (2000), *Voluntary Action in Health and Population – The Dynamics of Social Transition*, Sage: New Delhi.

Moses Chingono (2001), "AIDS Education and Prevention in Zimbabwe's Transport sector" in *Voices from Africa*, No. 10, UN-NGLS: NY.
http://www.unsystem.org/ngls/documents/publications.en/voices.africa/number10/a11chingono.htm

Mugisha, Frank, Harriet Birungi and Ian Askew (2005), "Are reproductive health NGOs in Uganda able to engage in the health SWAp?", *International Journal of Health Planning and Management*, 20(3), pp. 227–38.

Nadkarni, V., Rego, A. & Vasundhara, D. (2003), 'HIV/AIDS in India: An Annotated Bibliography of Selected Studies (1990-2000)' in *The Gender and Reproductive Health Research Initiative Mapping- A Decade of Reproductive Health Research in India.* CREA: New Delhi.

O'Gorman, Patrick & Paul Hardacre (2004), "Documentation of Best Practices and Needs Assessment of Service Providers in South Asian Association for Regional Cooperation (SAARC) Countries", *HIV POLICY.ORG*,
http://www.hivpolicy.org/bib/HPP000723.htm

Pachauri, S. (1994), *Reaching India's Poor – Non-Governmental Approaches to Community Health*, Sage: New Delhi.

Paul, Dinesh and Shanta Gopalakrishnan (2003), "Impact of training on knowledge regarding modes of transmission and prevention of sexually transmitted infections including HIV/AIDS of functionaries of non-governmental organizations", *Indian Journal of Community Medicine*, 28(4), pp. 161–64.

Putzel, James (2004), 'Governance and AIDS in Africa: Assessing the International Community's Multisectoral Approach' *Paper presented at the annual meeting of the American Political Science Association, Hilton Chicago and the Palmer House Hilton, Chicago.* http://cyber.law.harvard.edu/blogs/gems/politicshiv/putzel.pdf

Rajasekhar, D. (2000), "NGOs in India: Opportunities and Challenges", *Journal of Rural Development,* Vol. 19(2), pp. 249-275.

Rao, K.S., R.D. Pilli and B.R.Rao (1991), "Awareness of AIDS/ HIV among Voluntary Organisations in Andhra Pradesh", *Indian Journal of Sexual Transmission of Disease,* 1006(17): 19-21.

Roy, C.M. and Cain R. (2001), "The involvement of people living with HIV/AIDS in community-based Organizations: contributions and constraints", *AIDS Care,* Vol. 13, No. 4, pp. 421-432 http://www.socsci.mcmaster.ca/healthst/emplibrary/roy_cain_involvement.pdf

Salamon, Lester M. (1995), *The International Guide to Non-profit Law,* Wiley: New York.

Sarkar, A. (2005), *NGOs – The New Lexicon of Health Care,* Concept: New Delhi.

Sawadogo, Marie Rose (2001), 'Private and Community-based HIV/ AIDS Approaches in Burkina Faso'. In *Voices from Africa,* No. 10 , UN-NGLS: NY http://www.unsystem.org/ngls/documents/publications.en/voices.africa/number10/3sawadogo.htm

Tandon, R. (1994), 'Where are the people? Community Participation in Health'. In Pacauri (ed.) *Reaching India's Poor – Non-Governmental Approaches to Community Health,* Sage: New Delhi.

The International HIV/AIDS Alliance (2002), "Participation and empowerment in HIV/AIDS programming", *HIV POLICY.ORG.* http://www.hivpolicy.org/bib/HPP000597[1].htm

Tikku, Nirmal (2004), "NGOs in three north Indian states: Evaluation of NGOs working in the areas of nutritional and health status of women and children", *Social Change: Issues and Perspectives,* 34(3), pp. 34–52.

UNAIDS (2005), *A Scaled-up Response to AIDS in Asia and the Pacific.*
http://www.hivpolicy.org/bib/HPP000473.htm

Varma, Manish (2001), "Reproductive and sexual health of adolescents: An NGO experience", *Health for the Millions*, 27(3), pp. 42–44.

Vishnu and H. Sudarshan (2003), "Public sector-voluntary organisation partnership for primary healthcare services: The experience of Karuna Trust and Vivekananda Foundation", *Health for the Millions*, 29(4 & 5), pp. 52–57.

Williams Brian, Eleanor Gouws, Janet Frohlich, Catherine Campbell and Catherine MacPhail (2001), 'Lessons from the Front: NGOs and the Fight Against HIV/AIDS in South Africa'. In *Voices from Africa*, No. 10, UN-NGLS: NY.
http://www.unsystem.org/ngls/documents/publications.en/voices.africa/number10/8williams.htm

World Bank (1987), *Operational Manual Statement: Collaboration with NGOs'*, No. 5(30), p. 1.

3

Methodology

It is pertinent to note that so far there is neither national nor state level study available in the social science discipline on the topic of NGO response to HIV/AIDS. The methodology has been adopted keeping in view the nature of research problem, purpose of investigation, source and availability of data, observation, experience as well as capability of the researcher. The present study has tried to explore an unknown phenomenon.

Rationale of the Study

There is a long history of NGO activities in India. But the growth of NGOs is a phenomenon of late 1970s and early 1980s. During the last two decades there has been a shift towards greater reliance on market and NGOs for provision of service in the social sector. Thus inability of the government to invest coupled with the support from international donor agencies provided the impetus for the expansion of this sector in India. The private sector and NGOs are seen as more efficient, less bureaucratic and effective as compared to Government.

These NGOs are varied both in terms of size, level of operation and services provided. In the process of development, they carry out various programmes pertaining to education, income generation, welfare of handicapped, health and so on. Especially in the field of health, NGOs perform different roles. They provide clinical services, health awareness, health care training and at the same time conduct research. The National Health Policy document 2001 also envisages greater role for private sector and NGOs.

As stated earlier, HIV/AIDS is one of the major health issues in India. National AIDS Control Programme of the Government also envisages greater role for NGOs. In India some of the major NGOs engaged in HIV/AIDS care are Lawyers' Collective (Maharastra), SAHARAN (Delhi), Shalom (Manipur), Durbar Mahila Samanya Committee (West Bengal), etc. These are larger NGOs but there are several others who work at the grass root level. Review of available literature shows that there are very few state level studies on NGOs in health Care and these include Maharashtra (Duggal, Gupta and Jesani, 1986), Andhra Pradesh (Baru, 1987), Assam (Sarkar, 1998) and West Bengal (Sarkar 2005). We have also seen in the literature review that many studies were conducted on different aspects of HIV/AIDS in India. But no such state level study on the contribution of NGOs in HIV/AIDS care was undertaken so far. Thus, it is pertinent to explore and examine in detail on the responses of NGOs in HIV/AIDS care.

There is a need to generate baseline data through a critical examination of the functioning of the NGOs, the services they provide, organisational pattern, target group, programme components, programme execution strategy, source of funding, people's participation, beneficiaries' perception, impact of globalization, etc. In order to get some insights on these aspects, the present study has been conducted on NGOs engaged in HIV/AIDS care in West Bengal. The reason for selecting West Bengal is that it has a long and rich history of NGO activities. West Bengal is placed in the second group of States by NACO where HIV infection rate has crossed 5% or more among the high-risk behaviour groups. Besides it, West Bengal is one of the five states where Government of India initially started National AIDS Control Programme with the help of World Bank in 1987. Therefore, considering the importance of NGOs in HIV/AIDS care, it is quite relevant to study their contributions, so that beneficiaries may be better served.

Objectives

The specific objectives of the present study are as follows:

1. To get a state-level overview of NGOs engaged in HIV/AIDS care in West Bengal.
2. To study and examine the contribution of NGOs in HIV/AIDS care services through in-depth study in selected NGOs by focusing on organizational setup, target groups, nature and extent of services, programme execution strategies, involvement of various stakeholders, problem of stigmatization, ethical issues, sources of funding, perception of beneficiaries towards the working of NGOs, etc.
3. To explore the future trends of NGOs engaged in HIV/AIDS care in the context of globalisation.

Research Design

There is paucity of data in the proposed area of study. The main purpose of the proposed study was to explore and gain insight into the contribution of NGOs in HIV/AIDS prevention and care in West Bengal. It was necessary to explore different aspects and facts related to the services provided by these NGOs, target groups, intervention strategies, problem of stigmatization, ethical issues, sources of funding, perception of beneficiaries towards the working of NGOs and so on. Hence, the researcher had to do literature review, experience survey and case studies of some selected NGOs. Literature scanning was done to get an understanding on the state level overview of NGOs in HIV/AIDS care and future tends of such NGOs in the context of globalisation. Experience survey was also made through informal interviews and mailed questionnaires for the same purpose. Mailed questionnaires were sent to all NGOs implementing HIV/AIDS programme in West Bengal. Case study was initiated in the selected NGOs to understand and analyze various aspects pertinent to HIV/AIDS programmes. Thus, as already mentioned earlier that no such study was undertaken at the state-level, the present study has used exploratory design.

Types of Data Required

1. In order to fulfill the first objective, data related to geographical location of NGOs, background of organizations, year of starting the programme, target groups, nature and extent of services, source of funding, etc. were essential.
2. To fulfill the second objective, the types of data included were: historical background of NGOs, organizational setup, target group, preventive and supportive services, programme execution strategies, involvement of various stakeholders, problem of stigmatization, ethical issues, people's participation, perception of beneficiaries towards the working of NGOs, etc.
3. For the third objectives, types of data required were: sustainability of funding, nature of demand of the beneficiaries in future, networking with national and international agencies, impact of globalization, etc.

Sources of Data

Keeping in view the objectives, the data are collected from

the primary as well as secondary sources. First part of the data was collected by using both the sources i.e. through literature (Secondary source: Report of the West Bengal State AIDS Prevention & Control Society and SAATHII's "Red Ribbon" Directory of HIV/AIDS Services in India), informal interview with the key officials of Government and umbrella NGOs and mailed questionnaire to NGOs engaged in HIV/AIDS prevention and care (Primary Source) in West Bengal.

Second part of data has been collected by using primary sources i.e. six selected NGOs, selected staff and selected beneficiaries of these NGOs. Information related to organizational profile and HIV/AIDS programme was collected from the Chief and other functionaries of NGOs. Staff members of each NGO were selected from all level to know about their views on different key issues. Similarly, beneficiaries were selected from each NGO to know about their views towards the working of respective NGOs.

Third part of the data has been collected from both primary sources (NGOs and Key Informants) and secondary sources (relevant literature). The same mailed questionnaires were used for this objective and few key informants were also informally interviewed in this regard.

Tools and Technique of Data Collection

Data were collected through observation, interviewing and focused group discussion. Along with secondary data, the proposed study is mainly relied on the following tools for primary data collection:

1. In order to collect data regarding first objective, a mailed questionnaire was used to make a survey of NGOs engaged in HIV/AIDS care in West Bengal.
2. For collecting data on the second objective, an interview schedule was used during case study in the selected NGOs. The data on the basic information and programme activities were collected from the Chief

functionaries and Project Coordinators. Similarly, staff and beneficiaries were interviewed.

3. In order to fulfill the third objective, the same mailed questionnaire was used. Besides it, informal discussions with key informants (e.g. Government and Non-Government officials, academicians and experts etc.) were done. No tools were developed for these discussions.

Before the study, all tools are finalized through pilot study in SPARSHA, Kolkata.

Process of Data Collection

The process of data collection of the present study has been completed in the four phases, which are as follows:

- In the first phase, names and address of the NGOs engaged in HIV/AIDS care in 2006-07 was collected from various umbrella organizations (e.g. West Bengal State AIDS Prevention & Control Society, UNICEF, and Action AID) and HIV/AIDS Directory of SAATHII. Having put all names together, a comprehensive list of 60 NGOs engaged in HIV/AIDS care was prepared.

- In the second phase, questionnaires were mailed to all the NGOs from the above mentioned list and followed up with several reminders through e-mail and phone. The response was received from 27 NGOs, which has accounted 45% of total NGOs. This was done to collect necessary data to get a state level overview of NGOs in HIV/AIDS care in West Bengal.

- In the third phase, six NGOs i.e. Durbar Mahila Samanaya Committee (DMSC), Society for Community Intervention and Research (SCIR), Bhoruka Public Welfare Trust (BPWT), Human Development and Research Institute (HDRI), MANAS Bangla (MB) and SPARSHA were selected purposively based on certain criteria and studied in detail. In each NGO, emphasis was given on historical background, organizational structure, present activities, views of staff, beneficiaries' perception towards the working of NGOs, etc. to understand how far NGOs could contribute to HIV/AIDS prevention, care, support and treatment. In this phase, the researcher visited each NGO and their project sites several times and spent on an average 20 days in each selected NGO.

- At the last phase, the researcher had discussed informally with few key informants like academicians, experts, officials from NGOs and WBSAP&CS to know about their views on the impact of globalisation on NGOs working in the HIV/AIDS field. At the end of this phase, the researcher has done extensive literature review to know more about the impact of globalisation in this regard.

Sampling

Universe

The study was conducted in the State of West Bengal. A comprehensive list of 60 NGOs engaged in HIV/AIDS care in West Bengal was prepared with the help of government and umbrella non-governmental organizations and Directories of NGOs. These 60 NGOs were considered as universe of the present study.

Sample Size and Sampling Technique

- In the first phase of data collection, a comprehensive list of NGOs was prepared. In the second phase, questionnaires were mailed to all the NGOs of the comprehensive list. Therefore, sampling was not required in both these phases.

- In the third phase of data collection, out of the total sixty NGOs engaged in HIV/AIDS care in West Bengal, a sample of maximum six NGOs was selected by using purposive sampling technique. These six NGOs were of six different types based on the target groups. For instance, DMSC is working with Commercial Sex workers (CSWs), SCIR is with Injecting Drug Users (IDUs), HDRI is with Migrant Labourers (ML), BPWT is with Truckers, MB is with Men having Sex with Men (MSM) and SPARSHA is with People Living with HIV/AIDS (PLWHA). Following criteria were used to select each of the six NGOs:

(i) NGOs must be located within the territory of West Bengal.

(ii) NGOs must be registered, non-profit and welfare organization.

(iii) NGOs must be having at least one full-fledged HIV/AIDS related programme, which has specific project proposal, budget allocation and full-time paid staff.

Purposive sampling technique was used to select ten staff members from each selected NGO to know about their views on different key issues like problem of stigmatization and its effect, ethical issues, violation of human rights, etc. Efforts were made to include all types of staff (lower, middle and higher level) as per their availability. Similarly, fifteen beneficiaries were chosen from each selected NGO purposively to understand the beneficiaries' opinion about the contribution of the NGOs under the study. Except the group of PLWHA in SPARSHA, two groups of beneficiaries from two different places were formed in each NGO and their opinions were collected through focused group discussion.

- In the fourth phase, purposive sampling technique was used to select ten key informants on the basis of their experience and expertise on HIV/AIDS.

Analysis of Data

The present study is heavily relied on qualitative analysis. However, quantitative kind of analysis was also used for explaining some data of the study. For the first objective, quantitative analysis was made. At first available data were reorganized to develop a common framework for examining the same. The data, those were possible to code, were identified and grouped from each questionnaire. Then simple cross tabulation was done to understand the aspects mentioned in the objective.

For the second objective, the typical data analysis procedure of case study method has been used. First, the data have been organized from the interview schedule, field observation notes, annual reports and other relevant documents and all these data of six NGOs were put separately into six master files. Secondly, the data were analysed after careful reading and re-reading of available data. The data of each NGO were discussed qualitatively and presented through four parts. Chapter-6 has discussed the profile of selected NGOs on the basis of eleven aspects like historical background, vision, mission, present objectives, area of operation, target groups, organizational structures, infrastructure, present programmes, source of funding and future plan. Nature of HIV/AIDS programme sustainability of the selected NGOs is discussed in Chapter-7 on the basis of eight factors: (a) objectives, (b) components of the programme, (c) programme execution process, (d) people's participation, (e) monitoring and evaluation, (f) sources of funding, (g) innovative components and (h) local cooperation. Chapter-8 has qualitatively analyzed the views of selected staff members of six NGOs on six different issues such as stigmatization, ethical issues, violation of human rights, major barriers encountered, major reasons of spreading HIV/AIDS and future AIDS scenario and role of NGOs. The beneficiaries' perceptions towards the working of six selected NGOs under the study have been discussed qualitatively in Chapter-9 by using four criteria such as necessity of NGO's HIV/AIDS programme, cost and quality of services, staff's cooperation and scope of beneficiaries' participation. Simple cross tables were used to highlight the profile of staff members and beneficiaries of six selected NGOs.

For the third objective, data were analyzed both qualitatively as well as quantitatively. A future trend of NGOs in HIV/AIDS care in the context globalization was discussed in terms networking, advocacy, financial sustainability and future demands of beneficiaries.

Finally, the analysis of data were done from social work perspective and presented in a descriptive manner to support the specific objectives of the study.

Operational Definitions

AIDS: Acquired Immuno Deficiency Syndrome is a fatal transmissible disease caused by HIV. The term 'acquired' was chosen because the illness was neither genetically determined nor the result of other conditions. AIDS is the final stage of HIV infection, which is characterized by appearance of various opportunistic infections such as tuberculosis, pneumocytis, toxoplasmism, herpes, cytomegalovirus, etc. A group of various symptoms and signs caused by the HIV is called as 'syndrome'. Till date no medicine or vaccine has been developed to protect people from HIV infection. Death results from the unremitting growth of opportunistic infection or from the body's inability to fight off malignancies. It is an incurable disease.

ART: Antiretroviral therapy is a combination three or more drugs, provided to arrest the spread of virus within the body. Since HIV rapidly builds resistance to any single antiretroviral treatment, combination treatment is necessary for effective viral suppression. ART is not a cure, medicines need to be taken throughout life, expensive and having serious side effects. Some of these drugs are AZT, ddC, ddI, d4T, etc.

HIV: It means Human Immunodeficiency Virus, which causes AIDS. This virus slowly attacks and destroys the human immune system, body's defence against infection, leaving an individual vulnerable to a variety of other infections. HIV is transmitted by the direct transfer of body fluids, such as blood and blood products, semen and other genital secretions, or breast milk, from an infected person to an uninfected person. The pathology of HIV infection involves three stages – primary HIV infection, the asymptomatic phase and AIDS. HIV infected people can live symptom free lives for years. On an average it takes 8-10 years to develop AIDS after HIV infection, depending on the immune status of the individual.

HIV Positive: It is also known as seropositive or antibody positive. It means a person has developed antibodies to his immune system after HIV infection. An HIV antibody test will give a positive result for the presence of HIV antibodies. The person may look and feel perfectly well but is potentially infectious and can pass the virus on to the others.

HIV/AIDS Care: In the present study, HIV/AIDS care refers to NGO's multitude of services or interventions, which are provided by the NGO personnel to the individuals, families or communities in order to combat HIV/AIDS crisis. It includes all sorts of services such as preventive, curative, supportive, promotive and rehabilitative services.

Immunodeficiency: Immune system protects our body against the attack by bacteria, viruses and other such foreign organisms. Immunodeficiency means any decrement in the ability of the immune system to respond appropriately to foreign substances or organisms. Immunodeficiency results into an increased susceptibility to various infections.

NGO: It is voluntary formed and registered organization working towards development and amelioration of suffering with non-self serving aims and free from the state control in managing day to day affairs. The proposed study will consider those NGOs who execute at least one full-fledged HIV/AIDS related programme, which has specific project proposal, budget allocation and full-time paid staff.

NGO Response to HIV/AIDS: It refers to the contribution of the NGOs in combating HIV/AIDS crisis. Contribution refers to NGO's activity, support or help towards HIV/AIDS prevention, care, support and treatment.

Perception: According to the *Encyclopedia Americana* (1992), the core meaning of perception is immediate awareness. To perceive something is to become directly or immediately aware of it. For example, by means of our senses, we perceive or became aware of the objects, events and persons in our environment. As per the New Encyclopedia Britannica (2002), perception is the process whereby sensory stimulation is translated into organized or meaningful experience. Under the proposed study, perception refers to the way of seeing or awareness of beneficiaries towards the working of NGO.

Limitations

(i) This study has considered only those NGOs who are implementing HIV/AIDS programme in 2006-2007. Therefore, it has not included other NGOs who had previously implemented HIV/AIDS programme in West Bengal.

(ii) In the third phase of study, case studies (of six NGOs) have been done. It is important to note that outcome of case study may not be generalized everywhere in West Bengal.

(iii) The present study attempted to understand the future trends of NGOs in HIV/AIDS care in the context of globalisation. This may not be the real trend in future as the governance of HIV/AIDS is dependent on many national as well as international factors.

(iv) The study is not comprehensive due to selection of only two DICs/Clinics from the operational areas of each NGO to get the beneficiaries' responses about the contribution of NGOs in HIV/AIDS care. The study has also not encompassed all the beneficiaries in every studied DICs/Clinics.

(v) This study has been conducted in West Bengal. Hence, the entire findings of the study may not be applicable to other states as the response of NGO is influenced by the prevailing socio-political factors of the state.

4

West Bengal–An Outline and HIV/AIDS Scenario

Bengal represents the land that possesses a distinct culture with its indigenous art and crafts and makes it an important part of the Indian Union. We get a very high impression about the Bengal from the series of chronicles related to its history. For instance, people of this region were the first who crossed the seven seas of the world for the purpose of trade and commerce. The Bengalis were known for their spirit of independence from the very beginning of the history. They resisted the intrusion of Vedic culture into Bengal for long and evolved their own school of art and architecture. At that time, the *Viharas* (universities) of Bengal drew students from far and wide. At the same time, people of this region went to establish cultural colonies in different parts of Asia. Besides these, Bengal is also popular for the contribution of its many great sons like Ramakrishna Paramhansadeb, Swami Vivekananda, Rabindranath Tagore and many others; Renaissance of Nineteenth Century; art and literature of the Twentieth Century and its fight against the British Imperialism (Sur 1992). Since the present study is initiated in West Bengal, this chapter attempts to give a brief description about its history, socio-economic development and HIV/AIDS scenario.

Historical Background

During the period of the Vedic age Bengal was called Vanga and is said to have been inhabited by several groups of people belonging to various races. During the *Mahabharata* period this area was divided into small kingdoms and principalities ruled by chieftains. The Aryans inhabited Bengal during the post-Vedic period. Many dynasties exercised their control over Bengal. The Palas, Pundras, the Senas etc were a few whose rule was noteworthy. The Palas ruled for more than four hundred years. Owing to its favourable location this region had trade with Cambodia, Burma, Sri Lanka, the Deccan and the Persian Gulf. The navigable parts of Ganga made it favourable for internal trade and communication. In about the 3rd century the Mauryan and the Guptas established their rule. The Palas established their strong rule from about 800 A.D. till the 11th century after which the Senas ruled.

The economy, arts and culture of this region developed under the rule of the Hindu dynasties. In the beginning of the 13th century Bengal became a part of the Delhi Sultanate and later the Mughals. The influence of the Muslims led to conversions besides development of art and culture and cottage industries that produced items such as muslin, which were in great demand around the world.

The proximity to the sea also resulted in the influence with the foreigners – the Portuguese in the early 16th century, the Dutch in about 1632, the French influence between 1673–1676, the Danish in 1676 and British in 1690. The increased influence of the British resulted in conflicts with the Nawab. The diplomatic efforts with a series of conspiracies resulted in the ultimate capture of power in Bengal by the British. The Battle of Plassey (1757) and the battle of Buxar (1764) sealed the fate of the Mughal rule. Britishers took over the administration of Bengal in 1764. When Bengal was formed as a province, under the British rule, it included present Bihar, Orissa and expended upto Agra. Agra was detached from Bengal in 1861, but Assam was attached to it. Assam was constituted as a separate state in 1874.The British later brought forth the Dual system of administration. In 1905 the English partitioned Bengal on the basis of religion. Calcutta remained the Capital of the British Empire in India till 1911. After that the capital was shifted from Calcutta to Delhi.

In 1947 when India became independent Bengal was partitioned between India and Pakistan. India's share came to be known as West Bengal and Pakistan's share was called East Pakistan. Later, the state of Coochbehar and French enclave of Chandannagore were added to Bengal. Later on again, under the State Reorganization Act some parts of Bihar were added to West Bengal. Now the state is divided into 19 districts.

Georgraphical Characteristics

Location

West Bengal covers the bottleneck of India in the east, stretching from Himalayas in the north to the Bay of Bengal in the south. It is bounded on the north by Sikkim and Bhutan, on the east by Assam and Bangladesh, on the south by the Bay of Bengal and on the west by Orissa, Jharkhand, Bihar and Nepal. It has therefore, three international frontiers to the north, east and west. The state lies between 27°13'15" and 21°25'24" north latitudes and 85°48'20" and 89°53'04" east longitudes.

Physiography

West Bengal has two natural divisions. First, the Himalayan north comprising the districts of Darjeeling, Jalpaiguri and Coochbehar and second is the alluvial plain that lies south of it. West Bengal is essentially a flat, featureless alluvial plain large portion of it being a part of delta of river Ganga; only one per unit of its area in the far north is really mountainous. Temperature during summer fluctuates between 24 degree centigrade to 40 degree centigrade and during winter from 7 degree centigrade to 26 degree centigrade through. Rainfall varies from 1,006 mm to 2,933 mm. (*Manoroma Year Book, 2008*).

Rivers

The main rivers of West Bengal are Ganga, Bhagirathi, Damodar, Tista, Torsha, Jaldhaka, Ajoy, Hoogly, Subarnarekha, Mayurakshi, Kansabati, Jalangi, Churni, Bramhani, Kopai, Haldi, Sarswati, Silabati, Kapaleswari, etc.

Forest Area

In 1997, actual forest area of West Bengal was 8,349 sq. km, which increased to 12,343 sq. km in 2003. Out of this 12,343 sq. km, very dense forest is 2,303 sq. km; moderately dense forest is 3,742 sq. km and open forest is 6,298 sq. km. At the all India level, actual forest area in 1997 was 6,33,397 sq. km, which increased to 6,78,333 sq. km in 2003. Out of this 6,78,333 sq. km, very dense forest is 51,285 sq. km; moderately dense forest is 3,39,279 sq. km and open forest is 2,87,769 sq. km. (TERI 2005-06).

Demographic Characteristics

Population

As per the census of 2001, total population of West Bengal is 8,01,76,197. Out of this total population 4,14,65,985 are male and 3,87,10,212 are female. The Decadal Growth Rate of population has been decreased from 24.73 (1981-1991) to 17.77 (1991-2001) in West Bengal. Table 4.1 gives details regarding population of various districts in 2001.

Population Density

Table 4.2 shows the density of population in various districts of West Bengal. It is found that population density has increased from 767 (1991) to 904 in 2001. It also shows that Kolkata, Howrah and North 24 Parganas stand first, second and third respectively in terms of the density of population among the districts. In India, West Bengal occupies sixth place for population density. Delhi, Chandigarh, Pondicherry, Lakshadweep, Daman and Diu are ahead of this State.

Table-4.1

District-wise Population in West Bengal

Sl. No.	*Districts*	*Population 2001*	*Percentage (%)*	*Male*	*Female*
1.	Bankura	31,92,695	3.98	16,36,002	15,56,693
2.	Birbhum	30,15,422	3.77	15,46,633	14,68,789
3.	Burdwan	68,95,514	8.60	35,88,376	33,07,138
4.	Coochbehar	24,79,155	3.09	12,72,094	12,07,061
5.	Dakshin Dinajpur	15,03,178	1.88	7,70,335	7,32,843
6.	Darjeeling	16,09,172	2.00	8,30,644	7,78,528
7.	Hoogly	50,41,976	6.29	25,89,625	24,52,351
8.	Howrah	42,73,099	5.32	22,41,898	20,31,201
9.	Jalpaiguri	34,01,173	4.25	17,51,145	16,50,028
10.	Kolkata	45,72,876	5.70	25,00,040	20,72,836
11.	Malda	32,90,468	4.10	16,89,406	16,01,062
12.	Medinipur (E & W)*	96,10,788	11.98	49,16,370	46,94,418
13.	Murshidabad	58,66,569	7.32	30,05,000	28,61,569
14.	Nadia	46,04,827	5.75	23,66,853	22,37,974
15.	North 24 Parganas	89,34,286	11.15	46,38,756	42,95,530
16.	Purulia	25,36,516	3.16	12,98,078	12,38,438
17.	South 24 Parganas	69,06,689	8.62	35,64,993	33,41,696
18.	Uttar Dinajpur	24,41,794	3.04	12,59,737	11,82,057
	West Bengal	8,01,76,197	100.00	4,14,65,985	3,87,10,212

* On 1st January 2002, Medinipur district was divided into two districts – Purba (East) Medinipur and Paschim (West) Medinipur

Source: Directorate of Census Operations, West Bengal, 2001

Table-4.2
Population Density

Sl. No.	*District*	*Area (Sq. km)*	*Density (per sq. km)*		*Rank*
			1991	*2001*	
1.	Bankura	6,882	408	464	17
2.	Birbhum	4,545	562	663	14
3.	Burdwan	7,024	861	985	7
4.	Coochbehar	3,387	641	732	10
5.	Dakshin Dinajpur	2,183	555	677	13
6.	Darjeeling	3,149	413	510	16
7.	Hoogly	3,149	1,383	1,601	4
8.	Howrah	1,467	2,542	2,913	2
9.	Jalpaiguri	6,227	450	547	15
10.	Kolkata	185	23,783	24,760	1
11.	Malda	3,733	706	881	8
12.	Medinipur (E & W)*	14,081	592	685	12
13.	Murshidabad	5,324	890	1,101	6
14.	Nadia	3,927	981	1,172	5
15.	North 24 Parganas	4,094	1,779	2,181	3
16.	Purulia	6,259	355	405	18
17.	South 24 Parganas	9,960	574	694	11
18.	Uttar Dinajpur	3,180	604	778	9
	West Bengal	88,756	767	904	

Source: *(i) Directorate of Census Operations, West Bengal, 2001.*
(ii) India 2001- A Reference Annual, Ministry of Information and Broadcasting, Government of India: New Delhi.

Sex Ratio

Table 4.3 shows the sex ratio i.e. number of female per 1000 male. As per the Census Report 2001, sex ratio of West Bengal is 934, which is better than national sex ratio (933). It was 911 in 1981 and 927 in 1991. During last twenty years, the situation has improved considerably and now West Bengal has achieved seventeenth place with regard to sex ratio among all the states and Union Territories, which was twenty-third in 1991.

Table-4.3
Sex Ratio (Number of Female per 1000 Male)

Particulars	*1981*	*1991*	*2001*
India	935	927	933
West Bengal	911	917	934

Source: Manorama Year Book 2008 (Bengali Version).

SC, ST and Urban Population

As per the Census Report 2001, the percentages of people belong to SC and ST community is respectively 23.0% and 5.5% of the total population of West Bengal.

The corresponding figure in India is 16.2% and 8.2%. Table 4.4 shows the percentage of SC, ST and Urban people against the total population of each district. It is found that more than half of the people of Coochbehar and more than one-third of the people of South 24 Parganas and Jalpaiguri districts belong to SC community. Besides it, more that one-fourth of the people of Uttar Dinajpur, Dakshin Dinajpur, Nadia, Burdwan, Bankura and Birbhum district belong to SC community. Kolkata has the lowest number of SC people. With regard to people belong to ST community, Jalpaiguri, Purulia and Dakshin Dinajpur districts are having more numbers and Kolkata, Howrah and Coochbehar have very

Table-4.4
Percentage of SC, ST and Urban People (within the total population of the district)

Sl. No.	*District*	*SC (%)*	*ST (%)*	*Urban (%)*
1.	Bankura	31.37	10.34	8.29
2.	Birbhum	30.68	6.95	8.98
3.	Burdwan	27.44	6.21	35.09
4.	Coochbehar	51.76	0.61	7.81
5.	Dakshin Dinajpur	29.10	16.92	13.67
6.	Darjeeling	16.15	13.78	30.
7.	Hoogly	24.12	4.05	31.19
8.	Howrah	15.79	0.27	49.58
9.	Jalpaiguri	36.99	21.04	16.36
10.	Kolkata	6.45	0.20	100.00
11.	Malda	18.12	6.50	7.07
12.	Medinipur	16.34	8.28	9.85
13.	Murshidabad	13.40	1.30	10.43
14.	Nadia	29.01	2.35	22.63
15.	North 24 Parganas	21.49	2.33	51.23
16.	Purulia	19.35	19.23	9.44
17.	South 24 Parganas	34.45	1.23	13.30
18.	Uttar Dinajpur	28.97	5.41	13.13
	West Bengal	23.02	5.50	27.97

Source: *(i) Directorate of Census Operations, West Bengal, 2001.*
(ii) Manorama Year Book 2002 (Bengali Version).

few. So far as urban-based population is concerned, apart from Kolkata, few districts like North 24 Parganas, Howrah and Burdwan have significant number of urban people. As per Census Report 2001, West Bengal ranks fourth in terms of urban population after Maharashtra, UP and Tamil Nadu.

Social Characteristics

Employment

As per the Census Report 2001, the percentage of working population is 36.77 percent of the total population of West Bengal. It was 32.19 percent of total population in 1991. The percentage of male workers has increased from 51.40 percent (1991) to 53.99 percent of total male population in 2001. Similarly, percentage of female workers has increased from 11.25 percent to 18.32 percent of total female population in 2001. In 2007, total number of registered unemployed was 77.20 lakh (*Manorama Year Book, 2008*). But this data cannot give the actual information on unemployment scenario. It informs only about those educated unemployed who seek employment in the organized sector. On the other hand, total production has increased in both agricultural as well as in industrial sector and has generated employment opportunities for many people. Over the last few years, numbers of domestic and foreign companies have invested in West Bengal in various fields of industrial sector. In order to increase the employment rate in rural and unorganized sector, various programmes like Swarnjayanti Gram Swarojgar Yojana, Prime Minister's Rojgar Yajona, National Rural Employment Guarantee Scheme, Small Scale Enterpreneur Programme, Bangla Swanirbhar Karma Sansthan Prakalpa, etc., are in operation.

Education

There are eighteen universities in West Bengal. These include Bidhan Chandra Agricultural University, Burdwan University, Calcutta University, West Bengal University of Animal and Fishery Science, Jadavpur University, Kalyani University, Netaji Subhas Open University, North Bengal University, North Bengal Agricultural University, Rabindra Bharati University, Vidyasagar University, Gour Banga University, West Bengal State University, West Bengal

University of Health Sciences, West Bengal University of Technology, Bengal Engineering and Science University, The West Bengal National University of Juridical Sciences, and Visva-Bharati (Central University). Besides it, there are few premier institutes like Indian Statistical Institute, Kolkata; Indian Institute of Technology, Kharagpur; National Institute of Technology, Durgapur; and Indian Institute of Management, Kolkata. Over the last few years, numbers of private colleges have started different courses in the field of Engineering, Management, Para-Medical Science, Biotechnology, etc. Apart from the colleges and universities, there are 2,383 junior High Schools and junior Madrashas; 9501 high Madrashas, Secondary and Higher Secondary schools; 103 Senior Madrashas and 16 independent Higher Secondary Institutions in operation in 2001 (Education Department, West Bengal).

With regard to universal primary education, there are 52,426 primary schools and 13,117 Sishu Siksha Kendras (SSKs) or Child Education Centres in 2001 (Education Department, West Bengal). The State Government has started SSKs for those who do not get opportunity for formal education at the age of five to nine years. Local women are appointed as teachers. These SSKs are functioning under Gram Panchayat with the advice of Village Education Committee.

As per the Census Report 2001, the literacy rate has increased from 57.70 percent (1991) to 69.22 percent in 2001. Though the literacy rate has been increased, the position of West Bengal among all the states and union territories has not been much improved during last ten years. As per literacy rate, this State has now secured 18th place, which was 19th in 1991. Table 4.5 indicates the literacy rate in various districts of West Bengal. It is found that half of the total population in Uttar Dinajpur District is still illiterate. More than seventy five percent people of the total population are literate in

Kolkata, North 24 Parganas, Howrah, Hoogly and Medinipur. Few districts like Malda, Murshidabad and Purulia are lagging behind in this respect.

Table-4.5

District and Sex-wise Literacy Rate

Sl. No.	*District*	*Population*	*Literacy Rate (%)*		
			Total	*Male*	*Female*
1.	Bankura	31,92,695	63.84	76.76	49.43
2.	Birbhum	30,15,422	62.16	70.89	51.55
3.	Burdwan	68,95,514	71.00	78.63	60.95
4.	Coochbehar	24,79,155	67.21	75.93	56.12
5.	Dakshin Dinajpur	15,03,178	64.46	72.43	54.28
6.	Darjeeling	16,09,172	72.87	80.05	62.94
7.	Hoogly	50,41,976	75.59	82.59	67.21
8.	Howrah	42,73,099	77.64	83.22	70.11
9.	Jalpaiguri	34,01,173	63.62	72.83	52.21
10.	Kolkata	45,72,876	81.31	83.79	77.30
11.	Malda	32,90,468	50.71	58.80	41.25
12.	Medinipur	96,10,788	75.17	84.91	64.42
13.	Murshidabad	58,66,569	55.05	60.71	47.63
14.	Nadia	46,04,827	66.55	72.31	59.58
15.	North 24 Parganas	89,34,286	78.49	83.92	71.72
16.	Purulia	25,36,516	56.14	73.72	36.50
17.	South 24 Parganas	69,06,689	70.16	79.19	59.01
18.	Uttar Dinajpur	24,41,794	48.63	58.48	36.51
	West Bengal	8,01,76,197	69.22	77.58	60.22

Source: (i) Directorate of Census Operations, West Bengal, 2001.
(ii) *Manorama Year Book, 2008* (Bengali Version).

So far as female literacy rate is concerned; Kolkata, North 24 Parganas and Howrah are ahead of other districts. More than sixty percent of total female population in Purulia and Uttar Dinajpur and more than fifty percent in Malda and Bankura districts are illiterate.

Health Status

Table 4.6 indicates that birth rate, death rate and infant mortality rate have gradually come down in West Bengal as well as in India. It is found that the health status of West Bengal is better than the all India situation. But in the recent past, problems of mosquito born diseases along with death toll in low lying areas of Kolkata are being reported due to poor public health and hygiene.

Table-4.6
Birth Rate, Death Rate and Infant Mortality Rate (per thousand)

Year	*Birth Rate*		*Death Rate*		*Infant Mortality Rate*	
	India	*West Bengal*	*India*	*West Bengal*	*India*	*West Bengal*
1981	31.7	33.7	11.0	12.5	91	110
1991	27.0	27.0	8.3	9.8	71	80
2001	20.3	25.4	6.6	8.4	51	66
2004	20.3	24.1	6.6	7.5	46	58

Source: (i) Directorate of Census Operations, West Bengal, 2001.
(ii) Manorama Year Book 2008.

At present total number of health care institutions (primary health centre, sub-health centre, hospital and medical colleges) operating in government and private sector is 13,640. These institutions/centers are having total 92,315 bed facilities. (*Manorama Year Book 2008*).

Economic Characteristics

Agriculture

Like other states of India, agriculture plays an important role in the economy of West Bengal too. The amount of total land available in the state is 8,682.95 thousand hectares. Out of the total land, 13.53 percent are forest area, 20.19 percent are not fit for agriculture, 60.95 percent are cultivable land and 5.30 percent have infertile soil. The percentage of Farmers and Agricultural Labourers are respectively 19.03 percent and 24.92 percent of total population of West Bengal

(*Manorama Year Book 2008*). The land of the state is very fertile. Major agricultural products of the state are rice, wheat, oilseeds, potato, jute, vegetables, fruits, etc. Table 4.7 highlights the details of the production of major agricultural products.

Till 2005-06, under the Land Reform System, the government has distributed 6,62,159 hectares of land among the 15,32,870 people. Similarly, under the *Operation Barga System*, 28,96,881 sharecroppers have been registered and received 4,49,502 hectares of land. Apart from these, various facilities such as loans, high yielding seeds, fertilizers, insecticides and irrigation facilities have been extended to improve the agricultural production. The state government is also encouraging farmers for cash crops to increase their income. As a result of this, the production of tradition crops like Paddy, wheat, etc are decreasing slowly.

Table-4.7
Production of Major Agricultural Products during 2006-07

Sl. No.	*Agricultural*	*Products 1999-2000*	*Production (Lakh tonnes) 2005-2007*
1.	Rice	137.59	145.31
2.	Wheat	8.51	8.01
3.	Potato	78.82	74.62
4.	Oilseeds	4.06	6.23
5.	Jute	75.94 (Lakh Bales)	81.24 (Lakh Bales)
6.	Vegetables	99.32	115.56
7.	Fruits	18.16	23.01
8.	Milk	34.65	38.91
9.	Meat	4.36	4.87
10.	Fish	10.45	12.50

Source: Manorama Year Book (Bengali Version) 2002 and 2008.

Industry

The communist led government has changed their earlier policy and decided to go for liberalization. The state government declared New Industrial Policy in 1994 to attract more investment in the industrial sector. Total 2,474 proposals came for setting up of the industry in West Bengal during 1991 to 2000. Table 4.8 shows the details of project implementation in West Bengal. In 2001, the state government started 'Single Window System' for receiving and clearing the new proposals speedily to become more industrialists-friendly. The state Government has laid great emphasis for strengthening existing and building new infrastructure to encourage more investments. The State offers a relatively developed physical and social infrastructure that is now attracting the attention of investors both domestic as well as international. In order to develop, upgrade and maintain infrastructure facilities, the Government of West Bengal recognizes and encourages Public-Private partnerships. The state has already started to set up new ports, airports, Special Economic Zones (SEZ), IT Parks, Intelligent Parks and Growth Centers etc under this public-private partnership. At the moment, there are three SEZs operating in the State while several others have either been approved in principle or are in various stages of implementation. During the year 2001- 2002, the growth of State Domestic Product of West Bengal is 7.8% as against 5.4% growth of gross domestic product of the country over this period. As against the present growth rate of index of industrial production of 2.3% at the national level, the index of industrial production in West Bengal has been much higher at 4.6%.

Table-4.8
Industrial Projects Implemented since 1991

Year	*No. of Units*	*Investment (Rupees in Crores)*	*Employment Generated*
1991	26	84.36	767
1992	58	493.25	4017
1993	41	548.43	4932
1994	37	4831.55	19752
1995	15	251.21	2367
1996	40	665.79	4770
1997	35	556.74	3548
1998	49	537.24	4695
1999	95	1871.98	8735
2000	63	7740.11	8821
2001	86	2194.54	19748
2002	113	2325.95	19491
2003	137	2335.19	10772
Total	795	22101.15	102320

Source: West Bengal Industrial Development Corporation.

During last three years, West Bengal has received few big proposals from the companies like Salim Group of Industries, Malayasia, TELCO, Infosys, IBM, Zindal Group of industries and many more. Currently, West Bengal has become the favourite destination of national as well as international companies.

Energy

West Bengal is self-sufficient in terms of energy resources.

Table 4.9 and 4.10 give us an idea about the various energy resources available in this state. It is found that Coal resource is gradually increasing in the State. But, it was decreasing in 2000 in comparison to the situation of 1995. In case of power generation, the state has installed capacity of 3638.46 MW during 2005-06 and out which 93.92 percent is from thermal power plants. However, in case of Hydro and Renewable energy, West Bengal is lagging behind. It is found that more than two third households of total rural households in West Bengal are using firewood/chips for cooking, which is similar to the country level usage rate. On the other hand, near about half (47.1 %) of the total urban households are using LPG as major source for cooking in this state, which is nearer to the country level usage rate (50.7%). However, the rate of using Biogas is negligible both in West Bengal as well as in India. Considering the limited LPG and kerosene resources of our country and high import bill on oil, it is required to encourage people for increasing the use of Biogas for cooking.

Socio-economic Status of the Districts

At present, there are nineteen districts in West Bengal. An effort is made to develop a tentative idea on the socio-economic status of these districts through Table 4.13. It is found that all districts are not equal in terms of their prevailing socio-economic conditions. Few districts like Kolkata, Howrah, Hoogly, Burdwan and North 24 Parganas are developed; Jalpaiguri, Nadia, South 24 Parganas, Purba Medinipur and Paschim Medinipur are mediocre and the remaining nine districts are socio-economically backward. However, since last few years the state government has adopted several programmes for improving the socio-economic conditions of the people residing in these backward districts.

Table-4.9
Coal Resource (million tones).

State	2000				2005			
	Indicated	*Proved*	*Inferred*	*Total*	*Indicated*	*Proved*	*Inferred*	*Total*
WestBengal	10,894	10,779	4,236	25,909	11,878	11,383	4,553	27,814
India	89,501	82,396	39,697	2,11,594	1,19,800	95,900	37,700	2,53,400

Source: TERI, 2001; TERI 2006.

Table-4.10
Installed Capacities of Power (MW) as on 31.03.2006

State	Hydro		Thermal		Nuclear		Renewable		Total	
	MW	*%*	*MW*	*%*	*MW*	*%*	*MW*	*%*	*MW*	*%*
W.B.	161.70	4.44	3,417.06	9,3.92	0.0	0.0	59.70	1.64	3,638.46	100
India	32,325.77	26.01	8,2410.54	66.31	3,360	2.70	6190.86	4.98	1,24,287.17	100

Source: TERI, 2006.

Table-4.11

Socio-economic Status of the Districts in West Bengal

District	*Net Agricultural Land (%)*	*No. of Regd. Industry*	*No. of SSIs*	*No. of Health Care Institutions and Bed Capacity*		*No. of Family Planning Centre*	*No. of Banks & Cooperatives*		*Socio-Economic Status*
				Institutions	*Bed Capacity*		*Bank*	*PACS*	
1	*2*	*3*	*4*	*5*	*6*	*7*	*8*	*9*	*10*
Bankura	48.78	190	400	699	3,508	24	167	391	Backward
Birbhum	70.93	158	206	608	1,616	22	174	337	Backward
Burdwan	65.11	911	937	1,047	8,649	41	393	619	Developed
Coochbehar	74.48	40	278	474	1,882	14	110	231	Backward
Dinajpur (S)	84.70	97 (S+N)	48	285	1,130	9	63	128	Backward
Dinajpur (N)	86.48	—	106	389	982	11	81	192	Backward
Darjeeling	43.56	294	141	393	4,128	16	119	107	Backward

(Contd...)

1	2	3	4	5	6	7	8	9	10
Hoogly	70.08	626	324	928	5,618	26	259	484	Developed
Howrah	58.88	2,807	1,095	631	4,413	24	230	211	Developed
Jalpaiguri	54.06	518	280	653	2,805	17	136	160	Mediocre
Kolkata	—	962	1,762	335	23,426	38	1,041	—	Developed
Malda	59.74	54	419	590	1,724	16	148	218	Backward
Medinipur (W)	59.41	321 (W+E)	1,788 (W+E)	1,117	4,815	35	297	727	Mediocre
Medinipur (E)	74.14	—	—	899	2,646	27	197	925	Mediocre
Murshidabad	75.37	54	830	994	3,607	30	222	483	Backward
Nadia	74.74	187	528	620	6,024	21	184	360	Mediocre
North 24 Parganas	67 40	6,337 (N+S)	869	1,059	7,336	41	408	476	Developed
South 24 Parganas	39.04	—	918	1,303	4,660	35	239	483	Mediocre
Purulia	49.33	84	265	576	2,346	23	113	178	Backward

SSI = Small Scale Industry, Regd. = Registered.
Source: Manorama Year Book (Bengali Version) 2008.

HIV/AIDS Scenario in West Bengal

The first case of HIV infection in West Bengal was detected in 1986. According to data from voluntary counselling and testing centres (VCTCs) in the state, the number of new HIV infection cases in West Bengal was 304 in 1996. This figure grew to 371 in the year 1997, and further to 3638 in March 2007. Table 4.12, Table 4.13 and Table 4.14 give age-wise, year-wise and locality-wise information on total number of AIDS cases in West Bengal. In the last few years, the epidemic has spread to the general population and is no longer restricted to most high-risk populations only. The discussion of this part is mainly based on the annual report (2006-07) of WBSAP&CS. The current analysis has been done on the basis of data received from 103 blood banks, 32 VCTCs, 27 PPTCT centres, 33 STD Centres and 2 ART Centres. Besides it, data from Annual Sentinel Surveillance have also been incorporated in this part.

Table-4.12
Age Distribution of AIDS Cases in West Bengal (Since inception to May 2006)

Age group in years	*Number*	*Percentage of Cases*
0 - 14	236	4
15 - 29	2652	45
30 - 45	2298	39
45 +	707	12
Total	5893	100

Source: WBSAP&CS.

It is clearly evident from the above table that 84 percent youth in the age group of 15 years to 45 years, are the victim of this killer disease.

Table-4.13
Year-wise Break-up of AIDS Cases by Sex

Year	*Male*	*Female*	*Total*
1988	1	0	1
1989	0	0	0
1990	1	0	1
1991	0	0	0
1992	7	1	8
1993	10	1	11
1994	9	1	10
1995	7	2	9
1996	16	1	17
1997	29	8	37
1998	64	5	69
1999	184	42	226
2000	159	62	221
2001	153	54	207
2002	776	193	969
2003	480	131	611
2004	853	367	1220
2005	1300	731	2031
Total	4245	1668	5893
Percentage to Total	72.03	27.97	100.00

Source: WBSAP&CS.

Table-4.14: AIDS Cases by Locality

AIDS Cases	*Urban*	*Rural*	*Total*
No. of Cases	3713	2180	5893
Percentage to Total	63.01	36.99	100.00

Source: WBSAP&CS.

HIV and Sentinel Surveillance

Epidemiological Surveillance for HIV infection in the country is carried out annually on a regular basis. The purpose of epidemiological surveillance is to identify high-risk population groups, areas with high HIV prevalence and HIV trends. During the year 2006, the 10th round of Sentinel Surveillance was conducted in 47 sites in West Bengal. Out of these 47 sites, 13 sites were the ANC sites, 12 were the STD sites, and 5 were for IDU, 2 for MSM, 2 for the client of FSWs, 5 for truckers and 8 for FSWs. A total of 13372 persons were tested for HIV during the year 2006. Majority represented the ANC population and rests of the population groups were STD population, FSWs, IDUs and MSM. Among the high risk population West Bengal showed decreasing trend in all the groups other than MSM group where the prevalence rate increased from 0.54 in 2005 to 6.6 percent in 2006 (Sites changed in 2006). There were, however, considerable differences in the prevalence rates from district to district. HIV prevalence was >1% among antenatal mothers in Uttar Dinajpur and in Kolkata in the year 2006. The overall prevalence rate in ANC cases stood at 0.41 percent in the state. The Figure-4.1 clearly shows that the HIV epidemic has been stabilized over the years in the state, with a shoot in the year 2005. The HIV prevalence in ANC cases is considered as the HIV prevalence in general population. The prevalence rate remains somewhere at 0.4% over the years.

Figure-4.1: HIV Prevalence at ANC

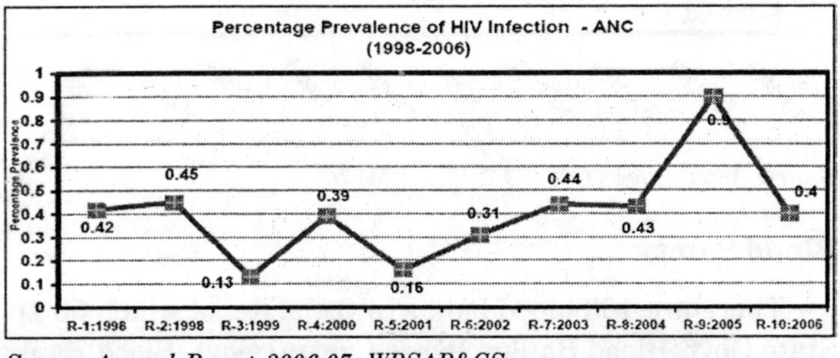

Source: Annual Report 2006-07, WBSAP&CS.

The 10th round of sentinel surveillance witnessed a declining trend in HIV prevalence in STD patients also. In 2006, it stood at 1.66% down from 2.79% in 2004 and 2.47% in 2005. This is depicted in the Figure - 4.2. The decreasing trend is noticed in all sentinel groups. HIV prevalence in FSW went down from 6.8% to 6.6% & prevalence in IDUs decreased to 4.64% from 7.41%; only MSM prevalence has seen an upward trend in the 10th round of surveillance where prevalence rate shot up from 0.54% to 6.6%, (Sites changed in 2006). Surveillance on truckers' population and among the clients of FSWs has been started from this year only and the HIV prevalence stood at 2.72% (N = 1248) among the truckers, whereas the prevalence in clients of sex workers stood at 3.41%. It can be derived from the surveillance data that the growth of the epidemic is arrested. The prevalence rate in general population stood at 0.4%, which is again a sign of stabilization of the epidemic over the years.

Figure-4.2: HIV Prevalence Percentage in STD Patients.

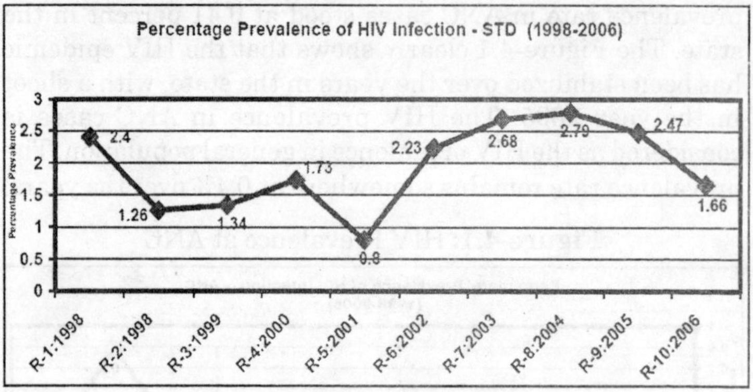

Source: Annual Report 2006-07, WBSAP&CS.

Blood Safety

There are 103 blood banks in the state, of which 58 are State Govt. Blood Banks, 16 are Central Govt. Blood Banks and 27 are Private Blood Banks. There are eight Regional Blood Transfusion Councils (RBTCs) under which 58 Govt. Blood Banks operate. The Table-4.15 shows that the total blood collection during 2006-07 was 640496 units. The total voluntary collection during the reporting period was 555850 units and the total replacement collection was 84646 units. The percentage of voluntary collection against the total collection of 640496 remained 87%, among the highest in the country. During the year 2006-07, a record number of 11049 blood donation camps were organized. Besides this, out of the total whole blood unit collected i.e. 640496, 152403 were separated component wise which is 24% of total whole blood units. The percentage of packed cells out of total blood components supplied in the reporting period are 50%, frozen plasma is 35%, Plasma and Platelets rich Plasma are 7% and 8% respectively. There are five government and twelve private blood components separating units working in West Bengal.

Table-4.15
Collection of Blood (units) from Blood Banks during 2006-07

Type of Blood Banks	*Voluntary Collection*	*Replacement Collection*	*Total Collection*	*Proportion of Voluntary Donation*	*Camp Organised*
Government	413085	51174	464259	89%	8696
Private	142765	33472	176237	81%	2353
Total	555850	84646	640496	87%	11049

Source: Annual Report 2006-07, WBSAP&CS.

Interestingly, the HIV positivity rate in Government Blood banks is significantly lower than the Private Blood banks. The overall HIV positivity rate in Government Blood banks stood at 0.36% comparing with that of Private Blood banks, which stood at 1.25%. HIV positivity rate stood between 0.51% and 0.76% in the four quarters, whereas overall positivity rate stood at 0.6% during 2006-07.

The Figure 4.3 shows that the HIV positivity rate in the blood collected through voluntary & replacement donors. The overall HIV positivity rate in the state stood at 0.36%, varied from 0.01% in Birbhum to 0.92% in Hoogly. It also shows that Paschim Medinipur, Malda, Darjeeling, Nadia, Howrah and Hoogly registered a high HIV prevalence, which is higher than the state average. Overall Programme indicators show a satisfactory performance for Blood safety in the state. However, there is scope for improvement on some issues like timely reporting and quality of reporting. Some districts also need more comprehensive monitoring system towards the better performance of the blood banks. However, overall the state picture is quite good when comparing with other states.

Figure-4.3: Trends in HIV Positivity in Govt. Blood Banks (District-wise distribution)

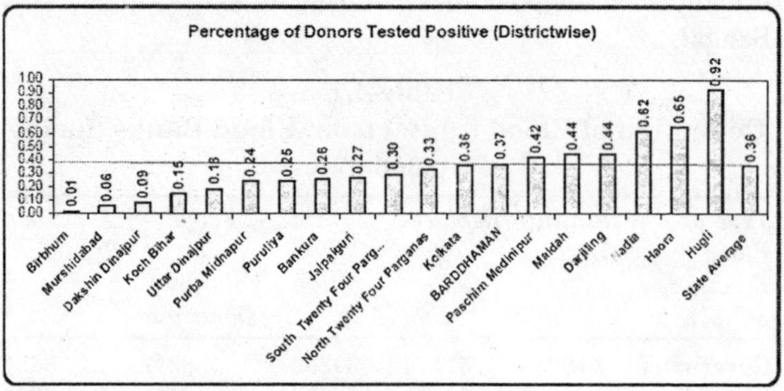

Source: Annual Report 2006-07, WBSAP&CS.

Voluntary Counseling and Testing Centres (VCTCs)

The Figure-4.4 shows the percentage of HIV positivity among the VCTC clients. There are 32 VCTCs till March 2007 in West Bengal. During 2006-07, total 41324 persons attended Pre-Test Counseling, 40594 persons underwent for testing and 3638 cases among the persons got tested were HIV positive i.e. 9% (approximately).

Figure-4.4: Percentage of HIV Positivity among VCTC Clients

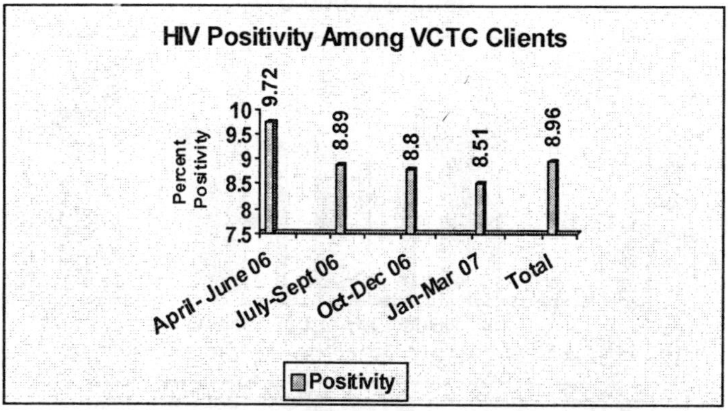

Source: Annual Report 2006-07, WBSAP&CS.

The routes of transmission reported among HIV positive male & female clients of VCTCs is mainly heterosexual contact, which is 90% and 93% respectively. Amongst the male clients, other routes are homosexual (1.0%), infected needles/syringes exchange (2.0%), blood and blood products (2.0%) and parent to child transmission (4.0%). Amongst the female clients other routes are parent to child (5.0%) and blood & blood products (2.0%). The Figure-4.5 shows the different routes of HIV transmission for male and female clients separately.

Figure-4.5: Routes of Transmission among the Clients in VCTC

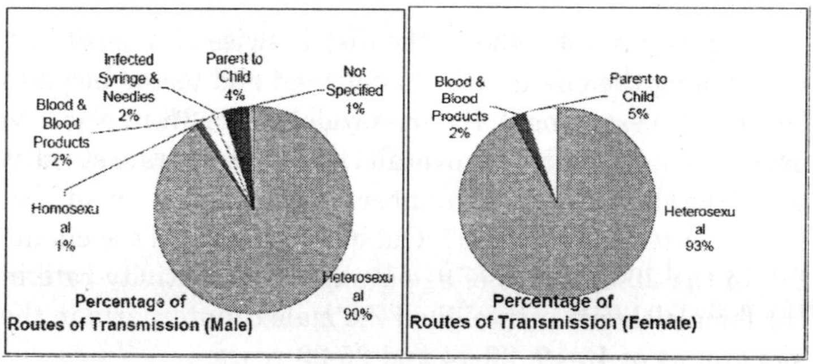

Source: Annual Report 2006-07, WBSAP&CS.

Figure-4.6: Number of clients undergone Pre-Test Counseling, Testing and Post-Test Counseling in West Bengal (2006-07)

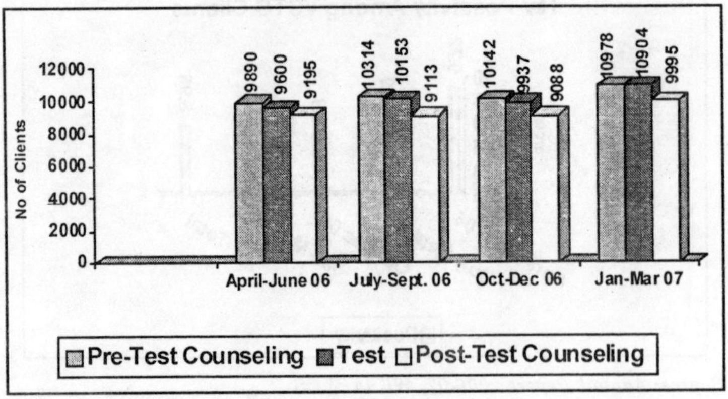

Source: Annual Report 2006-07, WBSAP&CS.

The details of pre-testing counseling, testing and post-test counseling are depicted in the Figure - 4.6. The acceptance rate of testing and post-test counseling remained quite high in the state over the last four quarters, for both male & female clients. Overall, 98 percent male clients who had undergone pre-test counseling accepted testing at the VCTCs and 92 percent clients came back for the reports and received post-test counseling. The figure remained same for female clients as well.

The Figure - 4.7 shows the district-wise HIV positivity rate among the clients who had visited and tested blood in VCTCs of West Bengal. It varies widely from 2% in Nadia to over 17% in Howrah. The overall HIV positivity rate stood at 9% in the state. The total number of persons underwent HIV testing is 40594 in 2006-07. Out of these, most of the clients fall in the 20-39 years of age group. HIV positivity rate in the female clients outweighed the male counterparts in the age groups of 15-19, 20-24 and 25-29 years.

Figure-4.7: District-wise HIV Positivity among clients of VCTCs

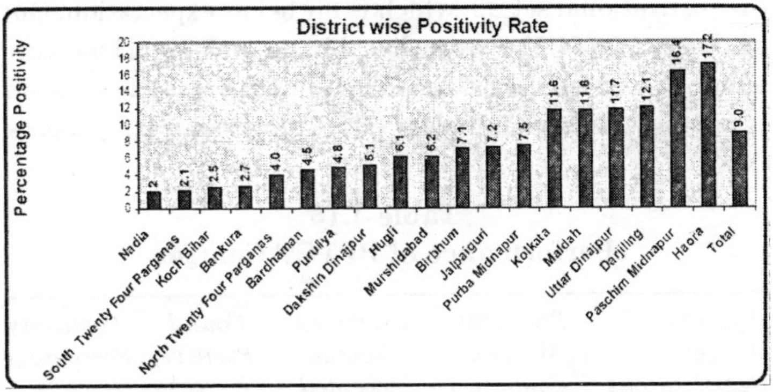

Source: Annual Report 2006-07, WBSAP&CS.

This may be attributed mainly to (a) early sex debut among females; (b) early marriage of females in West Bengal at the age of 15-20 years (median age -17years); (c) female sex workers are sexually active during the age group of 15-30 years; and (d) social and gender discrimination towards females mostly takes place in this age group. However, these observations may not be true for the general population as people attending the VCTC services may not be the representatives of the general population of the state. Positivity rate among males remained higher than females in 30-39, 40-49 and above 50 years of age group. The overall positivity rate in male and female clients remained 9.1% and 8.7% respectively. Male female ratio among VCTC attendees is 1.6:1.

Prevention of Parent To Child Transmission (PPTCT)

The analysis takes into consideration the reports (2006-07) from the 20 out of 27 registered PPTCT centers in CMIS from across the districts of West Bengal, since other seven units opened only in January' 2007. Out of the 202 positive mothers only 91 (45%) deliveries could be administered in the institutional set up; which is far below expectation. Out of these, 90 (44.5%) were live births and 83 (41%) were administered with MB pair NVP. Again there is a lot of scope to improve the services under PPTCT programme components.

Table-4.16
Performance of PPTCT Centres

Pregnant Women Registrations	*Pregnant Women Counseled (pre-test)*	*Pregnant Women Accepted HIV test*	*Found Positive*	*Positivity Percentage*
138997	128269	108530	202	0.19

Source: Annual Report 2006-07, WBSAP&CS

Anti Retroviral Therapy Programme (ART)

The Government of India launched free ART initiative on 1st April 2004 at eight Government hospitals in six high prevalence states. Since then, this is being scaled up in a phased manner and it is planned that free ART will be provided to 1,00,000 patients by the end of 2007 and 3,00,000 by 2011 in 250 centres across the country. In West Bengal, free ART initiative was launched at School of Tropical Medicine (STM), Kolkata since March' 2005 and then at North Bengal Medical College and Hospital (NBMCH), Siliguri since March' 2006. The target to provide ART service was set at 1500 for the year 2006-07. In the later half of 2007, two more ART Centres are opened in Burdwan Medical College and Hospital (BMCH) and Medinipur Medical College and Hospital (MMCH).

Figure-4.8: Details of ART Receiving Patients in West Bengal.

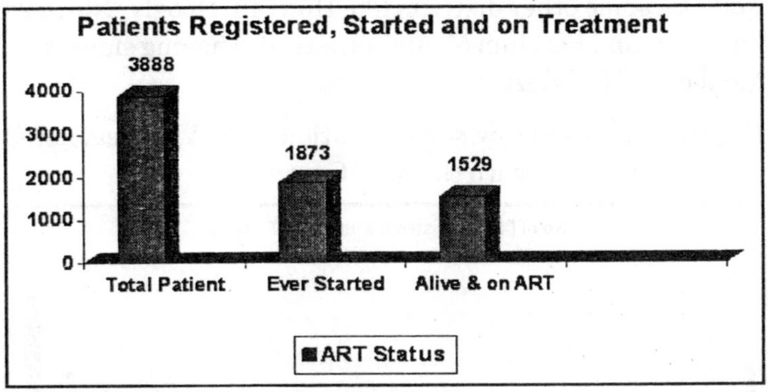

Source: Annual Report 2006-07, WBSAP&CS

The information in the Figure-4.8 is based on the report received from 2 ART centers based in School of Tropical Medicine, Kolkata and North Bengal Medical College and Hospital, Siliguri. Till the end of the reporting period, 15th April 2007, the total number of patients registered at ART center is 3888. Out of these 48 percent ever started the ART treatment and out of these 82 percent are alive and on ART. Out of the registered patients at ART Centres, 96% are adults and only 4% are children. Again out of the adult patients, 76% are male and 24% are female. There is a clear gender bias in accessibility of the treatment. The National ART Programme will also link with other programmes, such as the Revised National Tuberculosis Control Programme (RNTCP), Reproductive & Child Health (RCH) programme and National Rural Health Mission (NRHM). Strengthening of referrals and linkages to PPTCT programme is being carried out so that women and children living with HIV/AIDS have greater access to treatment.

The Figure-4.9 shows the number of patients from districts registered with the ART centres. The maximum number of

PLWHA is registered in Kolkata district and the number varies from 37 in Purulia to 691 in Kolkata. Apart from Kolkata, some other districts like Howrah, Hoogly, North 24 Parganas and Paschim Medinipur are also having significant numbers of PLWHA.

Figure-4.9: District-wise distribution of PLWHA registered with the ART Centres.

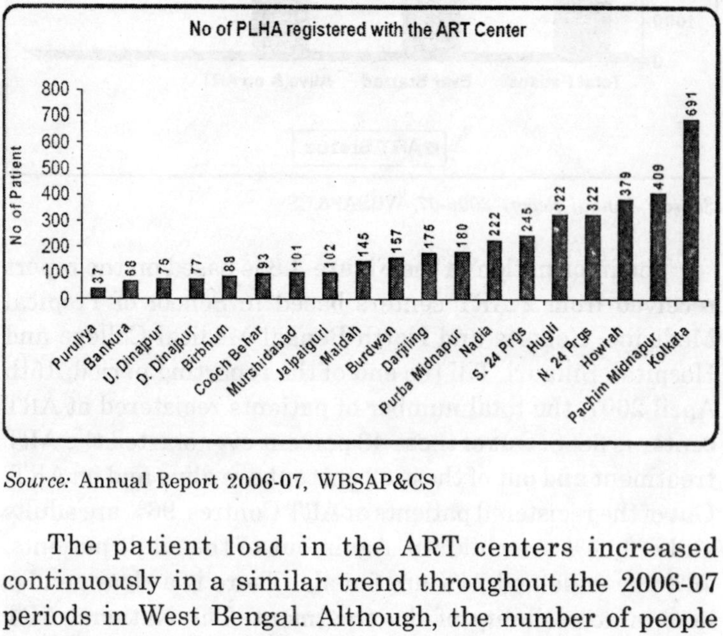

Source: Annual Report 2006-07, WBSAP&CS

The patient load in the ART centers increased continuously in a similar trend throughout the 2006-07 periods in West Bengal. Although, the number of people registering and receiving treatment increased continuously over the period, but it is still far way to reach even the 10 percent of the total estimated AIDS cases in the state.

West Bengal State AIDS Prevention and Control Society (WBSAP&CS)

National AIDS Control Organisation provides leadership to HIV/AIDS Control Programme in India, implementing NACP (National AIDS Control Programme) within one monitoring system. State AIDS Prevention and Control

Societies (SACSs) implement NACO programme at state level, but have functional independence to upscale and innovate. SACSs are autonomous and decentralised. Each State AIDS Prevention and Control Society has a governing body, its highest policy-making structure, headed either by the minister in charge of health or the chief secretary. It has on board representatives from key government departments, the civil society, trade and industry, private health sector and PLWHA networks, who meet twice a year. It approves new policy initiatives, annual plan and budget, appoints statutory auditors and accepts the annual audit report. For better financial and operational efficiency, administrative and financial powers are vested with the Executive Committee and the Programme Director of SACS.

Accordingly, West Bengal State AIDS Prevention and Control Society (WBSAP&CS) was established in 1992 to deal with the HIV/AIDS situation in West Bengal. The programme activities of WBSAP&CS can be broadly grouped under four categories namely – (1) preventive intervention programme for general people; (2) targeted intervention programme for high risk groups; (3) HIV/AIDS care, support and treatment programme; and (4) institutional strengthening programme. These activities are briefly discussed below:

1. Preventive Intervention Programme for General People

The HIV/AIDS epidemic is alarmingly pacing up in West Bengal, with its impact on the general population (beyond the most-at risk populations) becoming more and more visible. This requires sustained and coordinated activities instead of stand-alone, one-time programmes. The key elements of preventive interventions for the general population in West Bengal are as follows:

(a) Awareness Generation Campaigns

Preventive education for the general population, inclusive

of the most at-risk populations, has been brought under a consolidated media plan, which encompasses a range of BCC activities. These include messaging through print and audio-visual media, inter-personal communication and the use of traditional and unconventional folk media. Multi-media campaigns like the *Buladi campaign*, involving television, radio, newspapers and magazines, outdoor media, inter-personal communication, and social mobilization have also been implemented for extensive coverage both in urban and rural areas. As part of IEC programme to prevent HIV in general population a very unique effort has been launched to reach people throughout the state. A centralized system has been developed to provide counseling service on HIV/AIDS through telephone and the number was made toll free. The programme launched on August 2006 and generated a great response (WBSAP&CS, 2007).

(b) Voluntary Counselling and Testing Centres (VCTCs)

Voluntary Counseling and Testing (VCT) is the process that individuals go through to learn about their HIV status. The process is supposed to be voluntary, confidential and based on informed consent from the individuals concerned. It involves counselling prior to the HIV test, which helps people learn about HIV transmission and the likelihood of their being infected with HIV. It also helps them decide if they need an HIV test, and if yes, then to be mentally prepared for the outcome of the test. If the test is undertaken, counselling follows again irrespective of the test result. If people underwent test and are detected as HIV positive, post-test counselling helps them learn how to take care of their health. It also educates them on how to prevent passing on the infection to others and getting re-infected. If the result is negative for HIV, they learn about how to stay free of HIV infection. WBSAP&CS follows a specific protocol for VCT for HIV. Currently (end 2006) there are 46 VCTC centres located in various medical colleges and hospitals, district hospitals and sub-divisional hospitals in West Bengal. Three of these centres are community-based ones, one managed by an NGO i.e. Child In Need Institute (CINI), Pailan, South 24 Parganas district, another by a CBO named Durbar Mahila Samanway Committee (DMSC), Kolkata and the remaining one by another NGO named SHIS, Ghatakpukur, South 24 Parganas (WBSAP&CS, 2007).

(c) Blood Safety

The blood safety programme of WBSAP&CS has three major objectives namely – to ensure organized blood-banking services at the state and district levels, to educate and motivate people about voluntary blood donation and to enforce quality control of blood and blood products.

(d) Prevention of Parent to Child Transmission (PPTCT) Programme

The PPTCT programme of WBSAP&CS operates through 29 centres across West Bengal. The programme is a good example of integration of HIV/AIDS prevention, care, support, and treatment services with the reproductive and child health services in the state. Hon'ble Chief Minister of West Bengal, Mr. Buddhadeb Bhattacharya launched the programme on January 1, 2004. The programme started with 10 centres (at 9 medical colleges & 1 maternity home), scaled up to 29 centres in the year 2006-07 (WBSAP&CS, 2007).

(e) STD Care and Treatment Services

Sexually Transmitted Infections are well known to their wide prevalence, potential serious compilations and intricate relationships with the HIV infection. The present day evidences from different sources have proved beyond doubt that an early and effective management of Sexually Transmitted Infection (STI) is an important tool for the reduction of HIV infection. Thus an effective STI management is considered as one of the corner stone of any

STD control programme. In West Bengal, STD Control Programme is conducted through 44 NACO supported STD Clinics, State Government supported 23 clinics & 188 STD clinics of TI projects supported by WBSAP&CS. Beside this, STD diagnosis and treatment are also done by Gynecologist and Obstetrician in the out patient departments (OPD) of Medical College and Hospitals, District Hospitals, Sub-Divisional Hospitals, Rural Hospitals, State General Hospitals and in all OPD of Government set up to the level of Sub Centers (WBSAP&CS, 2007).

2. Targeted Intervention Programme for High Risk Groups

All over the world, it has been found that particular groups of people are more vulnerable than others to HIV/AIDS. These groups, because of their social circumstances and behavioural attributes, are likely to get HIV infection more quickly and spread the disease in a very short period. One of the ways of controlling the disease from further spread is to carry out targeted intervention (TI) programmes among these vulnerable groups through multi-pronged strategies. Therefore, TI programmes for most at-risk populations, are one of the most important components of the NACP and also the activity plan of WBSAP&CS. Currently, NACP considers the following as most at-risk populations – female sex workers, injecting drug users (IDUs) and males who have sex with males (MSM, a population that also covers male-to-female transgender groups, and male and transgender sex workers). Key elements of TI programmes are discussed below:

(a) BCC Strategies and Material Development

Behaviour Change Communication (BCC) forms the bedrock of a TI programme. The ultimate goal of a TI programme is to bring about such behaviour changes among all stakeholders that facilitate HIV prevention and alleviate the impact of HIV/AIDS. The BCC process is a continuum that consists of awareness generation, concern generation, building motivation for behaviour change, providing accessibility to the means for change and finally ensuring sustainability of the change. The activities needed to implement this process – outreach work, counselling, medical services, advocacy, training, community mobilization – are all part of the other elements of a TI programme. Therefore, BCC is integral to all other elements of a TI programme. Development of BCC strategies and material (also known as information-education-communication or IEC material) covers HIV/AIDS epidemiology, prevention, care, support and treatment and a range of related issues – gender, sexuality, human rights, sexual health, reproductive health, substance use, injecting practices, tuberculosis treatment and other mental and physical health issues. Provision of information on how to access services related to these issues is also included (WBSAP&CS, 2007).

(b) Condom Promotion

Availability of attractively packaged and technically superior condoms is considered as one of the important means for increasing acceptance and use of condoms. Currently WBSAP&CS promotes its "Jeevan" brand of condoms for both free distribution and social marketing of condoms. Peer educators and outreach workers of NGOs implementing TI programmes, form the backbone of the condom promotion programme of WBSAP&CS. Condom vending machines have also been installed at strategic sites all over Kolkata. WBSAP&CS is considering promotion of female condoms (or femmedoms). It is also supporting the availability of water-based lubes, which are helpful in reducing friction and chances of tearing of condoms during anal sex (WBSAP&CS, 2007).

(c) STI/HIV/AIDS Counselling

Majority of NGOs implementing TI programmes have

their own STI clinics, while others refer people to government and private services. In the STI treatment methodology emphasis is laid on syndromic management of STI cases. There are 188 STI clinics run by different NGOs. Along with STI treatment, the TI programmes also facilitate voluntary counselling and testing for HIV and AIDS care, support and treatment through referrals to VCTCs run by other NGOs and government bodies. Increasingly, TI programmes in West Bengal are also incorporating psychosocial counselling along with STI/HIV/AIDS services. Such counselling raises the self-esteem of people belonging to most at-risk populations, which are often also highly stigmatized and socially disadvantaged. Apart from improving the sense of self-worth, psychosocial counselling can also provide knowledge about health, human rights and legal issues. This in its turn can lead to an improvement in demand, delivery and acceptance of STI/HIV/AIDS services (WBSAP&CS, 2007).

(d) Creation of an Enabling Environment

This is another crucial element of TI programmes and includes a varied package of activities necessary for bringing about and sustaining the behaviour changes sought among different stakeholders. Advocacy, lobbying, networking, inter-sectoral collaborations, income generation programmes, drop-in centres (DICs), process documentation, research, infrastructure development, fund raising, training and other forms of capacity building – all contribute towards the creation of an enabling environment. A human rights based approach is important for the creation of such an environment, and this also entails provision of legal support to most at-risk populations and advocating for a non-discriminatory legal and larger social environment. The human rights approach, in its turn, is best adopted through a self-help approach, which involves community mobilization through peer education and formation of self-help groups and community-based organizations (CBOs) of the vulnerable populations or communities. Some of the largest TI programmes in West Bengal are implemented by CBOs. WBSAP&CS provides partial support to NGOs implementing TI programmes towards all these activities, encouraging them to develop other linkages and resources as well towards the creation of an enabling environment (WBSAP&CS, 2007).

(e) Other Specific Services

All the elements mentioned so far are common to all TI programmes in West Bengal, but there are also specific elements needed for certain programmes. For instance, TIs meant for IDUs often include harm reduction services like needle and syringe exchange and oral substitution therapy. Some TIs for IDUs prefer to adopt a de-addiction / detoxification and rehabilitation approach and provide associated services. Treatment for abscesses is another specific service that is part of TIs for IDUs (WBSAP&CS, 2007).

3. HIV/AIDS care, support and treatment programme

The one of the major objective of National AIDS Control Programme is to provide adequate care and support to PLWHA to improve the quality of life and strengthening prevention and care synergy. The number of people and families living with HIV/AIDS in West Bengal has been continuously increasing thereby increasing the demand for care and support at institutional, community, and family levels. To ensure effective implementation of Greater Involvement of People Living with HIV (GIPA) principles, PLWHA members were included in all decision making or other prominent forums and bodies - Executive Committee, Ethical Committee and sensitization programmes. The principle of Greater Involvement of PLWHA (GIPA) is also being adopted in the TI programmes, wherein support for PLWHA has been included as one of the key activities. Currently, 1873 PLWHA are receiving ART in government institutions in West Bengal. Government is committed to providing ART to those who need it most. NACP-III will scale up this service to a larger number of people. At the same time compliance and drug adherence will be ensured with community participation. To increase the number of eligible PLWHA on ART, linkages with VCTC/ICTCs/TIs/PPTCTs and PLWHA networks will be forged and strengthened. First line anti-retroviral therapy(ART) drugs are provided in the state free of cost through the School of Tropical Medicine (STM), Kolkata; North Bengal Medical College (NBMC), Siliguri; Medinipur Medical College and Hospital (MMCH), Medinipur; and Burdwan Medical College and Hospital (BMCH), Burdwan (WBSAP&CS, 2007).

Key features of the AIDS care, support, and treatment component:

(i) Involvement and participation of PLWHA through networks like Bengal Network for People Living with HIV/AIDS (BNP+) and its partners in the districts like Kolkata Network of HIV Positives (KNP+), SPARSHA, Kolkata and Sanghabaddho to name a few. Basically by working with these networks WBSAP&CS intends to mainstream GIPA through all the TI partners.

(ii) The uniqueness of WBSAP&CS Care, Support and Treatment programme lies in the short-stay homes for PLWHA in Drop-in-Centres (DIC). Each of the above-mentioned networks has two-three short-stay homes at remote rural bases. Apart from these short-stay homes, six Community Care Centres (CCCs) with the provision of 25 beds for long-term treatment of children, women and men are getting introduced in West Bengal.

(iii) Additionally, the earlier '*Bhalobasha*' care, support and treatment centre run by Bhoruka Public Welfare Trust (BPWT), Kolkata has been now developed as a full-fledged Capacity Building Resource Centre by WBSAP&CS.

(iv) In West Bengal, clinics for treatment of opportunistic infections function at all the nine Medical Colleges and Hospitals in the state. Apart from these, there are two Community Care Centres and five Drop-in-Centres in the state where drugs for opportunistic infections are also available.

(v) Tuberculosis (TB) and HIV are overlapping epidemics. There is increased risk of transmission to the general population on account of increasing TB cases amongst those infected with HIV. Thus importance is given to HIV-TB coordination in order to ensure optimal synergy between the two programmes for the prevention and control of both diseases. This coordination consists of cross-referrals between HIV-VCT centres and TB treatment centres in West Bengal. TB drugs are available in the state through Revised National Tuberculosis Control Programme (RNTCP) up to Sub- Health Centre level.

(vi) The post-exposure prophylaxis (PEP) drugs are made available from nine Medical Colleges and Hospitals in the State as well as from the District Hospitals and NGO Clinics (WBSAP&CS, 2007).

4. Institutional Strengthening Programme

(a) HIV Sentinel Surveillance

An HIV sentinel surveillance study consists of rapid collection of HIV prevalence data from a broad cross-section of a given population, which includes both most at-risk populations and other less vulnerable populations. An anonymous unlinked sampling procedure is adopted to calculate the HIV prevalence. This is as per the guidelines issued by NACO. The first annual HIV sentinel surveillance in West Bengal was conducted in 1998 at eight sites and the last surveillance (10th Round) was carried out in 2006 and conducted at 47 sites (WBSAP&CS, 2007).

(b) Behavioural Sentinel Surveillance (BSS)

There have been three BSS studies in West Bengal focused on the most at-risk populations. Initially, the BSS was conducted in two waves, one in 1999 and the next in 2001. The last study was completed in 2004. In the years in between NACO also conducted a BSS study in the state, covering the general population and most at-risk populations (WBSAP&CS, 2007).

(c) STI Surveillance

An STI surveillance study estimates the number of people infected or having a high chance of getting infected with STIs. This helps programme planners design appropriate health services. All 57 STI clinics in West Bengal report to WBSAP&CS monthly. NGOs engaged in TI programmes with an STI component also report to WBSAP&CS monthly (WBSAP&CS, 2007).

(d) AIDS Cases Surveillance

An AIDS case surveillance ensures reporting of AIDS cases as per the standard definition of an "AIDS case" adopted by specified institutions and trained physicians. The purpose is to capture the disease burden, and subsequently, design strategies for management of such cases. An AIDS case surveillance data can also supplement the HIV sentinel surveillance data in monitoring the HIV/AIDS epidemic and planning the provision of institutional and home-based care, support and treatment services. In West Bengal, AIDS cases surveillance is done through a process of reporting by the hospitals providing HIV/AIDS related treatment services. The bulk of information on AIDS cases in West Bengal is compiled at the School of Tropical Medicine, Kolkata and Calcutta Medical College and Hospital, Kolkata (WBSAP&CS, 2007).

(e) Training on HIV/AIDS and Related Issues

The training focus of WBSAP&CS consists of the following: (i) Training for field and institutional health workers; (ii) Training for nursing personnel of different hospitals; (iii) Training for public health care providers like doctors; (iv) Training for health care providers and NGO / CBO functionaries working in TI programmes; and (v) Training under inter-sectoral collaborations for workers of the Integrated Child Development Scheme (ICDS), municipal health officials, Panchayat functionaries, police personnel and others (WBSAP&CS, 2007).

In brief, first part of this chapter has portrayed the profile of West Bengal. Primarily, it is an agricultural state. West Bengal ranks fairly high in the country in terms of sex ratio, literacy rate and health status indicators. As far as industrial development is concerned, it has made remarkable progress during recent past and able to erase its previous image of anti- capitalists. The increasing rate of educated unemployment is a major concern for the state government. There is a growth of health services in West Bengal, but in comparison to other states, growth rate in private health sector is very slow. On the other hand, last part of this chapter highlighted the HIV/AIDS scenario in West Bengal and role of WBSAP&CS. Firstly, from the 10th round of Sentinel Surveillance report, it has discussed about various data regarding HIV positivity in ANC, STI clinics, VCTCs, PPTCTs and Blood Banks; routes of HIV transmission; blood safety; pre-test and post-test counseling; ART receiving clients; etc. It is a serious matter to see that HIV prevalence has gone up from 0.21 to 0.30 percent. During 2006, HIV prevalence was 1% among the antenatal mothers in Kolkata and Uttar Dinajpur District. Secondly, this part has also discussed about the different roles of WBSAP&CS in preventing and controlling HIV/AIDS in West Bengal. It has been playing four major roles namely – (i) preventive intervention programme for general people; (ii) targeted intervention programme for high-risk groups; (iii) HIV/AIDS care, support and treatment programme; and (iv) institutional strengthening programme. The next chapter now will give an overview of WBSAP&CS supported NGOs and their response to HIV/AIDS in West Bengal.

REFERENCES

Baru, R. (1998), *Private Health Care in India: Social Characteristics and Trends*, Sage: New Delhi, pp 74-80.

Government of India (2001), *India 2001- A Reference Annual,* Ministry of Information and Broadcasting: New Delhi.

Kar, Samit (2001), *WEST BENGAL – Beyond the Millennium,* Directed Initiative: Kolkata.

Malayalam Manorama (2002), *Manorama Year Book (Bengali Version)* 2002, Kottayam.

Malayalam Manorama (2008), *Manorama Year Book (Bengali Version)* 2008, Kottayam.

Office of The Registrar General (2001), *Census of India 2001,* Directorate of Census Operations, West Bengal, 2001. http://www.wbcensus.gov.in

Sarkar, A (2005), *NGOs: The New Lexicon of Health Care,* Concept: New Delhi.

Sur, A.K. (1992), *History and Culture of Bengal*, Best Books: Kolkata.

Tata Energy Research Institute (2002), *TERI Energy Data Directory and Year Book 2000-2001*, New Delhi.

Tata Energy Research Institute (2002), *TERI Energy Data Directory and Year Book 2005-2006*, New Delhi.

WBIDC (2006), 'Promotion of West Bengal as an Investment Destination'. http://www.wbidc.com/index.htm

WBSAP&CS (2007), Annual Report 2006-07, http://www.wbhealth.gov.in

WEBINDIA123.COM (2000), "Indian States and Union Territories". http://www.webindia123.com/states/index.htm

SECTION-II

NGO RESPONSE TO HIV/AIDS IN WEST BENGAL

5

State Level Overview of NGOs in HIV/AIDS Care

Development is commonly used to mean economic development. But true development is dependent on various aspects such as social and economic security of the people, social status of women, female literacy, internalization of investments to generate resources, and so on. These aspects can be improved through better income, health, education, information, gender justice, etc. and will ultimately lead to the development. The above cited preconditions of development have to be built on the expectation, aspirations and motivations of the people. Therefore, people's own organizations i.e. NGOs are emerging gradually and participating actively in the process of social and economic transformation (Sarkar 2005). Since health is an essential ingredient of the state's over all development and HIV/AIDS is causing a threat to this development, the state government with the help of central government and other agencies started to combat this killer disease through the involvement of NGOs. One of the objectives of the present study, which is the major thrust of this chapter, is to get a state level overview of NGOs engaged in HIV/AIDS care in West Bengal. The chapter, for better understanding, is divided and discussed separately in two parts. Part - A is based on the information collected from the secondary source i.e. from WBSAP&CS and Part - B is based on the information collected from the primary sources i.e., through mailed questionnaires.

PART – A

The discussion, in this Part, is based on the comprehensive list of sixty NGOs prepared in the first phase. The comprehensive list is prepared after collecting information about the NGOs engaged in HIV/AIDS care from key umbrella organizations like Solidarity and Action Against The HIV Infection in India (SAATHII), Society for Positive Atmosphere and Related Support to HIV/AIDS (SPARSHA), UNICEF, ACTION Aid, West Bengal Programme Support Unit (WBPSU) and West Bengal State AIDS Prevention and Control Society (WBSAP&CS). It is found that presently all HIV/AIDS related programmes are implemented by NACO through WBSAP&CS in West Bengal. The researcher has taken the financial year 2006-07 for the purpose of this study. Out of these sixty NGOs, nine NGOs are functioning in Darjeeling Gorkha Hill Council (DGHC) area and remaining fifty-one are in the other parts of West Bengal. In this part, focus is given to show the distribution of NGOs and their programmes that are meant for HIV/AIDS care in West Bengal. As per the WBSAP&CS, HIV/AIDS programmes are classified into four broad categories – (A) Drop-in-Centres, (B) Community Care Centres, (C) Multi-sectoral programmes and (D) Targeted Intervention programmes.

A. Drop-in Centres (DICs)

Few NGOs are running DICs exclusively for the People Living With HIV/AIDS (PLWHA). These DICs mainly function as out patient department and provide necessary counselling to the PLWHA as per their needs. Table 5.1 shows that five NGOs are running twelve DICs in different districts of West Bengal. It is found that only one DIC is functioning in DGHC area. Bengal Network of Positive People (BNP+) is running three DICs on each in the district of Burdwan, Bankura and Nadia. Similarly, Kolkata Network of Positive People (KNP+) and SPARSHA are running respectively four and three DICs in the above mentioned districts. In brief, there are ten DICs are in South Bengal and remaining two DICs are in North Bengal.

Table-5.1
NGO-wise distribution of DICs in West Bengal

Sl. No.	*Name of NGO*	*Target Group*	*No. of DIC*	*District*
1.	BNP+	PLWHA	3	Burdwan, Bankura and Nadia
2.	KNP+	PLWHA	4	Kolkata, Howrah, Hoogly and North 24 Parganas
3.	SPARSHA	PLWHA	3	Kolkata, Purba and Paschim Madinipur
4.	Sangobaddho	PLWHA	1	Jalpaiguri and Darjeeling (plain)
5.	Sankar Foundation	PLWHA	1	Darjeeling (DGHC area)
	Total		12	

Source: WBSAP&CS, 2006-07.

B. Community Care Centres (CCCs)

Community Care Centres are just like hospices and equipped with doctor, nurse and other inpatient facilities. Table 5.2 indicates that there are six CCCs operating in six districts during 2006-07. Out of these six CCCs, four are in South Bengal and two are in North Bengal. PLWHA get care, support and treatment from CCCs, whenever they feel sick and required to be admitted.

Table-5.2
NGO-wise Distribution of CCCs in West Bengal

Sl. No.	*Name of NGO*	*Target Group*	*No. of DIC*	*District*
1.	Gandhi Mission Trust	PLWHA	1	Paschim Medinipur
2.	Calcutta Diocesan Trust	PLWHA	1	Kolkata
3.	KNP+	PLWHA	1	South 24 Parganas
4.	SPARSHA	PLWHA	1	Howrah
5.	Jesu Ashram	PLWHA	1	Darjeeling
6.	Sangobaddho	PLWHA	1	Jalpaiguri
	Total		6	

Source: WBSAP&CS, 2006-07.

C. Multi-Sectoral Programmes

Multi-Sectoral Programmes are different from the Targeted Intervention Programmes (TIPs) in terms of target groups. Multi-Sectoral Programmes are not meant for the people with high-risk behaviour, but for the general people like industrial workers, Self-Help Groups (SHG) members, etc. Table 5.3 highlights about the different multi-Sectoral Programmes implemented by NGOs during 2006-07 in West Bengal. Out of nine programmes, five are Work Place Intervention (WPI) programmes for the industrial workers. Welfare of Indian Seamen's Everywhere (WISE) is running its WPI programmes in all districts of West Bengal through

Table-5.3
NGO-wise Distribution of Multi-Sectoral Programmes in West Bengal

Sl. No.	*Name of NGO*	*Target Group*	*Types of Progra-mmes*	*District*
1.	FXB India	Industrial Workers	Work Place Inter-vention	Howrah
2.	WISE	–Do–	–Do–	All 19 Districts
3.	VVM	–Do–	–Do–	Purba Medinipur
4.	BPWT	–Do–	–Do–	Kolkata
5.	WBVHA	–Do–	–Do–	Howrah
6.	Sree Ma Mahila Samity	Community People	SHG	North 24 Parganas, Nadia, Birbhum and Murshidabad
7.	SPADE	–Do–	–Do–	North 24 Parganas, Nadia, Coochbehar, Murshidabad and Malda.
8.	BPWT Network	PLWHA Centre	Resource Districts	All 19
9.	SLARTC	PLWHA Cell	Legal Aid Districts	All 19

Source: WBSAP&CS, 2006-07.

its six branch Unions. Similarly, Bhoruka Public Welfare Trust (BPWT) is functioning as Resource Centre for the networks of PLWHA in whole West Bengal. Socio Legal Aid, Research and Training Centre (SLARTC) is dealing with all legal issues related to PLWHA and helping them throughout the state. It is also found that two NGOs are working with the Self Help Groups (SHGs) of various districts. These SHGs are formed under Swarnajayanti Gram Swarojgar Yojana (SGSY) and are now being made aware about HIV/AIDS, so that they can convey the same to their neighbours. Basically both WPI and SHG programmes are preventive in nature and are providing awareness, counseling, etc. to the respective target groups.

D. Targeted Intervention Programmes (TIPs)

All over the world, it has been found that particular groups of people are more vulnerable than others to HIV/AIDS. These groups, because of their social circumstances and behavioural attributes, are likely to get HIV infection more quickly and spread the disease in a very short period. One of the ways of controlling the disease from further spread is to carry out Targeted Intervention Programmes among these vulnerable groups through multi-pronged strategies. Therefore, Targeted Intervention Programmes for most at risk population are one of the most important components of the NACP and WBSAP&CS.

1. *District-wise distribution of NGO and TIPs in West Bengal*

It is found from the Table 5.4 that total 46 NGOs are implementing 60 TI Programmes in West Bengal during 2006-07. This implies that there are few NGOs who are running more than one TI Programmes. It is also found that there are few NGOs who are working in more than one district. To overcome this problem, such NGOs are included in the districts wherein they got registered. But the targeted intervention projects implemented by them are shown in the particular district where the programme is actually going on. For example, in Darjeeling district, 12 TI Programmes are running by 12 NGOs, but the Table 5.4 shows that there are 10 NGOs in this district. This has happened because other remaining two NGOs are included in the Kolkata district as per their registration in Kolkata. Similar is the case with Howrah and Murshidabad districts.

Similarly, in some cases one TI Programme covers more than one district. In such cases also, the programme is shown in the district wherein its implementing NGO got registered. For example, CLPOA an NGO implementing one TI Programme for street children through out the state of West Bengal, but it shown under Kolkata district as it is registered in Kolkata. Similar is the case with DMSC, WISE, etc. These NGOs are working in other districts but included under Kolkata District. Therefore, Kolkata District is having maximum number of NGOs i.e. 10 (21.8%) of total 46 NGOs and 14 (23.3%) of 60 TI programmes.

Table 5.4 also indicates that there is no exclusive TI Programme in the districts of Bankura, Paschim Medinipur, Malda and Uttar Dinajpur. But these districts are partly covered under other TI programmes implemented by the NGOs from other districts. For example, DMSC a Kolkata based NGO, is covering Paschim Medinipur, Bankura and Malda through one of its TI Programmes. DMSC also covers Uttar Dinajpur through its North-Bengal TI Programme.

It is also found from the Table 5.4 that the number of NGOs and TI Programmes are, comparatively less in North Bengal than that of the South Bengal. Total number of TI Programmes in the six districts (including DGHC area) of North Bengal is 18 (30% of the total TI Programmes) and implemented by 12 local district based NGOs. Again out of these 18 TIPs, 12 i.e. 66.7% are running in Darjeeling districts only. This may be because of the geographical location, economic importance, and presence of more army units and being a tourist spot; the number of people with risk behaviour is more in Darjeeling district than other 5 districts of North Bengal. Darjeeling Gorkha Hill Council is another reason as out of twelve TIPs, eight Programmes are running in DGHC area.

Table-5.4
District-wise Distribution of NGOs and TI Programmes in West Bengal

Sl. No.	*District*	*No. of NGOs*	*No. of TI Programmes*
1.	Birbhum	2 (4.3%)	2(3.3%)
2.	Burdwan	2 (4.3%)	3(5.0%)
3.	Coochbehar	1(2.2%)	1(1.7%)
4.	Dakshin Dinajpur	1(2.2%)	1(1.7%)
5.	Darjeeling	10(21.8%)	12(20.0%)
6.	Howrah	2(4.3%)	3(5.0%)
7.	Hoogly	2 (4.3%)	2(3.3%)
8.	Jalpaiguri	4 (8.8%)	4(6.7%)
9.	Kolkata	10 (21.8%)	14(23.3%)
10.	Murshidabad	1 (2.2%)	3(5.0%)
11.	Nadia	1 (2.2%)	1(1.7%)
12.	Purulia	2 (4.3%)	2(3.3%)
13.	Purba Medinipur	2 (4.3%)	3(5.0%)
14.	North 24 Parganas	3 (6.5%)	5(8.3%)
15.	South 24 Parganas	3 (6.5%)	4(6.7%)
	Total	46(100%)	60(100%)

Source: WBSAP&CS, 2006-07

In South Bengal, most of the NGOs and projects are located in Kolkata and its adjacent districts like Howrah, Hoogly, North 24 Parganas and South 24 Parganas. These few districts are implementing 28 i.e. 46.7% of total TIPs in West Bengal through 20 i.e. 43.5% of total NGOs implementing TIPs. This may be because of presence of more red light areas in the big cities of these districts; and number of more migrated workers working in the cities, industries and ports of these districts. NGOs of these districts are more professional than other districts. Therefore, it is found that NGOs have a tendency in general to work in socio-economically developed area.

The districts that are located in the western part of the state namely, Paschim Medinipur, Birbhum, Bankura and Purulia, are not having much exclusive TI Programmes. Incidentally, these districts are also socio-economically backward than other parts of the State. Due to this backwardness, the rate of Intra-State and Inter- State migration is very high in these districts. And it is a known fact that migration is one of the major reasons for getting HIV infection and spreading it in a short time. Therefore, merely by opening one DIC or CCC in these districts will not be adequate to gain control over the situation.

2. *District-wise distribution of types of TIPs*

Table 5.5 highlights the district wise distribution of different types of TI programmes. It is found that out of 60 TIPs, 28 i.e. 46.7% of the total TIPs are for the CSWs. This is quite appropriate as more than 80% of HIV infection occurs in our country as well as in West Bengal through heterosexual intercourse. Again out of these 28 TIPs for CSWs, 16 i.e. 57.1% are centralized in Kolkata and its adjacent districts of Howrah, Hoogly, North 24 Parganas and South 24 Parganas. This is again justified, as most of the red light areas are located in the big and industrial cities.

Table-5.5
District-wise Distribution of Types of TI Programmes

Sl. No	*District*	*Types of TI Programmes (No.)*						*Total*
		CSW	*IDU*	*MSM*	*ML*	*Truckers*	*Street Children*	*No. of TIPs*
1.	Birbhum	1	-	-	-	1	-	2
2.	Burdwan	1	-	-	-	2	-	3
3.	Coochbehar	-	-	-	-	1	-	1
4.	Dakshin Dinajpur	-	-	-	-	1	-	1
5.	Darjeeling	3	4	1	3	1	-	12
6.	Howrah	1	1	-	-	1	-	3
7.	Hoogly	1	-	-	-	1	-	2
8.	Jalpaiguri	1	-	-	-	2		
9.	Kolkata	7	1	1	1	3	1	14
10.	Murshidabad	1	1	-	-	1	-	3
11.	Nadia	1	-	-	-	-	-	1
12.	Purulia	2	-	-	-	-	-	2
13.	Purba Medinipur	2	-	-	-	1	-	3
14.	North 24parganas	4	-	-	-	1	-	5
15.	South 24parganas	3	-	-	-	1	-	4
	Total	28(46.7%)	7(11.7%)	2(3.3%)	5(8.3%)	17(28.3%)	1(1.7%)	60(100%)

Source: WBSAP&CS, 2006-07

Next to CSWs, Truckers' programme occupies 28.3% of the total TIPs in West Bengal. All the 17 TIPs for Truckers are running in almost majority of the districts. So far other groups with high-risk behaviour are concerned only 11.6% of the total TIPs are for IDUs and 8.3% TIPs are for migrated Labourers (MLs). There is only one TIP for street children and two TIPs for MSM.

Surprisingly, out of the six TIPs for MLs, none of them is working in Burdwan district – which is one of the major industrial hubs of West Bengal. It is also found that another vulnerable group – prisoners are not covered under any TIPs of WBSAP&CS during 2006-07. Prisoners are vulnerable, because the incidences of drug abuse, homosexuality, etc. are common high-risk behaviour found among the prisoners. It is learnt that only one ICTC in running in Presidency Jail, Kolkata by WBSAP&CS. This is too inadequate for the prisoners of whole West Bengal. Thus, it is found that apart from the sex workers and truckers, TIPs for other vulnerable groups are comparatively less in West Bengal.

3. *Numbers of TIPs run by each NGO*

Table 5.6 gives an idea about the number of TIPs run by each NGO. It is found that 73.9% of the total NGOs are running only one TI programme, 21.8% NGOs implement two TI programmes and 4.3% NGOs each of whom carry out three TI programmes. Out of the 10 NGOs having two TIPs each, it is found that all of them are running both the programmes within the same districts. Out of the two NGOs running three TIPs each, society for Community Intervention and Research (SCIR) is working among IDUs in Kolkata, Murshidabad and Darjeeling districts. Another NGO – DMSC is implementing three TIPs for CSWs in Kolkata, Bankura, Burdwan, Paschim Medinipur, Malda, Uttar Dinajpur and Darjeeling Districts.

Table-5.6
Number of TIPs run by each NGO

Sl. No.	*No. of TIPs*	*No. of NGO*
1.	One	34(73.9%)
2.	Two	10(21.8%)
3.	Three	02(04.3%)
	Total	46(100%)

Source: WBSAP&CS, 2006-07

4. *District-wise Target Population Covered*

Table 5.7 shows different types of target population covered by the NGOs under 60 TI Programmes in West Bengal. It is found that 63,485 CSWs are covered through 28 TIPs i.e. on an average each project covers 2267 sex workers in West Bengal. So far districts are concerned, Kolkata has covered 26,907 CSWs through its seven TI Programmes and Darjeeling has covered 18,372 through its three TI Programmes.

Out of 10,000 IDUs covered under 7 TIPs, 53% of total IDUs are in Darjeeling district only and 25% are in Kolkata. The reason of higher numbers of IDUs as well CSWs in Darjeeling may be because of its geographical location (i.e. situated in the international borders) and being a tourist place. Table 5.7 also indicates that only two NGOs are implementing TIPs for 9000 MSM populations in West Bengal.

It is also found from the Table 5.7 that 36,000 migrated labour covered under five TIPs are working in the three districts of Kolkata, Darjeeling and Jalpaiguri. It may be noted here that five NGOs are implementing multi-sectoral programme (Work Place Intervention) among the industrial workers who are also migrated labourers. Out of five NGOs, four are working in Howrah, Kolkata & Purba Medinipur districts and the other NGO is working in all the districts of West Bengal.

As per Table 5.7, 17 truckers' intervention projects cover 2,67,000 truckers in almost all the districts of West Bengal excepting Nadia, Purulia, Bankura, Paschim Medinipur, Malda and Uttar Dinajpur. It means on an average each project covers 15,705 truckers. In terms of districts, Kolkata has covered 29.2% of the total truckers covered under the TIPs, which is higher than other districts like North 24 Parganas (11.2%), Purba Medinipur (11.2%), Burdwan (9.3%) and Jalpaiguri (9.3%).

The only NGO – CLPOA is covering 7,90,000 street children and working children through its 45 affiliated NGOs in all the districts of West Bengal. Thus, it is found that in West Bengal, 60 TIPs cover total 11,75,485 population representing major six target groups. According to WBSAP&CS, CSWs, IDU and MSM are high-risk groups and remaining three target groups are considered as bridge population at risk.

5. *Years of NGOs' Involvement with HIV/AIDS Programme*

The present analysis has been based on the list of NGOs collected from WBSAP&CS for the financial year 2006-07. WBSAP&CS updates this list time to time considering the performance of implementing NGOs. Therefore, the present list of 2006-07 does not include those NGOs who worked earlier in different districts of West Bengal, but currently not supported by WBSAP&CS. At the same time, there are many NGOs like HDRI, BPWT, etc. who have started HIV/AIDS programme much earlier. But they were supported by some international funding agencies (DFID etc.), not by WBSAP&CS at that time. Naturally, the Table 5.8 reflects only the numbers of years of involvement with WBSAP&CS.

Table-5.7
District wise Target Population covered during 2006-07

(As on 31.03.2007)

Sl. No	District	Types of Target Programmes (Nos.) CSW	IDU	MSM	ML	Truckers	Street Children	Total No. of Target Population
1.	Birbhum	2250	-	-	-	10000	-	12250
2.	Burdwan	1500	-	-	-	25000	-	26500
3.	Coochbehar	-	-	-	-	10000	-	10000
4.	Dakshin Dinajpur	-	-	-	-	15000	-	15000
5.	Darjeeling	18372	5300	2000	10000	5000	-	40672
6.	Howrah	300	700	-	-	10000	-	11000
7.	Hoogly	2500	-	-	-	9000	-	11500
8.	Jalpaiguri	300	-	-	16000	25000	-	41300
9.	Kolkata	26907	2500	7000	10000	78000	790000	914407
10.	Murshidabad	1566	1500	-	-	10000	-	13066
11.	Nadia	300	-	-	-	-	-	300
12.	Purulia	600	-	-	-	-	-	600
13.	Purba Medinipur	2350	-	-	-	30000	-	32350
14.	North 24pargonas	3090	-	-	-	30000	-	33090
15.	South 24pargonas	3450	-	-	-	10000	-	13450
	Total	63485	10000	9000	36000	267000	790000	1175485

Source: WBSAP&CS, 2006-07

Table-5.8
Years of NGOs' Involvement with WBSAP&CS

Sl. No	*No. of years involved with WBSAP&CS*	*No. of NGOs (%)*
1.	One year (since 2006)	19 (41.3%)
2.	Three years (since 2004)	7 (15.2%)
3.	Five years (since 2002)	2 (4.3%)
4.	Six year (since 2001)	12 (26.1%)
5.	Seven year (since 2000)	4 (8.7%)
6.	Eight year (since 1999)	1 (2.2%)
7.	Nine year (since 1998)	1 (2.2%)
	Total	46 (100%)

Source: WBSAP&CS, 2006-07.

It is found from the Table 5.8 that majority i.e. 41.3% of total NGOs implementing TIPs since 2006, 26.1% are involved with WBSAP&CS for a period of six years i.e. since 2001 and 8.7% are involved since 2000. DMSC and LAMP respectively are implementing TIPs of WBSAP&CS from 1999 and 1998. In brief, 43.5% of total NGOs are involved for more than 5 years with the HIV/AIDS programme of WBSAP&CS in West Bengal.

PART – B

It has already been mentioned that in the first phase, a comprehensive list of 60 NGOs engaged in HIV/AIDS Prevention and Care has been prepared. In the second phase, questionnaires (both hard copy as well as softcopy) were mailed to all these 60 NGOs. Having given several reminders, responses received from 27 NGOs, which worked out around forty five percent response rates. The data have been presented in this Part as per the responses received through the mailed questionnaires.

Background Information

1. Legal Status

The responses received from 27 NGOs show the particular year when they got registered and received legal status. Table 5.9 shows that 59.2 percent of the total NGOs (27) under the study have been registered during late 1970s and 1980s. It is also found that out of these NGOs, 88.8 percent are working both in urban and rural areas; 7.5 percent in urban area and remaining 3.7% in rural area only.

Table-5.9
Year of Registration

Sl. No.	*Year of Registration*	*No. of NGOs (%)*
1.	1970 – 1979	8 (29.6%)
2.	1980 – 1989	8 (29.6%)
3.	1990 – 2000	8 (29.6%)
4.	2001 and after	3 (11.2%)
	Total	27 (100%)

Source: Responses received through the mailed questionnaires.

2. Promoters' Background

Article 19 (1) (C) of the Constitution of India lays down that all citizens shall have the right to form associations or unions. Hence, any one can take initiative to develop or start an NGO. In the present study, doctors, group of like-minded people, school teachers, university teachers, activists of any movement, businessmen, untrained dedicated social workers, lawyers and others were found as promoters of NGOs. Table 5.10 clearly shows that almost half (i.e. 48.1%) of the total NGOs are developed by the untrained dedicated social workers. Apart from these social workers, doctors (14.8%) and group of like-minded people (11.2%) are the major promoters of the NGOs under the study. It is also found that people from all walks of life such as teachers, lawyers, businessman and social activist have also developed NGOs.

Table-5.10
Promoters' Background

Sl. No.	*Promoters' Background*	*No. of NGOs (%)*
1.	Doctors	04 (14.8%)
2.	Group of like-minded people	03 (11.2%)
3.	School teacher	01 (03.7%)
4.	University teacher	01 (03.7%)
5.	Activists of any movement	01 (03.7%)
6.	Businessman	01 (03.7%)
7.	Untrained dedicated social worker	13 (48.1%)
8.	Lawyer	01 (03.7%)
	Others	02 (07.4%)
	Total	27 (100%)

Source: Ibid

3. Types of Organisation

NGOs in West Bengal have been categorised as (A) Service organisation; (B) Development organization; (C) Research and Consultancy Organisation; (D) Action group and (E) Religious organization. There is no religious organization under the present study. Some of these NGOs are combination of these categories. Service organisations are basically service delivery oriented organisations work through socio-cultural ethos of people; development organizations are involved in the progress of human beings through self-sufficiency and sustain them; research and consultancy organizations carry out research activities and extend advice and guidelines; and action groups are involved in mobilization and organization of unorganized and marginalized sections of the society. Table 5.11 shows that out of the 27 NGOs under the study, almost half (44.4%) are service organizations and 7.4% are action groups. Apart from these two types of organizations, remaining 48.1% of total NGOs are combinations of above mentioned types.

Table-5.11
Types of Organisations

Sl. No.	*Types of Organisations*	*Nos. of NGOs (%)*
1.	A	12 (44.4%)
2.	D	02 (07.4%)
3.	AB	06 (22.2%)
4.	AC	03 (11.2%)
5.	BC	01 (03.7%)
6.	ABC	01 (03.7%)
7.	ABD	02 (07.4%)
	Total	27 (100%)

Source: Ibid

4. *Nature of Initial Programmes*

The present study points out that initially NGOs had various kinds of programmes, such as (a) Awareness, (b) Health, (c) Income generation, (d) Relief Work, (e) Social Movement, and (f) Research and Consultancy.

Table-5.12
Nature of Initial Programmes

Sl. No.	*Nature of Initial Programme*	*No. of NGOs (%)*
1.	B	4 (14.8%)
2.	D	1 (03.7%)
3.	F	1 (03.7%)
4.	AE	3 (11.2%)
5.	BD	2 (07.4%)
6.	AB	7 (25.8%)
7.	ACD	2 (07.4%)
8.	ABC	4 (14.8%)
9.	ABCDE	3 (11.2%)
	Total	27 (100%)

Source: Ibid

It is also found that many of the NGOs under study had more than one of these programmes. Table 5.12 indicates that initially more than three-fourth NGOs (77.8%) were having more than one programme. It is also found that only six NGOs running only one programme respectively in the field of health (4), relief work (1), and research & consultancy (1).

5. Present Programmes

The existing programmes of the NGOs under the study are of various types such as (a) HIV/AIDS intervention programme, (b) health programme, (c) permanent clinic, (d) running blood bank, (e) training of health workers, (f) Drug abuse, (g) anti-trafficking, (h) income generation, (i) community development and (j) educational programmes. Many of the NGOs have been running more than one of these programmes. As per Table- 5.13, one-third of the total

Table-5.13
Present Programmes

Sl. No.	*Types of Present Programme*	*No. of NGOs (%)*
1.	ABC	9 (33.3%)
2.	AHI	1 (03.7%)
3.	ABCE	5 (18.5%)
4.	ABCF	3 (11.2%)
5.	ABCG	2 (07.4%)
6.	ABCH	1 (03.7%)
7.	ABCI	2 (07.4%)
8.	ABCDE	1 (03.7%)
9.	ABCDEG	1 (03.7%)
10.	ABCFIJ	1 (03.7%)
11.	ABCGHJ	1 (03.7%)
	Total	27 (100%)

Source: Ibid

NGOs are having HIV/AIDS programme, health programme and permanent clinic. Apart from HIV/AIDS, health and permanent clinic, these NGOs are also running programmes on training of health workers, drug abuse, trafficking, income generation and community development. It is also found that 62.9% of total NGOs are presently running four or more programmes.

HIV/AIDS Programme Related Information

1. Year of starting HIV/AIDS Programme

In India, NACO started NACP-I (National AIDS Control Programme, Phase – I) in the year 1992. NACP-I was a five-year programme, but it continued up to March 1999.

Similarly, NACP-II started in April 1999 and continued up to May 2007. Table 5.14 highlights the responses with regard to the year of starting HIV/AIDS programme. As per the Table 5.14, 33.3% of the total NGOs under the study started HIV/AIDS programme during NACP-I and remaining 66.7% NGOs during NACP-II. Therefore, the number of NGOs is doubled in NACP-II. The same table also shows that 75% of total service organisations started HIV/AIDS programme during NACP-II, while all the action group organizations stated their HIV/AIDS Programme during NACP-I. However, amongst the organizations having combined approach, most of the NGOs started HIV/AIDS programme during NACP-II excepting AC type of organizations. In case of AC (Service and Research & Consultancy) type of organizations, 50% of NGOs started HIV/AIDS programme during NACP-I and remaining 50% NGOs during NACP-II. The reason of more number of NGOs starting HIV/AIDS programme in NACP-II is due to increase in the budget of NACO.

Table-5.14
Year of Starting HIV/AIDS Programme

Sl. No.	*Types of Organization*	*Year*		*Total*
		1992-1998	*1999 - 2004*	
1.	A	3 (25%)	9(75%)	12 (100%)
2.	D	2 (100%)	–	2 (100%)
3.	AB	1 (33.3%)	2(66.7%)	3 (100%)
4.	AC	3 (50%)	3(50%)	6 (100%)
5.	BC	–	1 (100%)	1 (100%)
6.	ABC	–	1 (100%)	1 (100%)
7.	ABD	–	2 (100%)	2 (100%)
	Total	9(33.3%)	18(66.7%	27(100%)

Source: Ibid

2. Target Groups addressed by NGOs

Part-A of this Chapter has already discussed about the major target groups covered by the NGOs during 2006-07 in West Bengal. It has been found that there are six major target groups namely CSWs, IDUs, MSM, MLs, truckers and street children. Table 5.15 shows the responses received from the mailed questionnaires with regard to the target groups covered by 27 NGOs.

Table-5.15
Target Groups addressed by NGOs

Sl. No.	Types of Target group	No. of NGOs NACP-I	NACP-II	Total
1.	CSWs	6 (50%) 66.7%	6(50%) 33.3%	12(100%) 44.4%
2.	IDUs	-	2(100%) 11.1%	2(100%) 7.4%
3.	Truckers	2(33.3%) 22.2%	4(66.7%) 22.2%	6(100%) 22.2%
4.	MSM	-	1(100%) 5.6%	1(100%) 3.7%
5.	PLWHA	-	3(100%) 16.6%	3(100%) 11.2%
6.	SHG	-	1(100%) 5.6%	1(100%) 3.7%
7.	MLs	1(50%) 11.2%	1(50%) 5.6%	2(100%) 7.4%
	Total	9(33.3%) 100%	18(67.3%) 100%	27(100%) 100%

Source: Ibid

It is found that two-third of the NGOs were implementing HIV/AIDS programme among the CSWs and none of the NGOs were working among the IDUs, MSM and PLWHA during NACP-I. The reason behind this is that both in India as well as in West Bengal, major source of HIV infection is heterosexual intercourse. As a result of it, at the initial stage i.e. in NACP-I, the problems of other target groups were not that much prevalent in West Bengal. Considering both NACP-I and NACP-II, majority i.e. 44.4% of the total NGOs under the study has been working among the CSWs and 22.2% of total NGOs are among the truckers. This is also quite similar with the trends, we have seen in Part-I (Table – 5.5). The table also indicates that out of NGOs working among the truckers, two-third of them have started the programme during NACP-II. All the NGOs working with IDUs, MSM and PLWHA have started their HIV/AIDS programmes only in NACP-II.

3. Nature of Approaches adopted by NGOs in HIV/AIDS Care

NGOs under the study fulfill the needs of beneficiaries (target groups) by means of adopting either only institutionalized approach or only by community-based approach or both institutionalized as well as community-based approaches. Institutionalize approach includes activities like running of health clinic for the treatment of STIs and OIs, providing medicines, collecting blood samples for HIV test, counselling, condom distribution, etc. It also includes in-patient facilities. On the other hand, community based approach includes outreach activities like awareness programme, distribution of IEC materials and condoms, organizing meeting with different stakeholders, etc. at the institutional level.

Table-5.16
Nature of Approaches adopted by NGOs in HIV/AIDS care

Sl. No.	Types of Target group	Nature of approaches adopted by NGOs in nos. (%)			Total
			Institutionalised	*Community based*	*Both*
1.	CSWs	–	1(8.3%) 33.3%	11(91.7%) 45.9%	12(100%) 44.4%
2.	IDUs	–	–	2(100%) 8.3%	2(100%) 7.4%
3.	Truckers	–	–	6(100%) 25.0%	6(100%) 22.2%
4.	MSM	–	–	1(100%) 4.2%	1(100%) 3.7%
5.	MLs	–	–	2(100%) 8.3%	2(100%) 7.4%
6.	PLWHA	–	1(33.3%) 33.3%	2(66.7%) 8.3%	3(100%) 11.2%
7.	SHG	–	1(100%) 33.3%	–	1(100%) 3.7%
Total		–	3(11.2%) 100%	24(88.8%) 100%	27(100%) 100%

Source: Ibid

4. *Types of Services provided by NGOs in HIV/AIDS Care*

The key elements of preventive intervention for the general population include awareness generation, ICTC, blood safety, PPTCT and STD care services. Similarly, key elements of TI Programmes for high-risk groups include BCC strategy and development of IEC material, condom promotion,

STD/HIV/AIDS counselling, creation of enabling environment and other specific services.

Table-5.17
Types of Services

Sl. No.	Types of services	No. of NGOs (%)
1.	Counselling for blood testing at ICTCs/PPTCTs	24(88.9%)
2.	Counselling for PLWHA	26(96.2%)
3.	Awareness for CSWs	14(51.8%)
4.	Awareness for Truckers	10(37.0%)
5.	Awareness for IDUs	06(22.2%)
6.	Education for vulnerable groups like slum dwellers	10(37.0%)
7.	Education for School/College Students & Youth	10(37.0%)
8.	Condom Distribution	25(92.5%)
9.	Advocacy for Protecting Human Rights of PLWHA	26(96.2%)
10.	Assistance in arrangement of ART	18(66.7%)
11.	Referred to other organizations	26(96.2%)
12.	Home visit and counselling of family Members, etc.	21(77.8%)
13.	Awareness among neighbors to remove stigma	20(74.0%)
14.	Mass Media Campaign	23(85.2%)
15.	Imparting Training to Health Staff, Volunteer, etc	17(62.9%)
16.	Organizing Health Check-up Camps	19(70.3%)
17.	Regular Permanent Clinic	22(81.5%)
18.	Mobile Dispensary	04(14.8%)
19.	Offering Treatment for STIs	24(88.9%)
20.	Running ICTC	2(07.4%)
21.	Developing and distributing IEC materials	26(96.2%)
22.	Awareness for Migrated Labourers	02(07.4%)
23.	Awareness for MSM, transgender, etc.	01(03.7%)

Source: Ibid.

The purpose of HIV/AIDS care support programme is to improve quality of life through counselling and medication (ART). As per the guidelines of NACO and WBSAP&CS, NGOs under the study have been providing various types of services to their respective target groups. Table 5.17 highlights the types of services provided by the NGOs during 2006-07 in West Bengal. It is found that about ninety percent or more of the total NGOs have been providing services like counseling for blood testing at ICTC, counselling to PLWHA, distributing condoms and IEC materials, advocacy for protecting human rights of PLWHA, making referral services to other organizations and offering care and treatment for STIs. Seventy to eighty percent of total NGOs have been providing services like organizing health check-up camps, awareness camps to remove stigma and prevent social boycott, home visit and counseling of family members, regular permanent clinic, and mass media campaign. In addition to these services, percentage of NGOs providing other services include assisting in the arrangement of ART (66.7%); awareness programme for CSWs (51.8%), for truckers (37%), slum dwellers (37%), students and youth (37%), and for IDUs (22.2%). Government medical colleges, hospitals and sub-divisional hospitals run most of the ICTCs in West Bengal and only three ICTCs are run by NGOs with the help of WBSAP&CS. Out of the 27 NGOs under the study, two NGOs run ICTC with the support of WBSAP&CS.

5. *Separate Staff for HIV/AIDS Programme*

Responses received from all the NGOs under the study have separate staff members for their respective HIV/AIDS programmes. These staff members are of two types – namely medical and non-medical staff. Most of the doctors are working as part-time paid staff in these NGOs. Non-medical staff members include Project Coordinators, Counsellors, Peer Counsellors, Outreach Workers, etc. Generally, these non-medical staff members are working as full-time paid staff,

Table-5.18
Total Number of Staff for HIV/AIDS Programme

Type of Staff	*Number of Staff (in no. of NGOs)*						*Total*
	01-10	*11-20*	*21-30*	*31-50*	*51-100*	*Above 100*	
Full Time	02 (7.4%)	07 (25.9%)	10 (37.0%)	05 (18.6%)	01 (3.7%)	2 (7.4%)	27 (100%)
Part Time	25 (96.2%)	-	-	01 (3.8%)	-	-	26 (100%)

Source: Ibid.

but it is contractual in nature. Because, WBSAP&CS approves the project for one year only and it renews the project again on the basis of new project proposal. Peer Educators are not treated as full-time or part-time staff as they work on honorarium basis as per WBSAP&CS rules. Table 5.18 shows the total number of full-time and part-time staff members of the NGOs. It is found that out of 27 NGOs under the study, 37.0% NGOs have full-time paid staff between 21 to 30 numbers and 25.9% have between 11 to 20 staff. Out of the two NGOs (7.4%) who have less than ten full-time staff members, one is working with SHGs and another NGO is working as legal aid cell for PLWHA. There are 8 i.e. 29.6% of total NGOs have more than 30 full-time paid staff, because they are running two or more targeted intervention programmes (TIPs). Out of these 8 NGOs, two NGOs are having more than 100 full-time paid staff. Out of the 27 NGOs, excepting one, remaining 26 NGOs have part-time staff members. The only NGO which is working with SHGs, does not have any part-time paid staff. Again out of 26 NGOs having part-time paid staff, 25 NGOs (96.2%) have staff members between one and ten.

6. *HIV/AIDS Budget*

Table 5.19 describes the HIV/AIDS budget of the NGOs

under the study for the financial year 2006-07. All the NGOs have separate HIV/AIDS budget as per the grants of WBSAP&CS.

Table-5.19
HIV/AIDS Budget of 2006-07

Sl. No.	*HIV/AIDS Budget (Rs. in lakh)*	*No. of NGOs.*
1.	Below	2 (07.4%)
2.	Rs.10 lakhRs.10 lakh to Rs. 20 lakh	7 (25.9%)
3.	Rs.21 lakh to Rs.50 lakh	13 (48.1%)
4.	Rs.51 lakh to Rs.1 crore	3 (11.2%)
5.	Above Rs.1 crore	2 (07.4%)
	Total	27 (100.0%)

Source: Ibid

It is found that almost half (48.1%) of the total NGOs under the study have the budget between Rs. 21 to 50 lakh, 33.3% have budget up to Rs. 20 lakh, and 18.6% over Rs. 50 lakh.

7. *Nature of Problems faced by the NGOs*

Table 5.20 shows the response of the NGOs under the study with regard to the problems faced by them. It is found that all the NGOs are facing more than one problem in implementing the HIV/AIDS programmes. Some of these problems are: (a) people's indifferent attitude due to stigma, (b) fear of people to be exposed and to be socially boycotted, (c) apathetic attitude of Government officer and health care personnel, (d) wrong policy of NACO/Donor agency, (e) financial problems, (f) staff related problem, (g) ART related problem, (h) inadequate infrastructure and resources to meet the demands of HIV/AIDS victims, and (i) migratory nature of clients. The table indicates that almost all the NGOs (96.3%)

are facing two major problems namely, people's indifferent attitude and fear of people to be exposed and socially boycotted. Next major problem is delayed disbursement of fund, which is expressed by more than half (55.5%) of the total NGOs. Other problems faced by the NGOs are - apathetic attitude of the Government officers and health personnel (33.3%); ART related problem (33.3%); staff related problems (25.9%); inadequate infrastructure and resources to meet the demand of PLWHA (25.9%); and migratory nature of clients (25.9%). Out of the 27 NGOs under the study, only one NGO talked about the wrong policy of NACO as one of the problems faced by it.

Table-5.20
Nature of Problems faced by NGOs

Sl. No.	*Nature of Problems faced by NGOs*	*No. of NGOs (%)*
1.	Indifferent attitude of the people due to stigma	26 (96.3%)
2.	Fear of exposure and social boycott.	26 (96.3%)
3.	Apathetic attitude of Govt. Health personnel	09 (33.3%)
4.	Wrong policy of NACO	01 (03.7%)
5.	Delayed disbursement of fund	15 (55.5%)
6.	Staff related problems	07 (25.9%)
7.	ART related problems	09 (33.3%)
8.	Inadequate infrastructure and resources	07 (25.9%)
9.	Migratory nature of clients	07 (25.9%)

Source: Ibid

In addition to the above mentioned problems, most of the NGOs have communicated that they would not be able to continue the programme, if funding is discontinued from WBSAP&CS. They are not in a position to run such projects through any other alternative funding sources.

8. *Suggestion of NGOs for overcoming the present problems*

NGOs under the study have suggested various measures to over come the present problems faced by them. Some of the suggestions are (a) Simplifying MIS and reporting system of WBSAP&CS; (b) More and regular fund flow; (c) mass awareness; (d) advocacy to get more cooperation from police; (e) more counseling; (f) network with other AIDS service organizations (ASOs); (g) introducing sex education at school level; (h) development of effective IEC materials; (i) opening up of more ART centres; (j) training for the government health staff; etc. Table 5.21 shows that NGOs suggested mass awareness (92.5%), more counselling (18.5%), development of effective IEC materials (7.4%) and advocacy (7.4%) for overcoming the problems of stigmatization and indifferent attitude of the people.

Table-5.21
Suggestions of NGOs for overcoming Present Problems

Sl. No.	*Types of Suggestion*	*No. of NGOs (%)*
1.	Simplifying MIS and Reporting System	06 (22.2%)
2.	More and regular fund flow	11 (40.8%)
3.	Mass awareness	25 (92.5%)
4.	Advocacy to get more cooperation from the police	02 (07.4%)
5.	More counselling	05 (18.5%)
6.	Network with other ASOs	01 (03.7%)
7.	Introducing sex education at school/college level	01 (03.7%)
8.	Development of effective IEC materials	02 (07.4%)
9.	Opening up of more ART distribution centre	02 (07.4%)
10.	Training of Government health staff	02 (07.4%)

Source: Ibid

Similarly, 7.4% of total NGOs suggested to open up more ART distribution centres to overcome the ART related problems. In addition to these suggestions, 22.2% of the total NGOs have opined for comparatively simpler MIS and reporting system of WBSAP&CS. Even one NGO suggested for the winding up of West Bengal Programme Support Unit (WBPSU) i.e. technical wing of WBSAP&CS to get rid of its interference in the activities of NGOs.

In addition to the above suggestions, most of the NGOs suggested that NGOs must be involved in policy making of NACO for delivering effective services. Some of the NGOs got a chance to participate in the preparatory discussion of NACP-III before its finalization. These NGOs were invited by the WBSAP&CS.

9. *NGOs' Opinion for the Effective Implementation of HIV/AIDS Programme*

Apart from suggesting the measures for overcoming the present problems they faced, NGOs under the study have also expressed their opinions for the effective implementation of HIV/AIDS programme. They feel that programmes can be implemented better by (a) developing network of all NGOs in HIV/AIDS care in West Bengal; (b) providing more technical support for the capacity building of NGOs; (c) providing more financial support; (d) rewarding the good NGOs for their performances; (e) changing the existing policy of NACO; (f) involving more NGOs to expand the coverage; (g) increasing the number of ICTCs, PPTCTs & ART distribution centres; (h) providing more fund to meet the general health care heads of the target group along with STI care services; (i) initiating more efforts for public-private partnership; etc. Many NGOs have suggested more than one measure in this regard. Table-5.22 highlights the opinions expressed by the NGOs. It is found that 81.5% of the total NGOs under the study have opined for more technical support for the capacity building of the implementing NGOs. They also include regular training for the staff to update their knowledge. Besides it, 74% of the total NGOs feel more financial support is required for effective implementation of the HIV/AIDS programmes and 29.9% NGOs feel that exchange of information and experiences among the NGOs is very much required, which can be done by developing network of NGOs engaged in HIV/AIDS care in West Bengal. Few NGOs (25.9%) have expressed that there is a need to change the existing policy of NACO. Some their specific views are i) inclusion of more vulnerable groups like hijras, etc; ii) increasing the supply of first line ART and starting of second

Table-5.22
NGOs' Opinion for the Effective Implementation of HIV/AIDS Programme

Sl. No.	*Opinions / Views*	*No. of NGOs (%)*
1.	By developing network of all AIDS Service Organization (ASOs)	08 (29.6%)
2.	By providing more technical support for capacity building of NGOs	22 (81.5%)
3.	By providing more financial support	20 (74.0%)
4.	By rewarding the good NGOs for their performance	02 (07.4%)
5.	By changing the existing policy of NGOs	07 (25.9%)
6.	By involving more NGOs to expand the coverage	03 (11.2%)
7.	By increasing the no.of ICTC,PPTCT & ART distribution Centre	03 (11.2%)
8.	By providing more fund to meet the general health care needs	04 (14.8%)
9.	By initiating more efforts to increase public-private partnership	02 (07.4%)

Source: Ibid.

Line ART medicines; iii) increasing in the salary of field level staff and provision of traveling allowances of the Peer Educators; iv) provision for the payment of conveyance to the PLWHA, who come from the distant palaces to collect medicines from the ART distribution centre in the city; v) development of more effective BCC strategy; etc. Some of the other measures as suggested by NGOs are – involving more NGOs to expand coverage (11.2%); opening of more ICTCs, PPTCTs, ART centre (11.2%); providing more funds to meet the general health care needs of the target groups (14.8%); and initiating more efforts to increase public private partnership (7.4%).

10. *Future Plans of NGOs*

Responses with regard to the future plan received from the NGOs under the study are many and diversified in nature. Majority of the NGOs want to increase the coverage of their target groups, form SHGs of PLWHA for income generation purpose, to build community ownership of the project and to maintain sustainability of the project. Few NGOS have expressed to start Day Care Centre for PLWHA, HIV-Positive children Care Centre, Home for aged CSWs, Centres for AIDS Orphans, etc. Some of these NGOs have also plan to establish research institutes and start need-based courses. For instance, they proposed to establish Research Centre for PLWHA, Research Institute for Drug Dependents, Research Institute for Social Health Intervention, etc. Some of the courses they wanted to start are Blood Banking Technology, Counselling Course on Drug Abuse and Vocational Training on different trades. In brief, all the NGOs under the study are committed and want to continue their effort in prevention and control of HIV/AIDS in West Bengal.

In brief, Part-A of this chapter has given an overview on the NGO-wise distribution of different HIV/AIDS programmes in different districts, district-wise distribution of types of TI programmes, target population covered by NGOs in different districts, number of TI programmes run by each NGOs, years of NGO's involvement with HIV/AIDS programme in West Bengal, etc. While Part-B of this chapter has highlighted the background information of NGOs under the study such as legal status of NGOs, promoters background, types of organizations, nature of initial progrmmes as well as present programmes. It also discussed about the different aspect of HIV/AIDS programme run by these NGOs. Some of these aspects are – year of starting HIV/AIDS programme, target groups, nature of approaches adopted by NGOs, types of services provided by them, nature of HIV/AIDS care staff, problems faced by the NGOs and their suggestions to overcome them, opinion of NGOs for effective implementation of HIV/AIDS Programme as well as their future plan.

6

Profile of Selected NGOs

The contemporary Indian society is undergoing through rapid changes in all spheres of life. The present society is characterized by many new and complex problems. The new economic policy of 1991 has shown some positive results, but at the same time it has also created too many negative results. It has contributed largely in destabilizing the national economy in terms of high inflation, collapse of large public sector undertakings (PSUs), increasing unemployment, etc. and thereby causing impoverishment of millions of people. Secondly, the revolution of information and communication technology along with its advantages, have adversely affected our traditional culture and value system. Thirdly, the rise of regional forces and their conflict with the federal political structure is hampering the objectives of decentralization of power at the grassroots level, which has been granted through 72nd and 73rd Amendments of Constitution of India. Fourthly, India still continues with the problems of poverty, casteism, religious unrest, illiteracy, gender discrimination, poor health care and so on. On the other hand, we are crazy again for information technology and nuclear energy. Under the above mentioned socio-economic and political context, NGO sector has been working in India. This situation is more bewildering than what we had seen on the eve of our Independence. In spite of the prevailing multidimensional problems, NGOs carry out their programmes for the betterment of the society.

NGOs of West Bengal are no exception. In West Bengal, NGOs work everywhere on various issues. In case of health care, they reach to the remote and distant villages, which are by and large, remain outside the purview of the government's health care services. The previous chapter has described the growth and distribution of NGOs engaged in HIV/AIDS care in West Bengal. But, it did not give details regarding the working of an NGO considering various aspects of programme, staff members, beneficiaries, etc. These information and issues are significant aspects of exploration. The present study intends to focus on NGOs' contribution in HIV/AIDS care in West Bengal. Therefore, the present chapter makes an effort to decribe the profiles of six selected NGOs. Similarly, chapter-7 deals with nature of programme sustainability; chapter-8 give details about staff members' views on different issues related to HIV/AIDS; and chapter-9 describes the beneficiaries' perception towards the working of NGOs. These chapters will help to develop an understanding on how much an NGO can contribute in HIV/AIDS prevention, control and care services. These six NGOs are: (i) Society for Community Intervention and Research (SCIR), (ii) Durbar Mahila Samanaya Committee (DMSC), (iii) Bhoruka Public Welfare Trust (BPWT), (iv) MANAS Bangla (MB), (v) Human Development and Research Institute (HDRI) and (vi) Society for Positive Atmosphere and Related Support to HIV/AIDS (SPARSHA). These six NGOs have been selected purposively on the basis of their direct involvement in HIV/AIDS prevention, control, and care and support services for different target groups by keeping in mind the objectives of the proposed study. The methodology chapter has given detail description about the process of selecting these NGOs.

A brief sketch of each of the NGO under the study is presented here. The profile of NGOs includes various aspects like background, vision, mission, present objectives, area of operation, target groups, organizational structure, infrastructure, present programmes, staff related information, financial information and future plans.

A. Society for Community Intervention and Research (SCIR)

Background

Late Sanjay Bhattacharya's initiative lies at the root of the birth of SCIR in 1996. It was in connection with the research activities at the National Institute of Cholera & Enteric Diseases (NICED) that he came in touch with drug users and was motivated into setting up of this organization for sustained work with this community. Initially, the Society was registered as 'Kolkata Taltala Society for Community Intervention & Research' in 1996, but the name was changed as 'Society for Community Intervention and Research (SCIR)' in 2003. SCIR did not receive any fund from external funding agencies for the first two years and managed with donations and subscriptions from the members. In the year 1998, SCIR got its first external fund from SAHARAN, New Delhi for conducting awareness programmes on HIV/AIDS, Drug abuse, etc. SAHARAN was the only funding agency for SCIR from 1998 to 2001. After receiving fund from NICED and SAHARAN, SCIR started Needle Syringe Exchange Programme (NSEP) in 2002. SCIR for the first time got financial assistance from West Bengal State AIDS Prevention and Control Society (WBSAP&CS) for conducting a 'Need Assessment Study' in 2003. It started Targeted Intervention Project (TIP) for IDUs in the year 2004 with the financial help of WBSAP&CS and has been continuing till today. From June 2006, SCIR started another two TIPs for IDUs at Siliguri (Darjeeling district) and Lalgola (Murshidabad district) respectively.

Vision

A society which respects each individual's self worth and dignity and ensures their empowerment.

Mission

People in society leading a life empowered through befriending, counseling, health care, rehabilitation and job skills training, practicing values and leading a healthy and meaningful life contributing to the upliftment of the community.

Present Objectives

The major objectives of SCIR are as follows: (i) To provide care and treatment services to drug abusers; (ii) To bring about behavioural change among the drug abusers and help them to lead a drug free life; (iii) To improve social status and quality of life of the drug abusers; (iv) To reduce the risk of HIV transmission from drug abusers to their partners and family members; (v) To create an enabling environment for the drug abusers; (vi) To establish vocational training centers for the economic rehabilitation of the ex-drug abusers; (vii) To make an arrangement for the education of the children of drug abusers; (viii) To establish a network with similar organizations; and (ix) To provide legal support to the drug abusers and their family members.

Area of Operation

SCIR is presently working in the four districts namely Kolkata, Howrah, Murshidabad and Darjeeling through its three Targeted Intervention Projects. The Kolkata project covers Kolkata and Howrah districts, Lalgola Project covers Murshidabad district and Siliguri project covers Darjeeling district (mainly Naxalbari and Siliguri area). Kolkata Project is having four drop-in centers at Park Circus, Goabagan, Mehdibagan and Buroshibtala.

The areas covered under these DICs are as follows:

(i) Park Circus DIC — Topsia, Tiljala, Beniapukur, Gobra, and Auddybag.

(ii) Buroshibtala DIC — Khidirpur, Ekbalpur, Mominpur, Lake Gardens, Kalighat, Tollygunj and Panchtala.

(iii) Mehdibagan DIC – Taltala, Sealdah, Janbazar and Alimuddin Street.

(iv) Goabagan DIC – Boubazar, Rajabazar, Kashipur, Dalpatty and Kalabagan.

Target Groups

SCIR is only working for the IDUs, their partners and family members. The number of IDUs and Shadow users registered during 2006-07 is 3366 in SCIR's Kolkata Project.

Infrastructure

SCIR is not having its own office buildings. Both Lalgola and Siliguri Project office is operating from rented building. The main office building of SCIR at Tiljala is owned by Railway. It was previously used as GRP office and later on handed over to SCIR for its noble purpose. Each office is well equipped with computer, Internet and telephone connection. While Lalgola and Siliguri Project is running one clinic each, Kolkata Project is running four clinics for health check-up and treatment of IDUs. There is one non-formal school for the slum children located in the first floor of SCIR's main office building.

Programmes

(i) *HIV/AIDS intervention Project for IDUs and their partners*

Kolkata project was started from 2004. Before conducting the project, in the year 2003 SCIR conducted a 'Need

Assessment Study' with the target groups in Park Circus, Tiljala, Buro Shibtala, Mehdibagan, Sealdah and Tollygunj areas. These areas were profiled and identified as HRB (high risk behaviour) sites. The study revealed that most of the IDUs were injecting drugs more than 2-3 times in a day; sharing needles with others; injecting cocktail drugs and subsequently developed wounds and abscesses and poor treatment seeking behaviour among IDUs. Considering the above findings, Kolkata Project started four drop-in centers at Park Circus, Goabagan, Mehdibagan and Buro Shibtala. The main objective of the Project is to reduce the risk of HIV infection among IDUs their partners and family members. The needle syringe exchange program (NSEP) is a process of befriending, and then through the process of counseling they are motivated to shift to the Oral Substitution Program (OSP). This program is a rehabilitative process that aims at gradually sending them for detoxification within a period of 4-6 months. The detail of this project is being discussed in chapter–7.

Based on the experience of its Kolkata project, SCIR started Siliguri Project under Darjeeling district and Lalgola Project under Murshidabad district of West Bengal in 2006. Both the projects were started after conducting 'Need Assessment Study' in the respective project areas. The project components are same as Kolkata project.

(ii) *Non-formal Education Centre*

SCIR is running this centre at its main office for the children of IDUs and local community for their better involvement. Community people are now spontaneously attending Parents-Teachers meeting and are being made aware about the personal health and hygiene. SCIR has also constructed a small garden cum Children Park in front of its main office. The children of the local slum community, who were used to play on dust and garbage for the whole day, are now coming to this Park and enjoying in a child friendly environment.

Organisational Structure

Chart 6-A: Organizational Structure of SCIR

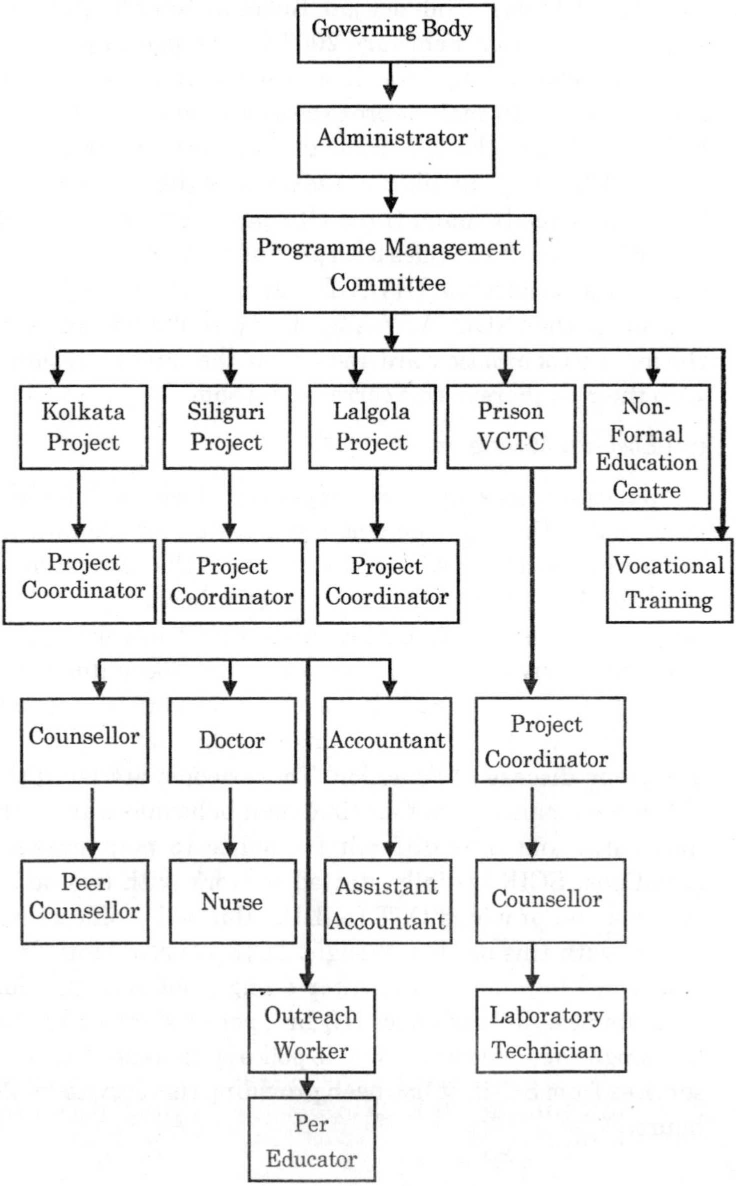

(iii) *VCTC*

WBSAP&CS entrusted the responsibility of starting a VCTC to SCIR at Presidency jail, Kolkata. Accordingly SCIR has started it from February 2007 for the prison inmates. From the counseling data, it was found that most of the inmates especially males were exposed to high-risk behaviour before coming to the jail. Some of them are still practicing high-risk behaviours (like anal sex) inside the jail premises. SCIR has already found three HIV positive cases out of 59 prison inmates. It provides both pre and post-Test counseling services, awareness on HIV/AIDS, drug abuse, etc. With the help of another NGO (AWAAZ), SCIR distributed clothes to the inmates of lunatic ward and gifts to the children residing with their mothers in this correctional home.

(iv) *Lock-up Management*

Basically Lock-up is a temporary place used for the detention of those people who are arrested for committing some crime. Lockup Management is one of the key activities of SCIR. The drug addicts are arrested basically for their involvement in petty crime for purchasing drugs or for their abnormal activities when they are under the influence of drugs. But it is observed that the locked-up addicts' cases are totally different from other criminals, as they are the patients of lifelong disease of addiction. These people are faced the withdrawal pain and at that time their behaviours are quite unnatural and it is difficult for police to manage such situations. SCIR initially started to work with two police stations and provided OST to IDUs. But police officers not agreed with this as they thought SCIR is promoting drug abuse in the jail/custody. After doing a lot sensitization programmes, Kolkata Police HQ gave permission to carry out this programme smoothly. Now 15 police stations are accessing services from SCIR. It has been providing this service for 24 hours.

(v) *Vocational Training Unit*

SCIR has one printing press and one leather unit where recovering IDUs can take training, if they are willing and interested. These two units were linked up with different organizations for getting orders and supplying the materials successfully. Both the units are running independently as Self-Help Groups.

Staff Related Information

SCIR is having total 109 full-time paid staff, 4 Part-time staff and one honorary staff. In its Kolkata Project, there are 27 full-time, 2 part-time (Doctors) and one honorary staff. Apart from it, 35 peer educators are working in the Kolkata project and almost similar numbers of peer educators are working in SCIR's Lalgola and Siliguri Project. Majority (80%-85%) of the staff members are either ex-drug addicts/ IDUs or recovering addicts/ IDUs. As far as volunteers are concerned, there is no specific organizational policy to use their help.

The Governing Body of SCIR has developed service rules for its staff. These are discussed here. All the Project Staff will report to the Project Coordinator at SCIR and work under his guidance. (a) Leave Rules: (i) A staff member can avail 20 days casual leave and medical leave as per doctor's advice. No leave will be granted without Permission and intimation for medical leave is compulsory. Medical Certificate is to be attached with medical leave application. (ii) A staff can take maximum 8 days leave at a stretch including Sunday and holidays. Special permission to be taken for leaves beyond 8 days. (iii) The official holidays declared by the organization will be considered as paid holidays. (iv) Three months paid maternity leave at a stretch can be sanctioned to a female employee and ten days Paternity leave to male employee. (b) All appointments are made on temporary and contract basis.

Every year contract should be renewed. Continuation service is subjected to availability of fund. (c) Minimum working hour is 7 hours per day and 40 hours per week (6 days in a week). Staff members may be asked for additional working days/hours as per the requirement of the office. (d) The appointment is terminable on either side by one month's notice or salary in lieu thereof. (e) The staff can be posted to work in any shift or office of work at any site managed by the Organization. He/she can be deputed to work in any sister concern of this Organization. (f) In case of harmful work against the interest of the organisation, the service of the concern employee will be terminated. (g) The Organization will reimburse starting fees for work or job related courses to encourage and motivate its staff. (h) Medical benefit –up to 50% of medical bills will be reimbursed as per the discretion of the Managing Committee. (i) All staff members will contribute (Optional) Rs. 50/- (fifty rupees only) from their monthly honorarium/salary towards the development, maintenance and functioning of the Staff Self Help Group (Staff Cooperative). (j) The prescribed Staff Regulations in force will govern and they may be amended and altered from time to time. (k) SCIR is also having Gender Policy and following the same.

SCIR is arranging training programmes regularly for its staff members. These programmes are organized internally as well as by external agencies. Some of these external agencies are WBSAP&CS, National Institute of Cholera and Enteric Diseases (NICED), Indian Institute of Health Management & Research (Jaipur), Murray Culshaw Consulting (Bangalore), Indian Institute of Bio-Social Research & Development (Kolkata), Hope Foundation (Ireland), etc.

Financial Information

SCIR's financial turn over in the year 2006-07 was Rs. 1,55,92,500/-. All together SCIR received Rs. 17,58,700/- from

WBSAP&CS for its three TI Projects at Siliguri, Lalgola and Kolkata. For its Kolkata Project, SCIR has received Rs. 5,55,900/- during 2006-07. During this period, various sources of funds were WBSAP&CS, World Vision, Assembly of God Church, Kolkata Municipal Corporation, AWAAZ, Public donations, etc. SCIR has no specific fund raising policy except for its Printing press and Leather Units. Every year SCIR is facing the financial problem at the beginning of new financial year due to the delay in releasing fund from the WBSAP&CS/NACO. But SCIR manages this situation with the help and full support of its staff members.

In order to manage the financial affairs, SCIR prepares annual budget considering expenditure mentioned in the project proposal, present market price, last year's expenditure, area needs, expected funds to be received, etc. Almost 5 percent to 10 percent money is spent for administrative purpose and 90 percent money used for the programme activities.

Future Plans

SCIR is trying hard to start the following activities in near future: (a) to establish a 'Research Unit' for undertaking research studies on different issues related to IDUs; (b) to start a State Level Resource Centre for helping the NGOs working on the drug addiction; and (c) to upgrade its existing vocational training unit by adding more units on different trades. But to do all these, SCIR requires more financial support from WBSAP&CS and other funding agencies.

To sum up, SCIR is mainly working among the IDUs and running its HIV/AIDS programmes for them in Kolkata, Murshidabad and Darjeeling districts of West Bengal. SCIR is reformative in its approach since it has been trying to reduce the risk of HIV infection among the IDUs, their partners and family members. Its approach of getting cooperation from the local community through running the non-formal school for their children is quite successful.

B. Durbar Mahila Samanwaya Committee (DMSC)

Background

WHO (Global Programme on AIDS) funded National AIDS Control Organization (NACO) in 1992 to undertake a study to assess the prevalence of STD (sexually transmitted diseases) and HIV among sex workers in Delhi, Mumbai, Chennai and Kolkata. In January 1992, Dr. M. Mehret, an AIDS consultant visited Kolkata and approached All India Institute of Hygiene and Public Health (AIIH&PH), a Government of India institution with a proposal for a community based study among the female commercial sex workers (CSWs) in Kolkata. The study was conducted by a team led by Dr. Smarajit Jana, an epidemiologist of AIIH & PH, in collaboration with Society for Community Development (SCD) – a local NGO. The study looked into issues of social demography of the locality, mapped the sexual behavioural practices among sex workers, their clients and partners; and assessed the prevalence of STD and HIV among them. The Kolkata experience proved to be a success because of the close rapport built up between the CSWs and Staff of the study team.

Following the baseline survey in 1992, AIIH&PH started the STD/HIV Intervention Programme (SHIP or popularly known as 'Sonagachi Project') at Sonagachi from September 1992 with the help of WHO and NACO. The word 'Sonagachi' stands out, as symbol of sex trade and it is an oldest as well as the largest red light area in Kolkata, having a population of 5000 CSWs. The 19th Century Bengali literatures on Kolkata's social history frequently referred Sonagachi, which ultimately became a proverbial term in the world of prostitution in Bengal. Kaliprasanna Singha, author of the famous social satire *Hutum Pencher Naksha* (1862) lamented that in Kolkata there was hardly a locality in which at least ten prostitutes did not stay.

The objective of SHIP was to control the spreading STD and HIV among the CSWs. The Programme incorporated three principal components: provision for health services including STD treatment, IEC and condom promotion and distribution. First a primary health clinic was set up at the Friend's Union Club at Imam Bux Lane. The clinic was later shifted to Rambagan area and finally to the Palatak club at 7/A, Maniruddin Lane, Sonagachi. The programme was put into operation through a network of government and non-government organizations by adopting a strong peer based outreach component. The project recruited sex workers as Peer Educators (PEs) and trained them for door-to-door awareness campaign about STD and HIV/AIDS. Soon, PEs of Sonagachi Project realized that sex workers were vulnerable to STIs and HIV infection not because of unsafe sexual behaviour but rather due to structural barriers that control their everyday lives. These structural barriers comprise of powerbrokers within the sex industry that coerce, exploit and oppress sex workers; mainstream society that stigmatizes sex workers and prevent them from accessing services otherwise freely available; and the law, which criminalises sex work through provisions of the Immoral Trafficking Prevention Act (ITPA).

Sex workers, therefore, realized that to ensure sustained change and safer sex practice, they needed to organize themselves to challenge and change these structural barriers. From this realization, Durbar Mahila Samanwaya Committee (DMSC) - a sex workers' forum, emerged with the direct support from the Project. It became an active partner of the programme (SHIP) on and from 1995. DMSC registered in 1995 with only 13 members. Finally, DMSC took over the management of STD/HIV Intervention Project from the AIIH&PH in the year 1999. Since then, there has been no looking back for DMSC. After taking full control of the programme, DMSC started replication of the basic principles and approach of the 'Sonagachi Project' in other red light areas of West Bengal. It took special initiatives to reach an increasing number of sex workers outside Kolkata.

DMSC rapidly expanded its activities and established different wings to run them effectively. Some of these wings are Usha Multi-purpose Cooperative Society Ltd. (cooperative bank), Komal Gandhar (cultural wing), Binodini Shramik Union (trade union), Srishti (vocation training centre), Shramajeebee Mahila Sangha (SHG), etc. In order to manage all these activities smoothly, a conglomerate of Sex Workers' Organisations under the name 'DURBAR' was established and all different wings including DMSC are working under it. Recently, to formalize the loose affiliation of all wings, an umbrella institution named as "Durjoy Durbar" has been registered. The word 'Durjoy' in Bengali language means which can't be defeated and 'Durbar' means unstoppable or indomitable. DMSC was running its project office from the head office of Durbar at 12/5, Nilmoni Mitra Street, Kolkata-6. In 2005, DMSC shifted its Project Office from the head office to 44, Balaram Dey Street, Kolkata-6. DMSC today is an organization of 65,000 sex workers with branches in 66 sex work sites throughout West Bengal.

Vision

Durbar seeks a world where all marginalized communities of the world live in an environment with due respect, rights and dignity. We hope for a social order where there is no discrimination based on class, caste, gender or occupation all people live in peace.

Mission

To enhance a process of social and political change in order to establish rights, dignity and improvement of social status including quality of lives of all sex worker communities of the world as part of the global movement to establish rights of marginalized people through:

1. Improvement of image and self-esteem of marginalized communities.
2. Influencing existing norms, policies and practices operating at all levels in the society.
3. Empowering communities through a process of collectivization and capacity building.
4. Addressing power relations within the sex sector and outside.
5. Formal and informal alliances with individuals, groups, institutions and movements.

Present Objectives

The major objectives of DMSC are as follows: (i) To fight for the recognition of 'sex work' as 'work' and 'sex workers' as 'workers'; (ii) To improve social status, dignity and quality of lives of all sex workers; (iii) To protect legal rights of sex workers and fight social injustices against sex workers; (iv) To reform laws that restrict human rights of sex workers, tend to criminalize them and limit their enfranchisement as full citizens; (v) To improve the image and self-esteem of sex workers; (vi) To empower and enable the sex workers community to assert their rights; (vii) To solve the social, economic and health problems of sex workers; (viii) To secure social existence of sex workers and their children; (ix) To establish non-formal education centers and vocational training centres for the sex workers; (x) To make arrangement for the education of sex workers' children; (xi) To form alliances with other like-minded organizations; and (xii) To prevent trafficking and entry of minor girls into sex work.

Area of Operation

At present 43 clinics of DMSC offer treatment for general

ailments with special emphasis on STD/HIV throughout West Bengal. Currently, DMSC is running five STD/HIV Intervention Projects (SHIP) namely, Sonagachi Project, Ganga Bhagirathi Project, Ultadanga Project, North Bengal Project and Cossipur Project. All the first four projects are working among sex workers and Cossipur Project is for truckers. Sonagachi Project covers Sonagachi, Khidderpore, Kalighat, Bowbazar and Lokermath. North Bengal project covers Coochbehar, Darjeeling (excluding Gorkha Hill Council Area) and Uttar Dinajpur districts. Ganga Bhagirathi Projects covers Burdwan, Howrah, Nadia, East and West Medinipur, Bankura, Malda and Hoogly districts. Ultadanga Project covers street-based (flying) sex workers and Cossipur Project covers Chitpur and Cossipur area of Kolkata. In general, Durbar is having 66 branches and covering around 65,000 sex workers in different districts of West Bengal.

Target Groups

The target groups of include female CSWs, male sex worker, lesbian, homosexual, transgender, etc. In addition, DMSC through its 43 clinics also serve the customers of sex workers, *babus* (non-paying fixed customers), pimps, etc.

Infrastructure

The head office of DMSC is operating from its own building. The Project Office of DMSC is operating from the rented building, which is owned by its sister organization — Usha Cooperative. Except the North Bengal Project, offices of the other four projects are situated in the same building. Its vocational training centre (SHRISTI) is also situated within its head office. Similarly, the residential schools (Rahul Vidyaniketan and Indubala Abasik Vidyalaya) for the children of sex workers are owned by DMSC. The Mamata Care and Treatment Centre is equipped with modern laboratories and in-house treatment of PLWHA. All the offices are well equipped with modern facilities like computers, telephones, Internet facilities, different audio-visual equipments, etc. About two-third of the total clinics run by DMSC are functioning from the rented premises. The clinics are well equipped with required facilities in general. But there are few clinics where space is comparatively small. In brief DMSC is having good infrastructure to run its different activities.

Programmes

Durbar is running numbers of different programmes through its different wings. The programme activities of DURBAR are depicted in the Chart - 6B. Some of the major programmes are being briefly discussed below.

(i) *Health Programmes*

(a) STD/HIV Intervention Programme

DMSC runs this programme in five project areas. The details are as follows: is presently running five such programmes throughout the state of West Bengal. These projects are Sonagachi Project (since 1992), Ganga Bhagirathi Project (since 2001), North Bengal Project (since 2004), Ultadanga Project (since 2000) and Cossipore Project (since 2006).

Ganga Bhagirathi Project (since 2001) is the one which divided into three zones – namely, Zone-1 (Durgapur under Burdwan district), Zone-2 (Seoraphuli under Hoogly district) and Zone-3 (Santipur under Nadia district). There are three Project Coordinators to look after the functions of three zones respectively. There are five clinics under Durgapur zone. These are: Asansol (Burdwan); Durgapur (Burdwan); Bisnupur (Bankura); Kharagpur and Ghantal (Paschim Medinipur). Similarly, there are six clinics under Seoraphuli zone. These are: Contai (Purba Medinipur), Domjur (Howrah), Uluberia (Howrah), Rajganj, Titagarh and

Seoraphuli (Hoogly district). Under Santipur zone, there are three clinics namely at Kalna (Burdwan), Santipur (Nadia) and Malda (Malda district).

North Bengal Project office is situated at Siliguri. There are three clinics under this project. These are located at Siliguri (Darjeeling), Islampur and Panjipara (Uttar Dinajpur district).

Ultadanga Project was started for street based sex workers (flying CSWs) and their clients covering a population of about 20000 CSWs. There are three clinics under this project. These clinics are located at DumDum (North 24 Parganas), Ultadanga and Rajabazar (Kolkata district).

Cossipur Project is for the truckers. All the five projects are funded by WBSAP&CS and having similar components. All the projects are running on the strong peer based approach. The details about Sonagachi Project are being discussed in chapter-7.

(b) VCTC

DMSC also runs a VCTC in its Mamata Care and Treatment Centre. This Centre provides HIV and VDRL testing facilities, pre-test and post-test counselling, diagnosis and treatment of opportunistic infections (OIs) like TB, etc. and ART to PLWHA. This initiative addresses the needs of PLWHA and their family members to cope with the social and psychological traumas associated with HIV/AIDS. It also provides weekly ration to the PLWHA. Apart from providing these services, the centre also aims at promoting positive attitude towards infected and affected people. DMSC also runs Community Based DOT programmes for PLWHA and CSWs as per Revised National Tuberculosos Control Programme (RNTCP). Because it is difficult for them to access the services from general PHCs as they are discriminated against.

(ii) *Educational Programmes*

(a) Adult Literacy Programme

This programme was first started in 1993 in the name of 'KOROK' and 'DIGANGANA' as more than 80% of CSWs were illiterate. This programme has helped DMSC in designing health and other intervention activities including empowerment and community mobilization. Currently 15 adult education centers covering almost 300 sex workers are run in Kolkata and other districts. In 1992, 84.4% of CSWs in Songachi were illiterate, which has come down to 69.9% in 2005.

(b) Educational assistance for the children of CSWs

A perennial problem with children of sex workers is questions raised by others about their father's identity. Once their identities are known, they become stigmatized and discriminated against. To address this problem, DMSC has adopted a special approach – 'Berabhenge' (Breaking fences). Basically it has three components viz. special assistance centers for school going children, education centers for school dropouts and special coaching centers for the children of higher classes. Classes are held in the evening, the time when most of sex workers are busy with their work and children have to fend themselves. Currently 15 Berabhenge centers are running in Kolkata and other districts covering almost 500 students. DMSC has started two libraries, one in Kolkata and another in Contai of Paschim Medinipur district.

(c) *Residential Homes for the children of sex workers*

DMSC has established two residential homes. Rahul Vidyaniketan is located at Baruipur, South 24-Pargana district and presently houses 48 school children in the age group of 5-14 years. All boarders of this home have enrolled in local mainstream schools and performing well. A small library was also started in this home. The other home – Indubala Abasik Vidyalaya is located in Ultadanga and presently houses 20 children in the age group of 4-10 years.

Organisational Structure

Chart 6-B.1: Organisational Structure of DMSC

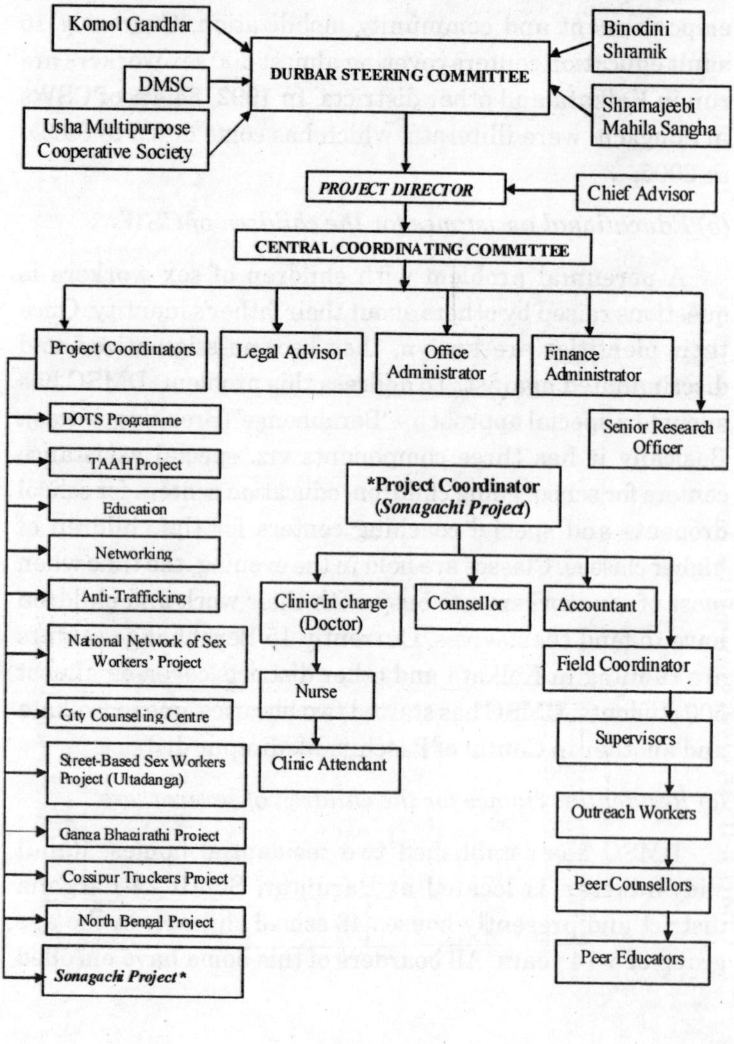

Chart 6-B: An Overview of the Activities undertaken by Durbar: A Conglomerate of Sex Workers' Organisations

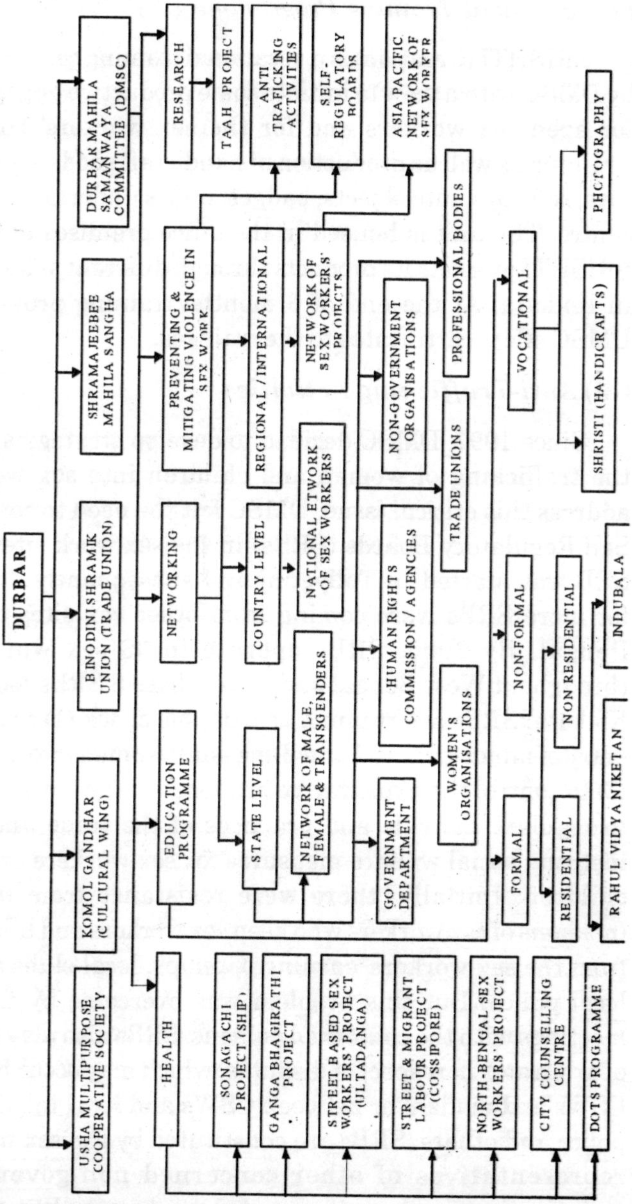

(d) Vocational Training Programme

SRISHTI (Creation) is a vocational training centre started by DMSC with a view to initiate some productive engagement for aged sex workers and for the sex workers' children. Training as well as production of handicraft goods (terracotta toys, soft toys, jute objects, badges, etc) is undertaken in this centre. The unit is housed in the office premises of DMSC. SRISHTI markets its products through different sales outlets in Kolkata. At the end of 6 months training programme, DMSC offers certificates to the trainees.

(iii) *Anti-Trafficking Activities*

Since 1997, DMSC decided to develop strategies to stop the trafficking of women and children into sex work. To address this critical issue, DMSC felt the need to constitute Self Regulatory Boards (SRBs) in the sex work sites. First SRB was started in Tollygunj and subsequently demands for more SRBs were coming from other sex sites of West Bengal. By 2006, SRBs operate in 33 sex work sites throughout West Bengal and out of these 8 SRBs located in Kolkata. SRBs are running as a double check (1) to prevent entry of minor girls and unwilling adult women into sex work, (2) to control the exploitative practices in the sex sector, (3) to regulate the rule and practices of the trade and (4) to institute social welfare measures for sex workers and their children. Initially, there were resistance from *malkins* (madams of sex workers who keep sex workers and take share from the sex workers' earnings), pimps, local clubs and the local police. But this problem was overcome by frequent meetings with the concerned persons. SRBs also play the role of arbitrator in respect of disputes, which may occur between CSWs and madam or between CSWs and local inhabitants, police and others. SRBs are constituted by the sex workers, representatives of other concerned non-government organizations and government departments like Health,

Labour, Social Welfare, Police, etc. During 1997 to 2007(June), DMSC had rescued 419 under age girls (below 18 yrs) and 86 unwilling women. These rescued girls and women were either sent to Government approved shelter-homes or to their respective families. DMSC teams also follow up these cases by visiting them. DMSC has collaborated with BPWT, UNDP and CARE-Bangladesh to address the issues around cross-border trafficking and established three SRBs at Hilly (Dakshin Dinajpur district), Changrabandha (Coochbehar) and Basirhat (North 24-Parganas). The percentage of minor girls in Sonagachi reduced from 25.29 percent in 1992 to 3.12 percent in 2001. Recently, DMSC has developed a detailed terms of reference for the constitution of SRBs at state, district and local level.

(iv) *Research activities*

Sonagachi Project was initiated following a community-based research study conducted in 1992 by AIIH&PH under the auspices of WHO and NACO. The project was unique as it inducted sex workers as peer educator. In 1998-99, Horizon (Population Council) sponsored a research project to enquire about community mobilization activities of DMSC and Sonagachi Project. A selected group of peer educators and sex worker activists were trained in conducting field interview and data entry. The success of this experience was overwhelming, but not sustained once project ended. Theory and Action for Health (TAAH) Group in collaboration with DMSC conducted a 3 years (2003-2006) Research Project. The objectives of this study are (1) to evaluate the social approaches that worked successfully in Sonagachi project, (2) to document the success, (3) to develop a model of the Sonagachi Project and (4) to develop learning resources for sex workers' groups, donor agencies, community leaders and policy makers at local, national and international level. DMSC-TAAH Project identified numbers of core values embedded in DMSC's programmes.

Following the first National Conference of Sex Workers in 1997 and global recognition of Sonagachi Project as 'Best Practice Model' by UNAIDS, DMSC, its sister organizations and sex workers became the 'subject' of research of by groups of film makers, researchers and many others. All of them were not completely satisfactory experiences as some of them failed to protect the rights, dignity and privacy of sex workers. DMSC felt an urgent need to set up norms and ethics of research on sex workers. Accordingly, the Ethical Review Committee on Research (ERCR) was born in DMSC for protecting the civil and human rights of sex workers who agreed to participate in research conducted by external researchers. Based on Helsinki Declaration, ERCR developed protocol that is needed to be adhered to by the willing researchers. For the present study, the researcher also had to go through ERCR of DMSC.

Staff related Information

DMSC is having total 302 full-time paid staff, 37 part-time staff and 400 Peer Educators who work on fixed honorarium as per WBSAP&CS rules. In its Sonagachi Project, there are 105 full-time and 15 part-time (Doctors) staff members. Apart from it, 232 peer educators are working in the Sonagachi project and remaining 168 numbers of peer educators are working in other four Targeted Intervention Projects of DMSC. As far as volunteers are concerned, there is no specific organizational policy to use their help. There are 80% to 85% staff members from sex workers' community including the Project Director. Most of them are working at different levels of the organization i.e. from Peer Educator to Project Director.

The Central Coordination Committee of DMSC has developed service rules for its staff. These are discussed here. All the Project Staff will report to the Project Coordinator at DMSC and work under his guidance. (a) Leave Rules: (i) A staff member can avail 18 days casual leave (12 days casual leave for peer educators) and 8 days medical leave in a year. No leave will be granted without permission and intimation for medical leave is compulsory. Medical Certificate is to be attached with medical leave application. (ii) A staff can take maximum 2 days leave at a stretch and special permission to be taken for leaves beyond 2 days. (iii) The staff members of DMSC enjoy almost all national holidays like government employees and the list of such holidays declared at the beginning of every year. The official holidays declared by the organization will be considered as paid holidays. (iv) Three months paid maternity leave at a stretch can be sanctioned to a female employee of DMSC. (b) All appointments are made on temporary and contract basis. The contract should be renewed on half-yearly basis. Continuation of service is subjected to availability of fund. (c) The working hour is 10.30 am to 6.00 pm for all staff except Peer educators who work from 10 am to 2 pm. Staff members may be asked for additional working days/ hours as per the requirement of the office. The staff members enjoy Compensatory Leave if they work on holidays, but it can be availed only with prior permission from the Project Director of DMSC. (d) The appointment is terminable on either side by one month's notice or salary in lieu thereof. (e) The staff can be posted to work in any office or at any site of the particular project managed by the Organisation. He/she can be deputed to work in any other projects also after getting his/her consent and approval of WBSAP&CS. (f) In case of harmful work against the interest of the organization; the service of the concern employee will be terminated. (g) The prescribed Staff Regulations in force will govern and they may be amended and altered from time to time. (h) DMSC is also having Gender policy and following the same.

DMSC is arranging training programmes regularly for its staff members. These programmes are organized internally as well as by external resource persons/agencies. There are two Training Officers apart from other key staff who impart internal training. Some of these external agencies are WBSAP&CS, CINI, etc. DMSC also sends its staff members to attend different seminars, workshops in different places within the country as well as in abroad too.

Financial Information

DMSC's financial turnover in the year 2006-07 was Rs. 5.0 crores (approximately). Sonagachi Project (SHIP) received Rupees 1,77,18,424.00 during 2006-07 from WBSAP&CS. All the five STD/HIV Intervention Projects are funded by WBSAP&CS and renewed annually. During this period, it received funds from various sources like WBSAP&CS, TDH, Action Aid, Clinton Foundation, Bill & Melinda Gate Foundation, UNAIDS, Kolkata Municipal Corporation, Public donations, etc. In spite of receiving fund from different funding agencies, the organization still feels that fund is inadequate to meet their requirements. DMSC has no specific fund raising policy. But keeping the interest and objectives of the organization in mind, DMSC approaches different funding agencies. Every year DMSC is facing the financial problem at the beginning of new financial year due to lack of timely disbursement of fund from the WBSAP&CS/NACO. But DMSC manages this situation with the help and full support of its staff members.

In order to manage the financial affairs effectively, DMSC prepares annual budget based on previous experiences, expenditure mentioned in the project proposal, present market price, last year's expenditure, area needs, expected funds to be received, etc. Almost 5 percent to 10 percent money is spent for administrative purpose and 90 percent money used for the programme activities.

Future Plan

Being a large organization, DMSC has a number of future

aspirations. Some of them are: (i) to set up a Day Care Centre for the HIV positive people; (b) to establish a Home for elderly and retired sex workers; (c) to start Educational and Vocational Training Centres in all sex sites of West Bengal; and (d) to register each Self Regulatory Board (SRB) as a separate body.

In brief, various types of programmes are run by DMSC. Few of them are welfare oriented; some programmes focus on relief services and the rest are having developmental and right-based approach. This kind of plurality in approach has emerged as a result of diversified needs and issues related with the sex workers' community. But, whatever may be the approach; DMSC becomes a best practicing model for its community mobilization activities in the world and UNAIDS recognizes its 'Sonagachi Project' as model Project.

C. Bhoruka Public Welfare Trust (BPWT)

Background

Late Shri Prabhu Dayal Agarwal established Bhoruka Public Welfare Trust (BPWT hereafter) in 1979. It was an initiative from the Transport Corporation of India (TCI) as a part of Charitable Trust. Shri P.D. Agarwal took birth in Bari Nangal – a small village in Rajasthan and shifted to West Bengal at the age of 13 years in search of earning a livelihood. He started his first job as a record-keeper and ultimately became the owner of a big diversified business empire through his hard work and vision. His job was to weigh and record the tea leaves plucked by the workers in Red Bank Tea Garden under Jalpaiguri district of West Bengal. His monthly wage was eight rupees only. His life story is no less interesting than a novel. Shri P. D. Agarwal established a number of trusts to carry out the social welfare activities throughout the country. The Indian Institute of Health Management, Jaipur is also under one such trust established by him. To him, "life means one long opportunity to be good and to do good: if that is religion, I practice it most ardently every moment'.

Initially, BPWT started with an aim to improve quality of life of general population by mainly promoting public health related issues. In the beginning, BPWT started its office in Transport Corporation of India's office at 'Foodnani Chamber' Kolkata. Later on, it shifted and started its independent office in its own building from January 1996. The head office of BPWT is located in its own building at 63,Rafi Ahmed Kidwai Road, Kolkata-16. Initially, it managed its activities with the financial assistance from TCI Foundation only. In 1982, Bhoruka Research Centre for Haematology & Blood Transfusion (popularly known as Bhoruka Blood Bank) was established by BPWT. Gradually, BPWT expanded its activities in different other fields with the help of different external funding agencies. Gradually, it has also extended its area of operation. Some of the major programmes of BPWT are HIV/AIDS intervention project for truckers, anti-girl trafficking project, RCH project, child watch project, HIV/AIDS infected and affected children's project, etc. Now BPWT is working in the States of Assam, Orissa, Bihar, West Bengal and Andhra Pradesh.

Vision

"We BPWT, provider of health care service to the society, are committed to build and sustain the organization as welfare oriented innovative service unit wherein QUALITY is the hallmark of every activity achieved through the teamwork and involvement of all employees in pursuit of excellence in all our endeavours".

Mission

BPWT seeks to improve the health status of the people in the society through providing quality blood and blood components efficiently; encouraging rationality in the use of blood; improving the quality of life by addressing the health needs and developing human resources for sustained quality services.

Present Objectives

The major objectives of BPWT are: (i) To improve the quality of life by addressing the health needs of the vulnerable section of the community; (ii) To reduce the incidence of HIV/AIDS among truckers; (iii) To develop a resource centre for PLWHA for providing technical assistance and capacity building of the positive networks in the different districts of West Bengal; (iv) To provide support to HIV/AIDS infected and affected children and their families; (v) To provide maternal and child health services to the poorer section of the society; (vi) To bring sustainable improvement in TB control activities at the community level; (vii) To provide healthy and congenial environment for the street children through drop-in-centres; (viii) To provide quality blood and blood components efficiently; (ix) To create an enabling environment for the adolescent girls and women to reduce their vulnerability of being trafficked; (x) To develop human resources for sustained quality services; and (xi) To undertake research on different health related issues.

Area of Operation

BPWT has been working in the five states namely Assam, Andhra Pradesh, Bihar, Orissa and West Bengal. In West Bengal, it covers Kolkata, Howrah, North 24 Parganas and Darjeeling district. The districts covered under other four states are Guwahati (Assam), Srikakulam (Andhra Pradesh), Ganjam (Orissa), East Champaran and Araria (Bihar).

Target Groups

BPWT has been working with the diversified group of people. Its HIV/AIDS intervention Projects are covering truck drivers, helpers and through them to their family members and sex workers. PLWHA and their networks are covered under its Resource Centre for PLWHA. It is also providing services to the street children and children infected and affected by HIV/AIDS. Adolescent girls and women are helped under the Anti-Trafficking projects. It also covers different categories of industrial workers through its Work Place Intervention project. BPWT provides services to all general people through its Blood bank.

Infrastructure

The head office of BPWT is operating from its own building. Its Blood Bank is also situated within its head office. Similarly, its other units like home for HIV/AIDS infected and affected children (*Snehneer*) and Resource Centre for PLWHA (*Bhalobasa*) are also located in its own building. Truckers' Intervention Project offices at Petrapole and KPT are running from rented building. The laboratory of BPWT is equipped with all modern equipments and machineries and has received ISO 9001 certificate. All the offices are well equipped with modern facilities like computers, telephones, Internet facilities, and different audio-visual equipments. The clinics and offices of truckers' intervention projects are comparatively small. Similarly, children's home (*Snehneer*) and care and support unit of PLWHA (*Bhalobasa*) are well furnished with all required facilities. There is one good library in its Resource Centre for PLWHA, which is operating from *Bhalobasa*. In brief, BPWT is having good infrastructure to run its different activities.

Programmes

BPWT is running different programmes in the five states of India. Some of the major programmes are being briefly discussed below.

(i) *Reproductive and Child Health Programme*

BPWT is running this programme in the states of Assam,

Bihar, Orissa, Andhra Pradesh and West Bengal. The project activities include information and awareness, training of the field workers and community health volunteers (CHV), activation and networking with existing service providers, organizing need based health camps and technical support to health care service providers. The RCH project is designed as a participatory intervention programme, where the target group will participate directly in the programme. Community Health Volunteers are working in the preventive aspect by creating enabling environment, promoting positive health seeking behaviour and smooth service access for the people.

(ii) *HIV/AIDS Programmes*

(a) HIV/AIDS Intervention Project for truckers

Truckers are vulnerable to STIs and HIV infections by nature of their job. They used to stay away from home for a long period and many of them visit sex workers to meet their sexual needs. Thus they are unknowingly getting infected with STIs and HIV infections. BPWT was one of the few organisations that initiated intervention among truckers in Uluberia check post in 1993. From the very beginning, BPWT is implementing the programme in Kolkata Port Trust (KPT) area. Currently, BPWT is running four such intervention projects in Guwahati (Assam), Ichchapuram (Andhra Pradesh), Raxaul (Bihar), Petrapole and Kolkata Port Trust (West Bengal). Respective States' AIDS Control Society financially supports these programmes. These projects are located at terminal points of highways or major transshipment centres, where trucks stop and wait for considerable amount of time. At every project, BPWT runs drop-in-centres cum clinics. These clinics offer a range of services: qualified doctors treat STIs and common ailments; counsellors help them recognize and assess their risks; various types of IEC materials and condoms are distributed. Apart from it, outreach workers and other field staff are regularly interact with the target group at the field to make them aware about STIs, HIV and AIDS and refer them to the clinic if needed. The details about the West Bengal project are discussed in Part-II of this chapter.

(b) Workplace Intervention Project among industrial workers

The prevalence of HIV/AIDS is increasing day by day among the working population. Relatively high mobility and prolonged absence from family and social support network may be partly responsible for it. BPWT has been running this project among the workers in different organizations of Kolkata with the financial support from WBSAP&CS. The main objective of the programme is to make the industrial workers aware about STD, HIV/AIDS and safer sex method. It also motivates the management to create a company policy regarding HIV/AIDS especially to avoid discrimination of positive people at work place. The project is now being implemented at the offices of Central Industrial Security Force, Food Corporation of India, Hindustan Jute Mill, ABC India Ltd. and Kolkata Port Trust (KPT) area.

(c) Resource Centre for PLWHA

WBSAP&CS has selected BPWT to act as a Resource Centre for providing technical assistance and capacity building of positive networks in all districts. It is felt that these network people need to build their capacity in terms of knowledge, information and technical know- how to fight against the disease more efficiently and effectively. The capacity building needs of network people are identified through Capacity Need Assessments. Since its inception in 2005, the Resource centre is actively involved in empowerment process of HIV positive people in West Bengal. It is imparting training to the PLWHA as well as those organizations that are extending services for positive people. It has completed capacity building process of PLWHA networks so far in eighty percent of districts in West Bengal.

Organisational Structure

Chart 6-C: Organizational Structure of BPWT

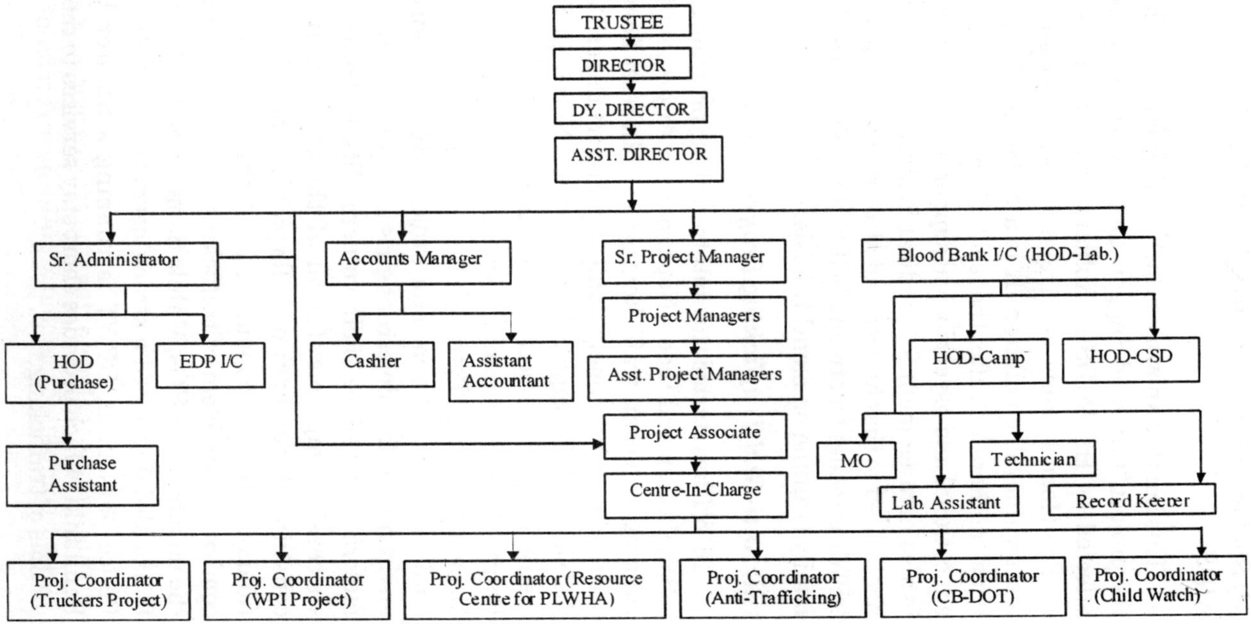

(d) Shelter home for children infected and affected by HIV/ AIDS

This home is known as 'Snehneer'. It is established under the project "Care and Support for the Children infected and affected by HIV/AIDS in Kolkata and suburbs" supported by The Hope Foundation, Ireland to ensure rights of these most vulnerable children. It is a 25 bedded home and two housemothers look after the residents. It provides nutritional, educational and psychological support to the children. There is also arrangement for medical facilities. The services are not limited to the children, but also provided to their families. BPWT provides treatment facility through OPD and organize family training on monthly basis.

(iii) *Anti-Girl Trafficking Programme*

BPWT has started this anti-trafficking programme at Indo – Bangladesh and Indo – Nepal border. At present BPWT is running three anti-trafficking projects. In West Bengal there are two projects namely Panitanki Project under Darjeeling district and Petrapole Project under North 24-Parganas district. Jogbani Project is under Araria district of Bihar. Both Panitanki and Jogbani Projects are functioning near Indo-Nepal borders and Petrapole Project is near Indo-Bangladesh borders. The main aim of the project is to create an enabling environment for adolescent girls and women to mitigate the factors that reduce their vulnerability to trafficking. For successful implementation of the Project, BPWT has constituted numbers of Village Vigilance Committee as fundamental component. It is a community led effort to combat the problem of trafficking. BPWT has also trained the members of SHGs, Mahila Samity and local youth clubs. It has also developed a strong network with BSF and local Police personnel. BPWT is running a Shelter Home at Panitanki, which provides short stay services to the rescued victims of trafficking.

(iv) *CB-DOT Programme*

BPWT, since 2005, has been implementing Community Based DOT (Direct Observation Treatment) Programme in Bongaon under North-24 Parganas district. The project sensitizes the people on tuberculosis and tries to increase the treatment compliance rate. BPWT has adopted community based partnership strategy to support the patients in completing their treatment. The project is working as a part of Revised National Tuberculosis Control Programme (RNTCP). The project reaches out to the beneficiaries through different IEC/BCC activities such as community sensitization meeting, kiosk programme, talking doll show, etc. A group of Community Health Volunteers (CHVs) is formed and trained, who work as a programme wheels in the community. The programme also sensitizes PRIs, CBOs, SHGs and other community stake holders.

(v) *Blood Bank*

Bhoruka Blood Bank is the first private blood bank in Kolkata aims to provide quality blood to the needy and promote blood donation. BPWT, at present, has been collecting nearly 10000 units of blood in partnership with nearly 180 NGOs, CBOs and Youth clubs. It has a very good laboratory and initiated screening of HIV, Hepatitis C, VDRL, Hepatitis B, etc. To ensure rational use of blood, BPWT has been preparing and supplying blood components to the patients requiring blood transfusion. The blood bank always gives emphasis on quality and has received ISO 9001 certificate for maintaining its quality system. It offers door steps services.

(vi) *Training and Research Activities*

BPWT is having a training unit, as it requires trained personnel for its diversified activities. This unit has also been imparting training for the staff of other organizations on various issues like counseling, BCC, HIV/AIDS, home-based care and support of PLWHA, RCH, gender sensitization, etc. Besides this, the unit has developed a number of manuals on AIDS and other health related issues. BPWT has also engaged in research activities and conducted studies on different issues. Currently, it is conducting a study to evaluate the impact of the use of Female Condom by CSWs and their clients in West Bengal. BPWT has also published few books/ reports on PLWHA, Call girls, Trafficking, Stigma, etc. to disseminate its experiences. BPWT is providing human resources for laboratory services for running the VCTC/ PPTCT centres across the state of West Bengal.

(vii) *Child Watch*

BPWT initiated its project for the street children in 2005. The Child Watch programme was started in 2006 with the children of Sudder Street, Royd lane, Rafi Ahmed Kidwai, Nonapukur, Marquis Street, etc. All children up to the age of 18 years are included in this project. The goal of this project is to protect children at high risk; to provide nutritive food and health support to street children in pursuance of minimizing the exploitation of this vulnerable population and thereby bringing about a positive change in their behaviour and attitude. One Drop-in Centre has been made in BPWT (*Bhalobasa*) where they spend considerable time and get all supports like food, life skill training, counseling, etc. The project also makes them aware regarding health and hygiene, HIV and AIDS.

Staff Related Information

BPWT has total 155 full time paid staff including 29 technicians of Blood Bank in West Bengal. In its Truckers' Project, there are 25 full-time and 3 part-time (Doctors) staff members. Apart from it, 21 peer educators are working in the Kolkata Port Trust (KPT) area and 24 peer educators are working in Petrapole area. As far as volunteers are concerned, there is no specific organizational policy to use their help in BPWT.

The Trustee of BPWT has developed service rules for its staff members. These are discussed here. All the Project Staff will report to the Project Coordinator at BPWT and work under his guidance. (a) Leave Rules: (i) A staff member can avail 10 days Casual Leave, 30 days Earned Leave and 5 days Medical Leave as per doctor's advice. In addition to above types of leave, staff are also entitled to 6 national holidays and 4 days optional leaves as per their conveniences. No leave will be granted without permission and intimation for medical leave is compulsory. Medical Certificate is to be attached with medical leave application. (ii) Staff are also entitled for compensatory leave if they work in holidays or Sundays. But this compensatory leave must be taken within that month only. (iii) A staff can take maximum 10 days leave at a stretch with permission. The service of a staff will be discontinued if s/he avails more than 7 days leave without permission. (iv) The official holidays declared by the organization will be considered as paid holidays. (v) Three months paid maternity leave at a stretch can be sanctioned to a female employee. (b) All appointments are made on temporary and contract basis except few staff members of Blood Bank. Every year contract should be renewed. Continuation of service for the Project staff is subjected to availability of fund. (c) Minimum working hour is 8 hours per day i.e. 9 am to 5 pm (6 days in a week). Staff members may be asked for additional working days/ hours as per the requirement of the office. (d) The appointment is terminable on either side by one month's notice or salary in lieu thereof. (e) The Centre In-Charge only can be posted to work in any site managed by the Organization. The project staff are generally not transferred to other project areas. (f) In case of harmful work against the interest of the organization, the service of the concern employee will be terminated. (g) The project staff members are not entitled to any medical benefit. But the direct staff of BPWT are entitled to Mediclaim and Accidental benefits. (h) The prescribed Staff

Regulations in force will govern and they may be amended and altered from time to time. (i) BPWT is also having Gender Policy like recruiting male and female staff at 50:50 ratio, rules to prevent the sexual abuse of female employees a work place, etc.

BPWT is arranging training programmes regularly for its staff members. These programmes are organized internally as well as by external agency like WBSAP&CS. It also organizes exposure visit for the staff members to other related NGOs.

Financial Information

The financial turnover of BPWT in the year 2006-07 was Rs. 2.67 crores. Its blood bank is running independently without any financial assistance. The State AIDS Control Societies of Assam, Andhra Pradesh, Bihar, Orissa and West Bengal are providing financial assistance for the truckers' projects of BPWT. Apart from it, BPWT also receives fund from European Commission, UNODC, TCI Foundation, Elton John AIDS Foundation, Care India, UNDP, Resource Centre for Sexual Health and AIDS (RCSHA/DFID) and International Commission on Research on Women (ICRW).

In order to manage the financial affairs, BPWT prepares annual budget through its competent Accounts section. Annual budget is prepared after considering the expenditure mentioned in the project proposal, last year's expenditure, expected fund to be received, present market price, etc. BPWT earmarks majority of funds for programme activities in its budget.

Future Plan

BPWT has a plan to start following activities in near future: (a) to expand its area of work and serve every individual infected and affected by HIV/AIDS all over the eastern part of the country; (b) to start a one year course on

Blood Banking Technology; (c) to introduce modern techniques for screening the transmissible viruses in the blood more efficiently; and (d) to campaign more among the doctors regarding 'rational use of blood' in West Bengal.

In brief, BPWT runs various types of programmes in the states of Assam, Andhra Pradesh, Bihar, Orissa and West Bengal. It has been working to serve the different categories of people like women, adolescent girls, children, truckers and PLWHA. Most of its programmes are health oriented. BPWT is having both institutional and community based services. It also assists other NGOs and CBOs through its Resource Centre for PLWHA. BPWT is also famous for research activities and therefore, has undertaken and completed many research projects with the support from UNDP, DFID, International Commission on Research on Women, UNIFEM and other such agencies.

D. MANAS Bangla (MB)

Background

NACO started the Phase-I of National AIDS Control Programme (NACP-I) in 1992. Accordingly all State AIDS Control Societies started to implement the Targeted Intervention Project for different high-risk vulnerable groups through NGOs. WBSAP&CS has also started many such projects for different vulnerable groups. But there was no project for males who have sex with males (MSM). In West Bengal, there were few NGOs were working with the MSM population in a scattered way with their limited resources. New Alipore Praajak Development Society (1994), Kolkata is one of the first agencies in West Bengal to focus on sexual health services for MSM. This NGO conducted a need assessment survey among MSM population. Later on, Palm Avenue Integration Society (another NGO) conducted similar survey in 2001. But findings of these surveys were confined to the respective NGOs only. Apart from these two NGOs, few other NGOs like PRANTIK, PRATYAY, SWIKRITI Society, AMITIE, etc. are also working with MSM. In the year 2003, one incidence took place, which triggered the formation of MANAS Bangla. Two outreach workers of an NGO working with MSM in Kolkata assaulted in a cruising area by local youth on 7th January 2003. The local police failed to take action. The NGO posted the news of assault on several e-mail forums. After one week, members of several other NGOs working with MSM in West Bengal had conducted a meeting and planned joint action in support of the aggrieved NGO. The idea of starting a network was also discussed in this meeting. During the Naz Foundation International's MSM Sexual Health Conference in New Delhi on 5th April 2003, several NGOs keen to form network, organised a meeting and set deadline for launching the MSM network. Finally, AMITIE (NGO), Chandannagar hosted first formal meeting of the network on 4th May 2003. MANAS Bangla (MB) – the first network of MSM in West Bengal started with seven constituent member NGOs. The names of these partner NGOs are: (1) AMITIE (Hoogly district); (2) ASTITVA (South 24-Parganas); (3) DumDum SWIKRITI Society (Kolkata); (4) PRANTIK (North 24-Parganas); (5) MITJYU (Darjeeling); (6) The Pratyay Gender Trust (Kolkata); and (7) Swapnil (Burdwan). The entire partner NGOs are CBOs i.e. started and managed by MSM themselves. Each of these NGOs has their own goals, activities and strategies. But they have realized the need for a greater level of commonality in policy and action. The network has been formed with the aim to coordinate and enhance their efforts in promoting health and general well being of MSM community. Initially, there was no office. Prof. Rajarshi Chakraborty – the General Secretary and one of the Key promoters of MB used his residence as office for time being. Later on, Praajak Development Society allowed MB to use its office, computers, etc. At the beginning, MB managed its activities with membership fees and later on SAATHII (an international NGO working on HIV/AIDS), Kolkata Branch provided support to it. Formally MANAS Bangla got registered under Society Registration Act in February 2004. In the later part of 2003, MB and Praajak Development Society jointly conducted a 'Need Identification Survey' among MSM population in west Bengal, with the financial support of WBSAP&CS. The findings revealed that about 10% of MSM are suffering from STIs. MB submitted a proposal of Targeted Intervention Project for MSM to WBSAP&CS. Finally, the proposal was approved and MB started *Male-to-Male Sexual Health Promotion and HIV Control Programme* w.e.f. July 2004. It is the first such intervention project for MSM in West Bengal as well as in the whole Eastern and North-Eastern India. The registered office of MB is located at 75, Jawpur Road and its Project Office is now located at E-31, Sreenivas Apartment, Rajdanga Nabapally, Kolkata-700107. MB is affiliated with Indian Network for sexual Minority (INFOSEM) of Humsafar Trust and with Naz Foundation Partners' Network.

Vision

The vision of MANAS Bangla is to coordinate and enhance the efforts of organizations working to promote the health and general wellbeing of MSM population in West Bengal.

Mission

With a primary focus on males who have sex with males (MSM), MANAS Bangla's mission is to empower socially excluded and disadvantaged males to secure social justice, equity, health and well-being for themselves.

Present Objectives

The broad objective of MB is to focus on the health concerns of MSM as a broader issue, inclusive of not just physical health, but also psychological and social health aspects. The major objectives of MB are as follows: (i) To run, maintain, manage and carry on the society for the welfare of the people of the localities; (ii) To promote awareness programmes on HIV/AIDS and sexual health among the people of localities; (iii) To prevent the spread of HIV/AIDS and other sexually transmitted diseases; (iv) To aware the people about their health and to arrange for free medical treatment to the needy patients by the qualified doctors; (v) To ensure proper sexual health services and facilities for those who require them; (vi) To provide advice regarding all aspects of sexual health by the qualified doctors; (vii) To print, publish, and distribute journals, periodicals, leaflets for the promotion of the objects of the society; (viii) To give necessary relief to the affected in times of flood, famine and other natural calamities; (ix) To impart and develop social awareness among the illiterate women and men by organizing awareness camps from time to time; (x) To improve the social and cultural life of the people by organizing various social and cultural programmes from time to time; and (xi) To engage and assist in all other philanthropic activities as may be deemed appropriate by the Executive Committee of the Society

Area of Operation

Being a network of CBOs, MB covers all parts of the West Bengal through its different partner organizations. It covers seven districts under its project of WBSAP&CS on 'Male to Male sexual Health Promotion and HIV control Programme'. Currently, MB has been running 8 Drop-in- Centres (DICs) at Baruipur (South 24-Parganas district); Bangaon (North 24-Parganas); Srirampore (Hoogly); Siliguri (Darjeeling); Kasba, Kadapara and DumDum (Kolkata) and Burdwan (Burdwan district). Srirampore DIC also covers Howrah district. It is also running partial DICs in the districts of Howrah, Nadia, and Jalpaiguri. Besides it, MB has been providing outreach services in Murshidabad, Coochbehar, Purba and Paschim Medinipur districts. It has also networking with different NGOs working with MSM in the districts of Malda, Birbhum, Bankura, Purulia and Uttar Dinajpur. MB has been covering around 9000 MSM population through this project in different districts of West Bengal.

Target Groups

Within the framework of MSM, there is a range of diverse sexual/gender identities, communities, networks, and collectivities like *Koti, Parikh, Dupli, Hijra,* Gay, Bisexual, married and single MSM, Male sex workers, etc. as well as just behaviours without any sense of affiliation to any identity or community. MB covers all these categories through its project. Apart from the MSM, non-MSM community members both males and females also come to DICs for counseling and treatment.

Infrastructure

MB is not having its own office building. Its registered office is actually the residential address of its General Secretary, Prof. Rajarshi Chakraborty. Its Project Office and all DICs are operating from the rented building. The Project Office of MB is well furnished with modern office equipments like computer, phone, Internet, library, etc. It is an ideal office accommodation for the Project Office. The DICs are comparatively having less space, but otherwise fit for running office as well as clinics.

Programmes

(i) *Male-to-Male sexual Health Promotion and HIV control Programme*

This is the only major programme run by MB since July 2004. This project is the only project under WBSAP&CS for MSM population in the state. MSM people are already stigmatized for their sexual behaviour as society yet to accept as normal sexual behaviour. And MSM who is infected by

Organisational Structure

Chart 6-D: Organisational Structure of MB

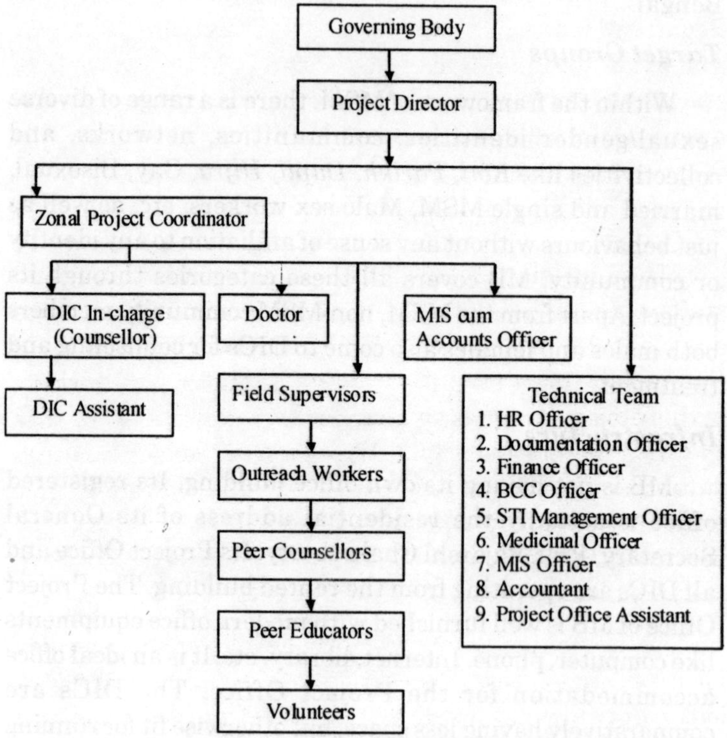

HIV is actually doubly stigmatized. Therefore, it is very challenging field to work. Presently, the project has been providing services to 9000 MSM through eight clinics in different districts of West Bengal. The details about the programme are discussed in Part-II of this chapter.

(ii) *Income Generating Programme*

MB has received financial support from the Social Welfare Department, Government of West Bengal for running an

Income Generating Project. Its project duration is 6 months only. Under this project, MB has organized and imparted training programmes on two trades i.e. Tailoring and Beautician courses for the willing MSM community members. The main purpose of this project is to help these people to start their own business after the completion of the training programme and lead an economically independent life. MB is in constant touch with these trained people.

Staff related information

MB is having total 50 full-time and 10 part-time paid staff members. Out of the 10 part-time staff members, there are eight doctors, one STI Management Officer and one Counsellor. Apart from it, 100 Peer Educators are working in this project. As far as volunteers are concerned, there is no specific organizational policy to use their help. Generally volunteers participate in event-based programmes (for example street play, etc.) of different DICs. Most of these volunteers regularly visit the DICs. In general, 80-85 percent staff members are from MSM community.

The Governing Body of MB has developed service rules for its staff members. The HR Officer in the Project Office looks after the staff related matters. At the DIC level, all staff members report to DIC in-charge who is working under the respective Zonal Project Coordinator. There are five Zonal Coordinators who work under the guidance of the Project Director. The service rules are discussed here. (a) Leave Rules: (i) A staff member can avail 14 days casual leave and 7 days medical leave as per doctor's advice. No leave will be granted without Permission and intimation for medical leave is compulsory. Medical Certificate is to be attached with medical leave application. (ii) The official holidays declared by the organization will be considered as paid holidays. (iii) Compensatory leave is given if any staff works on holidays or weekly holidays (b) All appointments are made on temporary and contract basis. Every year contract should be renewed. Continuation service is subjected to availability of fund. (c) Minimum working hour is 8 hours per day and 40 hours per week (5 days in a week). Staff members may be asked for additional working days/ hours as per the requirement of the office. (d) The appointment is terminable on either side by one month's notice or salary in lieu thereof. (e) In case of harmful work against the interest of the organization, the service of the concern employee will be terminated. (f) The Organization will reimburse starting fees for work or job related courses to encourage and motivate its staff. (h) Medical benefit – there is no medical benefits. Staff can consult the doctors of clinic at free of cost. (i) The prescribed Staff Regulations in force will govern and they may be amended and altered from time to time.

MB regularly arranges training programmes for its staff members. These training programmes are organized internally as well as by external agencies. Some of the external agencies are WBSAP&CS, Samikshani, Health Vision Research, DMSC, etc. MB used to organize centralized training programmes separately for its Peer Educators, Peer Counsellors, etc. with the support of WBSAP&CS. It also arranges exposure visits for its staff members to other organizations. Some of the staff members attended different seminars/workshops in India and abroad too.

Financial Information

MB's financial turnover in the year 2006-07 was Rs. 46.64 lakh approximately. Out of this, MB received Rs. 39,85,162.00 from WBSAP&CS and MB shared Rs. 6,78,961.00 as its contribution in the project. The project is funded by WBSAP&CS and renewed every year. Apart from WBSAP&CS, during this period MB has also received fund from Naz Foundation International; Social Welfare Department, Government of West Bengal; public donations and from internal sources. Internal sources include membership fees, registration fees at the clinics and social marketing of condoms and lubes. Naz Foundation assists in terms of supplying Lubes. MB has no specific fund raising policy. But keeping the interest and objectives of the organization in mind, it approaches different funding agencies. Delay in releasing fund from WBSAP&CS, inadequate clinical equipments, and no provision for traveling allowances for Peer educators, etc. are few major problems presently faced by the MB. However, it manages the situation with the help and active support of its staff members.

MB prepares annual budget in order to manage financial affairs smoothly. The Project Director prepares the budget with the help of other staff and submits it to the Managing Committee/Governing Body for approval. Annual budget is prepared on the basis of terms and conditions of funding agency, previous year's experience, present market price, etc. MB has to arrange different budget for its technical team for whom WBSAP&CS has no financial provision in its project for MSM.

Future Plan

Being a network of CBOs, MB has number of future plans. Some of them are: (a) to bring more districts especially rural areas under its coverage; (b) to initiate efforts for changing the traditional public notions on gender and sexuality; (c) to give more emphasis on psycho-social i.e. mental health aspects of MSM population; (d) to develop an enabling environment for MSM through income generation programmes; (e) to empower MSM community members to exercise their rights related to their identity and sexuality; (f) to work out a common policy for all member organizations on advocacy, outreach activities and referral system; (g) to frame guidelines and undertake research on sexual health related issues of MSM; and (h) to give more emphasis in developing network with other similar organizations at the national and international level.

In brief, MB runs only Male-to-Male Sexual Health Promotion and HIV control programme. It has adopted rights-based approach, which has emerged as a result of diversified issues related with MSM community. MB is the only organization, which has been running HIV/AIDS programme among the MSM community in West Bengal.

E. Human Development Research Institute (HDRI)

Background

Dr. D.P.Mallick, the present secretary and promoter of the organization is a medical practitioner by profession. Since his student life, Dr. Mallick was interested to do something for the betterment of the deprived section of the society. After the completion of his study, Dr. Mallick took up job and served many organizations. But he never forgot his desire to serve the people. During 1980s, drug addiction became a major problem in our country and Kolkata was not an exception in this regard. Dr. Mallick felt that something is to be done for these drug addicts, as there was no organization to deal with them in Kolkata at that time. Initially, HDRI was not a registered body. But later on, it was felt that without a registered organization, it would be difficult to work in the field of drug addiction. Accordingly, HDRI was registered in the year 1985. At the beginning, there was no office building. It was working from the residence of Dr. Mallick and sometime from the residence of Dr. S. Sinha who was president of the organization. HDRI first started a Day Care Centre for the drug addicts at the University Institute Hall, Kolkata. Initially there was no financial support from any external agency; HDRI managed its activities with donations from public and members of the General Body. For the first time, it has received fund from the Ministry of Social Welfare, Govt. of India in 1989 for running the project for drug addicts/

dependents. Then HDRI opened its project office along with the clinic and detoxification centre at Bidhan Sarani, near Hatibagan, Kolkata-11. Gradually, HDRI expanded its activities in other fields also. Later on, it has been registered under the Foreign Contribution Registration Act also. At present, the head office of HDRI is located at 45, Beniatola Lane, Kolkata-9. It has been running its full fledged 'Recovery De-addiction Centre at 43/C, Nimtolaghat Street, Kolkata-700006. Its old office of Hatibagan is now working as the project office for STD/HIV/AIDS Targeted Intervention Project for migrated labourers. Presently, HDRI is having a good reputation in West Bengal as well as in India.

Vision

HDRI seeks to enable the drug addicts to achieve total abstinence and to improve the quality of their lives by helping them and to give proper sexual health education to the target groups.

Mission

The mission of HDRI is to: (1) treat and rehabilitate the chemical dependents through psychotherapeutic programme; (2) provide and instill sexual health education to the chemical dependents as well as IDUs and migrated labourers; (3) treat and counsel STD cases along with general treatment; (4) provide good quality condoms and to facilitate them for safer sexual practice; and (5) perform networking and advocacy.

Present Objectives

The major objectives of HDRI are as follows: (i) To carry out sexual health education programmes among the migrated labourers, truckers and drug dependents; (ii) To provide STD treatment along with general health care services to the migrated labourers, truckers and drug dependents; (iii) To provide physical and psychological treatment for the drug dependents including vocational guidance and rehabilitation services; (iv) To reduce the incidence of STD and HIV infection among the migrated labourers, truckers, drug dependents and their family members and sex-partners; (v) To provide networking and advocacy at different levels of society; (vi) To promote sustainability at different components of existing intervention programmes; (vii) To prevent drug abuse among the students through school based primary intervention programme; (viii) To create awareness about drug abuse, HIV/AIDS among the general people of the society; and (ix) To undertake different community development programmes for the upliftment of poor and backward section of the society.

Area of Operation

HDRI is currently working in the four districts of West Bengal namely Kolkata, Howrah, Hoogly and Burdwan. It has been running STD/HIV/AIDS intervention programmes for truckers and migrated labourers at Kolkata district. Similarly it has been running its drug de-addiction programme at Howrah, Central and North Kolkata. Its school-based drug abuse prevention programme has been in operation in the five schools of Howrah, Hoogly, Burdwan and Kolkata. Its community development project is also being run in the Monteswar Block of Burdwan district.

Target Groups

HDRI has been covering 25000 migrated labourers under the Targeted Intervention Project in different areas of Kolkata. Similarly through its truckers' intervention project, HDRI has been covering 10000 truckers at Burrabazar, Kolkata. It is also covering IDUs and other drug dependents, their family members and sex-partners through its de-addiction and HIV/AIDS prevention programmes. HDRI is also running community development programme for the rural poor people and school based primary drug abuse prevention programme for the School children.

Infrastructure

The head office of HDRI is well furnished and equipped with all modern office equipments like computers, fax machine, telephone, Internet facility, etc. Fifteen-bedded 'Recovery De-addiction Centre' is well equipped with required infrastructure and manpower. The project office for migrated labourers is comparatively small in terms of space, but equipped with required infrastructure and manpower. The after care home run by HDRI for the recovering addicts, is also fit for use. Excepting the head office, all other offices and clinics of HDRI are operating from rented buildings.

Programmes

HDRI is implementing numbers of programmes through its different wings. Some of the major programmes are being briefly discussed below.

(i) *Programmes for drug dependents*

(a) Recovery De-addiciion Centre

This centre has started its journey with the support of Ministry of Social Justice and Empowerment, Govt. of India since 1993. It aims to help the addicts to achieve total abstinence and also to improve quality of their lives. Main objective of the centre is to treat and rehabilitate the drug abusers through psychotherapeutic programme. Major activities of the centre are: physical and psychiatric assessment, detoxification, psychological testing, psychotherapeutic programme (meditation, yoga, relaxation, counseling, etc.), awareness programme, vocational guidance, aftercare and rehabilitation. Total number of patients treated during 2006-07 is 1235 (old - 797 and new - 438). Every year this centre celebrates International Day against Drug Abuse on 26th June through meeting, seminar, street drama, audio-visual show, etc.

(b) G-86 Project

This project is being run for community empowerment to prevent drug abuse and HIV infection under the sponsorship on UNODC.HDRI carries out awareness generation, home visit, referral services, peer training, counseling, formation of SHG for women empowerment, etc. under this project. Besides it, school based primary prevention activity is also carried out by HDRI as a part of this programme. Group sessions are conducted among students, teachers, parents and community people. Preparation of slogan, quiz contests, etc are arranged for the students under this programme.

(c) H-13 Project

Prevention of transmission of HIV among drug users in SAARC countries Phase-1 Extension has been launched on November 2006 under the sponsorship of UNODC. The main goal of this project is to promote HIV/AIDS prevention; and care and support programme through comprehensive package approach. The comprehensive package includes referral services like STD treatment, low cost community based treatment camp, health check-up camp, Mid Day meal, volunteers' meeting, spouse meeting, safer injection training at DIC (Drop - in - centre) and other field area, abscess management at road side and at clinics. One such DIC was established at Shibpur, Howrah and providing all the above mentioned services. An Advocacy Forum was also formed in this regard.

(d) *I-49 Project*

This project is in operation especially for the women with the support from UNODC. As a Part of activity, data were collected from 60 women (10 female drug users and 50 female partners of drug abusers). Four women groups with a purpose of group sessions were formed. They were made aware about drug related HIV/AIDS, safer injecting practice, negotiation skill, STD and general health care, etc.

Organisational Structure

Chart 6-E: Organisational Structure of HDRI

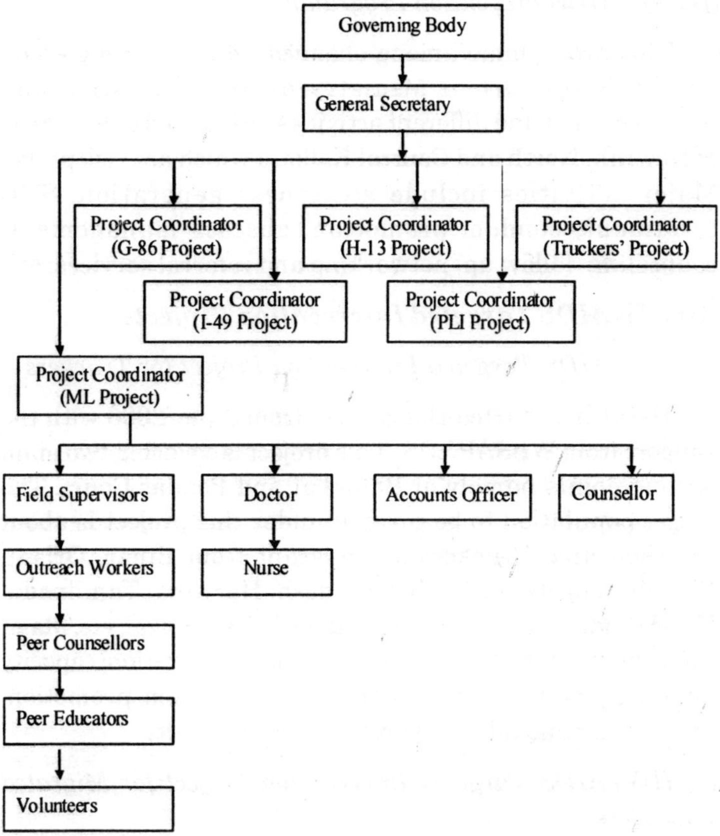

(e) PLI Project

This project is being implemented with the collaboration and under the sponsorship of DFID. Target areas of the project are Armenium Ghat and Sovabazar (Dalpatti). A base line survey was conducted among the drug users of the said areas. Target group was made aware about STD/HIV/AIDS, negotiation skills, effects of drug abuse, safer sex practice, etc. Group sessions and referral services are other important activities of the project.

(f) HIV/AIDS Prevention Programme

This programme among chemical dependents goes on with the support of Ministry of Social Justice and Empowerment and different activities are carried out in areas of Howrah, North and Central Kolkata which are risk prone. Major activities include awareness generation, STD treatment, condom promotion, abscess management, counseling, follow up, networking and referral services, etc.

(ii) *HIV/AIDS Targeted Intervention Projects*

(a) HIV/AIDS Targeted Intervention Project for Truckers

HDRI has started this project from June' 2006 with the support from WBSAP&CS. This project is covering two main halting points namely at Balughat and Poddar Court. The target population to be covered under this project is about ten thousand. Truckers are migrant from Bihar, Orissa, Punjab, Rajasthan, Andhra Pradesh, Haryana, Tamilnadu, Uttar Pradesh and interior districts of West Bengal, etc. Major components of the project are: awareness generation; capacity building; counseling; STD treatment; condom promotion; networking and advocacy; referral activity; etc.

(b) HIV/AIDS Targeted Intervention Project for Migrated Labourers

In 1992, on the recommendation of WHO, All India Institute of Hygiene and Public Health (AIIH&PH) started STD/HIV Intervention Programme at Sonagachi— the largest red light area of South East Asia. For this purpose, AIIH&PH developed a conglomerate of NGOs and HDRI was part of this. During this work, it was learnt from the sex workers that a large number of migrant populations used to visit them. Thus, they also become vulnerable for STD/HIV infection. In this perspective, HDRI started intervention programme for migrated labourers with the help of DFID (UK) in 1997. Later on the project was handed over to WBSAP&CS in 2001 and HDRI has been continuing the project. Now this project is covering 25000 migrant labourers of Burrabazar, Posta, Jorabagan, Mechua, Sovabazar and Ahiritola. By occupation, they can be classified as Sardars, Porters, Handcart pullers, labourers and others. There are five static clinics are operating at different target areas to serve the community people. The details of the project are being discussed in Part-II of this chapter.

(iii) *Community Development Programme*

HDRI has been running its community development programme in rural areas of Monteswar Block under Burdwan district for last 20 years. Patients having different problems have been provided treatment. Camps and awareness programmes on social menace like drugs and AIDS as well as other issues like family planning, leprosy, tuberculosis, etc. are organized for rural people. Besides rehabilitation programme for recovering addicts, HDRI has been helping rural poor through various programmes like primary health care, water treatment, fishery, improving agricultural outputs, etc.

Staff Related Information

HDRI is having total 66 full time paid staff members. There are seven part time paid staff, all of whom are doctors. There is no honorary staff in HDRI. The organization is having many volunteers, but exact number is not available. So far volunteers are concerned; HDRI is having a policy of using the services of volunteers. As per this policy, volunteers are selected on the basis of following criteria: (a) sobriety in case of ex-addicts; (b) concern volunteer's influence in the community; (c) his dedication and commitment; and (d) he is suited to HDRI's mission and vision.

The Governing Body of HDRI has developed service rules for its staff members. These are discussed here. All the Project Staff will report to the Project Coordinator at SCIR and work under his guidance. (a) Leave Rules: (i) A staff member can avail 12 days casual leave. There is no fixed number of days of medical leave, only if required as per doctor's advice. No leave will be granted without Permission and intimation for medical leave is compulsory. Medical Certificate is to be attached with medical leave application. (ii) Staff are entitled to 15-20 days national holidays and the list is prepared and intimated by HDRI at the beginning of the year. (iii) The official holidays declared by the organization will be considered as paid holidays. (iv) Three months paid maternity leave at a stretch can be sanctioned to a female employee. (v) The procedure of availing leave is different for the 'Recovery De-addiction Centre' as it works 24 hours like any hospital. Its staff can't take leave without alternative arrangement of duties. (b) All appointments are made on temporary and contract basis. Every year contract should be renewed. Continuation service is subjected to availability of fund. (c) Minimum working hour is 7 hours per day and 40 hours per week (6 days in a week). Staff members may be asked for additional working days/ hours as per the requirement of the office. (d) The appointment is terminable on either side by one month's notice or salary in lieu thereof. (e) The staff can be posted to work in any site of the same project managed by the Organization. (f) In case of harmful work against the interest of the organization, the service of the concern employee will be terminated. (g) The prescribed Staff Regulations in force will govern and they may be amended and altered from time to time

HDRI is regularly arranging internal as well as external training programmes for its staff members. It also arranges induction training programme for the new staff. The staff members are also time to time trained by the funding agencies and other external agencies. Some of these agencies are WBSAP&CS, NACO, UNODC, etc. Besides these, HDRI is also arranging exposure visit to other organizations for its staff members.

Financial Information

HDRI's financial turn over in the year 2006-07 was around one crore. It has received Rupees 34,89,026.00 (Rupees thirty four lakh eighty nine thousand twenty six only) from WBSAP&CS during 2006-07 for its HIV/AIDS intervention project for migrated labourers. During this period, it has also received funds for its other projects from various sources like WBSAP&CS, UNODC, DFID, Ministry of social Justice and Empowerment, Govt. of India, public donation, internal resources, etc. In spite of receiving fund from various funding agencies, HDRI still feels that fund is inadequate to meet the various requirements of the organization. Irregular flow of fund especially from the government funding agencies – is one of the problem faced by HDRI. Currently, HDRI is not having any specific fund raising policy. But considering the needs and objectives of the organization, HDRI approaches different funding agencies.

HDRI prepares annual budget in order to manage the financial affairs smoothly. It prepares annual budget on the basis of previous years' experiences, expenditure mentioned in the project proposal, last year's expenditure, expected fund to be received from the funding agencies, etc. But HDRI gives main emphasis on the terms and conditions of funding agencies in this regard.

Future Plan

Being an old and big organization, HDRI has a number of future plans. Some of these are: (i) to act as a Nodal Agency in the field of HIV/AIDS; (ii) to establish a Research Institute for undertaking different research projects on drug abuse and drug dependents; (iii) to establish a Regional Institute and offer regular Counseling courses on drug abuse to produce capable staff in this field; and (iv) to empower and hand over the project to community people to sustain the level of participation.

In brief, HDRI runs various types of programmes. Majority of these are on HIV/AIDS and Drug abuse. It has also few programmes for school children and rural poor people. HDRI has adopted developmental as well as right-based approach because of the diversified issues involved with migrated labourers, truckers and drug dependents. HDRI has got a good recognition for the services that it has been rendering since 1985 especially in the field of drug and chemical substance abuse.

F. Society for Positive Atmosphere and Related Support to HIV/AIDS (SPARSHA)

Background

In the late 1980s, a group of children and young adults with hemophilia (a genetically determined blood-clotting disorder) in West Bengal contracted HIV through transfusion of contaminated blood and blood products. The treatment, care and support needs of these youths remained un-addressed for long in the shadow of successful targeted HIV intervention projects for other population groups at risk in the state. No self-help group even existed till before 1998 although reported number of AIDS cases from West Bengal at that time was approximately 200. In the year 1994, Dr. Samiran Panda, one of the founder members of SPARSHA, was attached to ICMR and in 1997 he joined a research NGO named Society for Applied Studies in Kolkata. From these organizations, he used to treat and advice people living with HIV. These people with HIV, their friends and family members along with some more people from different walks of life joined hands to form a group in 1998 to reduce social discrimination and facilitate HIV/AIDS care and support, which ultimately culminated in the birth of SPARSHA later on. In this group, there were also people living with hemophilia who contracted HIV through blood transfusion. The group was started with 15 members only. Some of the key founder members of SPARSHA are Dr. Dilip Mahalnobis, Dr. Samiran Panda, Shri Umesh Kakarania, Shri Soumitra Poddar and Shri Apurba Mitra. Their active participation in forming the basic nucleus of SPARSHA and multifarious activities thereafter has been enormous. This was a pioneering effort, which was initiated in 1998 and paved the way for greater involvement of people living with HIV/AIDS (PLWHA) in West Bengal. The group eventually widened its platform for anybody living with HIV/AIDS irrespective of the way one got infected. Initially, there was no office premise. Sometimes, the offices, residences, etc of the above mentioned promoters were used to run the activities of this support group. There was no external funding support from any agency; the group managed its activities with the membership fees and donations from few well wishers. Finally, this group consolidated into a registered body named Society for Positive Atmosphere and Related Support to HIV/AIDS (SPARSHA) in November 2001 under the West Bengal Society Registration Act 1961. It started working on the creation of a supportive environment, to spread awareness and provide HIV/AIDS care and Support through networking. SPARSHA received its first funding support from the Australian Agency for International Development (AusAID) for a project entitled "Creation of a Support Network for People Living with HIV in West Bengal" in 2001 under the Indo-Australian Community Assistance Scheme (IACAS). Its participation in the Kolkata Book Fair in 2001 and 2002; and sensitization of journalists at Kolkata Press Club exemplify such initiatives. It is worth remembering that SPARSHA pioneered HIV care in West Bengal during a time when more emphasis used to be given to HIV prevention and awareness than on treatment.

In 2003, a small research project was entrusted to SPARSHA by WBSAP&CS on "Lessons learnt from HIV/AIDS Awareness Programme in Schools of West Bengal". The financial support for this activity came from the DFID, UK via Resource Centre for Sexual Health and AIDS (RCSHA), New Delhi. Within a short period of time, another project was entrusted to SPARSHA by the Government of West Bengal to assess the needs of HIV infected and affected families. Being satisfied with the result of these assessment studies, WBSAP&CS approved Care and Support Programme for PLWHA to SPARSHA in January 2004. In addition to it, currently it has been running different other programmes related to HIV/AIDS. HIV non-infected people remained as integral part of this movement since beginning of its formation that helped in effectively reducing stigma and discrimination against HIV/AIDS in the state. SPARSHA is presently run by a group of 'People Living with HIV/AIDS and Their Friends' (PLWHAF) and provides a platform where research as well as care needs with regards to physical, social, psychological and economic aspects of PLWHA are addressed.

Vision

We must ensure our next generation flying high in a world, free from fear and discrimination against HIV/AIDS.

Mission

Creation of enabling environment for HIV prevention, care, research and fulfillment of basic human rights with active participation of people living with HIV and those who are not infected with the virus is our mission, where engaging women and children will remain central.

Present Objectives

The major objectives of SPARSHA are as follows: (i) To provide care and support services to PLWHA; (ii) To facilitate HIV voluntary confidential testing and counseling; (iii) To disseminate information on HIV/AIDS and issues related to sex and sexuality; (iv) To provide counseling services with regard to stress management, ART, etc.; (v) To provide free anti-HIV medicines to reduce transmission of HIV from parent to child; (vi) To provide low cost clinical care including ART through referral network and lobbying with various pharmaceutical companies marketing Anti Retroviral medicines; (vii) To provide subsidized ART to a few HIV infected children belonging to impoverished family; (viii) To reach out to PLWHA in need of home-based care; (ix) To start income generation activities for women infected with HIV/ or affected by presence of HIV in someone in the family; and (x) To create awareness in the community to reduce stigma and discrimination against HIV/AIDS and physician's orientation programme for HIV/AIDS care and management.

Area of Operation

Under the HIV/AIDS Care and Support programme of WBSAP&CS, SPARSHA started three Drop-in Centres (DICs) and one Community Care Centre (CCC) – one each in the four districts of West Bengal. These DICs are located namely at Kestopur in North 24-Parganas district, at Sonakhali in Paschim Medinipur district, at Nandakumar in Purba Medinipur district, and only CCC at Uluberia in Howrah district. Apart from current projects, earlier (2003) SPARSHA conducted study entitled 'Lessons learnt from HIV/AIDS awareness programme in Schools of West Bengal' in Coochbehar, Bankura, Jalpaiguri and Darjeeling districts with an intention to assist future programme planning and development of School curriculum. Later on in 2004, SPARSHA conducted similar studies in Assam and Nagaland on the request of UNDP and UNICEF to assess the School AIDS Education Programme (SAEP).

Target Groups

SPARSHA is mainly working with the people living with

HIV/AIDS (PLWHA) and their family members since 1998. It has also given special focus on Women and Children infected with and / or affected by HIV/AIDS. Apart from it, SPARSHA has been conducting awareness programme on HIV/AIDS for general people.

Infrastructure

SPARSHA is not having its own office building. The head office is located at Kestopur and Kestopur DIC is also running from the same office. The head office and other three DICs are operating from the rented buildings. The Project office is well equipped with modern office equipments like computer, telephone, Internet, etc. The Uluberia CCC is having a 10-bedded hospice and also equipped with doctor, nurse and other necessary infrastructure. Similarly, the DICs of Sonakhali and Nandakumar are also fit for the project activities. SPARSHA is not having any official car, but got an ambulance from the Health and Family Welfare Department, Government of West Bengal for serving the general public of Habra-1 Block of North 24-Parganas district.

Programmes

(i) *STD/HIV/AIDS Care and Support Programme*

SPARSHA has been running the programme since January 2004 with the support of WBSAP&CS. The project is running through three DICs and one CCC located in the four districts of West Bengal namely at Howrah, North 24-parganas, Purba and Paschim Medinipur. Since 2004, the client base of SPARSHA has gone up from 152 to 1336 in 2007. The details of the programme activities are being discussed in Part-II of this Chapter.

(ii) *Community Support and Advocacy Programme (CSAP)*

The Save the Children (UK), Kolkata office, funds this

project. The programme is meant for the HIV infected and affected children and is implemented in three villages of Paschim Medinipur district. The names of these villages are Guchhati, Ajurya and Khatbarui. As the fear of stigmatization and discrimination still persists in the communities, it is decided to embrace all children irrespective of their HIV status in this project. This would serve as a good example of non-discriminatory practice in front of the whole community for positive support. In addition to medical treatment, this approach would facilitate better psychosocial development of the children. Before the starting of intervention, SPARSHA carried out a rapid base line survey visiting more than 800 households. This has generated a good qualitative database for measuring the expected change that would result from the intervention. The project has been started in 2006.

(iii) *Situation Assessment Research (SAR)*

Since July 2006, SPARSHA has started a research project entitled "Assessment of the Situation of Women and Children Infected with and / or Affected by HIV/AIDS" in West Bengal funded by DFID (UK) via Resource Centre for Sexual Health and HIV/AIDS (RCSHA). The project was implemented in Howrah and Paschim Medinipur districts. The study was of 8 months duration and ended in February 2007. It is found from the study that there was lack of income generation support for HIV infected women (many of whom had lost their husbands to AIDS) and affected families; and inadequate focus for children infected with HIV. Community at large was seen at places to mount strong discriminatory responses against people living with HIV and their families. Risk perception of HIV test uptake by women having spouses working as migrant labours was found to be low in this study.

(iv) *Child Development and Care Centre (CDCC)*

Dr. Bibhat Mandal and Ms. Cynthia Mandal from Manchester, UK floated the idea of sponsoring HIV positive children during their visit to SPARSHA. They publicized the sponsorship proposal widely in England through their contacts as well as articles published in R G Kar Ex-Students' (UK) Scientific Brochure. The aim of this programme is to provide developmental, material, medical and nutritional support for their children. Soon responses came forward for the three children and sponsorship programme began in October 2006. The sponsors are paying 250 pounds sterling per year for each child. A woman living with HIV from nearby village has been appointed as Childcare Community Worker to ensure appropriate care is provided to these children.

(v) *Income Generation Initiatives*

The women who lost their husbands to AIDS and those who are living with their ailing husbands are in abject poverty. Many of them had children, some of whom are HIV infected as well. SPARSHA has decided to augment their earnings through income generating initiatives by giving them vocational training. With this end in view, the first item selected was '*mangalsutra*' (a sacred necklace worn by married women). A team of five members living with HIV (one male and four female) was chosen for the training. After receiving training for three months in the beginning of 2006 in Sonakhali DIC, four team members (unfortunately the male member died in the meantime) began working. Since then programme is running smoothly and the beneficiaries claim that they are self-employed. Based on the same principle and approach, training was also given to four HIV positive women and one male HIV person in Uluberia DIC for '*zari*' work (silver or gold coloured thread work) on *sarees* during the last quarter of 2006. These women are fully skilled and started to enjoy the financial benefit from the programme. Both the above training programmes were financially supported by WBSAP&CS and the micro credit was supplied by SPARSHA's sister concern AASHA (Association for

Organisational Structure

Chart 6-F: Organisational Structure of SPARSHA

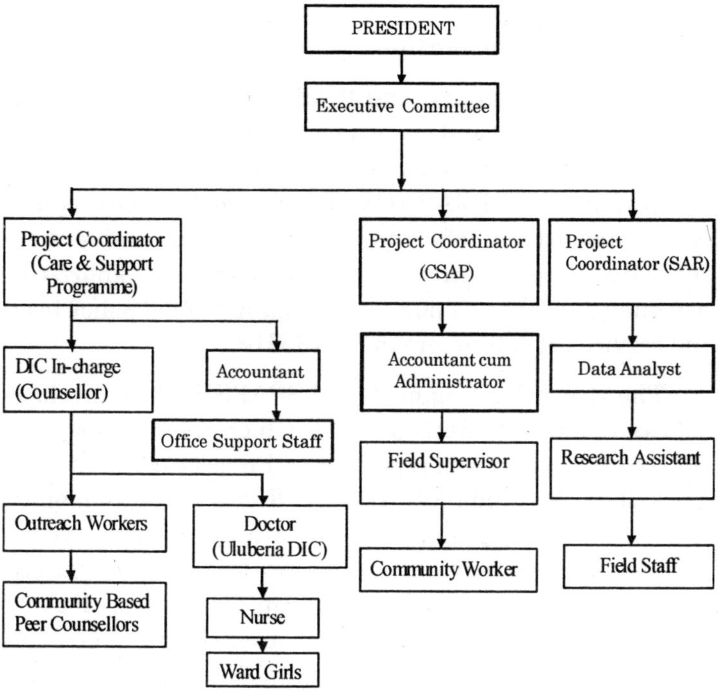

Acquiring Self-reliance through Handicrafts). In addition, training was also given in the making of jute and terracotta products to a number of the members of SPARSHA-family by Small Industry Service Institute (SISI). Government of West Bengal granted necessary permission to AASHA to produce and sell jute products in various fairs.

(vi) *Ambulance Services*

To meet the local needs of the people in Habra Block-1 of North 24-Parganas district, SPARSHA has started ambulance services. The Department of Health and Family Welfare, Government of West Bengal has provided the ambulance in December 2006. It runs on the basis of 'no loss, no profit basis'.

Staff related Information

SPARSHA is having total 42 full-time paid staff, one part-time staff (Doctor) and one honorary staff. Out of these staff, 30 staff members are working in HIV/AIDS Care and Support Programme of WBSAP&CS. There are no volunteers in SPARSHA except the interns of different universities including foreign universities, who visit for short-time assignments. There is no specific organizational policy to use the services of volunteers in SPARSHA.

The Executive Committee of SPARSHA has developed service rules for its staff members, which are discussed here. All the project staff will report to the Project Coordinator and work under his guidance. (a) Leave Rules: (i) A staff member can avail 15 days casual leave, 10 days privilege leave and 15 days medical leave in a year. No leave will be granted without permission and intimation for medical leave is compulsory. Medical Certificate or prescription or medicine bill is to be attached with medical leave application. (ii) A staff can take maximum 2 days casual leave at a stretch. Special permission to be taken for leaves beyond 2 days and it will be treated as medical leave. (iii) The official holidays (national holidays) declared by the organization will be considered as paid holidays. The number of such holidays is 15 days and intimated about the dates of these holidays to the staff at the beginning of every year. (b) All appointments are made on temporary and contract basis. Every year contract should be renewed. Continuation service is subjected to availability of fund. (c) Minimum working hour is 8 hours (10 am to 6 pm) per day. Except 2nd and 4th Saturday, SPARSHA is working 6 days in a week. Staff members may be asked for additional working days/ hours as per the requirement of the office. (d) The appointment is terminable on either side by one month's notice or salary in lieu thereof. (e) The staff members are selected and posted to work from the local area as SPARSHA works on community based approach and their jobs are not transferable. (f) In case of harmful work against the interest of the organization, the service of the concern employee will be terminated. (g) If required, any staff can stay and avail the treatment at short stay home of Uluberia DIC at free of cost. (h) The prescribed Staff Regulations in force will govern and they may be amended and altered from time to time.

SPARSHA regularly arranges training programmes for its staff members. These training programmes are arranged internally as well as by the external agencies. Some of the external agencies are WBSAP&CS, Kolkata Medical College and Hospital, RG Kar Medical College, School of Tropical Medicine, SAATHII (Solidarity and Action Against The HIV Infection in India), etc. SPARSHA also sends its staff to attend seminar and workshop in abroad too.

Financial Information

Total financial turnover of SPARSHA was Rupees 49,14,417.00 in the year 2006-07. The turn over for its HIV/ AIDS Care and Support Programme was 29,05,605.00 during 2006-07. During this period, SPARSHA has received fund from WBSAP&CS, Save the Children (UK), RCSHA (DFID, UK), public donation from within the country as well as from abroad, membership fees, beneficiaries contribution (1/3rd of cost) to avail ART for the children at subsidized rate, etc. SPARSHA has no specific fund raising policy. But keeping in the interest and objectives of the organization in mind, it approaches different funding agencies. Along with inadequate fund, lack of timely disbursement of fund from WBSAP&CS is one of the problems faced by SPARSHA.

In order to manage the financial affairs effectively, SPARSHA prepares annual budget based on the previous year's experiences, last year's expenditure, present market price, current needs of the organization, expected funds to be received, etc. Generally, SPARSHA considers 10% hike from the previous year's expenditure for preparing current year's annual budget.

Future Plan

Some of the major future plans of SPARSHA are: (i) to start a full fledged Research Centre for undertaking research on different issues related to HIV/AIDS in general and to PLWHA in particular; (ii) to establish a full fledged Child Development and Care Centre equipped with educational, nutritional, play and recreational facilities for HIV infected and non-HIV infected children; (iii) to bring more PLWHA under its Care and Support Programme; and (iv) to form more SHGs of PLWHA especially for women and start income generating programmes for them.

In a nutshell, SPARSHA runs various types of programmes and majority of them are for people living with HIV/AIDS. It has also given more emphasis for HIV infected with and / or affected women and children. SPARSHA has adopted developmental as well as right-based approach because of the diversified issues involved with PLWHA. Though small, but its initiative for the economic development of PLWHA through SHGs is a unique effort.

To sum up, this chapter is a discussion of different aspects (such as past background, objectives, organizational structure, infrastructure, present activities, future plan, etc) of six selected NGOs. It is found that DMSC, BPWT and HDRI are comparatively bigger organizations than SCIR, MB and SPARSHA in terms of financial turn over and volume of activities. Out of these six NGOs, DMSC and SPARSHA are CBOs and MB is a network of CBOs. The target groups for the HIV/AIDS programmes of SCIR, DMSC, BPWT, HDRI,

MB and SPARSHA are respectively IDUs, CSWs, truckers, migrated labourers, MSM and PLWHA. The promoters/chief functionaries of these NGOs are adequately experienced and interested to serve the society through their respective target groups. All the selected NGOs have multi-dimensional programmes and HIV/AIDS is an important aspect under their wide spectrum of activities. Despite of having many difficulties, NGOs of the present study are eye opener and pathfinder for the neglected, marginalized and poor masses. All of them have unique approach and are reformative in operation.

7

Nature of Programme Sustainability

In this chapter, initiatives have been taken to understand the nature and extent of services provided by the six selected NGOs under the study. HIV/AIDS programmes from each selected NGOs have been identified, discussed and interpreted. Researcher tries to find out how long these programmes will exist; whether they will be continued for long time (more sustainable) or short time (less sustainable) or will be stopped (unsustainable) when the project duration will be over or when funding agency will stop funding such NGOs. The programme activities are being discussed separately covering the different aspects of the programme. These aspects are: (a) objectives, (b) components of the programme, (c) programme execution process, (d) people's participation, (e) monitoring and evaluation, (f) sources of funding, (g) innovative components, and (h) local cooperation. Now programmes under each NGO are being analyzed below.

A. Society for Community Intervention and Research (SCIR)

At present SCIR is running three HIV/AIDS Intervention Projects for IDUs at Kolkata, Siliguri and Lalgola. Out of these projects, Kolkata Project was purposively selected, as other two projects were comparatively new and just started.

(a) Objectives of the Programme

The broad objective of the programme is to contribute to the reduction of HIV/AIDS incidence among IDUs, their partners and families and reduces the pool of infection. This will in turn contribute to increase the quality of life for IDUs in Kolkata and suburbs. The specific objectives of the programme are: i) to provide risk reduction services to IDUs, shadow users and partners; ii) to bring about Behaviour Change by switching from needle sharing to safer injecting practices and from injecting drug use to Oral Substitution Therapy; iii) to reduce the transmission of HIV from IDUs to their partners, offspring and the wider community by concerted condom promotion activities; iv) to create an enabling environment for PLWHA; and v) to empower and mobilize the community so as to ensure project sustainability.

(b) Components of the Programme

This programme has following major components: (i) counselling for blood testing at VCTC; (ii) counselling for PLWHA; (iii) Awareness for IDUs; (iv) awareness for vulnerable groups like slum dwellers; (v) awareness for college students and youth; (vi) condom distribution; (v) advocacy for protecting human rights of the PLWHA; (vi) making arrangement for Antiretroviral therapy (ART); (vii) referral services to other organizations; (viii) home visit and counselling of family members; (ix) awareness among neighbours to remove stigma and prevent social boycott; (x) imparting training to volunteers and staff of other organizations; (xi) organizing health check up camp; (xii) regular permanent clinic; (xiii) mobile clinic; and (xiv) treatment for STDs.

(c) Programme Execution Process

The Kolkata Project is having four (4) drop-in centers

(DIC) – namely, Park Circus DIC, Goabagan DIC, Mehdibagan DIC, and Buroshibtala DIC. Different types of staff execute this programme. For instance, Project Coordinator (PC) →DIC In-charge (Counsellor) →Outreach worker →Peer Counsellor →Peer educators →Volunteers. Apart from it, there are Accountant, Asst. Accountant, MIS Officer, Doctor and Nurse. As per WBSAP&CS, there are no posts of Assistant Accountant and MIS officer; but SCIR appointed some ORWs and Office Support Staff in these posts for effective implementation of the project. At the grassroot level, Peer Educators (PEs) with the help of Outreach workers (ORWs) and volunteers organize awareness camps; distribute condoms and IEC materials as per the pre-planned schedule. Other staff members also help the ORWs. In every DIC, clinics are held thrice in a week and attended by the doctor, nurse and counsellor. The DICs/Clinics offer counselling services for: (i) motivating the target group to comply with treatment (i.e. to complete the full course of medicine); (ii) abstaining from sex until recovery and proper condom, syringe and needle usage; (iii) treatment of their partners to prevent further infections; and (iv) exploring individual problems and helping them to develop safe health seeking behaviour. Park Circus DIC is located at the office of SCIR. All the doctors are working on part-time basis. Total 30 staff members (i.e. 2 Project Coordinators, one MIS officer, one Finance Administrator, 3 nurses, 4 counsellors, 4 peer counsellors, 10 ORWs, one accountant, one assistant accountant, 2 Doctors and one Consultant,) are involved in this project. The doctors and the consultants are part-time staff. Apart from it, 35 peer educators are also working in this project. Feedbacks of beneficiaries or field level staff reach to Project Coordinator through proper channel. Regular staff meeting is another platform to discuss about the plan, programme, progress and other related issues. Generally staff meetings are held twice in a month at the DIC. Meeting of all the project-staff are held at the HQ of SCIR once in a month. Besides it, meetings are held as and when required. SCIR is having one Core Committee to run the project effectively. This committee consists of PC, Counsellor, MIS Officer, Accountant, Counsellor, Peer Counsellor, Nurse, ORW (one) and Peer Educator (one).

(d) People's Participation

Beneficiaries (IDUs) of this programme are mostly selected through the referral. They are referred by the existing beneficiaries (recovering IDUs), volunteers, peer educators, police and community members. In SCIR, planning is done at the NGO level and before finalizing the plan; staff members were consulted in the staff meeting. Beneficiaries don't participate in planning, but their opinions are obtained through FGD/GD before implementing the plan. Apart from the staff, peer educators and volunteers actively participate in the programme implementation. It is noticed that beneficiaries received treatment in the clinic at free of cost. Recovering IDUs pay one rupee per day only if they are willing to take tea and lunch from SCIR. But it is optional, not compulsory. Considering the nature and personality of the IDUs, SCIR did not allow them to participate in monitoring and evaluation. Beneficiaries do not contribute any financial resources, but give physical labour in organizing awareness camps, putting up exhibition stall, etc. Thus, we find that beneficiaries participate in beneficiary's selection and programme implementation. But, they do not have any right to participate in programme planning, monitoring and evaluation. Therefore, the situation can be treated as partial participation of the people.

However, people's participation is duly recognized by SCIR. It is done through appreciating them in the meeting, giving them more responsibility and accepting their suggestions. Above all, majority of the existing staff at various levels are selected from among the beneficiaries. Even one Project Coordinator is an Ex-IDU.

(e) Monitoring and Evaluation

The programme is monitored every month as per the monitoring format of WBSAP&CS. The Monitoring and Evaluation Officer (MIS) of SCIR do this in every month. Besides it, the Programme Management Committee regularly monitors the staff members and finances. Financial monitoring is done on monthly basis as per programme budget. This Committee consists of two Project Coordinators, MIS officer, Accountant and Asst. Accountant. Staff members are supervised daily by the DIC in-charges. The Project Coordinator has the overall responsibility of monitoring the staff, programme activities and finance. It is done through monthly staff meeting. In this meeting, various documents (e.g. field visit diaries, etc) of the field level staff are checked and discussed. Besides this, PC sometimes made surprise field visit.

Apart from the internal monitoring, WBSAP&CS and NACO, Delhi also sends their team time to time for monitoring and evaluation of programme activities and performance of SCIR. Thus, it is understood how regular monitoring is done at SCIR's targeted intervention project for IDUs.

(f) Sources of Funding

SCIR has been running this programme for IDUs since 2003-04. This project is funded by NACO through WBSAP&CS and funded annually. Every year SCIR used to give its proposal and accordingly fund is granted by the WBSAP&CS. But this fund is granted for fixed programme components like BCC, cost of service, etc only. But there is no provision for providing food to the recovering addicts who are attending the Day Care Centre regularly. For this purpose, SCIR is getting help from Assembly of God Churches, Kolkata. Similarly except ART, for other medicinal support SCIR is getting 75% financial assistance from WORLD VISION and remaining 25% borne by SCIR itself. Another problem is financial crisis during the gap between the previous and current financial year. Fund is not granted immediately at the beginning of new financial year. During the first few months of every new financial year, SCIR and its staff had to face this problem.

(g) Innovative Components

In this project, few innovative components were found and these components helped to execute the programme in a better way. (1) The recovering IDUs who are attending Day Care Centre can get vocational training at free of cost at printing press and leather unit. (2) Primary school project mainly for the children of IDUs and for local slum children helps a lot as most of the IDUs don't have the financial capacity to pay school fees. (3) The strong referral network with different polyclinics helped the client to do the different types of pathological tests at subsidized rate. (4) By linking up with different traders, Printing Press and Leather unit of SCIR are running independently and generating fund. (5) SCIR is providing general health care facilities to the general people of the surrounding community, which helped it to receive active cooperation from the local people. Fund required for this purpose is managed by SCIR only.

(h) Local Cooperation

Out of the 4 DICs, Park Circus DIC is located at the main office of SCIR. The office is located in the slum area. Considering the good motive of SCIR, local people, local Councillor of Kolkata Municipal Corporation, local Police station, Chittaranjan National Medical College, local clubs, etc. extend their support to this programme as and when necessary. SCIR gets similar cooperation from all concerned in other three DICs. SCIR did not face any threat to carry out this programme from political parties or any other groups whose vested interests are not met. Befriending with the target group and local community is one of components in the targeted intervention project of WBSAP&CS. Thus cooperation of local people is satisfactory.

It is evident from the above discussion that the HIV/AIDS Intervention Project of SCIR under the study suffers from few bottlenecks. For instance, the delay in receiving funds and partial people's participation are the two major problems. At the same time, the programme has some positive and innovative components like committed and dedicated staff members most of whom are from IDUs, school for the children of IDUs, strong referral networking with various GOs and NGOs, etc. There is no alternative source of funding and the programme is totally dependent on the funding agency i.e. WBSAP&CS. So, it is evident that the programme of SCIR is less sustainable.

B. Durbar Mahila Samanwaya Committee (DMSC)

DMSC, at present, is implementing five STD/HIV Intervention Projects (SHIP) – namely, Sonagachi Project, Ganga Bhagirathi Project, North Bengal Project, Ultadanga Project, and Cossipore project. Sonagachi Project is purposively selected for this study as it is the oldest project (running since 1992) and got global recognition. DMSC started other projects simply by replicating the basic principles and guiding policies of Sonagachi Project.

(a) Objectives of the Programme

The broad objective of the programme is to reduce the incidence of STIs and HIV infections among the sex workers and their partners. The specific objectives of the programme are: (i) to bring about behaviour change for safer sex practices amongst CSWs; (ii) to reduce STI and HIV infection among sex workers; (iii) to prevent the transmission of STIs and HIV from their customers to CSWs and vice-versa; (iv) to provide STIs care and treatment services to CSWs; (v) to create awareness about STIs, HIV/AIDS, etc. among sex workers and their customers; (vi) to empower and enable the sex workers' community to assert their rights; and (vii) to provide advocacy services.

(b) Programme Components

Major components of the programme are: (i) pre-test and post-test counselling at VCTC; (ii) counselling for PLWHA; (iii) condom distribution; (iv) advocacy for protecting human rights of AIDS victim; (v) assistance for getting ARTs; (vi) referral to other such organizations; (vii) home visits and counseling for family members; (viii) awareness campaign to remove stigma and to prevent social boycott; (ix) mass media campaign; (x) imparting training to internal staff members as well as for the staff of other organizations; (xi) organizing health check-up camp; (xii) regular permanent clinics for STIs care and treatment; and (xiii) running VCTC aided by WBSAP&CS.

(c) Programme execution process

The Sonagachi Project is divided into two zones — known as SHIP-1 (North Kolkata) and SHIP-2 (South Kolkata). There are six clinics under SHIP-1 namely (i) Avinash clinic; (ii) Palatak Club clinic; (iii) Rabindra Sarani clinic; (iv) Rambagan clinic; (v) Seth Bagan clinic and (vi) Jorabagan clinic. First three clinics are run 6 days in a week, fourth and fifth clinics function 3 days alternatively in a week and Jorabagan clinic is run 2 days in a week. The timing of all the clinics is 11am to 2 pm except Rabindra Sarani clinic, which runs from 2 pm to 6 pm. Avinash clinic runs also in the evening from 6 pm to 8 pm. Similarly, there are seven clinics under SHIP-2 zone. These are: (i) Bowbazar clinic (4 days in a week); (ii) Kalighat clinic (4 days); (iii) Khiderpore clinic (6 days); (iv) Chetla clinic (5 days); (v) Lakermath clinic (one day); (vi) Ghoradanga clinic (2 days); and (vii) Bandhaghat clinic (2 days). The timing of all the clinics is 11 am to 2 pm. Only Bowbazar clinic also runs in the evening from 5.30 pm to 8.30 pm (2 days in a week).

The programme is executed through a logical process by involving different types of staff members. It is executed through a chain work i.e. Project Coordinator (PC) → Clinic in-charge (Doctor)→Counsellor →Field Coordinator →Supervisor →Outreach workers (ORWs) → Peer Counsellor →Peer Educators. In addition to these staff, there are nurses, clinic attendants, accountants, HR officer, Monitoring and Evaluation Officer, Training Officer, STI Management Officer, Legal Adviser, Finance Officer and Media & Advocacy officer. As per WBSAP&CS, there are no posts of Supervisor, Field Coordinator and Clinic Attendant; but DMSC appointed some ORWs in these posts for effective implementation of the project. The clinics offer counselling services for: (a) motivating the target group to comply with treatment (i.e. to complete the full course of medicine); (b) abstaining from sex until recovery and proper condom usage; (c) treatment of their partners to prevent further infections; and (d) exploring individual problems and helping them to develop safe health seeking behaviour. At the field level, peer educators visit brothel based sex workers time to time; make them aware about STIs, HIV/AIDS; refer STI cases to the clinic, distribute and do social marketing of condoms, and IEC materials as per pre-planned schedule. DMSC has been using various IEC materials like leaflets, calendars, flipcharts, etc. in this programme. All peer educators work in the field from 10.00 am to 1.00 pm and then return to the clinics/office. At the afternoon, they have regular literacy classes, meetings, trainings, etc. The Supervisors, ORWs and other staff help the peer educators in their activities. Generally, CSWs come to clinic in the morning hours and male patients in the evening hours. Apart from STI care, the clinics also provide treatment services for general ailments. Meetings with Police, *Babus, Malkins* (Madams who take rented rooms and keep CSWs; and takes shares from the earnings of CSWs), *Bariwalis* (Land ladies), shopkeepers and pimps are regularly held as per pre-planned monthly schedule. Regular staff meetings are another platform to discuss about the programme planning, progress, problems, and other related issues. The Clinic Level Committees look after each clinic's function and play an important role for their smooth functioning. This Committee consists of local branch committee members of DMSC along with other project staff. The basic approaches that DMSC adopted can be summed up as three 'R's: ***Respect, Reliance*** and ***Recognition.*** That is, *Respect* towards sex workers; *Reliance* on the knowledge and wisdom of the sex workers' community; and *Recognition* of sex work as an occupation, thereby protecting the sex workers' professional and human rights. In practice, the Project focused on translating this approach through building a relationship of mutual trust and rapport between the community of sex workers and the staff members of the project.

(d) Peoples' Participation

Most of the beneficiaries (sex workers and their customers) are selected through referral services. The existing beneficiaries, community members, peer educators and other staff members of DMSC refer them. Peer educators act as a via between sex workers and DMSC in this programme. In brothel based group meetings, needs and problems are discussed and reported to the NGO. In DMSC, planning is done at the NGO level, but before finalizing the plan beneficiaries' feedbacks were considered after thorough discussion. Beneficiaries expressed their needs to the peer educators and accordingly reported to the Project Coordinator by the peer educators. What should be the timing of the clinics (morning or evening), place of clinic, etc. were decided only after receiving feedback from the beneficiaries. Each beneficiary contributes Rs. 7/- as registration fee and avail the treatment at free of cost. They do not contribute any financial resources, but physically participate in different activities of DMSC. During brothel based awareness sessions, beneficiaries ensure their involvement by attending the programme, providing physical infrastructure (arranging chairs, etc.), controlling crowd, providing tea, etc. for the staff of DMSC. Beneficiaries also play an active role in monitoring and evaluation through Clinic Level Committee, which is represented by the branch committee members of DMSC. Whenever any external research team or evaluation team comes, beneficiaries extend full cooperation. Without beneficiaries' participation, it is impossible to implement this programme. Thus, beneficiaries' active participation is found in need identification; programme planning and its implementation; and monitoring and evaluation. Therefore, except financial resource contribution the situation can be treated as full participation of the people in DMSC and it is truly a community-based organization (CBO).

People's participation is duly recognized by DMSC. It is done through open appreciation in different meetings, giving them more responsibilities and accepting their suggestions. Above all, except doctors and few such other technical staff, majority of staff members (about 85 percent or more) are selected from among the sex workers and their children at all level. Even the present Project Director of DMSC also belongs to sex workers' community.

(e) Monitoring and Evaluation

The programme activities of Sonagachi Project are monitored every month as per WBSAP&CS's monitoring format. Clinic level activities are regularly monitored and evaluated by the concern Clinic Level Committee. The clinic level meetings are held once in a month and similarly meeting of all the project staff is held at the Project Office of DMSC once in every month. Besides these, need based meetings with different categories of staff are held as and when such need arises. For example, meetings of Peer Educators, ORWs, etc. are held separately. The overall responsibility of monitoring the staff, programme activities and finance is rested with the Project Coordinator. It is done through regular staff meetings. In these meetings, various documents of field-level staff (like field diaries, etc.) are checked and discussed thoroughly. Besides it, the Project Coordinator sometime makes surprise field visit. The Finance Administrator of DMSC does financial monitoring. At the top level, the Monitoring and Evaluation (M&E) Officer of DMSC and Central Coordinating Committee of DMSC regularly monitor all the projects, staff members and finances.

Apart from the internal monitoring, WBSAP&CS and NACO, Delhi send their teams for monitoring and evaluating the programme activities and performances of DMSC. Thus, it is understood that regular monitoring and evaluation are done in the Sonagachi Project of DMSC.

(f) Sources of Funding

The STD/HIV Intervention Project (SHIP) for CSWs is being at Sonagachi since 1992 by All India Institute of Hygiene and Public Health and by DMSC from 1999. The Project is funded by NACO through West Bengal State AIDS Prevention and Control Society (WBSAP&CS) annually and renewed every year after the submission of project proposal. DMSC bears 10 percent of the fund, while WBSAP&CS bears remaining 90 percent of fund in the project. But the fund is provided for some fixed components like Behaviour Change Communication, Programme Management, Enabling Environment, etc. Naturally this is not adequate fund to run the different activities initiated by DMSC. For example, for running Vocational Training Centre, Schools for sex workers and their children, etc. DMSC had to arrange from other funding agencies. Apart from SHIP, WBSAP&CS is providing financial assistance to DMSC for Mamata Care and Treatment Centre (VCTC). Lack of timely disbursement of fund from WBSAP&CS is a problem faced by DMSC. DMSC has no alternative sources of funding for the SHIP and fully dependent on WBSAP&CS. However, since 1992 Sonagachi Project is running successfully.

(g) Innovative Components

In Sonagachi Project, few innovative components were found which helped to execute the programme in an exceptionally better way. For instance, (1) a team of competent, committed and dedicated staff most of whom are selected from the sex workers' community. They are rendering services not as a salaried employee, but more as a community member. (2) Strong networking with different government and non-government agencies is instrumental in its successful advocacy programmes. (3) Vocational Training Centre for the aged and unwilling sex workers. (4) Formal and Non-formal Education Centres (both residential and non-residential) for CSWs and their children. (5) Linking up the sex workers with Usha Multi-Purpose Cooperative Bank and other sister organizations of Durbar. (6) Efforts for involving pimps, local shopkeepers, clubs, *Babus, Malkins, Bariwalis*, etc. and (7) Self-Regulatory Board for preventing trafficking and entry of under aged (below 18 years) girls.

(h) Local Cooperation

DMSC gets active cooperation from all concerned starting from the local MP, MLA, Ward Councillor of Kolkata Municipal Corporation, Police, Health, Social Welfare and other government and non-government agencies. Apart from it, local clubs, shopkeepers, pimps, *Babus, Malkins and Bariwalis* have also been extending all cooperation to field level staff members in executing the programme effectively. Initial threats from the local musclemen, etc. were conquered through DMSC's long and sustained efforts. Being a CBO, DMSC always receives more than required support from the sex workers' community in its different activities. Thus, cooperation of the local people is satisfactory. Being an outsider, the researcher did not face any problem due to good rapport between the project staff and local community.

Having made the above analysis, we understand that Sonagachi Project of DMSC is an integrated programme, not just merely a STD/HIV intervention project. The basic approach of the project is based on giving due respect to the sex workers, recognizing their profession and relying on their understandings. All activities of the programme are designed and implemented accordingly with an ultimate objective to enable and empower the sex workers. Though the main aim of the programme is STD/HIV/AIDS prevention, it has touched a chord deep down within the community of sex workers through multifarious project activities basically to empower sex workers' community. The active support from different sister organizations has made it is possible for DMSC. However, the programme suffers from few problems like irregularity in disbursement of fund and no financial provision for general health care by WBSAP&CS. Except financial resource contribution, there is full people's participation in the programme under the study. However, the programme is fully dependent on the funding agency i.e. WBSAP&CS. Hence, the programme is less sustainable.

C. Bhoruka Public Welfare Trust (BPWT)

BPWT runs HIV/AIDS Intervention Projects for truckers in West Bengal at two sites – namely at Petrapole (North 24 Parganas district) and Kolkata Port Trust (KPT) area (Kolkata). The KPT area is purposively selected for this Study, as it is the oldest truckers' intervention project (started since 1994) of BPWT and was initially funded by DFID. The WBSAP&CS started funding to this project since 2001. Later on, BPWT started other projects simply by replicating the basic principles of KPT Project.

(a) Objectives of the Programme

The broad objective of the programme is to reduce the

incidences of STI and HIV infections among the truck drivers, helpers and indirectly among their family members and sex workers. The specific objectives of the programme are: (i) To empower the truckers against AIDS with satisfactory level of information and awareness towards adoption of safer sexual practices; (ii) To reduce the incidence of STI among truck drivers, helpers and their clients (primarily sex workers) and maintain low prevalence rate among them; (iii) To undertake social marketing of condoms; (iv) To create an enabling environment for the project at a long term basis by sensitizing and involving truckers, transport industry, local people, civic, health and enforcement authorities on various issues related to HIV/AIDS; (v) To provide comprehensive supplementary and referral services to truckers along with HIV/AIDS related services; and (vi) To develop an internal system for monitoring and reviewing the effectiveness and quality of the programme.

(b) Programme Components

Major components of the programme are: (i) Counselling for changing high risk behaviour and blood testing at VCTC; (ii) Counselling for PLWHA; (iii) Awareness for truck drivers and helpers (iv) Condom distribution and social marketing of condoms; (v) Advocacy for protecting human rights of AIDS victims; (vi) Assistance for arrangement of Antiretroviral Therapy (ART); (vii) Referral to other such organizations for treatment, pathological tests; (viii) Awareness campaign to remove stigma and to prevent social boycott; (ix) Mass media campaign to improve the awareness among all concern; (x) Imparting training to internal staff members as well as for the staff of other organizations; (xi) Organizing Health Check-up camp; (xii) Regular permanent clinics for STI care and treatment; and (xiii) Development and distribution of IEC materials.

(c) Programme Execution Process

The objectives are being achieved through clinic

intervention, outreaching, STI case management, counselling and condom promotion. Smooth functioning of the intervention programme is ensured through various components by involving various categories of staff members. The programme is executed through a logical process by involving different types of staff members. It is executed through a chain work i.e. Project Coordinator (PC) →Clinic in-charge (Doctor) →Counsellor →Field Supervisor →Out reach workers (ORWs) →Peer Educators. In addition to these staff, there are Accountant, MIS officer and office assistant. As per WBSAP&CS, there are no posts of Field Supervisor and MIS officer; but BPWT appointed some ORWs in these posts for effective implementation of the project. In KPT Project area, there are two drop-in-centres cum clinics at major parking zones namely at Bhutghat, and Dhobiatala. The KPT area project office of BPWT is located at Bhutghat. The clinic of Bhutghat is open throughout the day and it is located in the Project office itself. Another clinic of Dhobiatala is open up to 1.00 pm. These clinics offer treatment of STI and other common ailments. Clinics provide STI treatment through syndromic approach, which helps to provide quick relief. This approach is adopted because of the low treatment compliance of truckers. Besides it, the clinics also offer counselling services for: (a) motivating the target group to comply with treatment (i.e. to complete the full course of medicine); (b) abstaining from sex until recovery and proper condom usage; (c) treatment of their partners to prevent further infections; and (d) exploring individual problems and helping them to develop safe health seeking behaviour. As per pre-planned schedule, Peer Educators (PEs) and Outreach Workers (ORWs) interact with the target group through one to one interaction and sometimes through group interaction at the parking zones. They also try to wipe out myths and misconceptions of the truckers about HIV/AIDS related issues. They also refer the individuals to these clinics for treatment. The PEs are selected from among the truck industry associated people (TIAP) like garage workers, local shopkeepers and local influential persons. They work purely on voluntary basis and do not take any honorarium like other projects of WBSAP&CS. Awareness programmes are organized in the field for dissemination of message on HIV/AIDS and STI. BPWT has been using various IEC materials like leaflets, calendars, flipcharts, talking doll shows, etc in this programme. BPWT initially started with free distribution of condoms supplied by the Health and Family Welfare Department, Government of West Bengal. Later on keeping in mind with demand of target population, BPWT started social marketing of condoms through small non-traditional outlets (*Paan* shops, tea stalls, hotels, etc.). The outreach workers do the monitoring of the condom outlets on a weekly basis. The programme planning, progress, problems and other related issues are discussed at regular staff meeting. Accordingly every staff member carries out his/her responsibilities. The Project Coordinator is regularly supervising all staff members and their performances and is also maintaining contact with the Head Office of BPWT.

(d) People's Participation

The existing beneficiaries, volunteers, peer educators, local community and truck industry associated people mostly refer the beneficiaries (truck drivers and helpers) of this programme. The truck industry associated people (TIAP) include the Truck Owners' Associations, the Truckers' Associations, the Loaders' Associations, employees of different transport agencies, trade unions of the workers engaged in transport agencies and transport agency officials. The local community represents people attached with *Paan* Shops, Tea Stalls, hotels/*Dhabas*, etc. Truckers are not always available in any place because of the nature of their jobs. Naturally, they could not take part in programme planning. However, their feedback/opinions are obtained through the field level project staff members and considered at the time of programme planning. However, local community members and truck industry associated people actively participate in programme implementation. It is noticed that Rs. 30/- is taken as registration fees from the beneficiaries and they avail the medicine at free of cost from BPWT clinics. This registration fee was taken so that wastage of medicines can be prevented and also it helps to generate some fund for general health care. Because, WBSAP&CS gives money for STI care only. They do not contribute any financial resources. Local truck industry associated people are extending all cooperation to the project staff members including physical labour at the time of organizing awareness camp, etc. They help in arranging chairs, controlling crowd, etc.

Thus, we find that beneficiaries participate in need identification, beneficiary's selection and partly in programme implementation. But they do not participate in programme planning, resource contribution, monitoring and evaluation. Therefore, the situation can be treated as partial involvement of beneficiaries. But this is mainly due to the nature of the beneficiaries' job. However, BPWT duly recognizes people's participation by accepting their suggestion.

(e) Monitoring and Evaluation

BPWT has developed a systematic MIS through which regular monitoring is done at the NGO level. The programme is monitored every month as per the monitoring format of WBSAP&CS. At the project level, the Project Coordinator has the overall responsibility of monitoring the staff, programme activities and finance. This is done through regular monthly staff meeting. In this meeting, programme activities, progresses of the work, problems, future plan, etc. are discussed. The Project Coordinator also reviews the progress of monthly plan in weekly staff meetings. Financial monitoring is done as per the programme budget on monthly basis. The Project Coordinator also makes surprise visit to the field. Besides it, Director and Administrative Officer of BPWT sometime make surprise visits to monitor the project activities. The Centre-in-Charge meets with all Project Coordinators to review the programme activities. Similarly, the Director and other senior officials of BPWT meet quarterly with all Project Coordinators and Centre-in-Charge for the same purpose.

Apart from the internal monitoring, the evaluation teams from WBSAP&CS and NACO also visit the project for monitoring and evaluating the programme and performances of BPWT. Thus, it is found that regular monitoring is done at this truckers' intervention project of BPWT.

(f) Sources of Funding

BPWT has been running this HIV/AIDS intervention project for truckers in KPT area since 1994. The Project is funded by WBSAP&CS annually since 2001 and previously the project was funded DFID. Every year WBSAP&CS asks project proposal and grants the fund after the project proposal is accepted and approved. But this fund is given for certain fixed components like Behaviour Change Communication (BCC), Cost of Service, Programme Management, etc. BPWT and other such NGOs are accordingly implementing the programme as per the guidelines of WBSAP&CS. But the project staff members felt that the fund is not adequate. There is no provision of providing medicines for the general health care, except STI care and management under this project. In KPT Project area, there is no near by health centre or hospital or nursing home. Naturally, in case of any health emergency, the truckers as well as truck industry associated people first approach the BPWT clinics for treatment. Lack of timely release of fund from WBSAP&CS is another problem. Especially, the delay in release of fund is occurred in the beginning of every new financial year. BPWT is fully dependent on WBSAP&CS and it has no alternative source of funding this project now. However, since 1994 BPWT is running the Truckers' project in KPT as well as in Petrapole area successfully.

(g) Innovative Component

In this project, few innovative components are found that helped to execute the programme in a better way. These components are: (1) Adoption of syndromic approach in the treatment of STI that gives quick relief is found very much useful. Because due to their migratory nature of job, the truckers have low treatment compliance rate; (2) Involvement of truck industries associated people and local shopkeepers, etc.; (3) Linking up with Bhoruka Blood Bank for blood test is an extra advantage for this project; (4) Annual sports is organized mainly with a view to recognise the contribution of local truck industry associated people and local community to ensure their participation in future too; and (5) Peer Educators work voluntarily and BPWT don't pay any honorarium to them like other TI projects of WBSAP&CS.

The basic approach adopted in this KPT project to empower the truckers against HIV/AIDS with satisfactory level are designed and implemented in accordance with the ultimate objective of the project i.e. to reduce the incidence of STI, HIV/AIDS among the truckers and their family members.

(h) Local Cooperation

BPWT gets active cooperation from the Kolkata Port Trust Authority without which it would have been difficult to run this programme within the port area. Besides it, BPWT also receives support from Health, Police, Social Welfare and other departments of government. This truckers' intervention project is operating in the parking zones/halting points of trucks within the KPT area. Therefore, it is not like other projects where local residents can participate in the programme activities. At the local level, there is one Advisory

Board consist of representatives from BPWT, Truck Owners' Association, Transport Companies, CISF, local Police Station, local MLA and local Councillor of Kolkata Municipal Corporation. The Advisory Board meets quarterly and discusses the progress, problems of the programmes, etc. Sometimes this Board also took initiative and arrange awareness programme with the help of BPWT staff. In short, BPWT is successful in getting support from all truck industry associated people. The Transport Companies, workers of different transport agencies, and trade unions of these workers, local shopkeepers — all extend necessary cooperation to the project staff.

It is evident from the above discussion that the Truckers' Project of BPWT suffers from few bottlenecks. For instance, it lacks full-fledged people's participation, delay in receiving fund, no provision for the general health care by WBSAP&CS, etc. On the other hand, the programme under the study has got some advantages like BPWT is having its own blood testing laboratory, active support from truck industries associated people, etc. But, the truckers' project of BPWT is fully dependent on WBSAP&CS for funding support. Hence, the programme is less sustainable.

D. MANAS Bangla (MB)

As already discussed in Chapter-6 that MB is the only organization, which is running Sexual Health Promotion and HIV Control Programme for MSM in West Bengal. Currently, MB is running this project through its eight DICs. These DICs are located at DumDum, Kadapara and Kasba (Kolkata district); Baruipur (South 24-Parganas); Bangaon (North 24-Parganas); Srirampore (Hoogly); Siliguri (Darjeeling) and Burdwan. Out of these eight DICs, DumDum DIC and Kasba DIC were purposively selected for this study as both of them are functioning since the inception of the project i.e. 2004.

(a) Objectives of the Programme

The broad objective of the programme is to reduce the incidence of STIs and HIV infections among the MSM and their partners. The specific objectives of the programme are: (i) to bring about behaviour change for safer sex practices amongst MSM population; (ii) to reduce STI and HIV infection among the MSM people; (iii) to prevent the transmission of STIs and HIV from MSM people to their partners and vice-versa; (iv) to provide STIs care and treatment services to MSM; (v) to create awareness about STI, HIV/AIDS, etc. among MSM people and their partners; (vi) to empower and enable the MSM community to assert their rights; (vii) to provide advocacy services; (viii) to prevent violence against MSM community members; (ix) to meet the health needs of MSM people; and (x) to reduce the stigma around gender or sexual identities of MSM among the common people.

(b) Programme Components

Major components of the programme are: (i) pre-test and post-test counselling for blood tests at VCTC; (ii) counselling for PLWHA; (iii) condom and lube distribution; (iv) advocacy for protecting human rights of HIV/AIDS victim; (v) assistance for getting ARTs; (vi) referral of clients to other such organizations; (vii) home visits and counseling for family members; (viii) awareness campaign to remove stigma and to prevent social boycott; (ix) mass media campaign; (x) imparting training to internal staff members, volunteers as well as for the staff of other organizations; (xi) organizing health check-up camp; (xii) regular permanent clinics for STIs care and treatment at DICs; and (xiii) developing and distributing IEC materials.

(c) Programme Execution Process

The programme is executed through a systematic process by involving different categories of staff members. MB has divided eight DICs into five Zones. There are five Zonal Project Coordinators (ZPC) to look after these DICs. For example, DumDum DIC and Bangaon DIC placed under one ZPC; Baruipur DIC and Kasba DIC under another ZPC; Srirampore DIC and Burdwan DIC look after by another ZPC; and remaining two ZPCs look after Siliguri DIC and Kadapara DIC respectively. It is executed through a chain work i.e. Zonal Project Coordinator (ZPC) → DIC in-charge (Counsellor) →MIS cum Accounts Officer →Field Supervisor →Outreach Workers (ORW) →Peer Counsellor →Peer Educators. In addition to these staff, there are one Doctor and one DIC Assistant in each DIC. The Project Director is the over all in-charge of the whole project. These DIC level staff are assisted by a Technical Team consists of HR Officer, Documentation Officer, Finance Officer, BCC Officer, STI Management Officer, Medicinal Officer, MIS Officer, Accountant and Project Office Assistant. The Project Director of MB heads this technical team. As per WBSAP&CS, there are no posts of Field Supervisor and MIS officer; but MB has appointed some ORWs in these posts for effective implementation of the project. The clinics offer counselling services for: (i) motivating the target group to comply with treatment (i.e. to complete the full course of medicine); (ii) abstaining from sex until recovery and proper condom and lube usage; (iii) treatment of their partners to prevent further infections; and (iv) exploring individual problems and helping them to develop safe health seeking behaviour. At the field level, peer educators and ORWs visit different Closing/ Meeting Points (for example, Railway Stations, Parks, etc.) where MSM people are assembled and make them aware about STIs, HIV/AIDS; refer STI cases to the clinic; distribute condoms, lubes and IEC materials as per pre-planned schedule. They also make efforts to build rapport with the local Police Stations, GRP, Clubs, etc. The Supervisors and other staff help peer educators in their activities. Peer educators are in regular touch with the target group people and take their feedback time to time about the services provided by MB. Regular staff meetings are held to discuss about the programme planning, progress, problems, and other related issues. During such meetings, individual tasks are assigned to each staff member. At the clinic level, Doctor provides treatment for STIs and other health problems, which is supplemented by the advice and counseling from the Counsellor. The Counsellor has been playing a very important role in the areas where contradictions regarding sex, gender, sexuality, sexual behaviour, sexual health, social norms and beliefs are confused with mental health issues. The timing of the clinics is 12'O clock to 8 pm and clinics are held 4 days in a week. In Baruipur DIC, the clinic is open for 5 days in a week, because every Sunday special clinic is held for *Hijras*. MB organizes number of community-based events to renew and enrich its old contracts as well as for possibilities in reaching out to other areas too. It also helps to form 'Support Group' where there is no such organization like MB. In practice, the Project focuses on building a relationship of mutual trust and rapport between the MSM community and the staff members of the project.

(d) Peoples' Participation

Beneficiaries, who regularly visit the DICs, directly participate in the meeting and involve in need identification. Most of the beneficiaries (MSM and their partners) are selected through referral services. The existing beneficiaries, community members, peer educators and other staff members of MB refer them. Sometimes regular visitors of DICs bring beneficiaries along with them. In MB, planning is done at the NGO level, but before finalizing the plan beneficiaries' feedbacks were considered after thorough discussion. Regular beneficiaries of DIC directly participate in GD/FGD and express their opinions. In case of outreach beneficiaries, their needs and problems are discussed and reported by the Peer Educators to the respective DIC and ultimately it reaches to

Project Director of MB. Each beneficiary contributes Rs. 2/- as registration fee and avail the treatment and medicines at free of cost. They pay separately for condoms and lubes, which are sold by peer educators through social marketing. They do not contribute any financial resources, but physically participate in different activities of DICs as and when required or asked for. Outreach beneficiaries also volunteer themselves in different outreach activities at the field level. Beneficiaries also participate in different activities of MB (for example community-based events, exhibition stall at fairs, etc.) as volunteers. Beneficiaries do not participate directly in monitoring and evaluation, but the project staff members consider their views and feedbacks. Beneficiaries extend full cooperation whenever any external research team or evaluation team comes to MB. Without beneficiaries' participation, it is impossible to implement this programme. Thus, beneficiaries' active participation is found in need identification, beneficiaries' selection, programme planning and its implementation; and to some extent in monitoring and evaluation. Therefore, except financial resource contribution the situation can be treated as full participation of the people in MB and it is truly a network of community-based organizations (CBO).

MB duly recognizes people's participation. The project staff members do it on the spot by appreciating or praising their contributions. It is also done through open appreciation in different meetings, giving them more responsibilities and accepting their suggestions. Above all, except doctors and few such other technical staff, majority of staff members (about 80 to 85 percent) are selected from among MSM community at all level.

(e) Monitoring and Evaluation

Within the DIC, Clinic level activities are regularly monitored and evaluated by the Counsellor (DIC in-charge) and MIS Officer of the concern DIC. The over all responsibility of monitoring the staff, programme activities and finance is rested with the Zonal Project Coordinators for the respective DICs placed under them. It is done through regular staff meetings. In these meetings, various reports and documents of field-level staff (like field diaries, etc.) are checked and discussed thoroughly. Besides it, the Project Coordinator sometime makes surprise field visit. At the top level, Project Director and the technical team members also time to time make visit to the DICs for the same purpose. The HR Officer, Finance Officer, MIS Officer, Documentation Officer, STI Management Officer regularly monitors and evaluates the activities of different DICs in their respective areas. The Governing Body members also time to time visit the Project Office and DICs. Besides this, the programme activities of MSM Project are monitored every month as per WBSAP&CS's monitoring format.

Apart from the internal monitoring and evaluation, WBSAP&CS and NACO, Delhi sends their teams for monitoring and evaluating the programme activities and performances of MB. Thus, it is understood that regular monitoring and evaluation are done in the MSM Project of MB.

(f) Sources of Funding

The Sexual Health Promotion and HIV Control Programme for MSM in MB is running from July 2004.The Project is funded by West Bengal State AIDS Prevention and Control Society (WBSAP&CS) annually and renewed every year after the submission of project proposal. MB bears 10 percent of the project cost and remaining 90 percent borne by WBSAP&CS. But the fund is provided for some fixed components like Behaviour Change Communication, Programme Management, Enabling Environment, Treatment Support, Desirable Support, Monitoring and Evaluation.

Naturally, it is not adequate fund to run the different activities of the project. For example, WBSAP&CS has no provision for meeting the expenditure incurred for general health care and treatment; for meeting the expenditure of traveling allowances of Peer Educators, etc. the allotted fund is also inadequate to purchase requires clinical equipments. Lack of timely disbursement of fund from WBSAP&CS is another problem faced by MB. It has no alternative sources of funding the MSM project and is fully dependent on WBSAP&CS.

(g) Innovative Components

In MSM Project of MB, few innovative components are found that help in executing the programme in better way. For instance, (1) purchasing medicines directly from CDMU, Kolkata at low price to reduce the cost and thereby serving more beneficiaries; (2) collecting medicines from Physician's sample for the same purpose; (3) people with MSM behaviour are by and large creative and MB has trained a batch of such people in stitching and embroidery who are now successfully earn their livelihood from it; (4) a team of competent, committed and dedicated staff most of whom are selected from the MSM community. They are rendering services more as a community member than as salaried employees; and (5) strong networking with different government, NGOs and CBOs is instrumental in its successful advocacy programmes.

(h) Local Cooperation

At the DIC level, MB gets cooperation from all concerned starting from the local Ward Councillors of Kolkata Municipal Corporation and other municipalities, Police, Health, Social Welfare and other government and non-government agencies. But still the cooperation received from the government agencies is not upto the desired level. The project did not face so far any threat from political parties or any group with vested interests. But there were some incidences where project staff were harassed and humiliated by the local people because of prevailing social attitude towards the MSM and their sexual behaviour. There are incidences where police refused to register FIR in case of such harassments of the project staff of MB. Orthodox and puritan nature of our social norms and beliefs regarding sex and sexual behaviour is one of the common problems faced by MSM community everywhere. The situation has improved through MB's long and sustained efforts. Thus, cooperation of the local people is not satisfactory to the desired extent. But being a network of CBOs, MB always receives more than required support from the member organizations and MSM community in its different activities.

It is found from the above analysis that the basic approach of the project is based on giving due respect to the MSM population, recognizing their sexual behaviours and relying on their understandings. All activities of the programme are designed and implemented accordingly with an ultimate objective of enabling and empowering the MSM community to assert their rights. Except the resource contribution, there is full- fledged people's participation. At the same time, the programme suffers from few problems like delay in receiving fund, no financial provision for the general health care and traveling allowances of PEs by WBSAP&CS, etc. On the other hand, the programme under the study has got certain advantages like committed and dedicated staff most of whom are from MSM community, strong referral networking, central technical team, etc. But, this MSM programme of MB is less sustainable as it is fully dependent on WBSAP&CS for funding support.

E. Human Development Research Institute (HDRI)

HDRI has been running HIV/AIDS Targeted Intervention Project for migrated labourers (ML) since 1997.

Initially, the programme was started with the help of DFID (UK) and it was handed over to WBSAP&CS in 2001. Presently, the project is covering 25000 migrated labourers of Burrabazar (8000), Posta (7000), Jorabagan (4000), Mechua (3000), Ahiritola (1500) and Sovabazar (1500). Out of these migrated laborers, 60% are Porters, 15% are Handcart pullers, 15% are Labourers, 5% are Sardars and 5% are engaged in other occupations. These people had to stay away from their family for a long time. Consequently, they wanted to fulfill their sexual desires by going to sex workers and thus become vulnerable for STD/HIV infections. This project is purposively selected for this study, as it is one of the oldest projects for MLs in West Bengal.

(a) Objectives of the Programme

The broad objective of the programme is to promote better sexual health among migrant labourers; and to reduce the incidence of STD/HIV infection among the ML, their family members and sex partners. The specific objectives of the programme are: (i) to provide sexual health education among ML; (ii) to bring about behaviour change for safer sex practice among ML; (iii) to reduce STD/HIV infection among ML; (iv) to prevent transmission of STD/HIV from ML to their family members and sex partners; (v) to provide STD treatment through syndromic approach along with general health care; (vi) to promote and distribute condoms through clinics and outreach activities; (vii) to provide networking and advocacy services at different level; (viii) to promote sustainability at different components of existing intervention programmes; and (ix) to empower and enable ML to assert their rights.

(b) Programme Components

Major components of the programme are: (i) counselling for changing high risk behaviour and blood testing at VCTC/ICTC; (ii) counselling for PLWHA; (iii) awareness for migrated labourers and other vulnerable groups like slum dwellers;

(iv) condom distribution and social marketing of condoms; (v) advocacy for protecting human rights of AIDS victims; (vi) assistance for arrangement of Antiretroviral Therapy (ART) through School of Tropical Medicine; (vii) referral to other such organizations for treatment, pathological tests; (viii) awareness campaign to remove stigma and to prevent social boycott; (ix) mass media campaign to improve the awareness among all concern; (x) imparting training to internal staff members and volunteers; (xi) organizing Health Check-up camp; (xii) regular permanent clinics for STD care and treatment; and (xiii) development and distribution of IEC materials.

(c) Programme Execution Process

HDRI has been running this project through five clinics. These clinics are: (1) Posta clinic, Burrabazar clinic, Ahiritola clinic, Mechua clinic and Sovabazar clinic. Posta and Burrabazar clinics open six days in a week; Ahiritola and Mechua clinics open 3days alternatively in a week and Sovabazar clinic opens twice in a week. The timing of the clinics is 8.30 am to 11 am. In each clinic there are doctor, nurse, counsellor and clinic attendant. The patients' names are recorded in the registers and case histories are maintained in the health cards of each individual patient. The clinics offer counselling services for: (i) motivating the target group to comply with treatment (i.e. to complete the full course of medicine); (ii) abstaining from sex until recovery and proper condom usage; (iii) treatment of their partners to prevent further infections; and (iv) exploring individual problems and helping them to develop safe health seeking behaviour. The programme is executed through a systematic process by involving different categories of staff members. It is executed through a chain work i.e. Project Coordinator →Clinic In-Charge (Doctors) → Counsellor →Outreach Workers (ORWs) → Peer Educators (PEs) → Volunteers. In addition to these staff, there are nurses, clinic attendants and accountant.

There are 36 PEs are working in this project and all of whom are selected from the migrated labourers' community. Most of these migrated labourers are available in *Gaddi* (place of work) and in *Thek* (place of group residence). Migrated labourers reside in group and work under one 'Sardar' (leader). At the field level, ORWs and PEs time to time visit these migrated labourers at their 'Gaddi' and 'Thek' as per the planned schedule. These field level staff members interact with the target population one to one or in group and make them aware about STD/HIV/AIDS, refer the STD cases to the clinics, distribute condoms and IEC materials, etc. They also issue health cards to the beneficiaries. Other staff members like Counsellor, Project Coordinator, etc. also help these ORWs and PEs. As per pre-planned monthly schedule, meeting with Sardars, Community Influencers, Trade unions, Merchant Associations, etc. are held to discuss about different aspects related to the programme activities. Regular staff meetings are another platform to discuss about the progress of the project, problems, programme planning and other related issues. At the clinic level, weekly staff meetings are held to plan clinic and field level activities. Monthly staff meeting for all project staff members is held at the Project Office of HDRI. For the smooth functioning, there are no formal clinic level committees to look after the function of each clinic. But usually the concern staff members of HDRI with the help of representatives from local target population and other associated organizations do it. In practice, the project is functioning through building a relationship of mutual trust and rapport between the migrated labourers and the staff members of HDRI.

(d) People's Participation

The project is implemented through Outreach workers and Peer educators at the field level. Beneficiaries' needs and problems were discussed in the group meetings with them and reported to the NGO. Here, Outreach workers and Peer educators act as a via between HDRI and beneficiaries. Most of the beneficiaries are selected through referral services. The existing beneficiaries, community members, peer educators and other field level staff members of HDRI refer them. Here planning is done at the NGO level and approved by the Governing Body of HDRI. There are three community members who are selected as member in the Governing Body. It is noticed that beneficiaries pay Rs. 10/- as registration fee to avail the treatment at free of cost from the clinics run by HDRI. Beneficiaries do not contribute any financial resources, but provide infrastructural support (arrangement of venue, electricity, chairs, etc.) during Annual Gathering, Sardar's meet, awareness camp, etc. They also physically participate and contribute in different activities of HDRI in terms of controlling crowds, arranging tea, etc. So far monitoring is concerned, beneficiaries do not actively involve in it. Beneficiaries do not have any role in evaluation of the project, but they extend full cooperation to the external evaluation team by participating in FGD. Thus, beneficiaries' active participation is found in need identification, beneficiary's selection, programme planning and implementation. But they have limited scope for participation in monitoring and evaluation. Therefore, the situation can be treated as partial participation of the people.

But people's participation is duly recognized by HDRI. Every year, HDRI organizes Annual Gathering programme for migrant labourers through organizing sports, games, audio-visual show and awareness generation programme. The whole programme is actually organized with the active support and participation of beneficiaries. Besides this, HDRI has recruited 36 Peer Educators from the migrant labourers' community. This indicates that HDRI recognized their contributions in the implementation of the project.

(e) Monitoring and Evaluation

All the programme activities are monitored on weekly,

monthly, quarterly, half-yearly and annual basis by different staff as per the monitoring and evaluation plan and strategy. The overall responsibility of monitoring the staff members, programme activities and finance is rested with the project coordinator. It is done through regular staff meeting. In such meetings review of progress, problems faced, plans, etc. are thoroughly discussed and suitable decisions are taken for the future. At the top level, Governing Body is continuously monitoring and evaluating the project. Sometimes GB members, Project Coordinators make surprise visit to the field for this purpose. In HDRI, there is 'exchange monitoring system' i.e. monitoring is done by the Project Coordinator of other project. Sometime the Project Coordinator of Truckers' Project make surprise visit to the Migrated Labourers' Project or vice-versa to ensure effective monitoring and implementation of the project.

Apart from the internal monitoring and evaluation, WBSAP&CS send its team for monitoring and evaluation. Sometimes such teams come from NACO, Delhi also. Thus, it is found that regular internal as well as external monitoring and evaluation are done in the HIV/AIDS Targeted Intervention Project of Migrated Labourers in HDRI.

(f) Sources of Funding

DFID (UK) funded the HIV/AIDS Targeted Intervention Project for ML from 1997 to 2001(March). Since April 2001, HDRI is receiving fund from WBSAP&CS. Every year the project is renewed after the submission of project proposal. Out of the project expenditure, WBSAP&CS bears 90 percent and HDRI bears remaining 10 percent of fund in the project. Lack of timely disbursement of fund from WBSAP&CS is a problem faced by HDRI. It has no alternative sources of funding for the project and fully dependent on WBSAP&CS. If funding is stopped, the programme could not be run in future. However, HDRI will try to strengthen its fund raising programme in near future. So it is evident from the above discussion that project cannot be continued for long time without the support of funding agencies. Anyway HDRI is running this project successfully since 1997.

(g) Innovative Component

Few innovative components are found in the Migrated Labourers' project of HDRI, which help to implement the programme in a better way. For instance, (1) linking up the ML project with the Truckers' project implemented by HDRI in the same area. Most of the migrated labourers are engaged in loading and unloading goods from these trucks. As a result, both the projects are running effectively; (2) similarly linking up the ML project with the Project for drug dependents also help in the effective implementation of each other, as many of the ML are drug dependents and they are getting help from the same NGO i.e. HDRI; (3) Annual Gathering programme for migrated labourers is a unique method for maintaining rapport with the community as well as for giving recognition to their contribution in the project; (4) strong networking with pathological Laboratories helping the beneficiaries to do the pathological tests at subsidized price; (5) strong networking with the different government and non-government agencies is playing an important role in its successful advocacy programmes; (6) Sardars are selected by HDRI as referral agents in their respective communities.

(h) Local Cooperation

HDRI gets active cooperation from all concerned. Initially, there was some resistance from the Merchant's Association. But with the continuous effort and persuasion by HDRI, now the same Merchants' Association is extending all cooperation towards the smooth implementation of the project. Similarly the trade unions of migrated labourers are also extending all possible cooperation. Cooperation is also received from local Ward Councillor of Kolkata Municipal Cooperation, MLA,

Police, Health, Social Welfare and other government departments. Thus, cooperation of the local people is satisfactory in implementing this HIV/AIDS intervention project of HDRI for migrated labourers.

From the above discussion, it is found that HIV/AIDS Intervention Programme for Migrated Labourers (ML Project) of HDRI is having few bottlenecks. For instance, partial participation of people, delay in receiving fund and staff mobility are the major problems. The programme under the study has got some positive aspects like representatives from MLs in the governing body of HDRI, strong referral networking, linking up with other projects of HDRI, etc. But, the programme is fully dependent on WBSAP&CS for funding support. Hence, the ML project is less sustainable.

F. Society for Positive Atmosphere and Related Support to HIV/AIDS (SPARSHA)

At present SPARSHA is running the STD/HIV/AIDS Care and Support programme through three DICs and one CCC located in four districts of West Bengal. Kestopur DIC, Uluberia CCC and Sonakhali DIC are purposively selected for the study and Nandakumar DIC is excluded for its recent origin.

(a) Objectives of the Programme

The broad objective of the programme is to provide care and support to the people living with HIV/AIDS (PLWHA). The specific objectives of the programme are: (i) to provide low-cost clinical care including ART through network; (ii) to provide counseling services with regards to stress management, ART, etc. for the PLWHA and their family members; (iii) to provide free anti-HIV medicines to reduce transmission of HIV from parents to child; (iv) to provide subsidized ART to a few HIV infected children belonging to poor family; (v) to reach out to PLWHA and train them and their family members on home-based care; (vi) to provide vocational training to the HIV infected/affected women for income generation activities; (vii) to facilitate HIV voluntary and confidential testing and counseling; (viii) to create support network for PLWHA; (ix) to document best practices on HIV/AIDS care and support for PLWHA; (x) to create awareness among the common people to reduce stigma and discrimination against PLWHA; (xi) to empower and enable PLWHA to assert their rights; and (xii) to provide advocacy services.

(b) Programme Components

Major components of the programme are: (i) pre-test and post-test counselling at VCTC; (ii) counselling for PLWHA; (iii) condom distribution; (iv) advocacy for protecting human rights of AIDS victim; (v) assistance for getting ARTs; (vi) referral to other such organizations; (vii) home visits and counseling for family members; (viii) awareness campaign to reduce stigma and discrimination; (ix) mass media campaign; (x) imparting training to internal staff members as well as for the staff of other organizations; (xi) awareness for vulnerable groups like slum dwellers; (xii) regular permanent clinics for care and treatment of People living with HIV; (xiii) runs Short Stay Home for PLWHA; (xiv) awareness for school students; and (xv) vocational training for HIV infected/affected women.

(c) Programme Execution Process

The programme is executed by involving different categories of staff through a systematic and logical process. It is executed through a chain work i.e. Project Coordinator (PC)→ DIC In-charge (Counsellor)→ Outreach Workers (ORWs)→ Community Based Peer Counsellor (CBPC). In addition to these staff, there are doctor, nurses, ward girls, accountant and office support staff. The doctor, nurses and ward girls are working in Uluberia CCC only. At the field level, ORWs and CBPCs as a regular activity visit and establish effective network with various government and private hospitals, health centers, nursing homes, DOT centers, etc. Physicians of these hospitals and health centres and local private doctors refer symptomatic clients to SPARSHA and it in turn assists them for blood testing, counseling, etc. at VCTC run by the government. These field level staff members also contact specialist doctors for free medical help. Further more, they make visits to clients' home for getting family members involved in caring people with HIV. They also conduct community sensitization programme to foster community acceptance and participation. The ORWs and CBPCs are also involved in the inclusion of new People living with HIV into the network, expanding and strengthening the network.

Besides the above activities, condoms are distributed from the DICs to enable clients to practice safer sex. Counselling by well-trained counsellors is also done from DICs with regard to various issues including adherence to ART, stress management, partner notification and legal rights for PLWHA. In addition, online information dissemination on HIV/AIDS, issues related to sex and sexuality, and relationships as well as tele-counselling are also undertaken by the counsellors. In each DIC, staff meetings are held weekly to review, plan and discuss about programme related activities. Apart from it, a group meeting of DIC staff and HIV positive clients and their family members is held in every month. These meetings serve as a platform for sharing each other's experience and prepare future planning. Such meetings are known as 'light house' in SPARSHA as it shows direction in time of darkness and depression. At the end of each financial year, a meeting involving all staff members is held at the head office, Kolkata. SPARSHA also provides subsidized ART to the poor children infected with HIV. The parents/guardians bear only 1/3rd of the cost of the medicines and remaining 2/3rd is contributed by SPARSHA from its core fund. The approach that SPARSHA adopted is to respect the PLWHA and recognize their rights like any other citizens of the country. In practice, the project focus on translating their approach through building a relationship of mutual trust and respect between PLWHA community and staff members of SPARSHA.

(d) Peoples' Participation

Beneficiaries participate in need identification through monthly group meetings of DIC, through FGD and sometimes through one to one individual discussion with the project staff members. Most of the beneficiaries are selected through referral services by the existing beneficiaries. It is like snow ball effect. Besides this, different government and private health centers/hospitals, staff members of SPARSHA, etc. refers beneficiaries. In SPARSHA, planning is done at the NGO level, but before finalizing the plan, beneficiaries' feedbacks are obtained through group meetings and FGDs held at DICs and considered seriously by the Governing Body. Beneficiaries do not contribute financially, but participate in the different programme activities of DICs run by SPARSHA. Beneficiaries ensure their involvement by attending the programmes, by providing physical infrastructure like sitting arrangements, providing tea for staff and resource persons during awareness camps, etc. Without their participation, it is impossible to implement the care and support programme of SPARSHA. Beneficiaries also take part in monitoring activities through interactions with DIC level staff as well as with the Programme Management Unit (PMU) of SPARSHA. They do not take part directly in evaluation, but extend support and take part in KABP and other study of WBSAP&CS.

Thus, beneficiaries' active participation is found in need identification, beneficiaries' selection, programme planning and its implementation, monitoring and evaluation.

Therefore, except financial resource contribution, the situation can be treated as full participation of the people and SPARSHA is truly a community based organization.

Peoples' participation is duly recognized by SPARSHA through giving them opportunity to express their needs, problems, etc. Fees are paid to them when they act as resource persons in different programmes of SPARSHA and other organizations. Above all, except few technical staff, majority of staff members (70% - 80%) are selected from among the PLWHA at all level including the Project Coordinator.

(e) Monitoring and Evaluation

SPARSHA is having Programme Management Unit (PMU) and Finance Management Unit (FMU) for monitoring and evaluation of care and support programme of WBSAP&CS. FMU is monitoring the financial aspects of each DIC. The secretary, PC and Accountant are the members of FMU. Similarly, the PMU is monitoring the programme activities of each DIC and CCC and it consists of Secretary, PC and other HIV positive persons. The Project Coordinator visits all DICs and CCC twice in a month to monitor the activities. The secretary visits each DIC once in a month, some times accompanied by the Vice-President, PC and Accountant. During their visit, they check the registers, bills, etc. maintained by the DICs. They also interact with clients in group meetings and also with different stakeholders to assess the need of the community to extend care components to the HIV infected/affected people. Besides this, FMU is also functioning in every DIC to monitor its financial activities of the concern DIC.

Apart from the internal monitoring and evaluation, WBSAP&CS time to time send its team to SPARSHA for the same purpose. Sometimes, such team from NACO, Delhi also visits to monitor and evaluate the project activities. Thus, it is found that regular monitoring and evaluation are done in HIV/AIDS Care and Support programme of SPARSHA.

(f) Sources of Funding

The STD/HIV/AIDS Targeted Intervention for Care and Support programme is running by SPARSHA since January 2004. The project is funded by WBSAP&CS annually and renewed every year. WBSAP&CS bears 90% of the project cost and remaining 10% by SPARSHA. But the fund is inadequate to run the different activities of SPARSHA. For example, there is no provision in the project for bearing the infrastructural and developmental cost. Besides this, the fund is too meagre to meet the demands of ART needed by the PLWHA. Though the Government is giving 1st line ART at free of cost, but there is nothing about 2nd line ART. The fund is also not sufficient for providing medicines for opportunistic infections (OIs). WBSAP&CS has no provision for funding the traveling expenses of the poor HIV positive people, who used to come from distant places to collect ART at the Government run ART centers. All these factors are preventing SPARSHA to expand its services to more number of PLWHA. Delay in releasing fund is another problem faced by SPARSHA. It has no alternative source for funding this project and SPARSHA is fully dependent on WBSAP&CS.

(g) Innovative Components

In the HIV/AIDS Care and Support programme of SPARSHA, few innovative components are found. These components are helpful in executing the project in a better way. Some of these components are: (1) a team of competent committed and dedicated staff and most of are selected from the people living with HIV. They are working more as missionaries than as salaried employees; (2) vocational training and formation of SHGs for helping the HIV infected/ affected women in order to make them economically independent; (3) linking of these SHGs with AASHA – its sister organization for marketing their products; (4) strong networking with different government and NGOs is instrumental for its successful advocacy programmes; (5) networking with pharmaceutical companies helps in providing ART at subsidized rate to the HIV infected children; (6) treatment preparedness initiatives to help the clients to cope up with the new ARV medicines; and (7) special emphasis on HIV infected/affected women and children.

(h) Local Cooperation

SPARSHA is getting active cooperation from all concerned starting from the local pathological laboratories, PHCs, Sub-Centres, Sub-Divisional Hospitals, Medical Colleges, Block Development Offices, Panchayats, etc. The Gram Panchayats exempt road taxes for the vehicles of SPARSHA. It has organized advocacy meetings at different Block Development Offices successfully with the support from the concern authorities. The project staff are getting necessary cooperation in executing the programme from all above mentioned agencies. Being a CBO, SPARSHA always receives more than required support from the PLWHA community, their family members and relatives. Thus, cooperation from local people is satisfactory.

It can be summarized from the above analysis that it is an integrated programme, not just merely a HIV/AIDS care and support programme. The basic approach of the programme is based on giving due respect to the people infected with or affected by HIV/AIDS; recognizing their basic human rights by reducing stigma and discrimination against them. Accordingly, activities are designed and implemented by SPARSHA with an ultimate objective of enabling and empowering PLWHA. It has touched the hearts of PLWHA through its empathetic approach and efforts. Except the financial resource contribution, people's participation is full-fledged in the programme under the study. It has got competent, committed and dedicated staff most of whom are HIV positive. However, the programme suffers from few bottlenecks like delay in receiving fund, inadequate funding provision for the treatment of opportunistic infections and no funding provision for traveling allowances to the poor people living with HIV who come from distant places to collect medicines from ART Centres of WBSAP&CS and so on. This programme of SPARSHA is fully dependent on WBSAP&CS for financial support. Hence, the programme is less sustainable.

Thus, this chapter attempts to discuss about the programme activities of six selected NGOs under the study. It is found that the programmes studied suffer from one or more problems. Some of the problems are common in all the programmes under the study. These problems are lack of timely disbursement of fund by WBSAP&CS, except STIs, no funding provision for the treatment of general health problems of target groups, no provision for meeting traveling expenditure of Peer Educators and People living with HIV, etc. In DMSC, MB and SPARSHA, people's participation is better than other three NGOs. One of the reasons for full people's participation is all the three above NGOs are CBOs or network of CBOs. Each programme has got some positive aspects and innovative components too. But, all the programmes are fully dependent on the funding agency i.e. WBSAP&CS. Therefore, all the programmes under the study are less sustainable and doubtful for their contribution in the someway in future.

8

Views of the Working Staff

The views of working staff are very important to understand the contribution of NGOs. This chapter has attempted to discuss about the views of staff members on different HIV/ AIDS related issues. In order to understand the staff's views, an interview schedule was used. The methodology chapter has given the details regarding the types of required data, sources of data, tools used for the collection of data and so on. In this regard, ten staff members from each selected NGO have been taken into consideration and views obtained from total sixty staff. A brief description of the profile of staff members and the views expressed by them are as follows.

Profile of Staff Members

(a) Sex of Staff Members

Table 8.1 gives an account for number of male and female staff members under six NGOs. Out of the purposively selected staff members, the numbers of males are found more as compared to females respectively in SCIR (80%), BPWT (70%) and MB (90%). On the other hand, numbers of female staff are more in DMSC (70%), HDRI (80%) and SPARSHA (60%). Similar trend is also found, if we consider the total staff strength of six NGOs under the study.

Table-8.1
Number of Male and Female Staff Members

Sl. No.	*Organization*	*Male*	*Female*	*Total*
1.	SCIR	8 (80%)	2 (20%)	10 (100%)
2.	DMSC	3 (30%)	7 (70%)	10 (100%)
3.	BPWT	7 (70%)	3 (30%)	10 (100%)
4.	MB	9 (90%)	1 (10%)	10 (100%)
5.	HDRI	2 (20%)	8 (80%)	10 (100%)
6.	SPARSHA	4 (40%)	6 (60%)	10 (100%)
	Total	33 (55%)	27 (45%)	60 (100%)

(b) Age of Staff Members

Table 8.2 shows that none of the NGOs is having staff, who are below 21 years. The age of maximum staff members is above 40 years in DMSC (70%) and SCIR (50%). While most of the staff members in BPWT (70%), MB (80%), HDRI (50%) and SPARSHA (50%) are aged between 21 years and 30 years. On the whole, out of 60 selected staff members, maximum (45%) belong to 21 years to 30 years category.

Table-8.2
Age of Staff Members

Sl. No	*Organisation*	*21years to30years*	*31years to 40years*	*41years & above*	*Total*
1.	SCIR	1 (10%)	4 (40%)	5 (50%)	10 (100%)
2.	DMSC	1 (10%)	2 (20%)	7 (70%)	10 (100%)
3.	BPWT	7 (70%)	2 (20%)	1 (10%)	10 (100%)
4.	MB	8 (80%)	1 (10%)	1 (10%)	10 (100%)
5.	HDRI	5 (50%)	5 (50%)	–	10 (100%)
6.	SPARSHA	5 (50%)	2 (20%)	3 (30%)	10 (100%)
	Total	27 (45%)	16 (26.7%)	17 (28.3%)	60 (100%)

Table-8.3
Educational Qualification of Staff Members

Sl. No.	*Organisation*	*Literate*	*Below SSC*	*SSC*	*HS*	*Graduate*	*Post Graduate*	*Total*
1.	SCIR	–	–	4 (40%)	3 (30%)	2 (20%)	1 (10%)	10 (100%)
2.	DMSC	5 (50%)	2 (20%)	1 (10%)	1 (10%)	–	1 (10%)	10 (100%)
3.	BPWT	–	–	–	–	7 (70%)	3 (30%)	10 (100%)
4.	MB	–	1 (10%)	–	1 (10%)	8 (80%)	–	10 (100%)
5.	HDRI	–	–	–	–	2 (20%)	8 (80%)	10 (100%)
6.	SPARSHA	1 (10%)	4 (40%)	2 (20%)	1 (10%)	2 (20%)	–	10 (100%)
	Total	6 (10%)	7 (11.7%)	7 (11.7%)	6 (10%)	21 (35%)	13(21.6%)	60 (100%)

(c) Qualification of Staff Members

Table 8.3 indicates that the staff members of DMSC (70%) and SPARSHA (50%) have less educational qualifications i.e. below SSC, while most of the staff members in MB (80%) and BPWT (70%) are graduates. In HDRI, maximum staff members (80%) are having post- graduate qualification. Out of the total 60 staff members under the study, more than fifty percent staff members are having graduate and above degree.

(d) Designation of Staff Members

It is evident from the Table 8.4 that 65 percent of the total sixty staff members under the study are field level workers i.e. Outreach Workers (51.7%) and Peer Educators (13.3%). Similarly, in each NGO between forty to eighty percent staff are field level workers and between twenty to sixty percent are middle level staff i.e. peer counselor, counselor, nurse and doctor.

View of the Staff Members

The staff members have expressed their views on different issues regarding (a) stigmatization, (b) ethical issues related to HIV/AIDS, (c) violation of human rights, (d) major barriers in implementing the programme, (e) major reason of spreading HIV/AIDS and (f) future AIDS scenario and role of NGOs. The views of staff members are being discussed NGO-wise qualitatively.

A. Society for Community Intervention and Research (SCIR)

Table-8.5 gives details of full-time paid staff of Kolkata IDU Project. Out of the total 30 staff members engaged in this Project of SCIR, 10 staff are purposively selected representing different levels of staff for the present study. Apart from the Project Coordinator (PC), five staff are selected

Table-8.4
Designations of Staff Members

Sl. No	*Designation*	*SCIR*	*DMSC*	*BPWT*	*MB*	*HDRI*	*SPARSHA*	*Total*
1.	PC	1 (10%)	–	1 (10%)	1 (10%)	1 (10%)	–	4 (6.7%)
2.	Doctor	–	–	1 (10%)	–	–	–	1 (1.7%)
3.	Nurse	1 (10%)	–	–	–	–	–	1 (1.7%)
4.	Counselor	1 (10%)	1 (10%)	1 (10%)	1 (10%)	2 (20%)	2 (20%)	8 (13.3%)
5.	Peer Counselor	–	1 (10%)	–	1 (10%)	1 (10%)	4 (40%)	7 (11.6%)
6.	ORWs	5 (50%)	3 (30%)	7 (70%)	6 (60%)	6 (60%)	4 (40%)	31 (51.7%)
7.	PEs	2 (20%)	5 (50%)	–	1 (10%)	–	–	8 (13.3%)
	Total	10 (100%)	10 (100%)	10(100%)	10(100%)	10(100%)	10(100%)	60(100%)

from Park Circus DIC and four from Goabagan DIC. By designation, there are five Outreach workers (ORWs), two Peer Educators (PEs), one Counsellor, One Peer Counsellor and one Project Coordinator. Out of these ten staff members, except the nurse, remaining nine are ex-IDUs.

Table-8.5
Characteristics of Full Time Paid Staff of Kolkata IDUs' Project

Sl. No.	*Designation*	*Nos.*	*Sex (M/F)*	*Qualification*
1.	Project Coordinator	2	M (1), F (1)	SSC, Graduate
2.	MIS Officer	1	F	Graduate
3.	Counsellor	4	M (1), F (3)	PG, Graduate& HS (2)
4.	Peer Counsellor	4	M (3), F (1)	HS, SSC (2) & VIII
5.	Nurse	3	F	SSC
6.	Outreach Workers	10	M (9), F (1)	Graduate, HS (4), SSC (4) & VIII
7.	Accountant	1	M	Graduate
8.	Asst. Accountant	1	M	Graduate
9.	Finance Administrator	1	M	PG
10.	Doctors*	2	M	MBBS
11.	Consultant#	1	M	PG
	TOTAL	30		

* *Part-Time; # Honorary*

(a) Stigmatisation

The entire staff members express that they are not affected by the HIV/AIDS related stigma. All of them are happy for working in this programme. They also inform that they would not change job or move to any non-HIV/AIDS projects, if they were given such offer with same salary. Because they are getting better job satisfaction by serving their own community members i.e. IDUs. The nurse is happy as she is serving these people who are neglected by the society. Their family members are aware about the nature of their jobs. They receive support and encouragement from their respective family members and friends. None of them have ever experienced that people are trying to avoid them after knowing their nature of job in the HIV/AIDS field; rather people want to know more about the disease. All of them have admitted that this job helped them get recognition and improve their social status. Therefore, the staff themselves are not stigmatized for working in the HIV/AIDS field. At the same time, they agree with the fact that due to fear of stigmatization, sometime even clients or their family members in spite of their awareness don't want to visit VCTC or such other organizations. These people are hidden in the society and are not coming under the targeted intervention project. Hence, the risk of spreading the HIV infection is very high. Most of the staff members have suggested that only mass awareness could reduce this fear of exposure and becoming a victim of social apathy. It is possible only through continuous effort by involving each and everybody. Few of them have also suggested that more counselling is required to motivate these people for blood testing.

(b) Ethical Issues

All of them are aware about the ethical guidelines related HIV/AIDS. But it is found that except the PC and Counsellor, their awareness is at superficial level. They are not well aware about the detailed guidelines except the issue of maintaining confidentiality about the client's HIV positive status and no discrimination against the HIV positive person. In SCIR, the doctor and counselor of the concern clinic can only know the

HIV positive status of the client. All the ten staff strictly follow and main confidentiality about case histories of their clients and never discuss it with their friends and family members. They are more careful because IDUs are doubly stigmatized for their drug-taking habits and for their vulnerability to HIV/AIDS.

(c) Violation of Human Rights

All staff members inform that they would protest and play the advocacy role if any incidence of human rights violation occurred or discriminatory practices done with PLWHA. Out of the ten staff, there is only one Project Coordinator (PC) who has narrated one such incidence. This is a case of depriving an HIV infected widow from her husband's property by her in-laws. Here, the PC played the advocacy role successfully. There are many incidences occurred where doctors and nurses refused to do the treatment of HIV positive people in the government run hospitals. On this issue, most of the staff felt that more training is required for the health personnel. While two of them feel that exemplary punishment should be given to such doctors/health personnel. Because one such incidence has far-reaching impact on the common people and all the awareness created earlier gone into wastage.

(d) Major Barriers Encountered

Regarding the major barriers encountered during the implementation of this project, most of the staff members agree with these three reasons namely, indifferent attitude of the people, fear of stigmatization and migratory nature of the IDUs. In addition to these, few of them feel that lack of shelter-home equipped with food, bathing facilities, etc. is another barrier. Because such shelter-home is very much essential for the environmental modification as well as for changing the behaviour of the recovering IDUs.

(e) Major Reasons of Spreading HIV/AIDS

Majority of the staff members have identified poverty, migration and ignorance as major causes responsible for spreading HIV/AIDS at a faster rate. Some of them have also pointed out that modern life-style (free mixing, etc.), effects of media (films, etc.) are also responsible factors.

(f) Future AIDS Scenario and Role of NGOs

Regarding the future scenario in relation to HIV/AIDS, four staff members feel that HIV/AIDS situation in India will be out of control. While remaining staff members feel that it would be within control if Government continues its effort by involving all other stakeholders. All of them also feel that NGOs would play the key role in the fight against this killer disease. Some of them have also suggested that Government should increase its coverage to include general population along with the vulnerable groups. Because, now the HIV infection is not restricted to high-risk groups, it spreads among all.

It is evident from the above analysis that staff members of SCIR under the study are not affected by HIV/AIDS related stigma. Majority of them are aware about the ethical issues related to HIV/AIDS and practice it always. They would definitely protest against the violation of human rights of PLWHA and have recommended more training for health personnel of government run hospitals to avoid such incidences in near future. Majority of them feel that fear of stigmatization, indifferent attitude of people and migratory nature of IDUs are the major problems that affecting the implementation of the programme. To them, ignorance, poverty and migration are the major reasons for spreading HIV/AIDS at a faster rate. Majority of them think that in future HIV/AIDS situation of our country will be within control, if government continues its present effort. All the staff members under the study feel that NGOs would continue its key role in the battle against the killer disease.

B. Durbar Mahila Samanwaya Committee (DMSC)

Table-8.6 shows the characteristics of full-time paid staff of Sonagachi Project for CSWs. Out of the total 121 staff members engaged in this Project of DMSC, 10 staff members representing different levels are purposively selected for the present study. Out of these 10 staff members, seven are selected from Avinash clinic and three from Rambagan clinic. By designation, there are two Outreach Workers (ORWs), five Peer Educators (PEs), one Counsellor, one Clinic Attendant and one Peer Counsellor. Five PEs, one ORW and one Counsellor are selected from Avinash clinic. Similarly, one Peer Counsellor, one ORW and the Clinic Attendant are selected from Rambagan clinic. Except the Counsellor, Clinic Attendant and one ORW, remaining seven staff members belong to sex workers' community.

Table 8.6
Characteristics of Full-Time Paid Staff of Sonagachi Project for CSWs

Sl. No.	*Designation*	*Nos.*	*Sex (M/F)*	*Qualification*
	1	*2*	*3*	*4*
1.	Project Director #	1	F	Graduate
2.	HR Officer	1	M	PG
3.	M & E Officer	1	M	PG
4.	Legal Adviser	1	M	LLB
5.	Finance Officer	1	M	Graduate
6.	STI Magt. Officer	1	M	MBBS
7.	Media Advo. Officer	1	M	PG

(Contd...)

1	*2*	*3*	*4*
8. Training Officer	1	M	PG
9. Accountant	3	M	Graduate
10. Office Asst.	2	M	Graduate
11. Project Coordinator	2	M	PG
12. Counsellor	10	M (4), F (6)	PG
13. Peer Counsellor	14	F	SSC (4), Literate (10)
14. Clinic Attendant	10	M	Graduate (6), HS (4)
15. Outreach Workers	45	F(44),M(1)	Graduate (5),HS(7),SSC(10), Literate (23)
16. Nurse	12	F	Diploma in Nursing
17. Doctors*	15	M (13), F (2)	MBBS
Total	121		

*# Honorary; * Part-Time*

(a) Stigmatisation

All the staff members express that they are happy in working with this HIV/AIDS intervention programme. All of them have said that they are not affected by the HIV/AIDS related stigma by nature of their jobs. But seven staff who are ex-CSWs, have said that they are affected by the social stigma related to sex workers. They also express that they would not like to change the present job or move to any non-HIV/AIDS projects. They would not even move to any HIV/AIDS project working for other target groups. Because they are getting better job satisfaction by serving their own community members i.e. sex workers' community. The

Counsellor, Clinic attendant and one ORW (who do not belong to sex workers' community) are happy as they are serving these people who are neglected and marginalized in the society. All of them informed that they receive support and encouragement from their respective family members and friends. None of them have ever experienced that people are trying to avoid them after knowing their nature of job in the HIV/AIDS field; rather people want to know more about the disease. All of them have admitted that this job helped them to get recognition and improve their social status. Therefore, the staff themselves are not stigmatized for working in the HIV/AIDS field. They also inform that sex workers are doubly stigmatized because of their profession and vulnerability to HIV/AIDS. Some sex workers simply avoid the clinics because they fear that they may be stigmatized and it will affect their earnings. Most of the staff members have suggested that this fear of exposure and becoming a victim of social apathy could be reduced only through mass awareness and continuous efforts of all.

(b) Ethical Issues

All of them are aware about the ethical guidelines related to HIV/AIDS. They are aware about the issue of maintaining confidentiality of the client's HIV positive status, informed consent of the person for blood testing and non-discriminatory practices against the HIV positive person. They have narrated one such incidence that took place in Sonagachi in 1994-95. One reputed NGO of Kolkata planned to conduct research on HIV prevalence among the sex workers without any consultation with the sex workers and utilized the services of local police. Sex workers protested and put a stop to this violation of ethics. In DMSC, the doctor and counselor of the concern clinic can only know the HIV positive status of the client. All the ten staff strictly follow and main confidentiality about case histories of their clients and never discuss it with other persons like their friends and family members. They are more careful because CSWs are doubly stigmatised for their profession and for their vulnerability to HIV/AIDS.

(c) Violation of Human Rights

All staff members would protest and take up the issue with appropriate authority if any incidence of human rights violation occurred or discriminatory practices done with PLWHA. They can go to any extent until justice is given to the victims. One of them narrates one such incidence that took place few years back in Sonagachi project. This is a case of a physician of dubious repute who claimed that he had invented a vaccine against HIV. This physician wanted to trial his vaccine among the sex workers of Sonagachi without any clearance from the Indian Council of Medical Research (ICMR). DMSC protested and successfully able to stop this so called vaccine trial. There are many incidences, where doctors and nurses have refused to do the treatment of HIV positive people in the government run hospitals. On this issue, most of the staff members feel that exemplary punishment should be given to such guilty doctors or other health personnel. Because one such incidence has far-reaching impact on the common people and will negatively affect the ongoing efforts to combat HIV/AIDS. But two of them feel that Government can open a separate Cell with specialized health personnel in every medical college to over come such problems.

(d) Major Barriers Encountered

The Sonagachi Project of DMSC is the oldest project for CSWs and is still functioning since 1992. Initially, DMSC has encountered so many problems in implementing this intervention project. Things were never smooth sailing. There is a vicious circle in every red light area like Sonagachi, controlled by vested interests, police-criminal-politician nexus. Here no one can live without negotiating with these elements. It is learnt from the experience that no headway could be made without negotiating with hoodlums and pimps who actually controlled the entire trade. There were resistances also from the *Malkins, Bariwalis, Babus* and even from the sex workers. Most of the sex workers were illiterate, ignorant and unorganized beset with factional and personal quarrels. All of them thought that this project would affect their earnings. It took long time for the project staff to convince them that the spread of AIDS may destroy their entire business. Gradually, the situation had been improved over a period of time as a result of the continued efforts of the staff members. Now most of these people are extending cooperation in implementing the project. All staff members inform that in recent times still there are two major barriers which affecting the implementation of this project. These two barriers are namely fear of stigmatization and migratory nature of street based or flying sex workers. Still many sex workers prefer private clinics instead of availing the services from DMSC run clinics at free of cost. Many sex workers also don't want to go for blood testing. Because they have the fear of stigmatization, which would ultimately affect their earnings by way of loosing customers. It is very difficult to work with flying sex workers, as they are not available regularly for intervention. In addition to these, few staff members feel that indifferent attitude of the people is another major barrier. Still social attitude towards sex workers and PLWHA are not positive. As a result of it, numbers of people are not approaching VCTC or such clinics.

(e) Major Reasons of Spreading HIV/AIDS

Majority of the staff feel that unsafe sex and contaminated blood are the major reasons of spreading HIV/AIDS at a faster rate. Still blood banks in West Bengal are not in a position to fulfill the demand and thereby compelling people to purchase blood, which may be contaminated. Besides these, two staff members are of the opinion that poverty, migration and ignorance are major causes responsible for spreading HIV/

AIDS at a faster rate. One of them also points out the modern life-style (free mixing, lack of parental control, etc.); effects of mass media (TV, films, etc.) as responsible factors.

(f) Future AIDS Scenario and Role of NGOs

Regarding the future scenario in relation to HIV/AIDS in our country, only two staff members feel that HIV/AIDS situation in our country will be out of control. While remaining staff members feel that it would be within control if Government continues its effort by involving all other stakeholders. They also feel that awareness about HIV/AIDS is increasing gradually among all section of people. There is no second opinion about the role of NGOs. All of them are of the opinion that NGOs would play a key role in the fight against this killer disease. Because NGOs are more effective than the government agencies and can reach out to any target group at any place. Some of them have also suggested that Government should increase the coverage to include general population under its intervention project. They are not agreeing with the fact that only high-risk groups are more vulnerable to HIV infection and to them everybody in the society is equally vulnerable.

It can be summarized from the above analysis that the staff members of DMSC under the study are not affected by the stigmatization because of their jobs, but seven staff (who are ex-CSWs) are affected by social stigma attached to sex workers. All of them are aware about the ethical issues related to HIV/AIDS and strictly follow them in practice. They would protest if any incidence of violation of human rights of PLWHA occurred and suggest exemplary punishment for the guilty health personnel to avoid the repetition of such incidences in future. Majority of them think that fear of stigmatization and migratory nature of street-based sex workers are the major barriers in implementing the project. Most of them are of the opinion that unsafe sex and contaminated blood are responsible for spreading HIV/AIDS at a faster rate. Majority of them are optimistic about the future AIDS scenario in our country and think it will be under control. There is no doubt among them regarding the major and effective role of NGOs in combating HIV/AIDS.

C. Bhoruka Public Welfare Trust (BPWT)

Table-8.7 highlights the detailed staff structure of BPWT's Truckers' Project. Out of the total 28 staff members engaged in this Project of BPWT, 10 staff representing different levels are purposively selected for the present study. It has already been mentioned in methodology chapter. Out of these 10 staff members, apart from the Project Coordinator (PC), six are selected from Bhutghat clinic and three from Dhobiatala clinic. By designation, there are seven Outreach workers (ORWs), one Counsellor, one Doctor and one PC. Out of the 7 ORWs, four are selected from Bhutghat clinic and three are from Dhobiatala clinic. Similarly, the Counsellor and Doctor are selected from Bhutghat clinic.

Table 8.7
Characteristics of Full Time Paid Staff of Truckers' Project

Sl. No.	*Designation*	*Nos.*	*Sex (M/F)*	*Qualification*
1.	Project Coordinator	2	M	PG, Graduate
2.	Counsellor	3	M (1), F (2)	PG
3.	Outreach Workers	16	M (9), F (7)	PG(5), Graduate (11)
4.	Accountant	2	M	Graduate
5.	Office Support Staff	2	M	Graduate
6.	Doctor *	3	M	MBBS
	Total	28		

* *Part-Time*

(a) Stigmatisation

All the staff members inform that the HIV/AIDS related stigma does not affect them. All of them have said that they are happy in working with this HIV/AIDS intervention programme. But they differ in terms of their reasons of happiness. Seven of them are of view that they are happy because of doing something good for the society, while others express about the challenging nature of the very job makes them happy. Majority of them said that they would not move to any non-HIV/AIDS project only because of stigma factor, if they were given any such opportunity. But, they could change the present job if they would have got better learning opportunities. All of them are of the opinion that their jobs don't involve any risk of getting HIV infection. The family members of all staff members are aware about their nature of job and always extend support to them. Therefore, majority of staff members themselves are not stigmatized.

At the same time, they agreed with the fact that in spite of all efforts made during last few years, still stigma is very much present in our society. Due to the fear of stigmatization, many well-informed people even do not want to visit the clinics or VCTC. Almost every staff member thinks that only mass awareness could reduce such fear. It is possible only through continuous effort from all. Few of them have also suggested that more counseling and sex education at school level could also play a vital role to reduce the social stigma attached with HIV/AIDS.

(b) Ethical Issues

All the staff members are aware about the ethical issues related to HIV/AIDS. But it is found that the knowledge is superficial among some of the field level staff. However, all of them are aware about these ethical issues like maintaining confidentiality about the patient's HIV-positive status, consent of the person before blood testing and no discrimination against the person on ground of his HIV positive status. The doctor and counselor of the concerned clinics can only know the information about the person's HIV positive status. All staff members inform that they strictly follow and maintain confidentiality about their clients. They even do not discuss it with their friends and family members. ORWs inform that even they maintain confidentiality with every client who attends the clinic. The doctor refers one such incidence of one truck driver who attended the clinic for treatment of STD; requested the doctor again and again for not disclosing it to his helper. Similarly peer educators and out reach workers inform that they take extra care in the field especially with those truckers who are not having any risk behaviour. These truckers are very reactive and are required to be dealt properly.

(c) Violation of Human Rights

In spite of the continuous awareness campaign, there are number of incidences when human rights of the HIV positive people are violated. Even today, doctors, nurse and other health personnel refuse to admit and offer treatment to the HIV positive people. On this issue, majority of the staff members feel that it is most unfortunate when such incidences occurred in the government hospitals. Only four staff members feel that only exemplary punishment of guilty health personnel can reduce such incidences. They have also justified their opinion with far reaching negative impact of one such incidence among the general people. While remaining staff members feel that more training is required for the health personnel. All the staff members inform that would always protest and play the advocacy role if such incidences occurred in front of them. The project coordinator informs that one such incidence of discrimination that occurred in KPT project when a truck driver lost his job because of his HIV status and it was successfully settled through advocacy. BPWT has a very good networking with different positive people's network in different districts of West Bengal being the Resource Centre for the network of PLWHA.

(d) Major Barriers Encountered

Majority of staff members admit that they have been encountering some problems in this truckers' intervention project. They mainly identify two problems namely migratory nature of the truckers and fear of stigmatization. Behaviour change is not possible through only one counseling session. It is very difficult to follow up the cases. Besides it, sometime truckers are not in a position to avail the counseling services for their preoccupations, fears, etc. Due to stigmatisation, even they are reluctant to visit doctors and thereby delay in treating STDs making them more vulnerable to HIV infection. The staff members also feel that inadequate fund is another problem. The salaries of the project staff have not increased and remain same over the years. In addition to this, except STD care and treatment, there is no fund from WBSAP&CS to address the general health problems of the target group. Four staff members feel that indifferent attitude of the people also sometime affect the smooth implementation of the project. Some truckers especially those without having any risk behaviour express their unhappiness for targeting them for HIV/AIDS. It is not easy to convince such kind of people.

(e) Major Reasons of Spreading HIV/AIDS

Most of the staff members are of the opinion that poverty, ignorance, migration and drug addiction/alcoholism are the major reasons of spreading HIV/AIDS at a faster rate in our country. So far truck drivers and helpers are concerned, all these factors make them more vulnerable. Their job compels them to stay away from their family for a long time and to get rid of this agony; many of them adopt high-risk behaviour like taking drugs, alcohol and other intoxicants; and visiting sex workers. Sometimes in spite of their awareness, they indulge in unsafe sex under the influence of intoxicants. In addition to these, two staff member blame the modern life style and consumerism that have destroyed the social and moral values. They feel that pre-marital sex, extra-marital affairs, sex with multiple partners, etc. are all bye-products of modern life style.

(f) Future AIDS Scenario and Role of NGOs

Six field level staff members think that the HIV/AIDS situation in our country will be out of control, if government did not change its policy. They feel that actual numbers of HIV infected people are much higher than the official figure. They also feel that unless economic conditions of the people are improved, AIDS will create havoc and destroy the nation. But remaining staff members are of the opinion that due to the efforts of Government, NGOs and other stakeholders, the situation will be under control. All the staff members also feel that the coverage of the project must be extended to include general population. Regarding the role of NGOs, all staff members strongly feel that in future NGOs will play a key role in controlling AIDS. They are always more effective than government agencies in reaching out grass root level target groups.

Having made the above analysis, it is found that none of the staff members of BPWT under the study are affected by HIV/AIDS related stigma. Most of the field level staff members are not well aware about the ethical issues related to HIV/AIDS. With regard to violation of human rights of PLWHA, none of them would tolerate such incidences if occurred in front of them and they have suggested training and exemplary punishment for guilty health personnel to avoid such incidences especially in government hospitals in future. They have encountered two major problems namely fear of stigmatization and migratory nature of truckers in implementing the programme. Majority of them feel that ignorance, poverty, migration and drug addiction are responsible for spreading HIV/AIDS. So far the future AIDS scenario is concerned, majority of them think that it would be out of control if government did not change its present policy. However, all of them agree that NGOs would play a key role in combating AIDS.

D. MANAS Bangla (MB)

Table-8.8 gives the characteristics of full-time paid staff of MSM Project. Out of the total 60 staff members engaged in this Project of MB, 10 staff members representing different levels are purposively selected for this study. Out of these 10 staff members, five each are selected from DumDum DIC and Kasba DIC. By designation, there are one Zonal Project Coordinator, one Counsellor (DIC in-charge), three Supervisors (ORWs), three Outreach Workers (ORWs), one Peer Counsellor and one Peer Educator. All the staff members except the Counsellor belong to MSM community.

Table-8.8
Characteristics of Full Time Paid Staff of MSM Project

Sl. No.	*Designation*	*Nos.*	*Sex (M/F)*	*Qualification*
	1	*2*	*3*	*4*
1.	Project Director	1	M	Graduate
2.	HR Officer	1	M	PG
3.	Document. Officer	1	M	PG
4.	BCC Officer	1	F	PG
5.	Finance Officer	1	M	PG
6.	STI Magt. Officer*	1	M	MBBS
7.	Medicinal Officer	1	M	Graduate
8.	Accountant	1	M	PG

(Contd...)

1	*2*	*3*	*4*
9. Office Asst.	1	M	Graduate
10. Zonal P C	4	M	SSC, Graduate
11. MIS Officer	9	M (8), F(1)	Graduate(6), PG(2),HS (1)
12. Counsellor	7	M	PG (4), Graduate (3)
13. Peer Counsellor	8	M	HS
14. Supervisor (ORW)	8	M	Graduate (4), HS (4)
15. Outreach Workers	7	M	Graduate(3), HS(3),SSC(1)
16. Doctors*	8	M	MBBS
Total	60		

* *Part-Time*

(a) Stigmatisation

All the selected staff members express that they are happy in working with this Sexual Health Promotion and HIV Control Programme for MSM. All of them inform that they are not affected by HIV/AIDS related stigma. But excepting the Counsellor, all of them are affected by MSM's sexual behaviour related stigma. Because, still it is neither socially approved nor legally accepted sexual behaviour in our country. Except the Counsellor, all of them express that even they would not like to work in any HIV/AIDS project meant for other target groups. Because, they are getting better job satisfaction by serving their own community members i.e. MSM population. The counselor informs that she feels more secure with these people and is happy with this project as she is serving these people who are marginalized group in the society. Their family members and friends are aware about their nature of jobs and receive full support and encouragement from them. But, at the same time, they reveal that initially family members were reluctant and discouraged them. Few staff inform that due to MSM related stigma, still their family members are not supportive. However, all of them inform that they do not tell about their nature of job to their relatives and neighbours because of this stigma. It is found that except the Counsellor, remaining nine staff members who belong to MSM community are not married. Therefore, it is quite doubtful that they properly inform about their nature of job to their parents, brothers or sisters. Five of them have experienced that people are trying to avoid them after knowing the nature of their jobs. Initially they felt bad and angry, but it is not against any particular person but against the prevailing social system that disapproves MSM's sexual behaviour and identity. All the staff members are of the opinion that their jobs do not involve any risk of getting HIV infections, but the working environment is risky as there are numbers of incidences of threat, harassment, humiliation, etc. from the local people, youth clubs, etc. Presently, the situation has been improved to some extent by the advocacy efforts of MB. All of them feel free in dealing with their clients because of their professional knowledge, skills, and rapport along with the advantage of belonging to the MSM community. Majority of staff members admit that their jobs helped to improve their social prestige and recognition, while three staff feel that they yet to receive such experiences. They also inform that MSM populations are doubly stigmatized because of their sexual behaviour and their vulnerability to HIV/AIDS. All of them agree with the fact that due to stigmatization many well informed clients or their family members do not want to visit the clinics. It is very difficult task to identify these hidden MSM populations. Hence, the risk of spreading HIV/AIDS through these people is very high. Most of the staff members have suggested that this problem can be reduced through mass awareness, introduction of sex education at schools, counseling for the clients and their family members, sensitization programme, etc. One of them suggests that policy makers will have to think about some new strategy to overcome such types of problems. After all life is precious than the stigma.

(b) Ethical Issues

Except two staff, all of them have said that they are aware about the ethical guidelines related to PLWHA. However, all of them are aware about the issue of maintaining confidentiality of the client's HIV positive status, informed consent of the person before blood testing and non-discriminatory practices against the PLWHA, etc. In MB, except the doctor and counselor of the concern DIC and ZPC, other staff members are not in a position to know about the HIV positive status of the client. All of them strictly follow and maintain confidentiality about case histories of their clients and never discuss it with other persons like their friends and family members. Being a member of the MSM community, most of the staff members used to take extra precaution in this regard. They are more careful because MSM people are doubly stigmatized for their sexual behaviour and for their vulnerability to HIV/AIDS.

(c) Violation of Human Rights

All the staff members are of the opinion that they would protest and take up the issue with appropriate authority if any incidence of human rights violation occurred or discriminatory practices done with PLWHA. They can go to any extent until justice is given to the victims. One Outreach worker has narrated one such incidence that took place one year back. One doctor misbehaved with one of the patients in School of Tropical Medicine (ART distribution centre). Immediately, the concern ORW protested and lastly the doctor accepted his fault. In recent times, there are many incidences, where doctors and nurses had refused to admit or provide the treatment to HIV positive people in the government run hospitals and medical colleges. On this issue, most of the staff feel that exemplary punishment should be given to such guilty doctors or other health personnel. Because one such incidence has far reaching impact on the common people and will destroy all the ongoing efforts to prevent and control HIV/AIDS through awareness. At the same time, most of the staff prescribe more training for the medical and para-medical staff. One of the Supervisors feels that the Network of PLWHA will have to play more effective role to reduce and avoid such unfortunate incidences. Another Supervisor feels that government should open specialized AIDS Cell equipped with suitable infrastructure and manpower in every medical college of West Bengal. Thus, it is found that staff members of MB are too much sensitive about the human rights of PLWHA.

(d) Major Barriers Encountered

The MSM Project of MB has been functioning since July 2004. Initially, MB encountered so many problems in implementing this intervention project because of the prevailing social attitude towards MSM and their sexual behaviour. Things were never smooth sailing. Landlords were not willing to rent their houses for the office or DIC purpose. Sometimes, landlord agreed but neighbours protested. The present Project Office of MB has faced same problem, but it is settled with the landlord's active support. Besides these problems, field level working environments were risky for the project staff. With the continuous efforts of MB, these problems have been reduced to some extent. In recent times too, project staff are facing different types of problems. All the staff members unanimously inform about three major problems that are affecting the implementation of the project. These are indifferent attitude of the people, fear of stigmatization and ignorance about sexual health, STD, HIV,

AIDS, etc. In addition to these problems, few staff members are of the opinion that inadequate finance and delay in disbursement of funds; migratory nature of clients and previous bitter experience of harassment, discrimination, etc. are also affecting the implementation of the project. Four staff members feel that it is very difficult to locate and identify the MSM clients for whom this project is going on. According to Zonal Project Coordinator, political non-cooperation, threat and harassment by the local people, youth clubs etc. are still going on. He has narrated one such incidence where one of the project staff was beaten up and his belongings are snatched by some unidentified youth while he was working with a client in one of the parks in Kolkata.

Thus, it is understood that prevailing social attitude towards MSM is one of the major barriers encountered in the implementation of the project. However, in spite of all these difficulties, MB is running this project with the help of its committed staff and strong networking and advocacy services.

(e) Major Reasons of Spreading HIV/AIDS

Majority of the staff feel that ignorance, migration and drug addiction are major reasons responsible for spreading HIV/AIDS at a faster rate in our country. Few of the staff members feel that modern life style of the present generation youth without having any parental or social control is also responsible for spreading HIV/AIDS, as these youth are having multiple sex partners. Besides these, two staff members are of the opinion that media is not playing its role properly. For example, through the different soaps and serials broadcasted in TV channels, a tendency of having multiple sex partners is developing gradually among the people. Regarding HIV/AIDS also, media never say that HIV/AIDS can also be spread through anal sex. This is most unfortunate part that NACO also continuing with the same instead of giving correct information to the people.

(f) Future AIDS Scenario and Role of NGOs

Regarding the future scenario in relation to HIV/AIDS in our country, all staff members are optimistic and feel that HIV/AIDS situation in our country will be within control and will become a manageable problem only. But it will be possible if Government continues its effort by involving all other stakeholders in its fight against this killer disease. There is no second opinion about the role of NGOs. All of them are of the opinion that NGOs would play a vital role in future too because of their efficiency and capabilities. The staff members have suggested few effective measures for preventing and controlling HIV/AIDS in our country. Some of these are: (i) to include more vulnerable groups like *Hijras*, etc. under the targeted intervention project; (ii) to involve more NGOs to expand the coverage of the project; (iii) to improve and increase the care and support services like supply of second line ART; (iv) to make arrangement for updating staff' technical knowledge and increase their salary to boost up the morale of the field staff especially; (v) to introduce sex education at the school level; (vi) to increase the number of VCTC, ART Centres, etc; (vii) to frame effective BCC strategies; and (ix) to include 'anal sex' as one of the sources of HIV transmission in all the media campaign of NACO, WBSAP&CS and other such organizations.

It can be summarized from the above analysis that staff members of MB under the study are not affected by HIV/AIDS related stigma, but affected by prevailing MSM related social stigma. Majority of them are aware about the ethical issues related to HIV/AIDS and practice them always. They would definitely protest against the violation of human rights of PLWHA and have recommended exemplary punishment for the guilty health personnel of government run hospitals to avoid such incidences in near future. Majority of them feel that ignorance, fear of stigmatization, indifferent attitude of people towards MSM community are the major problems that affecting the implementation of the programme. To them, ignorance, drug addiction and migration are the major reasons for spreading HIV/AIDS at a faster rate. Majority of them are optimistic and think that in future HIV/AIDS situation of our country will be within control, if government continues its present effort. All the staff members under the study feel that NGOs would play a more effective role in the battle against the killer disease.

E. Human Development Research Institute (HDRI)

Table-8.9 shows the characteristics of Migrated Laborers Project. Out of the total 26 staff members engaged in this Project of HDRI, 10 staff members representing different levels are purposively selected for the present study. It has already been mentioned in methodology chapter. Apart from the Project Coordinator (PC), five staff are selected from Posta clinic, three from Burrabazar clinic and one from Mechua clinic. By designation, there are seven Outreach workers (ORWs), two Counsellors and one PC. Out of the 7 ORWs, four are selected from Posta clinics and three are from Burrabazar clinic. Similarly, two Counsellors are selected from Posta clinic and Mechua clinic respectively.

Table-8.9
Characteristics of Full Time Paid Staff of Migrated Labourers' Project

Sl. No.	*Designation*	*Nos.*	*Sex (M/F)*	*Qualification*
1.	Project Coordinator	2	F	PG
2.	Counsellor	4	M (1), F (3)	PG
3.	Outreach Workers	14	M (9), F (5	PG(5),Graduate (7),HS (2)
4.	Accountant	2	M	Graduate
5.	Doctors*	4	M	MBBS
	Total	26		

* *Part-Time*

(a) Stigmatisation

All the staff members express that they are not affected by the HIV/AIDS related stigma by virtue of their involvement in this project. Majority of them inform that if they got an opportunity with same salary, they would not like to move and join any non-HIV/AIDS project. Few of them express that they will definitely accept better and interesting job offer, but it is nothing to do with HIV/AIDS field. They also feel that they are happy in working with this project for migrated labour. Some of them inform that they are getting better job satisfaction, as the nature of job is very challenging. All of them feel free to deal with their clients because of the training they have received in this regard. Except one, all staff members inform that their family members are aware about their nature of job and always receive support from them. The only staff member who has not informed his family members about his job says that he can't tell them that condom promotion is also part of his job. None of them have ever experienced that people are trying to avoid them after knowing their nature of job in the HIV/AIDS field. All of them are of the opinion that their jobs helped them to get recognition and improve their self-image. Therefore, the staff themselves are not stigmatized for being associated with HIV/AIDS intervention project for migrated labour. But at the same time all of them agree that due to fear of exposure and stigmatisation, many people don't want to visit clinics or VCTC. The Project Coordinator feels that the risk of spreading HIV/AIDS through such people is very high. Some of them have suggested that through more awareness and counseling such people can be motivated to visit clinics for treatment and blood tests. But two of the staff members blame few health staff of VCTC for breaking the confidentiality of client's HIV positive status. However, all staff members feel that though the situation has improved, but still lots to be done to remove HIV/AIDS related stigma from the society.

(b) Ethical Issues

Except one staff, all the staff members inform that they are aware about the ethical guidelines related to HIV/AIDS. All of them are aware about the issue of maintaining confidentiality about the client's HIV positive status, non-discriminatory practices against the HIV positive people, informed-consent of the person concern before blood testing, etc. The only staff member, who does not know about the ethical guidelines, has joined recently and so far not attended any training programme. Except one Outreach Worker, all other staff members don't share the case histories of their clients with their friends and family members. The concern Outreach worker says that he shares case histories without disclosing the client's identity with a view to make others aware about the issue for changing their attitudes towards HIV/AIDS related stigma. All of them always maintain confidentiality about the problems of their clients. The Project coordinator feels sometimes it is required to reveal the HIV positive status of the client for his betterment only. He has cited the example of arranging ART where the client's HIV positive status must be revealed to the doctor concerned. In HDRI, generally the HIV positive status of the client is restricted to the doctor, counselor and sometimes to the Project Coordinator.

(c) Violation of Human Rights

All staff members inform that they have not witnessed personally any incidence of human rights violation of PLWHA during their service life. But in reply of their reactions towards such incidences, five of the staff members told that they would protest and play the advocacy role in this regard. The remaining five staff members are of the opinion that they will take up the issue with appropriate authority, if any incidence of human rights violation occurred or discriminatory practices done with PLWHA. There are many incidences, where doctors or other health personnel had refused to admit or provide treatment to the HIV positive people in the government run hospitals or medical colleges. On this issue, surprisingly most of the staff do not express their views or opinions. Only two staff express their views in this regard. One of them feels that the guilty doctors will be punished severely by canceling their registration, while the other staff talks about the need for more training for the health personnel.

(d) Major Barriers Encountered

This HIV/AIDS intervention project for ML has been running by HDRI since 1997. Initially, things were not smooth sailing. The resistance was faced from the Merchants' Association and the migrated labourers mostly work under the different merchants of this Association. The Association at the beginning wrongly perceived that through this project, migrated labourers will be more right conscious and may create troubles for them through organized movements. Besides this, HDRI encountered many problems even from among the migrated labourers' community and their trade unions. It took long time and through continuous efforts of the project staff, HDRI able to convince them that the spread of HIV/AIDS may affect all and destroy the entire business. Gradually, the situation has been improved over a period a time. Now most of these people are extending cooperation in implementing the project.

Presently, most of the staff members inform that there are three major barriers which affecting the implementation of the project. These barriers are: (1) indifferent attitude of the people; (2) fear of stigmatization; and (3) ignorance of the people. Most of these migrated labourers are coming from rural and backward areas in search of earning their livelihood. Most of them are illiterate and totally ignorant about the HIV/AIDS. At the same time after becoming aware about the HIV/AIDS, they become too much worried. Besides this, the prevailing social attitude towards these migrated labourers and their occupations are not also good. These indifferent attitudes of the people thus become another barrier in implementing this project. As a result of these, many of them are not willing to visit the clinics for treatment or health check up. In addition to these three barriers, three staff members feel that migratory nature of the clients is another problem affecting the project. Many migrated labourers used to visit their native places during cultivation and crop harvesting seasons and not available for few months. Therefore, it is not possible to follow up these people and thereby affecting the smooth implementation of the project.

(e) Major Reasons of Spreading HIV/AIDS

Most of the staff members feel ignorance, migration and drug addiction are the major reasons for spreading HIV/AIDS at a faster rate. In addition to these reasons, few staff members are of the opinion that modern life style, poverty, effects of media especially about the free mixing, extra-marital relations, etc are also responsible for spreading HIV/AIDS. Interestingly, one staff points out that rape or forced sex is also responsible for spreading HIV/AIDS. However, the Project Coordinator feels that migration is the only reason responsible for spreading HIV/AIDS quickly in our society.

(f) Future AIDS Scenario and Role of NGOs

In relation to future HIV/AIDS scenario in our country, only two staff members feel that HIV/AIDS situation in our country will within control if Government and all other stakeholders continue their efforts in this regard. They also feel that gradually social attitude towards the PLWHA will be changed and stigma will be reduced. Surprisingly, the remaining eight staff members including the Counsellors don't express their views on this issue. However, all of them are of the opinion that NGOs would play a key role in the prevention and control of this killer disease. Because all of them feel that NGOs can reach to the grass root level and can work with any target group, which is not possible for any government agency. Besides this, services provided by the NGOs are better than government organizations in terms of quality and cost.

In brief, it is found that the staff members of HDRI under the study are not stigmatized and would not change their jobs for HIV/AIDS related stigma, but for better opportunities only. Majority of them are aware about the ethical issues related to HIV/AIDS and practice them always. With regard to the violation of human rights of PLWHA, they inform that they would protest against such incidences. But surprisingly, most of them do not express their views on the incidences of human rights violation and denial of treatment of HIV positive people in the hospitals and medical colleges run by the Government. They have encountered ignorance, fear of stigmatization and indifferent attitude of people as the major barriers in implementing the project. To them, ignorance, migration and drug addiction are the major reasons for spreading HIV/AIDS at a faster rate. Surprisingly, majority of them do not comment on the future HIV/AIDS scenario in India. However, they all are agreed with the fact that NGOs would continue to be the key player in controlling HIV/AIDS in future too.

F. Society for Positive Atmosphere and Related Support to HIV/AIDS (SPARSHA)

Table-8.10 highlights the characteristics of full-time paid staff of HIV/AIDS care and support programme. Out of the total 30 staff members engaged in this Project of SPARAHA, 10 staff members are purposively selected representing different levels for the present study. Out of these 10 staff members, four staff are selected from Kestopur DIC and three each from Uluberia DIC and Sonakhali DIC. By designation, there are two Counsellors (DIC in-charge), four Outreach Workers (ORWs) and four Community Based Peer Counsellor (CBPC). All the staff members except one are HIV positive and five of them are 'AIDS widow'.

Table 8.10
Characteristics of Full Time Paid Staff of HIV/AIDS Care Programme

Sl. No.	*Designation*	*Nos.*	*Sex (M/F)*	*Qualification*
1.	Project Coordinator	1	M	Graduate
2.	Counsellor	4	M (1), F (3)	PG, Graduate (2), School level(1)
3.	CBPC	9	M (2), F (7)	Graduate (1), School level (8)
4.	Outreach Workers	8	M (3), F (5)	PG (5), Graduate (1), HS (2)
5.	Accountant	1	M	PG
6.	Nurse	2	F	Graduate
7.	Ward Girl	2	F	School level
8.	Office Staff	1	M	Graduate
9.	Doctor*	1	M	MD
10.	Consultant #	1	M	MD
	Total	30		

* *Part-Time; # Honorary.*

(a) Stigmatisation

All the selected staff members express that they are happy in working with this HIV/AIDS Care and Support Programme. Because they have got an opportunity to serve some other unfortunate people like them and don't want to see them suffer like themselves. All of them inform that they are not affected by HIV/AIDS related stigma by nature of their job, but nine of them affected because of their own HIV positive status. Because, HIV positive people still are the victims of discrimination and stigmatization in the society. However, none of them would like to change the present job or move to any non – HIV/AIDS projects as they are getting better job satisfaction by serving their own community members i.e. PLWHA. The only HIV negative staff is happy with this project as he is serving these people who are marginalized group in the society and victim of social apathy. Majority of staff members' family members and friends are aware about the nature of their jobs, and receive full support and encouragement from them. But, at the same time, they reveal that initially family members were reluctant and discouraged them. Two staff inform that due to HIV/AIDS related stigma, their family members are not aware about their nature of job as well as their HIV positive status, as they don't want to put them in an embarrassing situation. However, all of them inform that they have not told about their nature of job to their relatives and neighbours because of this stigma. Out of the ten staff, there are three males and seven female staff. Out of the female staff, five are 'AIDS widow' and remaining two are unmarried because of their HIV positive status. It is found that all the three male staff are married including the HIV negative staff. Two male HIV positive staff members inform that their wives are also aware about their HIV positive status. Two of them have experienced that people are trying to avoid them after knowing the nature of their jobs. Initially they felt bad and angry, but it is not against any particular person but against the prevailing social system and because of their ignorance. But majority of them admit that the working environment is risky as there are numbers of incidences of threat, harassment, humiliation, etc. from the local people, neighbours, health personnel, etc. Presently, the situation has been improved to some extent by the advocacy efforts of SPARSHA, but not too much. All of them feel free in dealing with their clients because of their professional knowledge, skills, and rapport along with the advantage of their own personal experiences. Majority of staff members admit that their job has helped to improve their social prestige and recognition to some extent. Therefore, staff members themselves are not stigmatized for working in the HIV/AIDS project. All of them agree with the fact that due to fears of exposure and stigmatization, many well informed clients or their family members do not want to visit the clinics, DICs or such other organizations. Hence, the risk of spreading HIV/AIDS through these people is very high. Most of the staff members suggested that this problem can be reduced through mass awareness, community sensitization programme, introduction of sex education at schools, counseling for the clients and their family members, etc. One of them suggests that policy makers will have to think about some new strategy to overcome such types of problems.

(b) Ethical Issues

All the staff members are aware about the ethical guidelines related to PLWHA. It is found that all of them are aware about the issue of maintaining confidentiality of the client's HIV positive status, informed consent of the person before blood testing and non-discriminatory practices against the PLWHA, partner notification, etc. In SPARSHA, except the doctor and counselor of the concern DIC and PC, other staff members are not in a position to know about the HIV positive status of the clients. All them strictly follow and maintain confidentiality about case histories of their clients and never discuss it with other persons like their friends and family members. Being the HIV positive person, most of the staff members used to take extra-precaution in this regard. They are more careful because HIV infected and /or affected people are more vulnerable to stigma and discriminations.

The Counsellor of Sonakhali DIC recalls one such incidence. The DIC invited the Block Development Officer (BDO) of the concern Block in one of its community awareness programme, where the BDO openly refused to take tea offered by one of the DIC staff. The BDO also urged the community people to identify HIV positive people and isolate them from the locality for saving other people from infection. Later on, SPARSHA head office has made advocacy and able to settle the matter.

(c) Violation of Human Rights

All the staff members are of the opinion that they would protest and take up the issue with appropriate authority if any incidence of human rights violation occurred or discriminatory practices done with PLWHA. They can go to any extent until justice is given to the victims. One Outreach worker has narrated one such incidence that took place one year back. One doctor of a Sub-Divisional hospital in Howrah district marked HIV status of the patient in red ink and refused to admit him on the ground of other patients' safety. The staff members of SPARSHA protested and took up the matter with the concern Chief Medical Officer of Health (CMOH). Lastly the doctor accepted his fault, but no action was taken against him. The Counsellor of Sonakhali DIC informs that still the VCTC of Midnapore Medical College and Hospital is operating from only one room. There is no separate room for counseling and naturally it is not possible always to maintain the confidentiality of HIV positive persons. It is most unfortunate, because this is happening in a Medical College. In recent times, there are many incidences, where doctors and nurses refused to admit or provide the treatment to HIV positive people in the hospitals and medical colleges run by the government. On this issue, most of the staff members feel that exemplary punishment should be given to such guilty doctors or other health personnel. Because one such incidence has far reaching impact on the common people. At the same time, such incidences increase the sufferings of the concern HIV infected persons and their family members. Most of the staff also prescribe more training for the medical and para-medical staff; special AIDS Cell/Ward for PLWHA and recruit HIV positive persons as a staff in such Special Cell/Ward. At the same time, majority of them feel that the Network of PLWHA will have to play more effective role to reduce and avoid such unfortunate incidences. Thus, it is found that staff members of SPARSHA are too much sensitive about the human rights of PLWHA.

(d) Major Barriers Encountered

The HIV/AIDS Care and Support Programme of SPARSHA has been functioning since January 2004. Initially, SPARSHA encountered so many problems in implementing this intervention project because of the prevailing social attitude and stigma towards PLWHA and their family members. Things were never smooth sailing. Landlords were not willing to rent their houses for the office or DIC purpose. Sometimes, landlord agreed but neighbours protested. The present Project Office of SPARSHA has been facing some problem and will be shifting its office very soon. Besides these problems, field level working environments are risky for the project staff. With the continuous efforts of SPARSHA, these problems have been reduced to some extent. In recent times too, project staff are facing different types of problems. All the staff unanimously inform that five major problems that are affecting the implementation of the project. These are indifferent attitude of the people, fear of stigmatization, inadequate fund, migration and ignorance about sexual health, STD, HIV, AIDS, etc. In the Sonakhali DIC areas of Paschim Medinipur district, many people are working as goldsmith and migrated to Mumbai, Surat, Ahmedabad and other big cities for better income. Many of them has contracted HIV from these cities and subsequently infected their spouses in their respective native places. Thus, HIV spreads from cities to villages. Similarly, many people migrated to UP, Gujarat, Rajasthan, and other states from the areas under Uluberia DIC of Howrah district. These people are working as *zari* workers (silver and golden coloured thread work on *sarees* and some of them infected with HIV and later on infected their spouses residing in their respective native villages. Majority staff members complain about the discriminatory and non-cooperative attitude of the health personnel of government run hospitals. In addition to these problems, few staff members are of the opinion that inadequate finance especially for care and support with ART medicines and nutritious foods clubbed with delay in disbursement of funds has been affecting severely the implementation of the project. Previous bitter experiences of harassment, discrimination, etc. are also affecting the implementation of the project. Most staff members feel that it is very difficult to locate and identify the HIV clients for whom this project is going on. Because of the fear of stigmatization and social boycott, these people are not coming out for testing and treatment. HIV infected women are the worst sufferer as they are thrown out from their in-law's house as well as from parent's house. In most of the cases, they are blamed for the infection of their husbands. According to the Counsellor of Sonakhali DIC, political non-cooperation, threat and harassment by the local people, youth clubs etc. are still going on in different parts of the state.

Thus, it is understood that prevailing social attitude towards PLWHA is one of the major barriers encountered in the implementation of the project. However, in spite of all these difficulties, SPARSHA is running this project with the help of its committed staff and strong networking and advocacy services.

(e) Major Reasons of Spreading HIV/AIDS

Majority of the staff feel that ignorance, poverty, migration and drug addiction are the major reasons for spreading HIV/AIDS at a faster rate in our country. Few of the staff members feel that modern life style of the present generation youth without having any parental or social control is also responsible for spreading HIV/AIDS. Two ORWs also feel that poor health infrastructure of the government hospitals and poor work culture among the staff sometimes causes infection of HIV. There are many such incidences where hemophilia patients infected with the HIV simply because of the negligence of health staff. Besides these, few staff members are also of the opinion that media is not playing its role properly. For example, through films, different soaps and serials of TV channels, a tendency of having extra marital affairs, multiple sex partners, etc are developing gradually among the people. Regarding HIV/AIDS also, media mainly highlights unsafe sex as if the only source of HIV infection/transmission. But infection through contaminated blood could not be ignored, as Government and licensed private blood banks are still not capable of meeting the blood requirements in our country. Therefore, people are forced to use contaminated blood.

(f) Future AIDS Scenario and Role of NGOs

Regarding the future scenario in relation to HIV/AIDS in our country, majority staff members are pessimistic and feel that HIV/AIDS situation in our country will be out of control unless NACO changes its existing National AIDS Control Policy. The situation will be worst if vaccines are not invented in near future. But it will be possible if Government continues its effort by involving all other stakeholders in its fight against this killer disease. They also feel that awareness about HIV/AIDS is increasing gradually among all section of people. There is no second opinion about the importance of NGOs. All of them are of the opinion that NGOs would play a key role in future too because of their efficiency and networking capabilities. The staff members have suggested few effective measures for preventing and controlling HIV/

AIDS in our country. Some of these are: (i) to include more vulnerable groups like TB patients, hemophilia and thalassemia patients etc. under the targeted intervention project; (ii) to improve and increase the care and support services like supply of second line ART; (iii) to increase the number of VCTC, ART Centres, etc.; (iv) to involve more NGOs to expand the coverage of the project; (v) to introduce sex education at the school level; (vi) to make arrangement for updating staff' technical knowledge and increase their salary to boost up the morale of the field staff especially; (vii) to provide more fund for purchasing medicines for Opportunistic Infections; (viii) to provide financial assistance for paying conveyance to PLWHA for reaching the treatment centers, so that they can avail ART regularly; (ix) to introduce HIV treatment facilities at the doorsteps like at PHCs, Sub-health Centres, etc.; and (x) to involve HIV positive people in the care and support programmes for PLWHA.

It is evident from the above discussion that the staff members of SPARSHA under the study are affected by the HIV/AIDS related stigma not because of the nature of their jobs, but because of their HIV positive status. All of them are aware about the ethical issues related to HIV/AIDS and strictly follow them always in practice. They would protest if any incidence of violation of human rights of PLWHA would have occurred and have suggested exemplary punishment for the guilty health personnel of government hospitals to avoid the repetition of such incidences in future. Majority of them think that ignorance, migration, fear of exposure and stigmatization and inadequate fund are the major barriers in implementing the programme. Most of them are of the opinion that ignorance, poverty, migration and drug addiction are mainly responsible for spreading HIV/AIDS at a faster rate. Majority of them think that HIV/AIDS situation in our country will be out of control unless government changes its present policy. There is no doubt among them regarding the major and effective role of NGOs in combating HIV/AIDS in future too.

Thus, this chapter has highlighted the views of selected staff members of six NGOs under the study on different issues related to HIV/AIDS. It is found that no staff members of six NGOs are affected by HIV/AIDS related stigma because of the nature of their jobs. But staff members of DMSC, MB and SPARSHA are affected by prevailing social stigma related to CSWs, MSM and PLWHA respectively. It is to be noted that most of the staff members of these three organizations are selected from the respective target groups. But, SCIR is exception in this context because SCIR also selected most its staff from among the target group (IDUs). However, staff members of all the six NGOs have admitted the existence of HIV/AIDS related stigma in the society and have suggested mass awareness programmes, counseling, sex education at school, etc. to reduce it.

Majority of the selected staff members of six NGOs are aware about the ethical issues related to HIV/AIDS and always practice them. With regard to the violation of human rights of PLWHA, all staff members have said that they would protest against such incidences. On the issue of preventing such incidences occurred in government run hospitals, staff members of DMSC, MB, SPARSHA have suggested exemplary punishment for the guilty health personnel; staff of SCIR suggested more training and staff of BPWT suggested more training along with the punishment for the culprits. Surprisingly, majority of staff members of HDRI has not made any comments.

With regard to the major barriers encountered in implementing the project, selected staff members of all the NGOs have talked about ignorance, fear of exposure and stigmatisation, indifferent attitude of the people towards AIDS, migration and drug addiction. Staff members of six

NGOs differ in terms of their opinions on the major reasons for spreading HIV/AIDS at a faster rate. However, they have identified that ignorance, poverty, migration, drug addiction, unsafe sex are the major reasons responsible for spreading HIV/AIDS. Most of the staff members of SCIR, DMSC and MB are optimistic about the future AIDS scenario in our country. They think that the situation would be under control, if government continues its effort by involving all stakeholders. But staff members of BPWT and SPARSHA think that situation will be out of control, if government did not change its policy. Surprisingly, majority of staff members of HDRI have not expressed their views in this regard. However, all staff members of the six NGOs are of the opinion that NGOs would play a key and more effective role in combating HIV/AIDS in future too.

9

Perception of the Beneficiaries

Perception refers to the way of seeing or awareness/ understanding of beneficiaries towards the working of NGOs. Since the NGOs under study are engaged in HIV/AIDS care and their main thrust is to prevent and control the HIV infection and spread of AIDS, perception of beneficiaries is our centre of attention. In this context, two groups of beneficiaries from each selected NGO have been considered except SPARSHA. Only one group of beneficiaries (PLWHA) is formed with the permission of SPARSHA. Normally, it does not allow outsiders to interact directly with PLWHA, but they have considered the researcher for academic purpose only.

In order to understand the beneficiaries' perceptions, data collected from each group of beneficiaries are being discussed below NGO-wise separately. For understanding the perceptions of beneficiaries better, the discussion covers (a) necessity of NGO's HIV/AIDS programme, (b) cost and quality of NGO's services, (c) staff cooperation and (d) scope of beneficiaries' participation. A brief conclusion regarding the perception has been drawn at the end of discussion under each group. Table-9.1 shows the profile of the beneficiaries.

Table-9.1
Profile of the Beneficiaries' Groups

Sl. No.	Name of the NGO	Types of Target Group	Name of DIC/Clinic	No. of Members	
				Male	Female
1.	SCIR	IDUs	Park Circus DIC	11	-
			Goabagan DIC	12	3
2.	DMSC	CSWs	Avinash Clinic	-	12
			Rambagan Clinic	-	10
3.	BPWT	Truckers	Bhutghat Clinic	9	-
			Dhobiatola Clinic	8	-
4.	MANAS Bangla	MSM	DumDum DIC	10	-
			Kasba DIC	8	-
5.	HDRI	Migrated Labours	Posta Clinic	10	-
			Mechua Clinic	9	-
6.	SPARSHA	PLWHA	Kestopur DIC	10	6
			Total	87	31

A. Society for Community Intervention and Research (SCIR)

Group-1

It is formed with 11 male members at Park Circus DIC. The members belong to different background. The age group varies from 20 years to 57 years. All of them attending Day Care Centre regularly. Five of them are attached with SCIR since inception (1999).

(a) Necessity of NGO's HIV/AIDS Programme

Beneficiaries inform that before the starting of SCIR, there was nothing to look after the health conditions of IDUs in this region particularly. The present SCIR office is located in the slum and is near Gobra Railway station. Slum dwellers are residing both sides of the railway track. The present area was full of jungle and was a safe den for anti-socials and drug addicts especially after the evening. Now after the starting of SCIR's clinic, the IDUs and local people are getting the treatment and medicines from the qualified doctors at free of cost. SCIR is also distributing needles and syringes to reduce the use of contaminated needles, which also reduces the risk of HIV infections too. At the same time IDUs are getting Oral Substitution Therapy (OST) if they are willing to shift from injecting drug use under Harm Reduction Programme. SCIR is also providing necessary counseling to the IDUs and their family members. Besides these, recovering IDUs are getting vocational training at Printing Press and Leather units.

Beneficiaries also told that their children are getting education in the primary school run by the SCIR at Park Circus DIC. Children of local poor people are also getting education in this school. During FGD, majority of them expressed that to them SCIR is every thing and there is no alternative of it. All members pronounced that SCIR has contributed a lot in terms of creating awareness about HIV/AIDS and providing health services.

(b) Cost and Quality of NGO's Services

For general health care, medicines are provided totally at free of cost by SCIR. Similarly IDUs are getting new needles and syringes at free of cost under the Needle and Syringe Exchange Programme (NSEP). Those who opted for OST are also getting Buprenorphine at free of cost. Condoms are also distributed among the IDUs without charging any price for safe sex. Beneficiaries also informed that they are paying one rupee only per day to avail the food at SCIR. But it is not compulsory; they can take tea, etc outside SCIR also. They are very happy with these facilities. Beneficiaries are also happy with SCIR's networking with various polyclinics where they get concession for different pathological tests, x-ray, etc.

SCIR has also good network with other organizations for referral services. One member complained about the quality of food. But immediately other members pointed out that the project has no provision of giving food. SCIR has arranged it from other organization for their betterment only. Few members expressed their dissatisfaction about the doctor who comes in the first half for few hours only. None of the beneficiaries have clear and correct idea about the source of funding. In brief all members are happy and satisfied with the quality of services provided by SCIR.

(c) Staff Cooperation

Beneficiaries are of the opinion that doctors, nurse and other staff members are very cooperative. They can approach any staff without any hesitation and always receive good responses. Doctors attend their problems with patience and nurses also carefully clean and dress their wounds, abscess, etc. Few members also revealed their bitter experiences regarding apathetic attitude and rude behaviour that they received from the doctors and other health staff of Chittaranjan National Medical College. All members expressed that they never got such good behaviour and respect in any other place other than SCIR. Staff members are extending all cooperation in making alternative arrangement for those who are unable to pay for the medicines, pathological tests, etc. Outreach workers (ORWs) and Peer educators regularly visit the field and make people aware about AIDS, distribute needles and condoms. Members also told that even for solving other family problems, they consult and get advices from the staff.

(d) Scope of Beneficiaries' Participation

With regard to the scope of participation in SCIR's activities, beneficiaries have mixed views. They don't have any scope of participation in planning, monitoring and evaluation. However, they participate in beneficiary's selection by referring new IDUs. They don't contribute financially, but they offer physical labour when SCIR is organizing any awareness camp or putting up exhibition stall, etc. SCIR recognizes their contribution and selected ORWs, Peer Educators and other staff from among the recovering and ex-IDUs. The group members also cooperate the SCIR when Evaluation Teams come from the WBSAP&CS and other funding agencies. But beneficiaries don't take part in the selection process of the staff. All recovering IDUs of Day Care centre participate daily in various activities like gardening, arranging chairs for meeting/discussion, etc.

In a nutshell, beneficiaries have a better perception towards the activities of SCIR. They feel that SCIR's intervention is required more because of the indifferent attitude of the health personnel in government hospitals. They feel more homely and comfortable in SCIR.

Group-2

This group is formed in Goabagan DIC of SCIR with 15 members. All of them are attending the Day Care Centre regularly. In this DIC, clinic is held three days in a week i.e. on Monday, Wednesday and Friday. The timing of the clinic is 9.30 am to 12.30 pm. Out of these 15 beneficiaries, there are 12 male and 3 female members. The age of the members varies from 18 years to 45 years. Most of them are either unemployed or self-employed. Three female members are CSWs and one of them is HIV positive.

(a) Necessity of NGO's HIV/AIDS Programme

As like as the first group of Park Circus DIC, the members of this group informed that before the starting of this DIC by SCIR, they have faced lots of problem in government hospitals. The health personnel used to neglect them whenever they go for the treatment of abscess, injuries, etc. They don't have money to visit private doctors or hospitals and used to consult quack doctors. All of them have admitted they don't have any knowledge on HIV/AIDS and effects of needle/syringe exchange. Now after the starting of SCIR's clinic, the beneficiaries inform that IDUs are getting the treatment and medicines from the qualified doctors at free of cost. SCIR is also distributing needles and syringes to reduce the use of contaminated needles, which also reduces the risk of HIV infections too. At the same time IDUs are getting Oral Substitution Therapy (OST) if they are willing to shift from injecting drug use under Harm Reduction Programme. They also inform that in case of serious patients and detoxification, SCIR refers to other appropriate health care institutions. SCIR is also providing necessary counseling to the IDUs and their family members. The Goabagan DIC also runs a Day Care Centre for the recovering drug addicts. In reply of the researcher's question on where they would go if SCIR closed down this DIC, members inform that they could not imagine such situation. Majority of them expressed that to them SCIR is every thing and there is no alternative of it. All members pronounced that SCIR has contributed a lot in terms of creating awareness about HIV/AIDS and providing health services.

(b) Cost and Quality of NGO's Services

With regard to cost of medicines and other facilities, members of the present group inform that SCIR provides medicines totally at free of cost for the treatment of abscess and other general health problems. As like as the first group, this group also informs that IDUs are getting new needles and syringes at free of cost under the Needle and Syringe Exchange Programme (NSEP). Those who opted for OST are also getting Buprenorphine at free of cost. Condoms are also distributed among the IDUs without charging any price. Beneficiaries will have to pay in case of pathological tests like x-ray etc. But members of the present group are happy with SCIR's networking with various polyclinics where they get concession for such pathological tests. SCIR has also good network with other organizations for referral services. Everyday SCIR provides lunch to the beneficiaries of Day Care Centre at free of cost. Beneficiaries also inform that they are paying one rupee only per day to avail the tea at SCIR. But it is not compulsory; they can take tea, etc outside SCIR also. None of the beneficiaries have clear and correct idea about the source of funding. Some of them inform that fund may be given by the government. In brief, all members are happy and satisfied with the cost and quality of services provided by SCIR.

(c) Staff Cooperation

The members of this group are also satisfied with the doctor, nurse and other staff members of SCIR. All of them are very cooperative, kind and behave nicely with all beneficiaries. Doctors patiently hear their problems and nurses also carefully clean and dress their wounds, abscess, etc. All members expressed that they never got such good behaviour and respect in any government or private hospitals. According to the beneficiaries, staff members are extending all cooperation in making alternative arrangement for those who are unable to pay for the medicines, pathological tests, etc. They also inform that even they consult the staff members for their family problems and get advices from them. One of the female members appreciates the advocacy role of the staff members.

(d) Scope of Beneficiaries' Participation

With regard to the scope of participation in SCIR's activities, beneficiaries have almost similar views as like as the members of the first group. They don't have any scope of participation in planning, monitoring and evaluation. However, they participate in beneficiary's selection by referring new IDUs. They don't contribute financially, but they offer physical labour when SCIR is organising any awareness camp or putting up exhibition stall, etc. The group members also cooperate and participate when evaluation teams come from the WBSAP&CS and NACO. SCIR recognizes their contribution by selecting ORWs, Peer educators and other staff from the recovering and ex-IDUs. According to beneficiaries, majority of the staff members in SCIR are selected from the IDUs. But beneficiaries don't take part in the selection process of the staff. All recovering IDUs of Day Care Centre participate daily in various activities like arranging chairs for meeting, discussion, etc.

In a nutshell, beneficiaries have a better perception towards the activities of SCIR. They feel that SCIR's intervention has helped them to become aware about HIV, AIDS, safer injecting procedure, etc and has improved their self-esteems. They feel more homely and comfortable in SCIR.

B. Durbar Mahila Samanwaya Committee (DMSC)

Group-1

The group is formed with 12 members at Sonagachi red light area under Avinash Clinic of Sonagachi Project. All members belong to sex workers community. Out of 12 members, there are two *malkins* (madam) and 10 sex workers. The age group of sex workers varies from 20 years to 40 years and *malkins* are quite aged. *Malkins* are not now engaged in sex work.

(a) Necessity of NGO's HIV/AIDS Programme

Beneficiaries informed that before the starting of clinics run by DMSC, the health conditions of sex workers was very poor. Because of the apathetic attitude of health personnel as well as of general people towards sex workers, they were not able to go to government hospitals. They had to depend on the quack doctors practicing in and around mainly for the treatment of STIs and related problems. Majority of sex workers were illiterate and ignorant about these diseases.

Regarding treatment, they had to depend on the *malkins* and pimps for the advice. Only a few sex workers of high-income group used to avail treatment facilities at private nursing home. The economic conditions of the most sex workers were also bad. They had to give share from their earnings to *malkins, bariwalis* and pimps as per their demands. Similarly, sex workers were compelled to give 'tax' to the local dons and policemen. There was no unity among the sex workers. During the economic crisis, they had to take loans from the moneylenders at higher rate of interest.

In the context of above situation, all beneficiaries acknowledge the contribution of DMSC. They also informed that initially they resisted the STD/HIV intervention project (SHIP) started by All India Institute of Hygiene and Public Health (AIIH&PH). But later on when sex workers were recruited as peer educators and especially after the formation of DMSC in 1995 – they started to believe and took interest in the programme activities. As per the beneficiaries, now DMSC has multi-dimensional activities in Sonagachi. It runs SHIP, health clinics, non-formal schools for CSWs and their children, residential homes for the school going children of CSWs, vocational training centre for the aged CSWs, VCTC, etc. When the researcher asked about the necessity of the HIV/AIDS programme of DMSC, beneficiaries did not deny its importance. According to them, DMSC has been working for last 12-13 years. As a result of working for long period, the CSWs are now more aware about STIs, HIV, AIDS and safer sexual practices. Now CSWs insist their customers for using condoms and the rate of condom use has increased significantly since 1992. They also inform that most of the sex workers have their own bank accounts in Usha Cooperative Bank (sister organization of DMSC) and get rid of moneylenders. They are more secure now and the exploitation of local dons, police, etc. has reduced remarkably. They are also happy with the functioning of Self Regulatory

Board, which prevents trafficking, and entry of minor girls (below 18 years). All of them admitted that DMSC has enabled them to realize the strength of unity; increased their self-esteem and helped them to dream a better future of their children. All of them recognize the necessity of HIV/AIDS programme and other developmental programmes of DMSC in improving their overall status in general and health status in particular.

(b) Cost and Quality of NGO's HIV/AIDS Care Services

According to beneficiaries, DMSC provides medicines at free of cost for the treatment of STIs and other common health problems. It also provides treatment for TB under DOT programme. The clinic is not only open for CSWs but also for their customers. Timings of the clinic suits all concern i.e. morning clinic for sex workers and evening clinic for their customers. Beneficiaries pay only seven rupees as registration fee. This is done to reduce the wastage of medicines and to raise some funds for better functioning of the clinic. They don't have any grievance regarding registration fee, rather they are satisfied with this arrangement and feel it is justified. In case of medicines that are not available in the clinic, they purchase themselves from outside medical stores. In case of pathological tests, etc., Mamata Care and Training Centre (VCTC) of DMSC is having HIV and VDRL testing facilities with pre-test and post-test counseling. Beneficiaries also inform that DMSC has a very good networking with different polyclinics where they get concessions for different pathological tests. The project staff also regularly visit the sex workers to distribute condoms and IEC materials; and discuss about their problems. Having remembered the past stories, all beneficiaries said that they are far better now because of DMSC and its multi-dimensional activities.

(c) Staff Cooperation

Beneficiaries are of the opinion that all staff members of

DMSC are very cooperative. There is no doubt in it. They can approach the staff without any hesitation as most of them are from sex workers community. They feel free and homely at clinic also. The Doctor listen to them carefully and advice them meticulously. Peer educators visit and meet the sex workers in each building of the brothel regularly. Peer educators also organize group meetings for creating awareness; distributing condoms and IEC materials and motivate them to go to the clinic for any health problem. Beneficiaries and peer educators can understand each other well and feel comfortable, because all of them from the sex workers community. Beneficiaries narrated their experiences and compared the situation with government run hospitals where everybody hates them because of their profession. They are of the opinion that in spite of low salary, peer educators and other staff members of DMSC are very sincere, committed and do not neglect their duties. Beneficiaries are very happy with the staff members who treat them as their own family members.

(d) Scope of Beneficiaries' Participation

Group members have informed that there is ample opportunity for beneficiaries to participate in different programme activities of DMSC. Because, it is an organization of the sex workers, by the sex workers and for the sex workers. DMSC accepts and considers beneficiaries' valuable opinion at the time of planning the programme activities. Beneficiaries took part in need identification and beneficiary's selection. They also participate in programme implementation. They do not contribute financially, but they offer physical labour and participate in different activities of DMSC like in organizing awareness camps, All India Entertainment Workers' Conference, putting up exhibition stall, etc. Beneficiaries also participate in monitoring and evaluation through its local Branch Committee members. For smooth running of its each clinic, DMSC constituted the Clinic

Management Committee and includes beneficiaries' representatives from local Branch committee of sex workers.

In brief, we understand that beneficiaries have better perception towards the working of DMSC. Successes of various programmes completed previously and existing at present have contributed to make this perception. They acknowledge its contribution for improving their health status and awareness level on different issues like STIs, HIV, AIDS, safer sexual practices, etc. They prefer DMSC for its multi-dimensional activities and integrated approach. They feel that services of DMSC are more relevant than that of the government hospitals.

Group-2

This group is formed with 10 members at Rambagan clinic of Sonagachi Project. All the members are CSWs. The age of the group members varies from 22 years to 35 years. The summary of the FGD is being discussed below.

(a) Necessity of NGO's HIV/AIDS Programme

As like as the first group, the members of the present group have also narrated the same story of sufferings of the sex workers' community before the starting of STD/HIV Intervention Programme initially by AIIH&PH and later on by DMSC. There was none to extend help and support to the sex workers. According to the beneficiaries, the health and economic condition of the CSWs were very bad at that time.

In the context of above situation, all beneficiaries acknowledge the contribution of DMSC. DMSC has recruited many sex workers as staff in this project. This has given them lots of confidence as they are respected and recognized at least by some people of the society. Beneficiaries have appreciated various multi-dimensional activities of DMSC in Sonagachi like health clinics, non-formal schools for CSWs and their children, residential homes for the school going children of CSWs, vocational training centre for the aged CSWs, VCTC, etc. They are more secure now and the exploitation of local dons, police, etc. has reduced remarkably. Members express their happiness with the functioning of Self Regulatory Board (SRB) of DMSC. SRB is trying to prevent trafficking, and entry of minor girls (below 18 years) in sex trade. During this FGD with the members, the peer educators came with one such new CSW to the counsellor for knowing her case history and her opinion. She is not a minor. Members inform that if she is not willing, DMSC would help her to send to her home or rehabilitate in some other place. All of them have admitted that DMSC has enabled them to realize the strength of unity; increased their self-esteem and helped them to dream a better future of their children. The members reacted differently when researcher wanted to know where they would go if DMSC stopped the project in future. All members confidently informed that this would never happen as the whole sex workers community is involved with DMSC and they would extend all support to sustain the current project. In nutshell, all the members acknowledge the importance of DMSC.

(b) Cost and Quality of NGO's HIV/AIDS Care Services

The members of this group also inform that they get medicines at free of cost for the treatment of STIs and other common health problems from the clinic of DMSC. It also provides treatment for TB under DOT programme of the Government. They pay Rs. 7/- only as registration fees and are satisfied with this arrangement. This is done to reduce the wastage of medicines and to raise some funds for the treatment of general health problems as WBSAP&CS provides fund for STIs only. The clinic is open 3 days in a week for CSWs and their customers. Timings of the clinic suits all concern i.e. 11 am to 2 pm. Members express their happiness over the record keeping system of the clinic. Each patient's treatment record is maintained through individual card, which helps both doctor/counsellor and patients. In case of medicines that are not available in the clinic, they purchase themselves from outside medical stores. In case of pathological tests, Mamata Care and Training Centre (VCTC) of DMSC is having HIV and VDRL testing facilities with pre-test and post-test counseling. DMSC has a very good networking with different polyclinics where beneficiaries get concessions for different pathological tests. All the members inform that they are satisfied and feel far better now with DMSC and its multi-dimensional activities.

(c) Staff Cooperation

With regard to the staff cooperation like the first group, this group is also happy with the staff members of DMSC. The group members praise about the sincerity of the Outreach Workers and Peer Educators who regularly visit the field and doing their work as per the plan. The project staff members also regularly visit the sex workers to distribute condoms and IEC materials; and discuss about their problems. The peer educators bring patients on clinic days and organize meetings with different stakeholders on other days. The group members are also happy with the cordial attitude and behaviour of doctor, counselor and other staff members who always advise them like their own family members. They also inform that they feel comfortable in the DMSC's clinic, because most of the staff members belong to sex workers' community. Staff members extend all cooperation in making arrangement for pathological tests, referral to other organizations, etc. They also offer advises in their personal matters. In brief, beneficiaries are happy with the staff members of Rambagan clinic of DMSC.

(d) Scope of Beneficiaries' Participation

With regard to the scope of beneficiaries' participation in programme activities, members of this group also reply that there is ample opportunity. They participate in beneficiaries' selection, need identification, programme planning and implementation; monitoring and evaluation, but they do not make financial resource contribution. The project staff also consulted beneficiaries to know about their opinions about the programme activities. DMSC accepts and considers beneficiaries' valuable opinion at the time of planning the programme activities. They do not contribute financially, but physically participate in different activities of DMSC like in organizing awareness camps, putting up exhibition stall, etc.

To sum up, we understand that beneficiaries have better perception towards the working of DMSC. They acknowledge its contribution for improving their health status and awareness level on different issues like STIs, HIV, AIDS, safer sexual practices, etc. Lastly, they feel proud to be a part of the DMSC's battle for the rights of sex workers.

C. Bhoruka Public Welfare Trust (BPWT)

Group-1

The first group was formed in Bhutghat clinic. It was formed with 9 members. Out of these 9 members, six were truck drivers and remaining three were helpers. The summary of the FGD is being discussed below.

(a) Necessity of NGO's HIV/AIDS Programme

Kolkata Port Trust is situated in South-West Kolkata. Kolkata Port is an international transshipment point for cargo ships. The major halting points for trucks are Bhutghat, Babubazar and Dhobiatola. The truckers usually stay within the parking area until unloading and loading processes are over. Trucks are operating under different transport companies. The waiting/halting period for truckers varies from 2-3 days to 15 days. There is no other health centre or clinics except BPWT's clinic in the parking zone or near by. Three members of this group informed that they knew about the clinic run by BPWT since last 5 years. Except two members, others informed that they never personally visited clinic for their own treatment. These two members visited the clinic for fever, but none of them visited BPWT's clinic for the treatment of STDs. Most of them have not much idea about Kolkata city and about different hospitals and medical colleges. Being the outsiders, they are naturally worried about the cost of treatment and quality of treatment. There are few 'quacks' practicing nearby. All members are of the opinion that they feel secure in the presence of BPWT's clinic where at least one doctor is there to attend any emergency health problems. In case of referral also, they get all cooperation from the BPWT staff. All of them inform that now they are quite aware and alert about HIV/AIDS. Some of the group members revealed that many people from truckers' community have been availing treatment from the clinics run by BPWT. All of them recognize the necessity of BPWT's clinic and its HIV/AIDS programme. They feel more comfortable in this clinic as it is exclusively for truckers and truck industry associated people.

(b) Cost and Quality of NGO's HIV/AIDS Care Services

According to the beneficiaries, the BPWT run clinics provide them medicine at free of cost for the treatment of STD and other common diseases. The patients pay Rs. 30/- as registration fees. In case of medicines that are not available in the clinic, beneficiaries purchase themselves from outside medical stores. In case of blood test, the samples are collected in the clinic and sent to BPWT's modern laboratory. For other pathological tests, beneficiaries pay from their pocket, but the project staff members help them to avail these tests at a concession rate through its good networking with different polyclinics. The project staff regularly meet and discuss about AIDS etc. and distribute IEC materials to them. Their misconceptions regarding HIV/AIDS are now removed through such interactions with the project staff members. Two members expressed that earlier BPWT used to distribute condom at free of cost, but recently they have stopped the old system. Some of them are also of the opinion that all medicines for general health care are not available with the clinic. None of the members have clear idea about the source of funding for this project. In brief, members of this beneficiaries group are happy with the quality and cost of HIV/AIDS and STD care services. But they are not fully satisfied with BPWT's clinic as it lacks proper infrastructure to meet all health care needs of truckers.

(c) Staff Cooperation

Beneficiaries are happy with the staff of BPWT. They are of the opinion that in spite of dusts and other hazardous conditions, field level staff members are regularly visiting the field and patiently doing their work. They behave nicely with the target group. Normally, truckers feel awkward when they visit any doctor's chamber because of existing social class system. But in BPWT clinic, doctor carefully listen the beneficiaries' problems and advice them properly. The beneficiaries also inform that they feel comfortable in the BPWT's clinic as other than truckers and truck industry associated people, other people don't visit the clinic. Staff members extend all cooperation in making arrangement for pathological tests, referral to other organizations, etc. In brief, beneficiaries are happy with the staff members of BPWT.

(d) Scope of beneficiaries' Participation

With regard to the scope of beneficiaries' participation in BPWT's activities, beneficiaries are of the opinion that, due to their nature of job, they could not stay there for long time. Hence, they could not participate in all activities of the HIV/ AIDS project. However, they refer their colleagues (truck drivers and helpers) to BPWT for treatment, counseling, etc. Whenever BPWT organizes any awareness programme, etc. the project staff members invite the beneficiaries. The project staff also consulted beneficiaries to know about their opinions about the programme activities. Therefore, beneficiaries participate in beneficiary's selection, need identification, but they do not take part in resource contribution, programme planning, monitoring and evaluation. The situation can be called as partial participation of the beneficiaries.

In a nutshell, we find that beneficiaries have positive perception towards the working of BPWT. They acknowledge its contribution for improving awareness level on different issues like STD, HIV and AIDS, safer sex, etc. But they have certain grievances regarding the free medicines for general health care and social marketing of condoms. In general, they feel comfortable with BPWT's clinic and project staff.

Group-2

The second group was formed in Dhobiatola clinic. It was formed with 8 members. Out of these 8 members, four were truck drivers and remaining four were helpers. The summary of the FGD is being discussed below.

(a) Necessity of NGO's HIV/AIDS Programme

As per the information provided by these group members, there is no other health centre or clinics except BPWT's clinic in the parking zone. There are few 'quack doctors' practicing near by. Like the first group members, this group also has not much idea about Kolkata city and about different hospitals and medical colleges. Being the outsiders, they are naturally worried about the cost of treatment and quality of treatment. This group informed that they got different services from the clinic run by BPWT like treatment of STDs and medicines; free advice regarding safer sex, HIV/AIDS; condoms, etc. In case of referral for pathological tests, they get all cooperation from the BPWT staff members. All of them recognize the necessity of BPWT's clinic and its HIV/AIDS programme for the truckers in KPT parking zone.

(b) Cost and Quality of NGO's HIV/AIDS Care Services

As like as the first group of beneficiaries, this group replies that the clinic provides them medicine at free of cost for the treatment of STD and other common diseases and takes Rs. 30/- per patient as registration fee. When medicines those are not available in the clinic, beneficiaries purchase themselves from outside medical stores. Blood tests are done at free of cost in the BPWT's modern laboratory. For other pathological tests, beneficiaries pay from their pocket, but the project staff members help them to avail these tests at a concession rate through its good networking with different polyclinics. This group also acknowledges the efforts of project staff members in making the truckers aware about STD, HIV, AIDS, etc. Some of the group members are not satisfied, as all medicines for general health care are not available in the clinic. None of the members have clear idea about the source of funding for this project. In brief, members of this beneficiaries' group are happy with the quality and cost of HIV/AIDS and STD care services. But they are not fully satisfied with BPWT's clinic as sometime it fails to meet all health care needs of truckers.

(c) Staff Cooperation

With regard to the staff cooperation, this group is also happy with the staff members of BPWT. They praise about the sincerity of the field level staff members who regularly visit the field and doing their work as per plan. The group members are also happy with the behaviours of doctor and counselor who always advise them for the welfare of the beneficiaries. Staff members extend all cooperation in making arrangement for pathological tests, referral to other organizations, etc. In brief, beneficiaries are happy with the staff members of BPWT.

(d) Scope of Beneficiaries' Participation

With regard to the scope of beneficiaries' participation in

BPWT's activities, this group replies the same. Due to their nature of job, they could not participate in all activities of the HIV/AIDS project. However, they refer their friends (truck drivers and helpers) to the clinic of BPWT. Therefore, beneficiaries participate in beneficiary's selection, need identification, but they do not take part in resource contribution, programme planning, monitoring and evaluation. The situation can be called as partial participation of the beneficiaries.

In a nutshell, we find that beneficiaries have positive perception towards the working of BPWT. They acknowledge its contribution for improving awareness level on different issues like STD, HIV and AIDS, safer sex, etc. Few of them are aggrieved, as they are not getting all medicines for general health problems. In general, they feel comfortable and happy with the project staff members of BPWT.

D. MANAS Bangla (MB)

Group-1

The group was formed with 10 members at DumDum DIC. All members belong to MSM community. The age group of beneficiaries varies from 19 years to 36 years. Four of the group members associated with this DIC since inception of the project i.e. from 2004. The summary of the FGD is being discussed below.

(a) Necessity of NGO's HIV/AIDS Programme

Beneficiaries inform that the health condition of MSM population was very poor before the starting of the DIC/clinics run by MB. As already pointed out in Part-I of this chapter, there are few organizations working with MSM population with their limited funds and capacities. Beneficiaries have little or no knowledge regarding STIs, HIV, AIDS, etc. A good number of them are vulnerable to such communicable diseases. Because of the MSM related stigma, they were not able to go to government hospitals or private clinics. They are compelled to depend on the quack doctors mainly for the treatment of STIs and related problems that too in distant places. Because of the fear of exposure and stigmatization, even they were not able to consult any nearby doctors. At the same time they can't discuss their problems with their family members. As a result, they had to suffer from extreme psychological stress and anxiety. No one was there to help them. There was no channel of communication among the MSM community members. There was no safe place to meet with their partners other than railway station, park etc. but many a time they had to face trouble from local people, club members, police, etc.

In the context of above situation, all beneficiaries acknowledge the contribution of MB. At least now they can meet their community members at the DIC without any fear of harassment and humiliation by others. Here, they feel comfortable and shares their joys and sorrows with their fellow MSM community members. At the same time, they are getting different types of services from the clinic run by MB at this DIC. They are getting free health check-up, treatment and medicines from the doctor; counseling and advices for their psychosocial and health related problems from the counselor; learning condom use procedure through demonstrations by the staff; attending different awareness meeting on HIV, STIs, AIDS, Safer sex, etc. along with IEC materials. Above all, the environment of DIC is MSM friendly, where they can freely share their feelings, emotions and problems; and also get an opportunity to introduce with many new MSM community members. The native places of many beneficiaries are 20-30 km. away from the DumDum DIC. Two of them are residing near Bangaon DIC of MB, but attending this DIC due to fear of exposure in their locality and MSM related stigma. When the researcher asked about the necessity of the HIV/AIDS programme of MB, beneficiaries did not deny its importance. They all recognize the necessity of this programme in improving their over all status in general and health status in particular. All the beneficiaries are of the opinion that MB is everything for them and they cannot think of anything without MB. That is why in spite of financial problem, they are coming from long distances to attend the DIC and clinic of MB. All the group members admit that MB has enabled them to realize the strength of unity, increased their self-esteem and helped them to exercise their rights, instead of feeling guilty and marginalized in the society. All of them recognize the necessity of sexual health promotion and HIV/AIDS control programme run by MB.

(b) Cost and Quality of NGO's HIV/AIDS Care Services

According to beneficiaries, MB run clinic provides medicines at free of cost for the treatment of STIs and other common health problems. Ruptures, tearing etc. are very common in anal sex and doctor provides necessary advice and treatment for these problems too. Beneficiaries pay only Rs. 2/- as registration fee. This is done to raise some funds for better functioning of the clinic, reduce the wastage of medicines and to make them realize about the importance of such services. Beneficiaries are satisfied with this arrangement and feel it is justified. In case of medicines that are not available in the clinic, they purchase themselves from outside medical stores. MB supplies most of the medicines. It collects medicines from physicians' sample and purchase medicines from directly from CDMU, Kolkata at low price to cater the needs of its beneficiaries. In case of pathological tests like blood test, X-ray, etc., MB refers them to different polyclinics. Beneficiaries also inform that they get concessions for different pathological tests because of the MB's good networking with different polyclinics. Beneficiaries earlier used to get condoms and lubes at free of cost. But now due changes in the policy of WBSAP&CS, they have to pay for it. Few beneficiaries are not happy with this arrangement, but they have grievance against the government, not against the MB. For outreach beneficiaries, the ORWs and PEs regularly visit the field and interact with them to know about their problems. They also distribute condoms, lubes and IEC materials; refer them to clinic for treatment and invite them to visit DIC. Considering the past experiences, all beneficiaries feel that they are far better now because of MB and its different activities through DIC and clinics. But they also express that there is a need to open more DICs/Clinics to cover many MSM living in remote places for which it is difficult for them to access these few clinics located in the city. None of them have any detail idea about the source of funding for this project, but they guess that the government may sponsor it. In brief, they are satisfied with the cost and quality of services provided by MB.

(c) Staff Cooperation

According to beneficiaries, all staff members of MB are very cooperative. There is no doubt in it. The Doctors listen to them carefully and advice them properly in simple languages like their elder brother. The Counsellor also offers guidance and advice regarding their health problems, psychosocial problems and even for family related matters. They can approach the staff without any hesitation as most of them belong to their own MSM community. They feel free and homely at DIC and clinic. Beneficiaries, who regularly visit DIC, feel that they almost become family members of MB. At the field level, PEs and ORWs regularly visit and meet the clients. Being the member of same MSM community, both project staff and beneficiaries can understand each other well and feel comfortable to share their feelings, problems, etc. They are of the opinion that in spite of low salary, peer educators and other staff members of MB are very sincere, committed and do not neglect their duties. They work more as selfless social workers than merely as salaried employees. Some of the beneficiaries narrated their bitter experiences and compared the situation with any government or private run hospitals where everybody is indifferent and neglect them because of their sexual behaviour. In a nutshell, beneficiaries are very happy with the staff members of MB who treat them as their own family members.

(d) Scope of Beneficiaries' Participation

Beneficiaries inform that there is ample opportunity for them to participate in different programme activities of MB. Because, it is an organization of the MSM, by the MSM and for the MSM community members. Beneficiaries, who regularly visit DIC, directly participate in need identification, beneficiaries' selection, programme planning and its implementation. In MB, planning is done at the NGO level, but it accepts and considers beneficiaries' opinion received through project staff. Outreach beneficiaries' feedbacks are obtained and considered through PEs and ORWs. Beneficiaries do not contribute financially, but they offer physical labour and participate in different activities of MB (for example, organizing awareness camps, putting up exhibition stall, street play, etc.) as volunteers. Beneficiaries do not directly participate in monitoring and evaluation, but their feedbacks are obtained through GD/FGD by the project staff. They extend cooperation to the external evaluation team of WBSAP&CS by participating in GD/FGD.

To sum up, we understand that beneficiaries have better perception towards the working of MB. They acknowledge its contribution for improving their health status, self-esteem and awareness level on different issues like STIs, HIV, AIDS, safer sexual practices, etc. They prefer MB for its multi-dimensional activities and rights-based approach. They cannot imagine a situation if MB stops working for them for any reason in future.

Group-2

The group was formed with 8 members at Kasba DIC.

All members belong to MSM community. The age group of beneficiaries varies from 18 years to 40 years. Two of the group members associated with this DIC since inception of the project i.e. from 2004. The summary of the FGD is being discussed below.

(a) Necessity of NGO's HIV/AIDS Programme

As like as the first group, this group also narrated the same story of sufferings of the MSM community before the starting of MB's sexual health promotion and HIV control project. There was none to support them. In the context of this situation, all the members acknowledge the contribution of MB. Now they can come and meet their fellow community members without any fear of harassment or humiliation. They feel very homely and comfortable in the DIC and in its clinic. The DIC offers numbers of services like health check-up and treatment for STIs and general health problems, counseling and advice for different problems, awareness on STD, HIV, AIDS, safer sex, etc. Above all, DIC provides a platform to meet with new community members, share their joys and sorrows together and develop a support base. Like the first group, this group members also admit that MB helps them realize the strength of unity, increased their self-esteem and helped them to exercise their rights. All of them recognize the necessity of sexual health promotion and HIV/AIDS control programme run by MB.

(b) Cost and Quality of NGO's HIV/AIDS Care Services

This group of beneficiaries also informs that they get treatment and medicines at free of cost from the clinic. They pay Rs. 5/- as registration fee to avail the services of the clinic and are satisfied with the arrangement. In case of medicines not available in the clinic, they purchase it from the outside. But generally most of the medicines are available in the clinic run by MB. In case of pathological tests, etc. the project staff make necessary arrangement for referral services to other polyclinics. Beneficiaries inform that because of MB's good networking with other polyclinics, they get concessional rates for such tests. Considering the past experiences, all group members inform that they are better now because of the MB's efforts. But none of this group is aware about the source of funding for MB's project clearly. But they guess that it may be by government or any foreign funding agency.

(c) Staff Cooperation

With regard to the staff cooperation like the first group, this group is also happy with the staff members of MB. The group members praise about the sincerity of the Outreach Workers and Peer educators who regularly visit the field and doing their work as per plan. The group members are also happy with the cordial attitude and behaviour of doctor, counselor and other staff members who always advise them like their own family members. They also inform that they feel comfortable in the MB's clinic, because most of the staff members belong to MSM community. As a result they understand each other nicely and there is hardly any misunderstanding takes place. Staff members extend all cooperation in making arrangement for pathological tests, referral to other organizations, etc. They also offer advises in their personal matters. In brief, beneficiaries are happy with the staff members of Kasba DIC of MB.

(d) Scope of Beneficiaries' Participation

With regard to the scope of beneficiaries' participation in programme activities, this group also replies that there is ample opportunity. They participate in need identification and beneficiaries' selection. The project staff also consulted beneficiaries to know about their opinions about the programme activities. In MB, programme planning is done at the NGO level, but after giving due consideration to the beneficiaries' feedback. The beneficiaries who visit DIC regularly directly participate in different meetings, GDs and

FGDs and express their opinions and views. The feedbacks of outreach beneficiaries are obtained through PEs and ORWs. Thus, they also participate in the programme planning and its implementation. They do not contribute financially, but physically participate in different activities of MB. Therefore, beneficiaries participate in beneficiaries' selection, need identification, programme planning and implementation, but they do not take part in resource contribution, monitoring and evaluation. But they extend cooperation to the external evaluation teams of WBSAP&CS.

In brief, it is found that beneficiaries have better perception towards the working of MB. They acknowledge the necessity of MB and its contribution in improving their health status, self-esteem and awareness level on different issues like STIs, HIV, AIDS, safer sexual practices, etc. In general, they feel comfortable and happy with the project staff members of MB.

E. Human Development Research Institute (HDRI)

Group-1

The first group was formed in 24/C, Jorabagan Street under Posta Clinic of HDRI. It was formed with 10 members. Out of these 10 members, six were porters and remaining four were labourers. The summary of the FGD is being discussed below.

(a) Necessity of NGO's HIV/AIDS Programme

The geographical area covered under the HDRI's HIV/ AIDS intervention project covers a large area, which includes Burrabazar, Posta, Jorabagan, Mechua, Sovabazar and Ahiritola. The total number of migrated labour working in this area is around one lakh. Most of them are rural poor people who are forced to leave their native place in search of livelihood. They are working as porters, handcart pullers, sardars, labourers, hawkers and workers of different shops.

They are hardly educated and having little or no knowledge and information about STD, HIV, AIDS, safer sex, etc. A good number of them are vulnerable to STD, HIV or other communicable disease and may endanger the life of their innocent family members in their respective native places. With this background information, the researcher tries to know about the beneficiaries' perception about the contribution of HDRI.

Beneficiaries inform that the health condition of migrated labourers was very poor before the starting of clinics run by HDRI. Because of the apathetic attitude of health personnel towards the migrated labour and poor infrastructure, they were not able to go to government hospitals. They had to depend on the quack doctors practicing in and around mainly for the treatment of general health problems and STD related problems. Majority of them are illiterate and ignorant about these diseases. Regarding treatment, they had to depend on the Sardars and local shopkeepers for the advice. Most of them belong to low-income group and can't afford to do treatment in private nursing home or under reputed doctors. There was no unity among the migrated labourers and divided region wise like *Biharis, Oryas,* etc. During the economic crisis, they had to take loans from the moneylenders at higher rate of interest.

In the context of above situation, all beneficiaries acknowledge the contribution of HDRI. They also informed that initially they resisted the HIV/AIDS intervention project. But later on when Peer Educators were recruited from among them, they started to believe and took interest in the programme activities of HDRI. As per the beneficiaries, now HDRI runs health clinics for the general health problems as well as for the treatment of STDs. When the researcher asked about the necessity of the HIV/AIDS programme of HDRI, beneficiaries do not deny its importance. According to them, HDRI has been working for last 10 years. As a result of working for long period, the migrated labourers are now more aware about STD, HIV, AIDS and safer sexual practices. Now the rate of condom use has increased significantly. All of them admitted that HDRI has enabled them to realize the strength of unity; increased their self-esteem and helped them to dream a better future. All of them recognize the necessity of HIV/AIDS programme of HDRI in improving their overall status in general and health status in particular.

(b) Cost and Quality of NGO's HIV/AIDS Care Services

According to beneficiaries, HDRI run clinics provide medicines at free of cost for the treatment of STD and other common health problems. Beneficiaries pay only Rs. 10/- as registration fee to avail the services from the clinic. The registration fees are taken to reduce the wastage of medicines and to raise some funds for better functioning of the clinic. Beneficiaries don't have any grievance regarding registration fee, rather they are satisfied with this arrangement and feel it is justified. In case of medicines that are not available in the clinic, they purchase themselves from outside medical stores. In case of pathological tests like X-ray etc. HDRI refers them to different polyclinics. Beneficiaries also inform that HDRI has a very good networking with different polyclinics where they get concessions for different pathological tests. For blood tests, blood samples are collected in the clinic of HDRI itself. The project staff also regularly visit them in their *Gaddi* (place of work) or *Theks* (place of group residence) to distribute condoms and IEC materials; and discuss about their problems. Having remembered the past incidences, all beneficiaries said that they are far better now because of HDRI and its different programme activities. None of the group member has any idea about the source of funding for this project. Few members guess that the fund may be coming from the government.

(c) Staff Cooperation

Beneficiaries inform that all staff members of HDRI are

very cooperative. They can approach the staff without any hesitation. They feel free and homely at clinic also. The doctor and nurse listen to them carefully and advice them properly in simple languages. The counselor explains and guides them like their own family members. Peer Educators and Outreach Workers visit and meet them regularly. These field level staff also organize group meetings for creating awareness; distributing condoms and IEC materials and motivate them to go to the clinic for any health problem. Beneficiaries and peer educators can understand each other well and feel comfortable, because all of them from the same community. Beneficiaries narrated their experiences and compared the situation with government run hospitals where everybody neglects them because of their occupations. They are of the opinion that in spite of low salary, peer educators and other staff members of HDRI are very sincere, committed and do not neglect their duties. Some of them requested the researcher to do something to increase the salary of field level staff of HDRI. Beneficiaries are very happy with the staff members.

(d) Scope of Beneficiaries' Participation

Group members have informed that there is opportunity for beneficiaries to participate in different programme activities of HDRI. It is working for their betterment. Beneficiaries took part in need identification and beneficiaries' selection. HDRI accepts and considers beneficiaries' valuable opinion through Outreach Workers and Peer Educators at the time of planning the programme activities. The Governing Body approves the programme planning. Three members from the migrated labourers' community are representing in the Governing Body of HDRI. They also participate in programme implementation. They do not contribute financially, but they offer physical infrastructural support (like arrangement of venue, electricity, chairs, etc.) during Annual Gathering, Sardars' Meet, awareness camp, etc. They also physically participate and contribute in different activities of HDRI in terms of controlling crowds, arranging tea, etc. Beneficiaries do not participate in monitoring and evaluation. But they extend cooperation to the external evaluation teams of WBSAP&CS by participating in focused group discussion (FGD).

In brief, we understand that beneficiaries have better perception towards the working of HDRI. They acknowledge its contribution for improving their health status and awareness level on different issues like STD, HIV, AIDS, safer sexual practices, etc. They feel that services of HDRI are more relevant to them than that of the government hospitals.

Group-2

The second group was formed in 314/B, Rabindra Sarani (Kachauri Gally) under Mechua Clinic of HDRI. It was formed with 9 members. Out of these 9 members, there were three Handcart Pullers, three Porters, one Sardar and two Hawkers. The summary of the FGD is being discussed below.

(a) Necessity of NGO's HIV/AIDS Programme

As per the information provided by these group members, there is no other Government's health centre or clinics except HDRI's clinic in their area. The Sardar informs that there were few private nursing homes and 'quack doctors' practicing nearby. But they can't afford the treatment facilities of nursing homes. This group has not much idea about different hospitals and medical colleges in Kolkata. Being the outsiders, they are naturally worried about the cost of treatment and quality of treatment. The group members have informed that they get different services like treatment of STDs and general health problems; free advice regarding safer sex, HIV/AIDS; condoms, etc. from the clinic run by HDRI. In case of referral for pathological tests, they get all cooperation from the HDRI staff members. All of them recognize the necessity of the clinics run by HDRI and its HIV/AIDS programme for the migrated labourers.

(b) Cost and Quality of NGO's HIV/AIDS Care Services

As like as the first group of beneficiaries, this group replies that they receive medicines from the clinic of HDRI at free of cost for the treatment of STD and other common diseases. They pay Rs. 10/- only as registration fee. The medicines, which are not available in the clinic, beneficiaries purchase themselves from the outside medical stores. Blood tests are done at free of cost and samples are collected in the clinic itself. For other pathological tests, beneficiaries pay from their pocket, but the project staff members help them to avail these tests at a concession rate through HDRI's good networking with different polyclinics. This group also acknowledges the efforts of project staff members in making them aware about STD, HIV, AIDS, etc. Some of the group members are not satisfied, as all medicines for general health care sometimes are not available in the clinic. None of the members have clear idea about the source of funding for this project. In brief, members of this beneficiaries' group are happy with the quality and cost of HIV/AIDS and STD care services. But they are not fully satisfied with HDRI's clinic as sometime it fails to meet their all health care needs.

(c) Staff Cooperation

With regard to the staff cooperation like the first group, this group is also happy with the staff members of HDRI. The group members praise about the sincerity of the Outreach Workers and Peer educators who regularly visit the field and doing their work as per plan. The group members are also happy with the behaviours of doctor, nurse and counselor who always advise them as their own family members. They also inform that they feel comfortable in the HDRI's clinic. Staff members extend all cooperation in making arrangement for pathological tests, referral to other organizations, etc. They also offer advises in other personal matters. The Sardar informs that the project staff members of HDRI once helped them on the issue of poor bonus payment made by their employers. In brief, beneficiaries are happy with the staff members of HDRI.

(d) Scope of Beneficiaries' Participation

With regard to the scope of beneficiaries' participation in programme activities, this group also replies that there is ample opportunity. They participate in need identification and beneficiaries' selection. The project staff also consulted beneficiaries to know about their opinions about the programme activities. They also participate in the programme planning through their representatives in the Governing Body of HDRI. They do not contribute financially, but provide infrastructural support like venue, chairs, electricity, etc. at the time of various programmes of the project. They also physically participate in different activities of HDRI. Therefore, beneficiaries participate in beneficiaries' selection, need identification, programme planning and implementation, but they do not take part in resource contribution, monitoring and evaluation. But they extend cooperation to the external evaluation team of WBSAP&CS. The situation can be called as partial participation of the beneficiaries.

In a nutshell, we find that beneficiaries have positive perception towards the working of HDRI. They acknowledge its contribution for improving awareness level on different issues like STD, HIV and AIDS, safer sex, etc. In general, they feel comfortable and happy with the project staff members of HDRI. But some of them are not happy with the general health care services of its clinic.

F. Society for Positive Atmosphere and Related Support to HIV/AIDS (SPARSHA)

The researcher is grateful to the Secretary of SPARSHA for allowing him to interact directly with the beneficiaries who came to attend the monthly group meeting of HIV positive people at Kestopur DIC. The group was formed with 16 members at Kestopur DIC. Out of the 16 beneficiaries, there are ten male and six female members. The age group of beneficiaries varies from 22 years to 47 years. Five of the group members associated with this DIC since inception of the project i.e. from 2004. Majority of them are unemployed, few of them are daily wage earners and self-employed.

(a) Necessity of NGO's HIV/AIDS Programme

Beneficiaries inform that before the starting of the DIC run by SPARSHA, the conditions of HIV positive people was very poor. As already pointed out in the profile of SPARSHA. there were no organizations working with the HIV positive people in West Bengal at that time. One of the old beneficiaries informs that they have little or no knowledge regarding HIV, AIDS, safer sex, etc. They felt quite helpless when they came to know about their HIV positive status. Because of the HIV/AIDS related stigma, they were refused and denied treatment in government hospitals. The behaviours of the health personnel towards the HIV positive persons were so terrible that they don't want to recall those bitter experiences. Because of the fear of exposure and stigmatization, even they were not able to consult any private doctors or go to private hospitals. They are compelled to depend on the quack doctors mainly for the treatment of STD and other related health problems that too in distant places. At the same time they can't discuss their problems with their family members. As a result, they had to suffer from extreme psychological stress and anxiety. No one was there to help them. There was no channel of communication among the HIV positive members. Therefore, when they came to know about SPARSHA, they consider it as a gift from the god only.

In the context of above situation, all beneficiaries acknowledge the contribution of SPARSHA. In DIC, they feel comfortable and shares their joys and sorrows with their fellow HIV positive community members. At least now they can meet their fellow community members at the DIC without any fear of harassment and humiliation by others. Besides it, they are getting different types of services from the SPARSHA through this DIC. They are getting free health check-up, medical advices, treatment and medicines for common health problems from the doctor; counselling and advices for their psychosocial and health related problems from the counsellor; attending different awareness meeting on HIV, STD, AIDS, safer sex, etc. along with IEC materials. Two female beneficiaries inform that they have received vocational training on making jute products with the help of SPARSHA. All of them inform that SPARSHA also helps to get ART from the School of Tropical Medicines and now five of them are taking ART regularly. One female beneficiary informs that her child is getting ART at the subsidized rate. Majority of them inform that they have received advocacy support from SPARSHA as and when they required it. Above all, the environment of DIC is PLWHA friendly, where they can freely share their feelings, emotions and problems; and also get an opportunity to introduce with many new HIV infected members. The native places of many beneficiaries are 30-40 kilometers away from the Kestopur DIC. Even two of them are residing in Purba Medinipur district, but attending this DIC due to fear of exposure in their locality and stigma. When the researcher asked about the necessity of the HIV/AIDS programme of SPARSHA, they all recognize the necessity of this programme in improving their overall status in general and health status in particular. All the beneficiaries are of the opinion that SPARSHA is everything for them and they are alive because of it. That is why in spite of financial problem, they are coming from long distances to attend the DIC and group meetings of SPARSHA. All the group members admit that SPARSHA has enabled them to realize the strength of unity, increased their self-esteem and helped them to exercise their rights, instead of feeling guilty and marginalized in the society. All of them recognize the necessity of HIV/AIDS care and support programme run by SPARSHA.

(b) Cost and Quality of NGO's HIV/AIDS Care Services

According to beneficiaries, SPARSHA run clinic provides medicines at free of cost for the treatment of STD and other common health problems. The doctor at Uluberia DIC provides necessary advice for maintaining healthy life and how to take necessary precautions to prevent the spread the HIV infection. In case of other DICs, SPARSHA is having a very good networking with different local specialist doctors to help the beneficiaries as per their needs. Beneficiaries will have to fill up a Membership Form to avail the services from DICs. No membership fee or registration fee is charged from the beneficiaries. In case of pathological tests like blood test, X-ray, etc., SPARSHA refers them to different polyclinics. Beneficiaries also inform that they get concessions for different pathological tests because of the SPARSHA's good networking with different polyclinics. The Outreach Workers and Community Based Peer Councellors regularly visit and maintain effective network with various government and private hospitals, health centers, nursing homes, etc. They also regularly keep in touch with each PLWHA. The DICs also distribute condoms, and IEC materials; refer them to clinic for treatment and advice them to visit DIC regularly. Counselling is an important part of the care and support programme of PLWHA. Beneficiaries inform that they receive counseling with regard to various issues like adherence to antiretroviral medicines, stress management, partner notification, legal rights of PLWHA, etc. Considering the past experiences, all beneficiaries feel that they are far better now because of SPARSHA and its different activities through DIC and clinics. But they also express that there is a need to open more DICs or clinics to cover many PLWHA living in remote places for whom it is difficult to access the services from these few DICs. Few of them inform the difficulty of bearing the cost of traveling for collecting ART or CD4 testing at free of cost from School of Tropical Medicine, Kolkata. Because it is far away from their native places. But they do not have any grievance against SPARSHA in this regard. They feel that government should consider this aspect of suffering by the PLWHA also. At the same time, two beneficiaries from Purba Medinipur inform that sometimes SPARSHA bears their traveling cost. None of them have any detailed idea about the source of funding for this project, but they guess that it may be sponsored by the government and by public donations. In brief, they are satisfied with the cost and quality of services provided by SPARSHA.

(c) Staff Cooperation

Beneficiaries inform that all staff members of SPARSHA are very cooperative. The Doctor and the Counsellor listen to them carefully and also offer guidance and advice regarding their health problems, psychosocial problems and even for family related matters. They can approach the staff without any hesitation, as majority of them are HIV positive. They feel free and homely at the DIC of SPARSHA. Beneficiaries, who regularly visit DIC, feel that they belong to a single family of SPARSHA. At the field level, Community Based Peer Counsellor and Outreach Workers regularly keep contacts with their clients. In case of emergency, they also make home visit to help the beneficiaries. If required, they conduct community sensitization programmes and advocacy meetings to reduce stigma among the community people. Being the member of same PLWHA community, both project staff and beneficiaries have good understanding with each other and feel comfortable to share their feelings, problems, etc. They are of the opinion that in spite of low salary, peer counsellors and other staff members of SPARSHA are very sincere, committed and do not neglect their duties. The staff members work more as social workers than merely as salaried employees. Some of the beneficiaries narrated their bitter experiences and compared the situation with health personnel of any government or private run hospitals where everybody is indifferent and hate them because of their HIV positive status. In a nutshell, beneficiaries are very happy with the staff members of SPARSHA who treat them as their own family members.

(d) Scope of Beneficiaries' Participation

According to beneficiaries, there is ample opportunity for them to participate in different programme activities of SPARSHA. Because, it is an organization of the PLWHA and for the PLWHA. Beneficiaries directly participate in need identification, beneficiaries' selection, programme planning and its implementation through the monthly group meetings of DICs. In SPARSHA, planning is done at the NGO level, but it accepts and considers beneficiaries' opinion received through project staff of DICs. Beneficiaries do not contribute financially, but they offer physical labour and participate in different activities of DICs run by SPARSHA. Beneficiaries ensure their involvement by attending the programmes, by providing physical infrastructure like sitting arrangements, providing tea for staff and resource persons during awareness camps, etc. Beneficiaries also take part in monitoring activities through interactions with DIC level staff as well as with the Programme Management Unit (PMU) of SPARSHA. Beneficiaries do not directly participate in evaluation, but they extend cooperation to the external evaluation team of WBSAP&CS by participating in GD/FGD. SPARSHA also recognizes beneficiaries' participation by recruiting them as project staff at different level including the Project Coordinator.

In brief, we understand that beneficiaries have better perception towards the working of SPARSHA. They acknowledge its contribution for improving their health status, self-esteem and awareness level on different issues like STD, HIV, AIDS, safer sexual practices, ART and its side effects, CD4, etc. They prefer SPARSHA than any other organizations for its multi-dimensional activities and rights-based approach. They cannot think of a situation if SPARSHA stops working for them for any reason in future.

In a nutshell, this chapter has highlighted the beneficiaries' perceptions towards the working of six selected NGOs under the study. Out of eleven groups, eight groups have expressed positive perception and few members of remaining three groups have shown dissatisfaction. By and large, beneficiaries have better perception towards the working of respective NGOs. The HIV/AIDS programmes of the respective NGOs are satisfactory to the beneficiaries. These NGOs have helped them in improving their health status and awareness level on various HIV/AIDS related issues. These programmes include more preventive services and less curative services. Out of the six NGOs, SPARSHA only runs HIV/AIDS Care and Support services for PLWHA. So far anti-retroviral medicines (ART) are concerned, it is distributed by the government through a very few ART distribution centers in West Bengal. Majority of the beneficiaries use these NGOs as a stepping-stone for better referral health services and to avoid the indifferent attitude and apathy of the health personnel in government-run hospitals.

So, we can conclude from the case studies (discussed in Chapter 6, 7, 8 and 9) that an NGO engaged in HIV/AIDS prevention and care in West Bengal can help in improving the health status and awareness on HIV/AIDS by providing more preventive and less curative services. These NGOs can also supplement the government run health care institutions in combating HIV/AIDS in the state. But, the programmes of these NGOs would be less sustainable after the project duration. Therefore, for the continuation of a full-fledged programme, that project has to be on with adequate funding support.

SECTION-III
AIDS, NGOs AND GLOBALISATION

10
Globalisation and NGO Response to HIV/AIDS

Globalisation has affected all facets of life. In recent years, we have witnessed an unprecedented debate on globalisation. Attention has been focused on the origin and main features of globalisation and its potential impact on world economic, political and social order. This policy debate is quite understandable, as the pace and consequences of globalisation have implications for every individual, community or nation. It is changing the lives of people in developed as well as in developing countries. Recent financial and economic regional crises ranging from Mexico to Russia and East Asia, the failure of the New Millennium 'Development' Trade Round in Seattle, hot debates at the UNCTAD-10 Conference in Bangkok, and the recent South-South meeting in April 2000, have brought the discussion on globalisation to a new peak of rhetoric and passion (McCarty, 2001). Several statements and judgements are made by different distinguished personalities on the nature of globalisation, but the debate is still far from over. Some of the common questions asked by the people are: What is globalisation? Is it good or bad for human development? Is it something new, or part of a longer historical process? How does it affect the developing countries? How to protect vulnerable groups from the volatility of the globalisation wave?

What is Globalisation?

The term "globalisation" has been given a number of meanings. The definition of globalisation can be quite elastic, going beyond economic integration of the world to encompass political and cultural integration as well (Osmani 2005). At its broadest, it has been used as a term encompassing any form of societal change with transnational dimensions. In general, globalisation is the term used to characterise the processes of growing interconnection and interdependence in today's world, generated to a large degree by growing international economic, cultural and political cooperation and links, as well as by the need to respond together to global problems which can be solved only on a planetary scale (Dommen 2001). Globalisation is a process of change. It is a process, which increases economic and other interactions between countries due to the persistent decline in international transaction costs. According to Prof. Galal Amin (1999), "Globalisation is a multifaceted phenomenon, which includes the acceleration of international trade, of the flows of labour, capital and technology as well as of the transfer of ideas and patterns of living."

Some of the specific characteristics of globalisation include the rapid development and expansion of information technology, including internet links and cellular phones; the speed of communications, including cheaper and faster international transport; the intensification of international trade and foreign direct investment flows; the increase of financial flows, with globally linked foreign exchange and capital markets, operating 24 hours a day; the growth in the size and power of private corporations; global business competition and global consumer choice; and the sheer number of people affected by globalisation. In this sense globalisation has been defined as "a process of rapid economic integration among countries, driven by the liberalization of trade, investment and capital flows as well as rapid technological change" (Held 1999); and one of its main characteristics is the convergence of globalising tendencies within all the key domains of social interaction.

The numerous definitions of globalization emphasize different aspects of the process and in doing so express different evaluations and ideological stances (Went, 2000). For example (Osmani, 2005)*:

- The intensification of global linkages across a wide sphere - across transnational corporate business structures, international finances, people's mobility (migration, tourism), global cultural exchange, global environmental issues, and technology and electronic communication.
- Globalization not only refers to economic processes or the development of economic institutions, but also describes the interconnection between individual life and global features; the process of increasing economic, political, and social interdependence and global integration that takes place as capital, traded goods, persons, concepts, images, ideas and values diffuse across state boundaries. Routes of globalisation are in the industrial revolution and *laissez-faire* economic policies of the last century.
- Globalization and liberalization are a fast, new express train and countries have been told that all they need

*These definitions are taken from a very useful discussion on the internet by Tamara Hattar, Debra Berliner, and Flavio Casoy, dated October 17, 2000 and entitled *Globalization: Health Promoter or Health Hazard*?

to do was get on aboard...those that fail to get aboard will find themselves marginalized in the world community and world economy.

- New "actors" and "agents" which transcend national boundaries, for example the World Trade Organisation (WTO). Such agencies may have or claim to have authority over governments. Indeed the role and potential for action of nation-states – with the exception of the largest and most powerful, the US – may be questioned by the existence of such global organisations. Some multinational corporations have global reach and more economic power than many states. Some NGOs are able to mobilise globally in opposition to and independently of states.

Globalism is a state of the world involving networks of interdependence at multicontinental distances. Globalisation refers to the increase of globalism. In comparison with interdependence, globalism has two special characteristics (Keohane and Nye, 2000). Firstly, globalisation refers to networks of connections (multiple relationships), not simply to single linkages. Secondly, it refers to the shrinkage of distance but on a large scale, which can be contrasted with localization, nationalization, or rationalizations. Interdependence and globalisation are both multidimensional phenomena. Analytically, Keohane and Nye have differentiated following dimensions according to the types of flows and perceptual connections that occur in spatially extensive networks:

(i) *Economic globalism* involves long-distance flows of goods, services and capital, and the information and perceptions that accompany market exchange. It also involves the oganisation of processes that are linked to these flows: for example, the organization of low-wage production in Asia for the USA and European markets.

(ii) *Environmental globalism* refers to the long distance transport of materials in the atmosphere or oceans or of biological substances such as pathogens or generic materials that affect human health and well-being. Examples include the depletion of stratospheric ozone layer, global warming and the spread of AIDS virus from central Africa around the world beginning at the end of the 1970s.

(iii) *Military globalism* refers to long-distance networks of interdependence in which force, and the threat or promise of force are employed. A good example is the "balance of terror" between the USA and Soviet Union during cold war.

(iv) *Social and cultural globalism* involves movements of ideas, information, images, and of people— who of course carry ideas and information with them. It also includes imitation of one society's practices and institutions by others: what some sociologists refer to as 'isomorphism'.

Almost all forms of globalisation have political implications. For example, WTO, Non-Proliferation Treaty (NPT), Montreal Convention, and UNESCO — are responses to economic, military, environmental and social globalisation. Globalisation occurs in other dimensions as well. The division of globalisation into separate dimensions is inevitably somewhat arbitrary. But it is useful for analysis, because changes in the various dimensions of globalisation do not necessarily co-vary. Thus, without an adjective, general statements about globalisation are often meaningless or misleading (Keohane and Nye, 2000).

Globalisation is Not New

Globalisation is not a new phenomenon. The oldest form of globalisation is environmental: climate change has affected the ebb and flow of human population for millions of years. Migration is a long-standing global phenomenon. The human species began to leave Africa (place of origin) about 1.25 million years ago and reached the Americas sometime between 30,000 and 13,000 years ago. One of the most important forms of globalisation is biological. The first smallpox epidemic is recorded in Egypt in 1350 B.C. It reached China in 49 A.D.; then Europe after 700; the Americas in 1520 and Australia in 1789 (Barquet and Domingo, 1997). Similarly, the plague or Black Death originated in Asia, but its spread killed a quarter to a third population of Europe between 1346 and 1352 (McNeill, 1977). Military globalisation dates back at least from the time of Alexander the Great's expeditions of 2,300 years ago, which resulted in an empire that stretched across three continents from Athens to the Indus through Egypt. Indeed, Alexander's conquests were arguably most important for introducing Western thought and society, in the form of Hellenism, to the eastern world (McKay, 1991).

When people make comments like "globalisation is fundamentally new" only make sense in this context but are yet misleading. It is better to speak of globalism as a phenomenon with ancient roots and of globalisation as the process of increasing globalism, now or in the past. The issue is not how old globalism is, but rather how "thin" or "thick" at any given point of time (Held, 1999). The Silk Road provided an economic and cultural link between ancient Europe and Asia is an example of "thin globalisation". But the route was used by a small group of traders and the direct impact of the trade was primarily on small and relatively elite consumers along the road. In contrast, "thick globalisation" involves many relationships that are intensive as well as extensive: long-distance flows that are large and continuous, affecting the lives of many people throughout the world. Often, contemporary globalisation is equated with Americanisation, especially by non-Americans, who resent popular culture of USA and the capitalism that accompanies it. If we think of the content of globalisation being "uploaded" on the Internet and then "downloaded" elsewhere, more of this content is uploaded in USA than anywhere else.* However, the ideas and information that enter global networks are downloaded in the context of national politics and local cultures, which act as selective filters and modifiers of what arrives. Political institutions are often more resistant to transnational transmission than popular culture. Globalisation today is America-centric and the central position of USA in global networks creates "soft power": the ability to get others to want what Americans want (Nye 1990). But the processes are reciprocal in many respects, rather than one way only. Soft power is a reality, but it cannot be credited with USA in all areas of life, nor it is the only country to possess it. This historical background is important as it shows that transport and communication inventions and innovations have been causing dramatic economic upheaval and development throughout the past 200 years. Globalisation refers to this process between countries, but it also happens within one country, as the economic history of America shows.

Is there anything about globalism today, which is fundamentally different? Historians can always find precursors in the past for phenomena of the present, but contemporary globalisation goes "faster, cheaper and deeper" (Friedman 1999). The thickness of globalisation is giving rise to increased density of networks, increased institutional velocity and increased transnational participation. As a result, it is expected that globalisation will be accompanied by uncertainty. On the one hand, there will be a continuous competition between increased complexity and uncertainty;

---

*Professor Anne-Marie Slaughter of Harvard University Law School used the expressions of "uploading" and "downloading" content, at John F. Kennedy School of Government Visions Project Conference on Globalisation, Bretton Woods, N.H., 1999.

and efforts by the governments, market participants and others to grasp and manage these complex interconnected systems, on the other.

General Impact of Globalisation

The impact of globalisation as it becomes evident in economic sphere has not left social and political sphere untouched. In the economic sphere as there is greater emphasis on privatisation and opening of economy for foreign capital. In political sphere too, the first world's institutions and standards are projected as a model. Individualism is re-emphasized in recognition of not only a form of individual's freedom of creating wealth and property but also as living a life of dignity that entails availability of basic necessities of life like food, water and shelter. Freedom from want, fear and insecurity is the basic condition to be human. Overall, many aspects of the functioning of the new global economy are still poorly documented and understood. This state of relative ignorance has provided fertile ground for the growth of anxiety over the effects of globalisation.

There are both positive and negative impacts of globalisation. A world-wide wave of trade and investment liberalisation (but, notably, not of general labour market liberalisation) is an important factor behind globalisation in recent decades, spurred in part by the rejection of central planning and similar protectionist development models in many countries (McCarty 2001). The average tariff rate across all countries has fallen steadily from 40 percent in 1940 to about 5 percent in 1995 (Dicken 1998). Globalisation is now also being driven by the notable improvement in the quality and declining cost. Mobile phones, facsimile machines, and the Internet have introduced new communication choices. The worldwide number of Internet hosts increased from about 3 million in 1994 to over 50 million in 1999 (World Bank 2000). The movement of financial and capital flows across borders is both a cause and effect of this "information revolution" and the liberalisation trend: the daily turnover of foreign exchange markets increased from $US1.1 billion in 1992 to $US1.6 billion in 1995; international liquid capital flows grew at an average 25% per annum during 1980-1995; and global foreign direct investment increased from US$193 billion in 1990 to US$400 billion in 1997 (World Bank 2000). Thus, while globalisation may not be new, it is different: faster, and driven by new information-based technologies and liberalising reforms to exploit the comparative advantages of nations. It is also, arguably, becoming more inclusive.

But in spite of all these advantages, why are we all not applauding globalisation? Because, a number of processes associated with globalisation have been considered to have had negative impacts. In normal use, globalisation tends to refer to just business transactions. So it values business transactions above all others – the social, cultural and other transactions between people. Therefore, globalisation really tends to be used to mean globalisation of markets, not the globalisation of society. But that is not the only problem. Agriculture has been devalued by the processes of globalisation. If we look at the wealth gap not between rich and poor countries, but between the rich and poor people, we will find that the gap is widening continuously and rapidly. In 1960, the poorest 20 percent of the global population received 2.3 percent of the global income. By 1991, their share had sunk to 1.4 percent and today it is only 1.1 percent of the global income. The ratio of income of richest 20 percent of the people to that of poorest 20 percent was 30:1 in 1960, and by 1995 that ratio stood at 82:1 (Rao, 2008). This is based on distribution between rich and poor countries, but when maldistribution of income within countries taken into consideration, the richest 20 percent of the world's people got at least 150 more than poorest 20 percent (UNDP 1992). This richest 20 percent of highest income countries account for 86 percent of the global consumption, while poorest 20 percent, only 1.3 percent. It has been argued that "globalisation is proceeding largely for the benefit of the dynamic and powerful countries" (UNDP 1997). It can also be perhaps described as a neo-colonial marriage between metropolitan financial interests and metropolitan industrial interests (Patnaik, 1999). The supporters of globalisation may argue that the gap between North and South is reducing, not increasing. It is true that over recent years the growth rate of Southern countries is slightly ahead of Northern countries. It is because of just few countries, China and India in particular. If we take out China from the picture, we would see that developing countries are still falling behind the industrialized countries. Even if growth rate might be higher for the southern countries, it is not same as catching up with the North. The growth of an economy is like acceleration of the economy, its not to do with the over all size. "To say that the developing countries are catching up with the North is a little bit like saying that a bicycle that sets off to try to catch a racing car that is going at full speed. If we are able to maintain the acceleration, it would take 74 years at the current growth rate for the developing countries to catch up with the industrialized countries. And for the first 50 years of that progress, the absolute gap between North and South would continue to widen" (Clark 2003). Another thing is that inequalities are not just between North and South; it is very much present within different regions of the country, particularly between rural and urban areas.

From human rights perspective also, globalisation has many negative impacts. The debt situation of the third world countries – itself a product of first world's lending policies in the past – became the vehicle for neo-colonial onslaught. Future loans from IMF and World Bank are linked with broad package of macroeconomic policies in the form of

'Structural Adjustment Programme (SAP)'. Indebted countries were obliged to accept this in order to qualify for loan rescheduling and continued international assistance (Gershman and Irwin, 2000). The fundamental feature of SAP included a reorganization of poor countries' economic and social policy structures in line with the ideology of economic neoliberalism. The role of the state was minimized, the private sector deregulated, and market forces freed. SAPs forced the privatization of many government assets, sharp public sector budget cuts especially on health and education, scaling back of labour protections, the elimination of price controls and subsidies on food, and the imposition of "user fees" for health services and education. In theory, SAPs were intended to stimulate growth and help reduce the burden of poverty; but in practice, the austerity measures often exacerbated poverty (Schoepf *et al.* 1992). The quality and provision of basic services in many countries are either decreased or privatized. It can result in significantly reduced poor people's ability to access to these services which are essential for the enjoyment of the rights recognized in human rights instruments such as the International Covenant on Economic, Social and Cultural Rights (ICESCR) and the Convention on the Rights of the Child (CRC). A decrease in the availability of public services can result in adverse effects on the rights to education, to health, to an adequate standard of living, and on women's rights. The right of everyone to social security may not be ensured by arrangements that rely entirely on private arrangements and on private schemes. The reduced quantity and quality of basic services can be further reduced if elites and middle classes "opt out" of national level systems of service (Dommen, 2001). At the UN Millennium Summit in September, 2000, countries recognized the potential of globalization but noted that it was also characterized by risks and uncertainties that could further exacerbate existing imbalances and further polarize the "haves" and "have nots".

Thus, the problem is not with the globalisation per se but with the selective way that the globalisation has been managed in a way that widens inequalities of wealth and power. Good governance of globalisation is a reality. One cannot escape its forces. And there is no denying that globalisation has led to the marginalisation of a large number of already vulnerable sections of society. The challenge before the state is not how to fight globalisation but how to manage it with good governance. The good governance is linked with what UNDP's Human Development Reports call "building capabilities and widening the choices of all". Of course, the capability building approach is better than the so called basic needs or minimum needs approach (Raj, 2002). As Prof. Amartya Sen points out, needs is a more passive concept than capability and it is arguable that the perspective of positive freedom links naturally with capabilities (what can the person do) rather than with the fulfillment of their needs (what can be done for them).

Globalisation and Health

There are two broad views of how globalisation affects health. The optimistic view sees the increased interdependence attendant upon globalisation resulting in an increased willingness of nations to work together in pursuit of improved health because this would serve their rational self-interest. This offered an optimistic analysis of the health benefits of globalisation to poor countries and to poor communities in rich countries. This view argues that increased pace of cross-national exchanges should facilitate diffusion of technological innovations such as new and effective contraceptive methods, techniques for enabling access to clean water, inexpensive refrigeration, efficient transport and communication technologies, and new and effective systems for prevention and treatment of infectious disease (Barnett, 2000). From cultural and political level, it also includes acceptance and application of common human rights throughout the world. Globalisation can play a positive role in facilitating exchange of information on health policies and exchange of health services. Globalisation can also facilitate the realization of human rights such as the rights to information and to education, which in turn are important for the realization of the right to health.

On the other hand, the pessimistic view sees globalisation as a phenomenon, which because of the increasing loss of sovereignty by nation states means that states are less willing to pool resources (Barnett 2000). Increased movements of people seeking employment, changes in behaviour, and increased movement of goods across the world, for instance, have contributed to the more rapid spread of diseases such as malaria, HIV/AIDS, and tuberculosis. The adverse health effects associated with this are exacerbated by reductions in basic services as limited resources in developing countries constrain the governments' capacity. The right to health should not to be understood as a right to be healthy, but that it does embrace a range of socio-economic factors that promote conditions in which people can lead a healthy life, and extends to the underlying determinants of health, such as food and nutrition, housing, access to safe and potable water and adequate sanitation, safe and healthy working conditions, and a healthy environment.

In addition to the fact that multinational pharmaceutical companies have fought to keep prices of important drugs high, making it harder for governments to protect and fulfill the right to health. These companies also tend to invest more into research into diseases that affect rich countries rather than those that affect the poorest inhabitants of the low-income countries. For the more readily available large profits from treatments of diseases in rich countries, they have been paying less attention to the needs of the poor countries. That's why the pursuit of an HIV/AIDS vaccine has been of less interest to big pharmaceutical companies as they get more profit from development of treatments than vaccines. These concerns have been particularly evident in the some pharmaceutical companies' efforts to ensure strong patent protection for their products, and their obstruction of production of cheaper, generic versions of important medicines. Pharmaceutical companies have brought cases against countries like South Africa and Philippines for their initiatives to make drugs available at lower cost through compulsory licensing or parallel imports. The US government has brought legal challenges against Thailand, Brazil and other countries' initiatives to allow compulsory licensing for production of inexpensive generic versions of expensive drugs to treat HIV/AIDS.

In this context, role of the international agencies are also need to be discussed. Although neo-liberal economic ideologies and the World Bank have not always been identical, they have certainly been very close. The World Bank has had a profound influence on health provision in poor countries as the largest external financer of health activities in low and middle income countries. It has also been a major voice in national and international health policy debates and an important contributor to health policy research. Over the past two decades, the thrust of the World Bank's strategies was to emphasize the role of the market in health care provision. Government's role was to be mainly regulatory, by supervising the marketplace, insurance legislation, ensuring "acceptable" levels of access. But, it ignores the social ethics of health care and defines health services as commodities to be delegated to the market sector of an economy; ignores the provision of public goods such as immunization and public sewage; and generally seeks to shift the larger burden of curative services to the private sector, which makes it available to foreign investment. The WHO, whose work in this area is underpinned by human rights concerns because of its focus on equity of access to drugs, has taken a number of initiatives to this end. WHO says that patents should protect the interest of the patent-holder while safeguarding public health, and supports measures, which improve access to essential drugs (WHO 2000; WTO 2001). But, World Trade Organisation (WTO) did not agree to change Trade Related aspects of Intellectual Property Rights (TRIPs).

In addition to all these, brain drain is another problem. Less than a decade ago, the biggest problem in global health seemed to be the lack of resources available to combat the multiple scourges ravaging the world's poor and sick. Today, there is an extraordinary and unprecedented rise in public and private funding; more money is being directed toward pressing health challenges than ever before. But poor countries could be pushed even further into trouble, unless these efforts are properly coordinated and directed mostly at specific high-profile diseases rather than at public health in general; and unless the braindrain from the developing world can be stopped. This danger exists despite the fact that today, for the first time in history; the world is poised to spend enormous resources to conquer the diseases of the poor (Garrett, 2007). Virtually no provisions exist to allow the world's poor to say what they want, decide which projects serve their needs, or adopt local innovations. Besides it, the world is now short well over four million health-care workers and this fact is all too often ignored. As the populations of the developed countries are aging and require even more medical attention, they lure away local health talent from developing countries. As per the *Journal of the American Medical Association* (JAMA), already one out of five practicing physicians in the United States is foreign-trained and estimated that if current trends continue, by 2020 the United States could face a shortage of up to 800,000 nurses and 200,000 doctors. Data from international migration-tracking organizations show that health professionals from poor countries worldwide are increasingly abandoning their homes to take up jobs in wealthy countries. In Ghana, 604 out of 871 medical officers trained in the country between

1993 and 2002 now practice overseas. Zimbabwe, similarly, trained 1,200 doctors during the 1990s, but only 360 remain in the country today (Garrett, 2007).

Thus, we find that effective interventions exist for many priority health problems in low income countries; prices are falling, and funds are increasing. However, progress towards agreed MDGs related to health remains slow. There is increasing consensus that stronger health systems are key to achieving improved health outcomes. There is much less agreement on quite how to strengthen them. As a result, the health world is fast approaching in the road of uncertainty. The years ahead could witness remarkable improvements in the health of billions of people, or they could see poor societies pushed into even deeper trouble. The emerging outcome will depend on whether it is possible to expand the developing world's local talent pool of health workers, restore and improve crumbling national health infrastructures of developing countries, and devise effective local and international systems for disease prevention and treatment.

AIDS, NGOs and Globalisation

Globalisation forces have reduced state controls over the economy at the national level, increase pressure for democratic accountability, or raise questions about state sovereignty. These developments have created political space for civil society organizations as alternative sources of services once provided by the state, as watchdogs over and advocates for government policy formulation and implementation, as policy entrepreneurs or implementers with state partners, and as social innovators to guide improved services. In general, however, the more open the country is to globalisation, the more we would expect civil society organisations to become important actors in the country's development. This is a function of three factors: (1) globalisation has impacts on consciousness—both liberating and counter-revolutionary–

that are likely to be expressed via civil society organisations; (2) globalisation is likely to place enhanced emphasis on the political ideologies of individualism, freedom, and equal rights for which NGOs are both a product and an exemplar; and (3) globalisation invites in international actors (INGOs, international agencies) that actively promote and strengthen the emergence of national civil societies (Brown *et al.* 2000). When globalisation expands political space, civil society actors may emerge to respond to the concerns of impoverished and marginalized groups that would remain voiceless under prior regimes (Brown *et al.* 2000). Of course, neither globalisation, nor a form of international governance, nor the emergence of a kind of transnational civil society undergirded by nongovernmental organisations is entirely new. NGOs and civil society alliances have been active in international governance and policy-making for many years. What is new is the recent explosion in numbers, activity, and visibility of international initiatives by civil society actors on a variety of issues, at least in part linked to the rapidly declining cost of communication. The emergence of international NGOs, networks, coalitions, and social movement organizations as potentially important political actors at both national and international levels has been stimulated by the need to create collective responses to threatening circumstances created by globalisation. By the count of the *Yearbook of International Organizations*, the number of international NGOs has grown more than fourfold (i.e. from 6000 to 26000) in the last decade (*Economist* 1999). While there is a great deal of variance in the size and activity of the civil society across countries, the sector is growing rapidly in many countries and regions. It is estimated, for example, that more than 100,000 civil society organisations have emerged in Eastern Europe since the fall of the Berlin Wall, and more than 1,000,000 NGOs are operating in India (Smith *et al.* 1997). International NGOs and NGO alliances are emerging as increasingly influential players in international decision-making. The focus of NGOs on official UN deliberations on the international policy agenda was evident at a number of major UN conferences and their preparatory meetings. Some of these conferences are: UN Conference on Environment (Rio de Janeiro, 1992), World Conference on Human Rights (Vienna, 1993), International Conference on Population and Development (Cairo, 1994), Fourth World Conference on Women (Beijing, 1995), World Summit for Social Development (Copenhagen, 1995), UNGASS (2001) and many more. These conferences attracted an unprecedented number of NGOs. There has been a dramatic increase in their importance in many arenas over the last two decades. This change has been characterized as a "global associational revolution" that may as important to the end of the 20th century as the rise of the nation-state was a century earlier (Salamon, 1994). NGOs formed coalitions and played a significant role in the accords to ban landmines, to establish International Criminal Court, to introduce code of conduct for baby food sales, to include women's reproductive health rights and on many more issues. NGO are also increasingly active in many different arenas like global warming, debt relief for heavily indebted poor countries (HIPC), elementary education for all children, trade related intellectual property rights (TRIPS), etc. At the international level NGOs and NGO alliances have identified emerging problems, articulated new values and norms, created or reformed institutional arrangements, fostered innovations in international practice, and helped to resolve conflicts and manage differences.

Thus, the role of NGOs in society can't be ignored. This is true also in the field of prevention and treatment of HIV/AIDS. Two years after its first appearance in 1981, the AIDS virus had spread to 60 countries and it rapidly became a global pandemic. Globalisation is midwife both to the spread of the disease, as modern travel facilitates rapid dissemination of HIV infection across national borders, and, through concerted global action, triumphant conqueror over its devastating impact and expansion. William McNeill (1977) was among the first to draw our attention to the role of epidemic disease in human history. Many subsequent authors have noted its importance, and most recently Jared Diamond (1998) has informatively discussed its role in the increasing integration of human society and economy over the past 13,000 years (which may be another way of talking of "globalisation"). HIV/AIDS is a global pandemic affecting the ultimate metapopulation – the entire human community. Its distribution is unequal: spatially, in terms of countries and parts of countries; socially, in terms of social and cultural groups; and economically, in terms of income and wealth classes (Barnett & Whiteside 2000).

In 1980s, when AIDS started gaining public attention, close friends, family members and other individuals came from the same interest group. People living with HIV/AIDS (PLWHA) were amongst the first to provide care and support. Despite reluctance and slow actions from many governments, these NGOs, particularly AIDS Service Organistions (ASOs) came forward to provide critical care and support to HIV affected people mainly because of their closeness and trust of the people on the ground. Beyond this personal support, many of these organisations have evolved into effective advocates who helped put issues squarely on to the national agenda (Bogasao, 1998). Several CBOs and NGOs have since emerged from these groups hardest hit by AIDS. AIDS is no longer a concern for just health authorities. The potential impact of AIDS makes it a challenge in economic, political, social and religious spheres as well. Amongst the organisations responding to the crisis, NGOs are emerging as a powerful force in the effort to contain the epidemic. Diverse groups at risk of HIV infection have been reached by NGOs in a wide variety of innovative programmes (Mercer *et al.* 1991). In areas of the industrialized world hardest hit by AIDS, NGOs helped set trend that have now been institutionalized within AIDS prevention. In the developing world, the NGO response to HIV/AIDS emerged somewhat more slowly. It reflects both lack of resources and experience, and a widespread reluctance to publicly acknowledge or recognize the threat. However, as the epidemic progressed, both well established and newly formed NGOs among the first to respond, promoting the need for PLWHA to have access to counseling, support and health care. They have mobilized impressive efforts for training, education and other supportive services while official declarations denied the existence of the problem (Morna and PANOS 1991; Haslegrave, 1988; Mercer *et al.* 1991). The importance of NGOs in the NACP of developing countries has also evolved overtime.

The journey from the denial of early years to the AIDS bandwagon, and from these into infinitely complex world of HIV/AIDS awareness and control, has brought perceptible shifts of emphasis in interventions. Until the late 1990s, the governments of the majority of acutely threatened African States were silent about AIDS – the epidemic that ravaging their countries. The UN was of little help either. Its agencies were slow and resistant to responding to the threat that HIV posed to developing states, prone to intense institutional rivalry and bickering, and overly protective of vulnerable, established budgets and mandates. As the epidemic of HIV/AIDS continues to expand to all corners of globe, it is clear that every sector of the society must respond. It was not until 1987, six years into the pandemic that the WHO, the UN's leading public health arm, responded to the reality that millions of people had been infected with HIV in all continents. The WHO established the Global Programme on AIDS (GPA) in 1987 under the leadership of late Dr. Jonathan Mann. GPA successfully mobilized national responses, initiated needed research and became a voice for those living with AIDS. At that time, it was the WHO's largest programme.

But it soon was plagued by conflict with other bodies of UN system. These rivalries, as well as concerns over WHO's senior leadership, an increasing preference by the wealthy nations for bilateral programmes in the face of declining foreign aid budgets and for UN reform after the cold war – led to calls for a more multi-sectoral response (Merson, 2005). Accordingly the decision was made in1996 to disband GPA and replace it with a Joint UN Programme on AIDS (UNAIDS), to coordinate AIDS targeted programmes. In its leading advocacy role for worldwide action against HIV/AIDS, UNAIDS along with its eight co-sponsors – United Nations Children's Fund (UNICEF), United Nations Development Programme (UNDP), United Nations population Fund (UNFPA), United Nations Educational, Social and Cultural Organisation (UNESCO), United International Drug Control Programme (UNDCP), International Labour Organisation (ILO), World Health Organisation (WHO), and World Bank (WB) – states its mission to " lead, strengthen and support an expended response to HIV/AIDS epidemic aimed at preventing the transmission of HIV, providing care and support for those infected and affected by the disease, reducing vulnerability of individuals and communities to the HIV/AIDS and alleviating the socio-economic and human impacts of the epidemic" (UNAIDS, 2002). UNAIDS is actively engaged with leading global advocacy efforts, establishing baseline global facts on the pandemic, and coordinating accordingly the efforts of its eight co-sponsoring agencies, all of which maintains their own substantial HIV/AIDS programmes. The ILO focuses on the pandemic's impact on the workers and employers; UNICEF focuses on disproportionate impact of HIV/AIDS on children and mothers; UNDP and World Bank have taken leadership roles in addressing the threat to development posed by HIV/AIDS in building national capacities across key ministries; UNDCP increasing focuses on preventing HIV transmission through illicit drug use; the UNFPA focuses on the connection between reproductive health and HIV. Later on, United Nations High Commissioner for Refugees (UNHCR) and the World Food Programme (WFP) are also included in UNAIDS as co-sponsors. The Figure 10.1 shows the spending of UN Agencies on HIV/AIDS during 1996-2005.

Figure-10.1: UN Agency Spending on HIV/AIDS

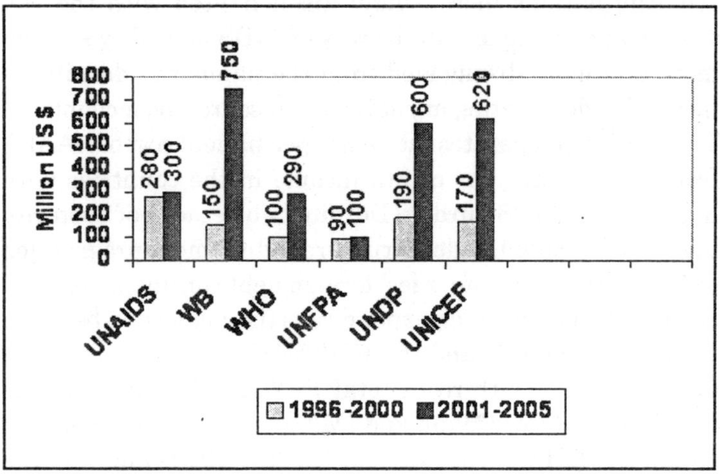

Source: UNAIDS 2007.

During 1990s, all countries established National AIDS Control Programme and adopted strategies and intervention to prevent the spread of HIV/AIDS. The strategies broadly included: (a) preventing HIV infection and (b) providing care and support to those living with HIV/AIDS. Lessons learnt from the experiences of last two decades clearly indicate that national responses should not wait for AIDS cases to soar. Instead they should focus on responding quickly, mobilizing all sectors and recognizing and collaborating with NGOs and the private sector. Involving vulnerable groups at every step of policy and programme development and implementation is crucial for programme success.

In 1996, the same year when UNAIDS was established, researchers announced a new therapy to prolong the lives of people with AIDS. This highly active antiretroviral therapy (HAART) promptly saved millions of lives in developed countries. The HAART costs over US $ 10,000 per patient per year – a price affordable to few in developing countries. Wealthy nations increasingly disenchanted with the UN system and facing less in the way of AIDS mortality seemed more and more disengaged from the pandemic, despite its increasing devastating impact on the resource- poor countries. This wide gap separates the yearly per-patient cost of HAART from the average per capita income in the countries with highest HIV/AIDS burden. Despite two decades of austerity measures adopted under structural adjustment programme (SAP), many poor countries' foreign debt continues to grow. A recent Oxfam briefing paper draws the connection between unsustainable debt and the HIV/AIDS pandemic. It points out that the one-third of total PLWHA live in countries classified by World Bank and IMF as heavily indebted poor countries (HIPC). Through out the late 1990s and into the present decade, activist organizations like AIDS Coalition to Unleash Power (ACT UP), Health Global Access Project (Health GAP), South Africa's Treatment Action Plan (TAC) and others have carried on sustained campaign targeting large multinational pharmaceutical firms to introduce different pricing system for the developing countries that would open the possibility for government and NGOs to purchase ARVs at discounted rates (Irwin et al 2003). Activists' direct actions were complemented by the policy and advocacy work of US watchdog Consumer Project Technology (CPT), Health Action International and Medecins Sans Frontieres (MSF). In October 1999, MSF was awarded the Nobel Peace Prize and became a vocal leader in demanding AIDS treatment for the world. A month later, AIDS activists joined anti-globalisation protesters at the "Battle for Seattle"— the venue of WTO meeting, which led to a violent clash and grabbed more international attentions. They made similar protests during subsequent WTO and G-8 Summits for changes in the TRIPS and cancellation of debts of HIPCs along with other demands. Jubilee 2000 (another NGO, who launched 'Drop the Debt' campaign for African countries) pointed out that Africas' debt repayment totals around US$ 15 billion annually – far surpassing the US$ 10 billion needed for the global AIDS treatment. In response, Accelerating Access Initiative (AAI) was started in May 2000 and began to provide steeply discounted drugs to the least developed countries based on country's GNP. The AAI is an alliance between five UN organizations and five big pharma companies (later six), but it failed to deliver enough treatment to Africans. In the same month, the big firms made a complain with WTO to prevent Brazil from acquiring and making generic drugs and two months later they revived their lawsuits against South Africa (D'Adesky 2004). The turning point in the global battle was the pioneering decision by Cipla–a leading Indian generic drug manufacturer to offer ARV medicines to the frontline groups of African countries like MSF for $360 a year (i.e. less than $ 1 a day per patient) or for $ 600 if purchased by the governments. Overnight, the single biggest obstacle to global access fell away; setting the stage for what has become the era of treatment (*Reuters* 2001). Responding to the pressure of public opinion and market competition from the generic drug companies, major research based pharma companies announced initiatives to lower their own prices on AIDS medications in poorer regions. Later on, they also settled the matter with Brazil and withdrew the lawsuit against South Africa (D'adesky, 2004).

However, NGOs' roles are not just restricted to the role of advocacy and implementing agencies in the HIV/AIDS field. It is also actively participating in the decision making process at the local, national, regional and international level. Since

UNAIDS was set up in 1996, civil society or NGO has been a key partner. Among the various UN entities UNAIDS has had one of the most diverse and extensive set of civil society partners. Historically, the relationships with civil society developed at a time when many governments were reluctant to even acknowledge AIDS. Early partnering started with AIDS activists and gradually expanded to a wide diversity of civil society partners. UNAIDS was the first United Nations programme to have formal civil society representation on its governing body. At present, the Programme Coordinating Board (PCB) allows for an NGO Delegation of 5 representatives and 5 alternates. The Delegates have formal

Figure-10.2: Structure of Country Coordinating Mechanisms (CCMs).
(Entities participating in preparation of Round Four proposals.
100% = All representatives of all 78 surveyed CCMs.)

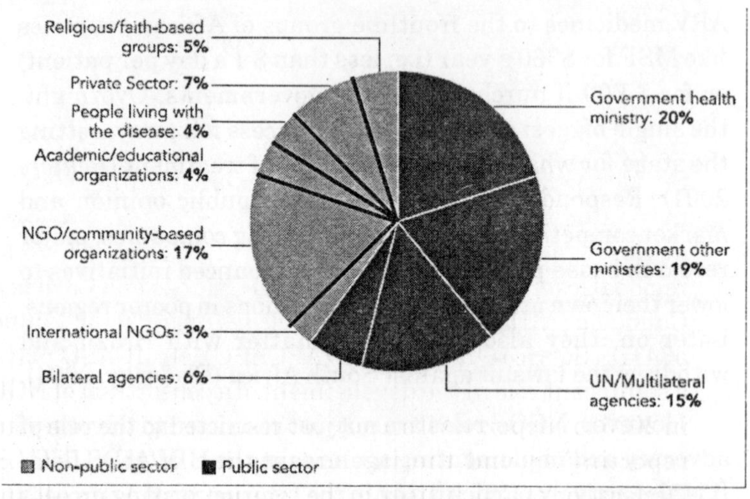

Source: GFATM

terms of reference, can serve for up to three years and have non-voting status. The UNAIDS model helped inform the governing structures of the GFATM. Civil society members hold three seats on the GFATM Board, namely the Developed Country NGO, the Developing Country NGO and the Communities Affected by the Diseases (referred to as the "Communities Delegation"). Each of these constituencies has full voting rights. Country Coordinating Mechanism (CCM) is central to the Global Fund's commitment to local ownership and participatory decision making (See Figure 10.2). These country-level partnerships develop and submit grant proposals to the Global Fund based on priority needs at the national level. After grant approval, they oversee progress during implementation.

NGOs are also represented in other UN bodies and similar international organizations. They are also engaged in training, research, documentation, networking and consultancy work. In 1992, the Global Network of People Living with HIV/AIDS (GNP+) was officially launched, which had a huge impact at the regional and national level. For example, Asia Pacific Network of People Living with HIV/AIDS (APN+) and Indian Network for PLWHA (INP+) were formed respectively at the regional and national level. Another organization – International Council for AIDS Service Organisation (ICASO) similarly influenced and maintains a strong network with other such organizations at the regional and national level. For example, there are regional level organizations like Latin America and Caribbean Council of AIDS Service Organisation, Asia Pacific Council of AIDS Service Organisation (APCASO), etc. ICASO played a significant role in the development of a consortium of NGOs in 2005 to support civil society-led monitoring, advocacy and reporting around the implementation of the UNGASS Declaration of Commitment. The International AIDS Alliance produced a toolkit to help NGOs evaluate and build their capacity to respond to the epidemic (International AIDS Alliance, 2004). In December 2004, NGOs from around the world came together and created the nongovernmental organization HIV/AIDS Code of Practice. It provides a set of principles of good practice for advocacy and AIDS programming, to which NGOs can commit themselves and be held accountable. Thanks to the combined efforts of organizations and networks, the basic principle of ensuring meaningful involvement of civil society, and particularly of people living with HIV, is now being written into the policies and strategies of many organizations, institutions and AIDS programmes.

Around the turn of the millennium, several key changes made these same rich nations to be receptive again to UNAIDS advocacy. Firstly, the significant spread of HIV into Russia, China and India in a post - 9/11 environments prompted concern that AIDS could destabilize global political and economic systems. Secondly, the agitation of international NGOs led to generic production of ART drugs at a globally reduced price. Brazil showed the way in demonstrating how the use of these drugs could dramatically reduce AIDS mortality in a developing country setting. Thirdly, after their long reluctance, the politically powerful faith-based communities in USA extended support to this global fight including support for condom promotion. As a result of all these changes, millions of persons saw the impact of the pandemic, when the XIII International AIDS Conference was held in 2000 for the first time in a developing country (Durban, South Africa). This has resulted in increasing partnerships, greater involvements and enhanced political commitments to scale up effective interventions to fight this global adversary (GFTAM, 2002; WHO, 2001). For example, United Nations Millennium Development Declaration adopted unanimously in 2000 by all members, encompasses eight Millennium Development Goals (MDGs), three of which are health related: reducing child mortality, improving maternal health and to have halted and begun to reverse the spread of HIV/AIDS and the incidence of malaria and other diseases by 2015. In June 2001, the ground-breaking UN General Assembly Special Session on HIV/AIDS (UNGASS) mobilized political and financial commitments from both the developed and developing countries. In Doha Summit (November, 2001), WTO issued a ruling allowing the poorest countries to use compulsory licensing and other trade mechanisms to access generic drugs in case of public health emergencies such as AIDS, TB and malaria. But, it put a condition that generic drugs could only be produced for domestic consumption, not for export. This ruling affected many poor countries, who don't have the capacity to produce the generic drugs. In January 2002, the Global Fund to Fight AIDS, TB and Malaria (GFTAM) was established. The Global Fund is a unique global public-private partnership between governments, civil society, the private sector and affected communities represents a new approach to international health financing. The Global Fund works in close collaboration with other bilateral and multilateral organizations to supplement existing efforts dealing with the three diseases. The Global Fund provides more than 20 percent of international funding to fight AIDS, as well as two-thirds of international funding to fight malaria and tuberculosis. This provided an unprecedented opportunity to mobilize and disburse additional resources through public-private partnerships to enable countries to substantially scale up interventions to check the spread of HIV/AIDS (WHO, 2001). Since its creation in 2002, the Global Fund has become the dominant financer with approved funding of US$ 8.6 billion for 450 programs in 136 countries *(*GFATM, 2007*)*. In September 2003, the WHO set a target of providing ART to 3 million people in developing countries by 2005 ('3 by 5' initiative). But, it took two more years to achieve the target. Besides these, many international organizations have been set up to assist in funding and implementing HIV prevention and care programme and related health initiatives worldwide. These include the President's Emergency Plan For AIDS Relief (PEPFAR) set up by George W. Bush, the Global Alliance for Vaccines and Immunization (GAVI), the Global Health Council, the Bill and Melinda Gates Foundation, the Rockefeller Foundation, the World Bank's Multi-country AIDS Programme (MAP), the William J. Clinton Presidential Foundation, etc. In 2003, PEPFAR pledges US $ 15 billion for a period of 5 years to fund AIDS programme in 12 African nations, Haiti and Guyana. But most of the money would be spent through USAID (i.e. through bilateral arrangement) and only US $ 1.0 billion was channeled to GFATM. Despite global progress in expanding HIV treatment access, including in some of the world's most resource-limited countries, more than 70% of individuals who were medically eligible for antiretrovirals lacked access to these drugs in 2006(UNAIDS, 2007). As HIV disease progresses among HIV-infected people who are not yet on therapy, the number of people needing therapy will grow much larger in the future.

In 2005 (14-16 September), UN General Assembly World Summit adopted a resolution towards the universal access to HIV prevention, treatment, care and support by 2010. The African Union and the G-8 countries have also endorsed this move. In 2006 at a High Level Meeting of the UN General Assembly, countries embraced a Political Declaration on HIV/AIDS that committed UN Member States to "pursuing all necessary efforts to scale up nationally driven, sustainable and comprehensive responses to achieve broad multisectoral coverage for prevention, treatment, care and support, with full and active participation of people living with HIV, vulnerable groups, most affected communities, civil society and the private sector, towards achieving the goal of universal access to comprehensive prevention programmes, treatment, care and support by 2010." (UNAIDS, 2007). Considering the national specificities with the need for global accountability, the Political Declaration on HIV/AIDS encouraged countries to develop their own national targets for key interventions and to report on progress as an integral part of existing monitoring obligations. As of June 2007, 93 countries had established time-bound targets to move towards universal access.

However, despite marked increases in financing for the HIV response during this decade, the Figure 10.3 shows the gap between resources available and the amounts needed during 2005-2007.

Figure-10.3: Funding Gap between Resource Needs & Resource Availability (2005-07).

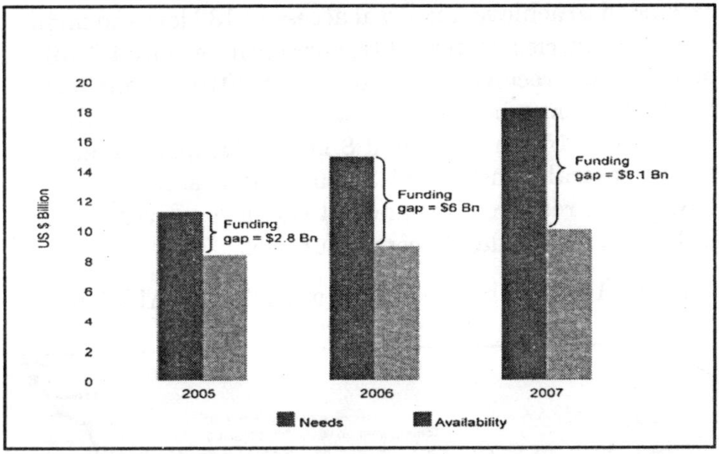

Source: UNAIDS, 2007.

This gap would be wider over the next several years if current funding trends continue. Substantial progress has been achieved in bringing essential HIV services to those in need in the low and middle-income countries where 95 per cent of all people living with HIV reside. The number of people receiving antiretrovirals in these countries increased five-fold between 2003 and 2006, and declines in HIV prevalence have been reported in several countries following the implementation of strong HIV prevention measures. If the scale-up of HIV services continues at the same pace as in the recent past, the necessary funding is projected to reach US$ 15.4 billion in 2010 (US$13.4 – US$ 17.6) and US$ 22.5 billion in 2015 (US$ 18.8 – US$ 26.9). Yet the current pace of scale-up will not achieve universal access by the agreed target date of 2010, endangering the world's ability to halt and begin to reverse the HIV epidemic by 2015, as provided in the Millennium Development Goals (MDGs). If current trends continue, only 4.6 million people would receive antiretroviral in 2010, or roughly two-thirds of the number of people who needed antiretrovirals in 2006. By 2015, an estimated 8 million people would be on antiretrovirals, instead of 21.85 million as estimated by UNAIDS if resources expanded to achieve universal access in 132 low and middle-income countries. If current trends continue, only 4.6 million people would receive antiretrovirals in 2010, or roughly two-thirds of the number of people who needed antiretrovirals in 2006. By 2015, an estimated 8 million people would be on antiretrovirals, instead of 21.85 million as estimated by UNAIDS if resources expanded to achieve universal access in 132 low and middle-income countries.

Figure-10.4: Global Resources available for AIDS during 1986 to 2007

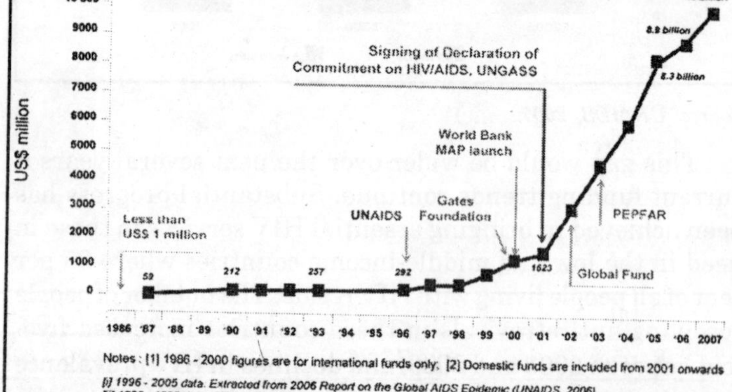

Source: UNAIDS, 2007.

The Figure 10.4 indicates the global mobilization of resources from 1986 that is unprecedented with respect to the management of chronic illness in low- and middle-income countries – generating an estimated US$ 10 billion in financing in 2007.

An urgent worldwide mobilization of technical resources is required over the next three years to overcome the many impediments that have slowed programme implementation and scale-up, such as weak procurement and supply management systems and overburdened health delivery systems. Table 10.1 shows that to meet the goal of global universal access by 2010, available financial resources for HIV must be more than quadruple by 2010 compared to 2007– up to US$ 42.2 billion (US$ 31.9 – US$ 51.4) – and continue to rise to US$ 54.0 billion by 2015 (US$ 44.6 – US$ 63.3).

Table-10.1
Financial Resources Needed for HIV Services by Scenario

(US$ Billion)

Sl. No	*Types of HIV Services*	*2009*	*2010*	*2015*
1.	Prevention	11.4	15.0	15.4
2.	Treatment & Care (including palliative care)	10.8	15.4	22.7
3.	Orphan and vulnerable children	2.4	4.4	4.5
4.	Programme costs	5.0	6.1	10.1
5.	Prevention of violence against women	0.6	1.3	1.3
	Total	30.2	42.2	54.0
	Range	(24.7 - 36.1)	(31.9 - 51.4)	(44.6 - 63.3)

Source: UNAIDS, 2007.

UNAIDS also calculated the financial resources needed to achieve universal access by the countries in terms of the income category. Table 10.2 shows the breakdown of resource needs by income level of country. As in the past, upper-middle income countries will continue to finance almost the totality of their responses to HIV, particularly in Latin America, Eastern Europe and Asia. Thus, it is anticipated that domestic public sources will supply roughly one-third of the global amounts needed to close the looming resource gap. External sources will be required to cover roughly two-thirds of the global amounts needed to achieve universal access, with the majority of such assistance focused on low-income countries, especially in sub-Saharan Africa.

Table-10.2

Financial Resources Needed Categorized by income category

(US$ Million)

Sl. No.	*Countries*	*2008*	*2009*	*2010*
1.	Low income	9,117	13,916	20,286
2.	Lower - Middle income	5,814	8,944	12,511
3.	Upper - Middle income	5,276	7,308	9,448
	Total	20,207	30,168	42,245

Source: UNAIDS, 2007.

Although the level of resources needed for HIV is higher than comparable estimates for other MDGs, it is important to note that nearly one quarter of total resources required for HIV will support health systems strengthening, which in turn will substantially buttress efforts to achieve other health-related MDGs. Table 10.3 indicates the UNAIDS estimated financial resources needed to achieve universal access in terms of activity area. These investments in the health sector include those with both direct and indirect impact on the epidemic. Overall, approximately one-third of these HIV resource needs estimates are for selected activities addressing the social drivers of the epidemic, for social mitigation and other services that are termed non-health activities. Cross-cutting activities include: civil society strengthening, global advocacy and coordination policy, human rights and stigma. UNAIDS has calculated the financial requirements by computing the number of people in need, the target coverage and the unit cost of the intervention, with amounts expressed as funds needed for each year as cash flows.

Table-10.3
Financial Resources Needed Categorized by Activity Area

(US$ Million)

Sl. No.	*Activity Area*	*2008*	*2009*	*2010*
1.	HIV specific health services	10,060	15,068	20,807
2.	Health system strengthening and cross-cutting activities	4,938	6,019	7,227
3.	Non-Health services	5,209	9,081	14,211
	Total	20,207	30,168	42,245

Source: UNAIDS, 2007.

The high levels of funding that will be needed to move towards universal access in the coming years reflect the world's failure to respond to the epidemic before it achieved crisis dimensions. Had the world made prudent investments 10-20 years ago – in prevention, in strengthening health systems in low and middle-income countries, in preserving and building essential human resources, in addressing the corrosive effects of gender inequities and other drivers of the epidemic – much smaller amounts would be required today. This same principle holds true today-we cannot afford the costs of inaction. A comprehensive, scaled-up HIV prevention response would avert more than half of all new infections that are projected to occur between 2005 and 2015 (Stover *et al.* 2006). Unless we can prevent new infections, future treatment costs will continue to mount. While these obstacles are significant, the global community stands a better chance of overcoming them than ever before. Never before has this level of funding been achieved. Never before have major world leaders focused so intensively on a global health problem. The challenge now is for all players – including recipient nations – to continuously surmount the national obstacles to a unified AIDS response. Only then real progress will be made in addressing this disease that threatens to kill 60 million more people in the next 15 years (Merson, 2005).

So far as India is concerned, NGOs like other countries were first to respond especially in the initial years when response to HIV/AIDS from the government was slow. This has been already discussed in detail in the Chapter-I. In response to international as well as national pressure created by the NGOs, the government of India started a medium term plan in 1989 for three years in collaboration with WHO. Since its establishment in 1992, NACO recognized the importance of NGOs and involved them in NACP-I (1992-1999) and NACP-II (1999-May 2007). NACO in consultation with SACS and representatives of NGOs prepared a comprehensive guideline for the involvement of NGOs in different activities of NACP. NACP-III (2007-2012) was prepared after thorough discussion with NGOs, PLWHA and other stakeholders, which took more than a year. The plan outlays of NACPs are increasing significantly as per the demand of services required in the country. NGOs put pressure on government to provide ART at free of cost, to improve health infrastructure, to ensure protection of human rights of PLWHA, etc. The government introduced free ART from April 2004. At the national level, Indian Network of

PLWHA (INP+) along with its different state branches established strong network with regional (e.g. APCASO, APN+, etc.) and international level organizations like GNP+, ICASO, etc. They have also tied up with different International NGOs and implementing different projects financially aided by these INGOs. With this strong networking, Indian NGOs have been putting more pressure on the government by demanding introduction of second line ART, amendment of Immoral Traffic Prevention Act, abolition of Indian Penal Code (IPC) Section 377 that treats MSM behaviour as a crime, recognition of sex workers as workers and provision of social security through labour laws, etc. Because of their efforts, NACP-III has incorporated several provisions like supply of second line ART, introduction of 'Smart Card' for PLWHA receiving ART, establishment of PLWHA's Network and Civil Society Forum at the district level, promotion and active involvement of CBOs more in future, etc. But, within the country, there is no networking between NGOs in HIV/AIDS care and NGOs working in other fields. Even there is no federation of NGOs working in HIV/AIDS field at the national and state level. However, Indian NGOs are represented in different international forums like UNAIDS, GFATM, etc. They are participating in GFATM through CCM and Figure 10.5 indicates the structure of Indian CCM. Thus, in India too, NGOs are actively participating in decision-making process, advocacy, training and capacity building, research and documentation along with service delivery work.

In West Bengal, the situation is no way exceptional from the national scenario. WBSAP&CS regularly consults NGOs and implementing different programmes of NACP through NGOs in the state. There is no state level federation or networking among the NGOs in HIV/AIDS care, nor with NGOs working in the other field. It implies that may be HIV/AIDS is considered by the NGOs as an isolated phenomenon, not as a threat to the development of the country. To know about the impact of globalisation on the NGOs working in HIV/AIDS field, mailed questionnaires were sent to all implementing NGOs of West Bengal. Out of 60 NGOs, responses received from the 27 (45%) NGOs are discussed below.

Figure-10.5: INDIA-CCM Structure & Inter-relationships.

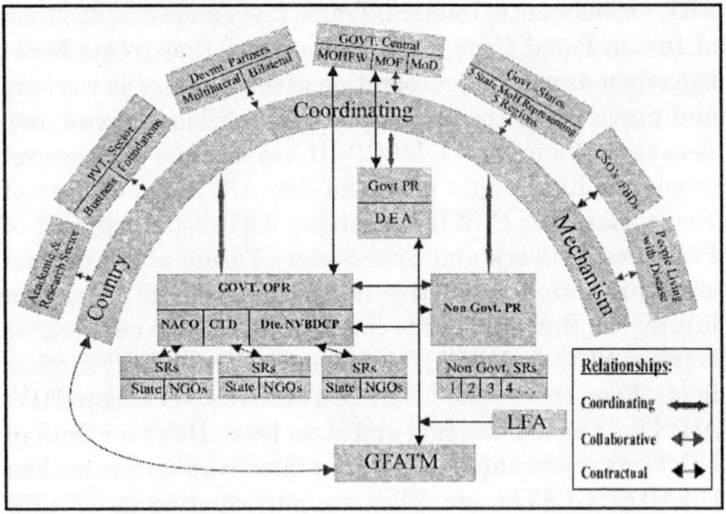

Source: GFATM.

It is found that 81.5% of the NGOs are of the opinion that fund flow will increase due to globalisation. All the NGOs feel that the role of NGOs will also be increased in the era of globalisation and justified their opinion with reasons. Some of these reasons are: (A) government is not capable alone, (B) NGOs are more effective and (C) this is a global trend. Table-10.4 shows that 44.4% of total NGOs under the study feel that NGOs' role will be increased due to government's inability and global trend (AC). While 37% NGOs feel that the government is not capable alone and NGOs are more effective than the government (AB).

Table-10.4
Reasons responsible for the Increasing Role of NGOs.

Sl. No.	*Reasons*	*No. of NGOs (%)*
1.	A	3 (11.2%)
2.	B	1 (3.7%)
3.	AB	10 (37.0%)
4.	AC	12 (44.4%)
5.	ABC	1 (3.7%)
	Total	27 (100%)

Source: Responses received through mailed questionnaire.

All the NGOs under the study are of the opinion that networking with national and international NGOs will help to fight against HIV/AIDS. They have also expressed the benefits of networking in this regard. Some of these are: (A) through exchange of information, (B) through training and exposure of staff in abroad or foreign NGOs and (C) by creating pressure on the policy makers. Table-10.5 indicates that about 70% NGOs under the study feel that all the above benefits will be available from networking, while 22.2% NGOs think about first two benefits only.

Table-10.5
Benefits of Networking

Sl. No.	*Benefits of networking*	*No. of NGOs (%)*
1.	B	1 (3.7%)
2.	AB	6 (22.2%)
3.	AC	1 (3.7%)
4.	ABC	19 (70.4%)
	Total	27 (100%)

Source: Ibid.

Considering the increasing future needs and demands of PLWHA, NGOs have expressed their views on the ways through which these demands can be fulfilled. Some of the ways are: (A) unified efforts of the government, NGOs, private companies and common people, (B) multinational companies will have to lower price for ART drugs for the developing countries, (C) government will have to ensure supply of ART at free of cost and (D) international agencies like WHO, UNICEF, ILO, etc. will have to play more active role for the developing countries. Table-10.6 shows that most (88.9%) of the NGOs under the study have suggested all the above mentioned measures for meeting the future demands of PLWHA.

Table-10.6
Ways to Meet the Future Demands of PLWHA

Sl. No.	*Ways to meet future demands*	*No. of NGOs (%)*
1.	A	1 (3.7%)
2.	D	1 (3.7%)
3.	AB	1 (3.7%)
4.	ABCD	24 (88.9%)
	Total	27 (100%)

Source: Ibid.

With regard to the over all impact of globalisation on NGOs working in HIV/AIDS care, none of the NGOs under the study express that impact will be worst. While 66.7% of them feel that impact will be good, remaining 33.7% NGOs can't predict the impact just now.

From the above discussion, we understand that HIV/AIDS is considered as a global problem and this globality of the disease has given importance in the international development and aid policy agendas. Alongside this, certain practices for coordination, communication and implementation are established. This formulation around the HIV/AIDS pandemic is very much similar with Gordenkar and Weiss's (1996) definition of global governance: "efforts to bring more orderly and reliable response to social and political issues that go beyond capacities of the states to address individually". We also find that globalisation has created enough space for the NGOs to play a more active role in all spheres including HIV/AIDS prevention, care, support and treatment. Globalisation has also helped to strengthen the networking at the national, regional and international level not only among the NGOs working in HIV/AIDS field, but also with NGOs working in the other fields. It has also brought together NGOs of the North and of the South. These networking help the NGOs in terms of sharing experiences, capacity building, training, research, etc., not just advocacy and seem to continue in future too.

We, from the above discussion, have also tried to understand the role of NGOs within the emerging international governance of HIV/AIDS and its impact in the national and local level governance of the disease. The international policy makers believe that the existing intervention mechanisms are providing correct channels for policy interventions and have recognized that lack of adequate funding as one of the most important challenges in scaling up HIV/AIDS. As a part of the existing intervention mechanisms, civil society organizations or NGOs have been at the centre for HIV/AIDS pandemic in the world. So far, NGOs were successfully able to bring more funds by their advocacy efforts especially from the reluctant industrialized countries. Recently, US House of Representatives sanctioned US$ 50 billion to PEPFAR for next five years (2009-2013) and out of it, US$ 2 billion will be channeled to GFATM for 2009 (*Washington Post*, 2008). In September 2007, Donors meeting held at Berlin and pledges US$9.7 billion over three years to GFATM. The pledges constitute the largest single financing exercise for health ever, and it will allow the Global Fund to move towards annual commitments of US$6 - 8 billion by 2010 (GFATM 2007). Therefore, it is expected that financial sustainability will be continued in future too.

However, considering the large number of NGOs, it is difficult to conclude whether the interventions of these NGOs are coherent or sustainable and whether they will have a societal impact in the long run. The external resource dependency of NGOs is one of the reasons for this situation. In the governance of HIV/AIDS, most NGOs choose the intervention mechanism as prescribed by the donors or policymakers (e.g. NACO in India). Otherwise their participation would be questioned leading to their exclusion from the system. Due to the same reason, local NGOs and networks of PLWHA are not raising their voices about the problems and issues associated with the intervention programmes. Because, it is considered to be controversial and may influence the support and funding arrangements that resemble a competitive market whereby donors/policymakers are choosing those NGOs who are willing to accept and implement their policies and priorities. Besides it, their activities like condom distribution, STI management, VCT counseling, training workshops, etc. are evaluated respectively on the basis of exact numbers distributed, treated, tested and trained. But, to effect a change in the behaviour of the target group, the concern NGO requires sustaining the efforts over long term to eliminate the causes of disease, while at the same time dealing with immediate problems. This reflects the donors'/policymakers' interests in concrete measurable outcomes for accountability purposes within a limited project cycle instead of an assessment of actual long-term impact of an intervention. In this way, the relationship between the donors/policymakers and the implementers once again influences the way latter function (Seckinelgin 2005).

In some ways, it is possible to agree with Fowler (1997) and suggest that NGOs are rich in potential capacities, but very much limited in their capabilities, which according to Giddens (1984), is creating poverty in the NGOs. At the same time, a new challenge that NGOs will have to face is the side effects of ART and huge number of PLWHA. Because of the increased access to ART, the life span of PLWHA will be increasing. As it is already known that ART has many side effects, which requires special attention and professional services. NGOs must be prepared and ready to deal with such new demands successfully in future. But, there is no doubt that innovative and effective interventions are created and implemented by NGOs.

Thus, globalisation brings with it many benefits in addressing the spread of HIV throughout the world. However, these benefits can only be realized if appropriate programmes are available in areas of need. As part of the generous supply of aid aimed at addressing problems specific to HIV/AIDS, attention needs to be paid to building capacity in recipient countries so that such funds may be effectively disseminated and the epidemic effectively curbed.

To sum up, governments, donors and civil society, as in the past, will remain at the forefront of efforts to move towards universal access to HIV prevention, treatment, care and support. Governments will have to increase funding for AIDS – both domestically and as development assistance. It will be critical, for example, to ensure that the Global Fund and other important initiatives, such as PEPFAR, are fully funded. Therefore, efforts must be made to develop new funding sources and mechanisms (such as the recent Airline Tax for AIDS, TB and Malaria). The philanthropic foundations will have to play an increasingly prominent role as core AIDS funders, and business community must rapidly accelerate action on AIDS. Civil society or NGOs will have to continue and fulfill their vital functions as advocate, watchdog, advisor and implementer – keeping AIDS high on the political and public agenda.

REFERENCES

Amin, G. A. (1999), "Globalisation, Consumption Pattern and Human Development in Egypt", Working paper No. 9929, *SSRN*. http://papers.ssrn.com/sol3/papers.cfm?abstract_id=217075

Bagasao, T.M.P. (1998), 'Moving forward through community response: Lessons learned from HIV prevention in Asia and the Pacific'. In S. Gruskin, J. Mann and D. Tarantola (eds.) *Health and Human Rights*, Harvard School of Public Health: Boston, pp. 8-19.

Barnett T, and Whiteside, A. (2000), *AIDS in the Twenty-First Century: Disease and Globalization,* Palgrave-Macmillan: Basingstoke.

Barnett, T. (2002), "HIV/AIDS and Globalization: What is the epidemic telling us about economics, morality and pragmatism?", *AIDS Economics*, July 2002, IAEN.
http://www.policyproject.com/pubs/other/SOTAecon.pdf#page=18

Barquet, N and Domingo, P. (1997), "Smallpox: The Triumph over the Most Terrible of the Ministers of Death," *Annals of Internal Medicine,* October 15, 1997, pp 36-38.

Brown L.D. et al. (2000), 'Globalization, NGOs and Multi-Sectoral Relations'. In J. S. Nye and J. D. Donahue (eds.) *Governance in a Globalizing World*, Brookings Institution Press: Washington D. C.

Clark, J. (2003), 'Globalisation and Rural Development: Limits and Possibilities'. In *Asian NGO Leadership Amidst Globalisation: A Documentation of the Asian Rural NGO Leaders' Dialogue, October 27-31, 2003, Cyberjeya, Malaysia,* Asia DHRRA: Quezon.

D'Adesky, AC (2004), *Moving Mountains: The Race to Treat Global AIDS,* Verso: London.

Diamond, Jared (1998), *Guns, Germs and Steel: a short history of Everybody for the last 13,000 years,* Vintage House: London.

Dicken, P. (1998), *Global Shift: Transforming the World Economy*, Paul Chapman: London, p.93.

Dommen, C. (2001), Background Note of the Workshop on "The impact of globalisation on the full enjoyment of economic, social and cultural rights and the right to development", held at Kuala Lumpur, Malaysia, 8-10 May 2001.

Economist, (1999), "Citizen's Groups: The Nongovernmental Order, Will NGOs Democratize or Merely Disrupt Global Governance?", *The Economist*, December 11, 1999; Boli, J., & Thomas, G. M. (1999).

Fowler, A. (1997), *Striking a Balance: A Guide to Enhancing the Effectiveness of Non-Governmental Organisations in International Development*, Earthscan: London, pp. 43-68.

Friedman, T. (1999), *The Lexus and the Oliver Tree: Understanding Globalisation*, Farrar Straus Giroux, pp. 7-8.

Garrett, L. (2007), "The Challenge of Global Health", *Foreign Affairs*, January/February 2007. http://www.foreignaffairs.org/2007/1.html

Gershman, J. and Irwin, A. (2000), 'Getting a Grip on the Global Economy'. In Jim Yong Kim, J.V. Millen, A. Irwin and J. Gershman (eds.) *Dying for Growth: Global Inequality and the Health of the Poor*, Common Courage Press: Maine.

GFATM (2002), *Report of Global Fund to Fight AIDS, T.B. and Malaria, 2002*. www.globalfundatm.org

GFATM (2007), Global Fund to Fight AIDS, T.B. and Malaria, *Press Release*, 27th September 2007. www.theglobalfund.org

Giddens, A. (1984), *The Constitution of Society: An Outline of the Theory of Structuration*, Polity Press: Cambridge, p. 9.

Gordenker, L and Weiss, T.G. (1996), 'Pluralizing Global Governance: Analytical Approaches and Dimensions'. In Gordenker and Weiss (eds.), *The UN and Global Governance*, Lynne Rienner: Boulder, p. 17.

Haslegrave, M. (1988), 'Resource guide to NGOs concerned with AIDS in Africa based in UK'. In *AIDS in Africa: The Social and Policy Impact*, Meller Press: Lewiston, New York.

Held, D. and others (1999), *Global Transformations: Politics, Economics and Culture*, Stanford University Press: Stanford, pp. 21-22.

Irwin A, J. Millen and D. Fallows (2003), *Global AIDS: Myths and Facts- Tools for Fighting the AIDS Pandemic*, South End Press: Cambridge, MA.

Keohane, R.O. and Nye, J.S. (2000), *Power and Interdependence: World Politics in Transition*, 3rd ed., Addision-Wesley.

McCarty, A. (2001), "Globalisation and Human Development", *International Trade*, Econ WPA. http://ideas.repec.org/p/wpa/wuwpit/0110001.html

McKay, J.P. and Others (1991), *A History of Western Society*, 4th ed. Houghton Mifflin, pp. 106-07.

McNeill, W.H. (1977), *Plagues and Peoples*, Basil Blackwell: Oxford.

Mercer, M.A., L.Liskin & S.J. Scott (1991), "The role of NGO in the global response to AIDS", *AIDS Care*, 3(3): 265-270.

Merson, M. (2005), "HIV/AIDS: A Truly Global Response Needed For a Global Scourge", *Yale Global*, 20 November 2005, New Haven.

Morna, C.L. and PANOS (1991), "South African NGOs Seize the Initiative", *World AIDS*, 12:5-9.

Nye, J.S. (1990), *Bound to Lead: The Changing Nature of American Power*, Basic Books: NY, pp. 31-32.

Osmani, S. R. (2005), "Globalisation and the Human Rights Approach to Development" – *The paper was presented at a High Level Seminar on the Right to Development on the Occasion of the Sixtieth Session of the Commission on Human Rights*, organized by the Office of the High Commissioner on Human Rights in Geneva during 9-10 February, 2004.

Osmani, S. R. (2005), 'An Essay on the Human Rights Approach to Development'. In A. Sengupta (ed.) *Reflections on the Right to Development*, Sage Publications: New Delhi.

Patnaik, P. (1999), 'The Political Economy of Structural Adjustment: A Note'. In Mohan Rao (ed.) *Disinvesting in*

Health: The World Bank's Prescriptions for Health, Sage: New Delhi.

Raj, P. (2002), "Globalisation and Human Rights", *PUCL Bulletin*, July 2000. http://www.pucl.org/index.htm

Rao, M. (2008), " The Political Economy of Health in the Second Phase of Globalisation", *Health For The Millions*, Feb-Mar. 2008, Vol. 33, No. 6 & Apr-May 2008, Vol. 34, No. 1.

Reuters (2001), "Indian Firm Offers AIDS Cocktail for $ 1 a day", *Reuters*, February 9, 2001.

Salamon, L. M. (1994), "The Rise of the Nonprofit Sector", *Foreign Affairs, 73*, 109-116.

Schoepf, Schoepf, and Millen (1992), 'Theoritical Therapies, Remote Remedies'. In Steven Feierman and John M. Janzen (eds.) *The Social Basis of Health and Healing in Africa*, University of California Press: California.

Seckinelgin, H. (2005), "A Global Disease and Its Governance: HIV/AIDS in Sub-Saharan Africa and the Agency of NGOs.", *Global Governance*, Boulder: Jul-Sep 2005, Vol. 11, Issue 3.

Smith, J., Chatfield, C., & Pagnucco, R. (eds.) (1997), *Transnational Social Movements and Global Politics: Solidarity beyond the State*, Syracuse University Press: New York.

Stover J, et al. (2006), "The Global Impact of Scaling Up HIV/ AIDS Prevention Programs in Low- and Middle-Income Countries", *Science*, 10 March 2006: Vol. 311. no. 5766, pp. 1474 – 1476.

The Times (1995), *Atlas of World History* (4th Edition), Lomdarda, Milan.

UNAIDS (2002), *Report on the Global HIV/AIDS epidemic*. http://www.unaids.org

UNAIDS (2007), *Financial Resources Required to Achieve Universal Access to HIV Prevention, Treatment, Care and Support*, UNAIDS.

http://data.unaids.org/pub/Report/2008/20080801_jc1509_universal_access_en.pdf

UNDP (1992), *Human Development Report, 1992*. Oxford University Press: New York.

UNDP (1997), *Human Development Report, 1997*. Oxford University Press: New York.

Washington Post (2008), "Politics and Policy- President Bush Signs PEPFAR Reauthorization Bill", *Washington Post,* 31 July 2008.
http://proquest.umi.com/pqdweb?index=1&did=884766741

Went, R. (2000), *Globalization: Neoliberal Challenge, Radical Response,* Pluto Press: London.

WHO (2000), *WHO Policy perspectives on Medicines, Globalisation, Trips and Access to Pharmaceuticals, 2000,* WHO: Geneva.

WHO (2001), *Report of the Commission in Macroeconomics and Health.* Jeffry Sachs (ed.), WHO: Geneva.

World Bank (2000), *World Development Report 1999/2000: Entering the 21st Century,* Oxford University Press: New York.

WTO (2001), WTO/WHO Secretariats Workshop on *Affordable Drugs,* 2001. www.wto.org/english/tratop_e/trips_e/tn_hosbjor_e.htm

SECTION-IV
CONCLUSION

11

Discussion and Conclusion

AIDS is the leading infectious cause of adult deaths in the world. Within two years of its first appearance in 1981, AIDS has spreaded to 60 countries and later on to all the countries across the globe. The current revised estimate suggests that globally 33.2 million (30.6 – 36.1 million) people are living with HIV/AIDS in 2007 (UNAIDS, 2008). Out of this, 30.8 million (28.2 – 33.6 million) are adults, 15.4 million (13.9 – 16.6 million) are women and 2.1 million (1.9 – 2.4 million) are children under 15 years (UNAIDS, 2008). More than 25 million people have already died. AIDS is now considered not only as a health problem, but also as a developmental and security threat. Although AIDS epidemic began in USA more than 25 years ago, up to 95 percent of new HIV infections now occur in developing countries, which are unfortunately also least equipped to effectively respond to the challenge. It is now well recognized that the epidemic is affecting developed and developing countries differently. AIDS in developed countries is now a chronic disease and a manageable health problem. In developing countries, however, AIDS is destroying societies, nations and communities. The antiretroviral treatments that have increased longevity of patients in industrialized countries are unfortunately beyond the reach of those in the developing world. The disease is, therefore, widening the gap between 'haves' and 'have nots', between rich and poor nations, thereby presenting a new ethical and human rights dilemma.

In India, the first HIV infection was reported in 1986 and within a short period of time, it has evolved as one of the most serious public health problems across the country. The current revised estimate suggests that 2.5 million (2.0-3.1 million) people are infected with HIV/AIDS in India (NACO/HSS 2006). This is equivalent to approximately 0.36 percent of the adult population (prevalence rate for males is 0.43% and for female is 0.29%). Maharashtra, Tamil Nadu, Karnataka, Andhra Pradesh, Manipur, Mizoram and Nagaland are declared as high prevalence states, where the HIV infection rate has crossed one percent in antenatal women. Similarly, Gujarat, Goa, Pondicherry and West Bengal are placed in moderate prevalence states category. The HIV infection rate has increased 5 percent or more among the high-risk groups in these states. The remaining states are placed in low prevalence category, where HIV infection rate is below one percent among antenatal women and below 5 percent among high-risk groups. NACO has also identified 156 districts as high prevalence districts and out of which four districts are in West Bengal (NACO/HSS 2006). Like other countries, in India too, NGOs were first to respond to HIV/AIDS. Later on, after the establishment of NACO, it has involved NGOs as partners in the National AIDS Control Programmes.

It is true that there is a long history of NGO activities in India. But the phenomenal growth of NGOs has taken place during late 1970s and 1980s. There are numbers of factors responsible for it. Major among them are implementation of SAP as prescribed by the World Bank and IMF; and influence of INGOs as well. Thus, state's inability coupled with funding support from international donor agencies and other INGOs provided the impetus for the expansion of NGO sector in India. It has been found from the previous studies that NGOs are varied in terms of size, capacity, levels of operation and services provided. They carry out various programmes pertaining to income generation, education, welfare of the weaker sections, health and so on. Especially in the field of HIV/AIDS, NGOs perform different activities. They provide clinical services, counseling, awareness, advocacy, care and support as well as conduct research. In India, some of the prominent NGOs engaged in HIV/AIDS care are SHALOM in Manipur, SAHARAN in Delhi, DMSC in West Bengal, Lawyers Collective in Mumbai, MASUM in Pune and Seva Mandir in Udaipur. But, there is little information on the characteristics, distribution and activities of such NGOs at the all India and state levels. In order to get some insights into these aspects, this study has been conducted on NGOs in HIV/AIDS care in West Bengal. The reason for selecting West Bengal is that it is placed in moderate prevalence states category where HIV infection rate is more than 5 percent among high-risk groups; four districts are declared as high prevalence and four districts as moderate prevalence districts as well. Besides it, West Bengal is one of the five states where Government of India initially started National AIDS Control Programme with the help of WHO in 1987. The review of literature suggests there are few studies done on NGOs in health care at the state level and these include Maharastra (Duggal, Gupta and Jesani 1986), Andhra Pradesh (Baru 1987), Assam (Sarkar 1998) and West Bengal (Sarkar 2005). But, similar studies are not conducted on NGOs in HIV/AIDS care at the state level. In this context, the present study has tried to understand the case of West Bengal with regard to HIV/AIDS care. It has made an effort to get a state level overview of such NGOs, to understand their distribution and contributions as well as future trends of such NGOs in the context of globalisation.

An exploratory design has been used in the present study. The study has been carried out in four phases. In the *first phase*, names and address of the NGOs engaged in HIV/AIDS care were collected from various umbrella organizations (e.g. West Bengal State AIDS Prevention & Control Society, UNICEF, ACTION-AID and SAATHII's directories of NGOs). Having put all names together, a comprehensive list of 60 NGOs engaged in HIV/AIDS care in West Bengal was prepared. In the *second phase*, questionnaires were mailed to all the 60 NGOs and followed up with several reminders through e-mail and phone. The response was received from 27 NGOs. This was done to collect necessary data to get a state level overview of NGOs in HIV/AIDS care. In the *third phase*, six NGOs (i.e. Durbar Mahila Samanaya Committee, Society for Community Intervention and Research, Bhoruka Public Welfare Trust, Human Development and Research Institute, MANAS Bangla and SPARSHA) were selected purposively based on certain criteria and studied in detail. In each NGO, emphasis was given on historical background, organizational structure, present activities, views of staff, beneficiaries' perception towards the working of NGOs, etc. to understand how far NGOs could contribute to HIV/AIDS prevention, care and support. At the *last phase*, the researcher had discussed informally with few key informants like academicians, experts, officials from NGOs and WBSAP&CS to know about their views on the impact of globalisation on NGOs working in the HIV/AIDS field. At the end of this phase, the researcher has done necessary literature review to know more about the impact of globalisation in this regard.

Now, the important issues, which have been observed in this study, are being discussed below.

(i) Typology of NGOs

There are different ways to classify NGOs. In order to

avoid the complexity, present study has classified the NGOs of West Bengal in terms of their activities into five categories. These include religious organizations, development organizations, research and consultancy agencies, and action groups. The Chapter-5 (Part-B) shows that the HIV/AIDS care programmes are mostly carried out by the service organizations, research & consultancy agencies and development organizations.

(ii) Growth and Initial Activities of NGOs

It is observed in Chapter-5 (Part-B) that NGOs has grown in numbers during late 1970s and 1980s in West Bengal. Most of the NGOs were initially engaged in awareness generation and health related programmes. It is also found that mostly the dedicated untrained social workers, medical practitioners and group of like-minded people have promoted these NGOs. This may raise a question like what was the reason for rapid growth of NGOs during this period. We find the answer in Sarkar's (2005) study on "NGOs in Health Care in West Bengal". The Sixth and Seventh Five Year Plans have given more importance on human resource development and expressed the need for greater involvement of NGOs. At the same time, a paradigm shift was also taking place from welfare approach to development approach at that time. All these led to the growth of most NGOs during late 1970s and 1980s (Sarkar, 2005). With regard to promoters of NGOs, more involvement of dedicated untrained social workers and a group of like-minded people was due to their humanitarian attitude and zeal to do something for the poor people; and involvement of medical practitioners was due to the availability of fund from the government for initiating health care programmes through NGOs.

(iii) Present Activities of NGOs

The Chapter-5 (Part-B) also shows that most of the on-going programmes of NGOs are related to HIV/AIDS and health. They are also running permanent clinics and organizing training for health workers. Few programmes are related to drug abuse, anti-trafficking of women, community development, etc. So far HIV/AIDS programme is concerned, most of the NGOs (66.7 %) have started this during NACP-II (i.e. in between 1999 and 2006). Most of these programmes are initiated for a particular section of people like women, children, people vulnerable to HIV/AIDS, etc. As a result of this trend, the principle of universality of public health approach gets undermined – since the needs of entire population are not met.

(iv) District-wise Distribution of NGOs

In the Chapter-5 (Part-A), district-wise distribution of NGOs in HIV/AIDS care in West Bengal has been discussed. This has clearly brought out the fact that 50% of total NGOs are situated in Kolkata and its adjacent areas (i.e. Howrah, Hoogly, North and South 24 Parganas). Out of the total NGOs implementing targeted intervention programmes (TIPs), 43.5% NGOs situated in these districts and implementing 46.7% of total TIPs in West Bengal. It means NGOs prefer to work in socio-economically developed areas. The similar trend was found in the study of Maharashtra (Duggal, Gupta & Jesani, 1986), Andhra Pradesh (Baru, 1987), Assam (Sarkar, 1998) and West Bengal (Sarkar, 2005). This kind of trend has an implication on the principle of universality, accessibility and availability. As a result of this kind of approach, HIV/ AIDS care services do not reach to all areas and sections of society. For example, there is no full-fledged TIP in Bankura, Malda, Paschim Medinipur and Uttar Dinajpur districts. This lack of attention might have led to increase in HIV infection rate as NACO (2008) identified Uttar Dinajpur, Purulia and Burdwan as high prevalence and Medinipur (Purba and Paschim) as moderate prevalence districts.

(v) Target Groups addressed by NGOs

The Chapter-5 (Part-A) has discussed about the target

groups addressed by NGOs in HIV/AIDS care. It is found that almost half (46.7%) of the total TIPs are for sex workers and 28.3% for truckers. However, the coverage of high-risk groups like IDUs (11.7%) and MSM (3.3%) are comparatively less. This may be the cause of increasing trend of HIV infection among the IDUs and MSM in West Bengal as indicated by NACO (2008). However, most of the NGOs have been working in both urban and rural areas by adopting institutional as well as community-based approaches.

(vi) Problems faced by NGOs

NGOs have been facing various problems in the implementation of HIV/AIDS programme. The Chapter-5 (Part-B) shows that majority of them have identified indifferent attitude of people due to stigma (96.3%), fear of exposure and social boycott (96.3%), delay in disbursement of fund (55.5%), apathetic attitude of government health personnel (33.3%) and ART related problems (33.3%). NGOs have also pointed out about staff related problems, inadequate infrastructure and resources to meet the demands of HIV/AIDS victims, migratory nature of target groups and wrong policy of NACO/WBSAP&CS. Case studies in selected NGOs (discussed in chapter-8) have also supported these views. It is surprising that NGOs are not hesitant to point out the defects in the donor's (i.e. WBSAP&CS /NACO) policy.

(vii) Suggestions of NGOS for Effective Implementation of HIV/AIDS

In Chapter-5 (Part-B), various suggestions given by NGOs for the effective implementation of NGOs have been discussed. Majority of NGOs (92.5%) think that stigma related problems could be overcome through mass awareness and counseling. With regard to financial problem, 74% of total NGOs have asked for financial support to meet the needs of target population. Other suggestions include developing network among the NGOs in HIV/AIDS care in West Bengal;

bringing necessary change in the existing policy of NACO; opening of more ICTC and ART distribution centers; and simplification of MIS and Reporting system. These suggestions are justified and important. Most of these issues are considered and taken care of in NACP-III (2007-2012).

(viii) Organisational Setup

Case Studies, in Chapter-6, bring to our notice that there is a variation in organizational structures of NGOs. For instance, SCIR, HDRI, SPARSHA and MB have very simple or flat type of organizational structures. But BPWT and DMSC have very complex or hierarchical organizational set-up and both the organizations have very wider coverage. While BPWT tries to reach all sections of community, DMSC has adopted an integrated approach for the sex workers and their children. As a result of this kind of plurality, it is understood that all NGOs do not contribute equally. However, all of these six NGOs are working as per the guidelines of WBSAP&CS/NACO.

(ix) Nature of Programme Sustainability

In chapter-7, nature of programme activities of the six selected NGOs has been discussed in detail on the basis of eight requisite criteria. These are: (a) objectives of the programme, (b) components of programme, (c) programme execution process, (d) people's participation, (e) monitoring and evaluation, (f) source of funding, (g) innovative components and (h) local cooperation. Some commonality is found in six NGOs as all of them are implementing the programme as per WBSAP&CS guidelines. But they differ from each other, as each of them working with different target groups. It is found that the programmes of all six NGOs under the study suffer from one or more problems. Some of the problems are common in all the programmes under the study. For instance, lack of timely disbursement of fund by WBSAP&CS, no funding provision for addressing the general health problems of target groups and for meeting traveling expenditure of Peer Educators. In every NGO, there is some internal mechanism for monitoring and evaluation of the programme. At the same time, each NGO's programme has got some positive aspects and innovative components too. But, all the programmes are fully dependent on the funding agency i.e. WBSAP&CS. Therefore, all the programmes under the study are less sustainable. This kind of trend expresses that NGOs can't contribute in the community for a long time.

(x) Extent of People's Participation

The chapter-7 has discussed people's participation on the basis of their participation in need identification, beneficiary selection, programme planning, programme implementation, resource contribution, and monitoring & evaluation. It is found that comparatively people's participation is better in CBOs like DMSC, MB and SPARSHA. In SCIR and BPWT, beneficiaries don't have scope to participate in programme planning, monitoring and evaluation. However, they participate in the evaluation of external team (i.e. WBSAP&CS/NACO) by proving information. Beneficiaries of all six NGOs do not contribute financially except the registration fees. But, they physically participate in the programmes of NGOs, provide physical infrastructure (e.g. chair, table, etc.), control public gathering, arrange refreshments for resource persons, etc. However, they have no right of getting a programme sanctioned that they need, which is seen as management level affairs. Thus, top-down approach of public sector is very much present in NGOs too. Government funding may be one reason of replicating this in NGOs.

(xi) Innovative Components

Case Studies, in chapter-7, analyze the innovative components of each selected NGOs in detail. It is found that comparatively CBOs like DMSC, MB and SPARSHA are better than remaining three NGOs. These CBOs have got a team of committed and dedicated staff members, most of whom are selected from among the target groups that they serve. All six NGOs under the study are having strong networking with government, private and other NGOs. Especially, their networkings with pathological laboratories help the beneficiaries to avail the concessions. DMSC, SCIR and SPARSHA have made provisions for the vocational training of their respective target groups. These arrangements help in the rehabilitation of marginalized groups like CSWs, IDUs and PLWHA. DMSC and SCIR also run schools for the children of their respective target groups, which has helped to win the confidence of their respective beneficiaries. Having own blood testing facility and ICTC is an added advantage respectively for BPWT and DMSC, as beneficiaries are getting such facilities from the respective NGOs. World Health Organisation has declared the Sonagachi Project of DMSC as 'Model Community Based Project for Sex Workers' in the world for its peer-based approach.

(xii) Sources of Funding

India has adopted "Three Ones" principles as suggested by UNAIDS. These principles include one national AIDS control authority, one national strategic framework and one national monitoring and evaluation system. Therefore, all funds are routed through NACO and from NACO to State AIDS Control Societies. It is observed in Chapter-6 that there is plurality in sources of funding – self-generated resources, state government, central government and foreign funding agencies are the main sources. So far as HIV/AIDS programmes are concerned, NGOs are receiving fund from WBDSAP&CS. However, some research activities are funded by bilateral and international funding agencies. As all NGOs are dependent on WBSAP&CS for funding, it is less likely that programmes would be sustainable in absence of such external funding. NGOs have also complained about the inadequate and irregular flow of funding.

(xiii) Staff's Views

The Chapter-8 highlights the views of selected staff members of six NGOs under the study on different issues related to HIV/AIDS. These issues are (a) stigmatization, (b) ethical issues, (c) violation of human rights, (d) major barriers encountered, (e) major reasons of spreading HIV/AIDS, and (f) future AIDS scenario and role of NGOs. It is found that no staff members of six NGOs are affected by HIV/AIDS related stigma because of the nature of their jobs. But staff members of DMSC, MB and SPARSHA are affected by prevailing social stigma related to CSWs, MSM and PLWHA respectively. It is to be noted that most of the staff members of these three organizations are selected from among the respective target groups. However, staff members of all the six NGOs have admitted the existence of HIV/AIDS related stigma in the society and have suggested awareness programmes, counseling, sex education at school level, etc to reduce it. With regard to ethical issues related to HIV/AIDS, majority of the selected staff members of six NGOs are aware and always practice them. With regard to the violation of human rights of PLWHA, all staff members have said that they would protest against such incidences. On the issue of preventing such incidences occurred in government run hospitals, while staffs of SCIR and BPWT suggested more training, staff members of DMSC, MB, SPARSHA suggested exemplary punishment for the guilty health personnel. Surprisingly, majority of staff members of HDRI did not make any comments.

The selected staff members of all the NGOs have talked about ignorance, fear of exposure and stigmatization, indifferent attitude of the people towards AIDS, migration and drug addiction as major barriers encountered in implementing the project. Most of the staff members of SCIR, DMSC and MB are optimistic about the future AIDS scenario in our country. They think that the situation would be under control, if government continues its effort by involving all stakeholders. On the other hand, staff members of BPWT and SPARSHA think that situation will be out of control, if government did not change its policy. Surprisingly, majority of staff members of HDRI have not expressed their views in this regard. However, all staff members of the six NGOs are of the opinion that NGOs would play a key and more effective role in combating HIV/AIDS in future too.

(xiv) Perception of Beneficiaries towards the Working of NGOs

The beneficiaries' perceptions towards the working of six selected NGOs under the study have been discussed in Chapter-9. Out of eleven groups, eight groups have expressed positive perception and few members of remaining three groups have shown dissatisfaction. By and large, beneficiaries have better perception towards the working of respective NGOs. The HIV/AIDS programmes of the respective NGOs are satisfactory to the beneficiaries. These NGOs have helped them in improving their health status and awareness level on various HIV/AIDS related issues. These programmes include more preventive services and less curative services. Out of the six NGOs, SPARSHA only runs HIV/AIDS Care and Support services for PLWHA. So far as anti-retroviral medicines (ART) are concerned, it is distributed by the government through a very few ART distribution centers in West Bengal. Majority of the beneficiaries use these NGOs as a stepping-stone for better referral health services and to avoid the indifferent attitude and apathy of the health personnel in government run hospitals.

(xv) Impact of Globalisation on NGOs in HIV/AIDS Care

The Chapter-10 has thoroughly discussed about the impact of globalisation on NGOs in HIV/AIDS care. Globalisation, like other spheres, has affected both positively as well as negatively to the NGOs in HIV/AIDS care. The impact of globalisation is discussed in terms of networking, sustainability of funding, future demands of services, etc. It is found that globalisation has reduced states' capacity to fulfill its social responsibility towards the people, which has created a space for the NGOs. Thus, globalisation has helped in the growth of more NGOs and made them active throughout the world. Globalisation has also helped to strengthen the networking at the national, regional and international level not only among the NGOs working in HIV/ AIDS field, but also with NGOs working in the other fields. It has also brought together NGOs of the North and of the South. But at the domestic level, such networking is missing among the NGOs in HIV/AIDS care in India as well as in West Bengal. Similarly, NGOs have been playing advocacy role successfully at the international level; but at the local level, NGOs are not able to play advocacy role properly because of their dependency on external funding resources. They can't raise their voices against the policies of the donors. With regard to financial sustainability, considering the increasing number of multilateral, bilateral and private philanthropic donors and their increasing contributions to HIV/AIDS, it is expected that financial sustainability will be continued in future too. At the same time, new avenues for funding must be explored in order to achieve the goal of universal access to HIV/AIDS prevention, care, support and treatment by 2010. However, the policy of getting quick outcome in terms of quantity within a limited period may not have societal impact in the long run. So far as the future demands of services are concerned, NGOs will have to cope up successfully with the side effects of ART related problems; as increased access to ART will increase both the life span of PLWHA and their numbers gradually. In brief, governments, donors and civil society, as were in the past, will have to remain at the forefront of efforts to move towards universal access to HIV prevention, treatment, care and support by 2010.

The present study has given many new insights. It has confirmed following two hypotheses. The first hypothesis was developed for the first time in the study of Maharashtra (Duggal, Gupta & Jesani, 1986) and was confirmed by the studies of Andhra Pradesh (Baru 1987) and Assam (Sarkar 1998). The second hypothesis was developed in the study on "NGOs in Health Care: A Study of West Bengal" (Sarkar 2005).

(i) There is an association between socio-economically developed areas and location of NGOs.

(ii) Contribution of NGOs varies with the nature of financial sustainability of the programme.

The present study has also developed two new hypotheses. These are:

(i) CBOs are more effective than NGOs in HIV/AIDS prevention, care, support and treatment.

(ii) There is a positive correlation between globalisation and NGO response to HIV/AIDS care.

Implication for Social Work

The key findings of the present study demonstrate the relevance of 'Structural Social Work' perspective in HIV/AIDS prevention, control, care and support activities. More specifically, the findings of the study identified the crucial need for a holistic social work practice. There are two-fold goals of structural social work. First, it alleviates negative effects of structural exploitation on the people; and second, simultaneously transforms the social structure through social reforms and social change initiatives. The study illustrates that the selected NGOs have been working to strike a balance between the social care and social change in their battle against HIV/AIDS. It has been demonstrated by their involvement in social care activities such as running drop-in centres, community care centres, clinics and vocational training centres; counseling, etc. for the people infected and affected by HIV/AIDS. At the same time, NGOs have initiated social change activities such as awareness generation programmes, community organization, protest march, and evolving strategies to reduce stigma and discrimination against people living with HIV/AIDS (PLWHA), men having sex with men (MSM), etc. to bring social transformation. Therefore, NGOs are successful instruments and initiators of structural social work practice. Thus, the present study indicates the importance of 'structural social work' as holistic social work practice for empowering the marginalized section such as PLWHA, MSM, CSWs, etc.

The findings and observations of the present study are significant for current social work practice. The different approaches, strategies, programmes and field experiences found in the study are relevant to the body of social work knowledge. These experiences of the study are useful information for the social workers committed to the pursuits of social justice and equality. The successful implementation of structural social work by NGOs in HIV/AIDS prevention care and support will inspire social workers and civil society to take initiatives against the stigmatization and discrimination of PLWHA. The holistic approach of NGOs in HIV/AIDS care raises issues before current social work practitioners to adopt structural social work practice, if they really believe in the core professional values of social justice, equity and commitment to marginalized groups in society. Thus, the present study is the important source material for the social work education to adopt structural social work perspective as model to address the issues of marginalized and promote social justice in the society.

Conclusion

There is plurality among the NGOs in HIV/AIDS care in

West Bengal in terms of their emergence, promoters' background, organizational setup, nature of activity, etc. In West Bengal, NGOs are found as suitable means to provide HIV/AIDS prevention, care and support services; but can't contribute much in providing treatment services for PLWHA. People having received the awareness from NGOs and understanding the need of treatment services, go to public sector hospitals especially for HIV test and ART. This kind of trend proves that health services provided by government are complementary for NGOs in HIV/AIDS care in West Bengal. There is a need of more integration and coordination of services of all stakeholders in providing better HIV/AIDS care services. It is also important to note that NGOs in HIV/AIDS care prefer to work in socio-economically developed areas in West Bengal and can't continue to work for a long time due to their external resource dependency. It is expected that major findings of the present study will be worth for the government in formulating appropriate policy and useful to donors and NGOs to be careful in designing, implementing and monitoring HIV/AIDS programmes. The present study suggests that there is a need to initiate further research in the following areas: (a) Role of FBOs in HIV/AIDS care in West Bengal, (b) Comparative study between CBOs and NGOs in HIV/AIDS care and (c) Interface between Government and NGOs with regard to HIV/AIDS care in West Bengal.

REFERENCES

Baru, R. (1987). 'Factors Influencing Variations in Health Services–A Study of Selected District of Andhra Pradesh', *M. Phil. Dissertation,* CSMCH, SSS, Jawaharlal Nehru University, New Delhi.

Duggal, R.; Gupta, M. and Jesani, A. (1986), *NGOs in Rural Health Care,* Foundation for Research in Community Health, Mumbai.

NACO/HSS (2006), *HIV Sentinel Surveillance Report*, NACO, New Delhi.

NACO (2007), *UNGASS Country Progress report: India*, NACO, New Delhi.

UNAIDS (2008), *Report on the Global AIDS Epidemic 2008*, Geneva.

Sarkar, A. (1998). 'Characteristics of NGOs: An Exploratory Study in Assam', *M. Phil. Dissertation*, CSMCH, SSS, Jawaharlal Nehru University, New Delhi (Unpublished).

Sarkar, A. (2005). *NGOs: The New Lexicon of Health Care*, Concept Publishing Company: New Delhi.

APPENDIX-I

MAP OF WEST BENGAL

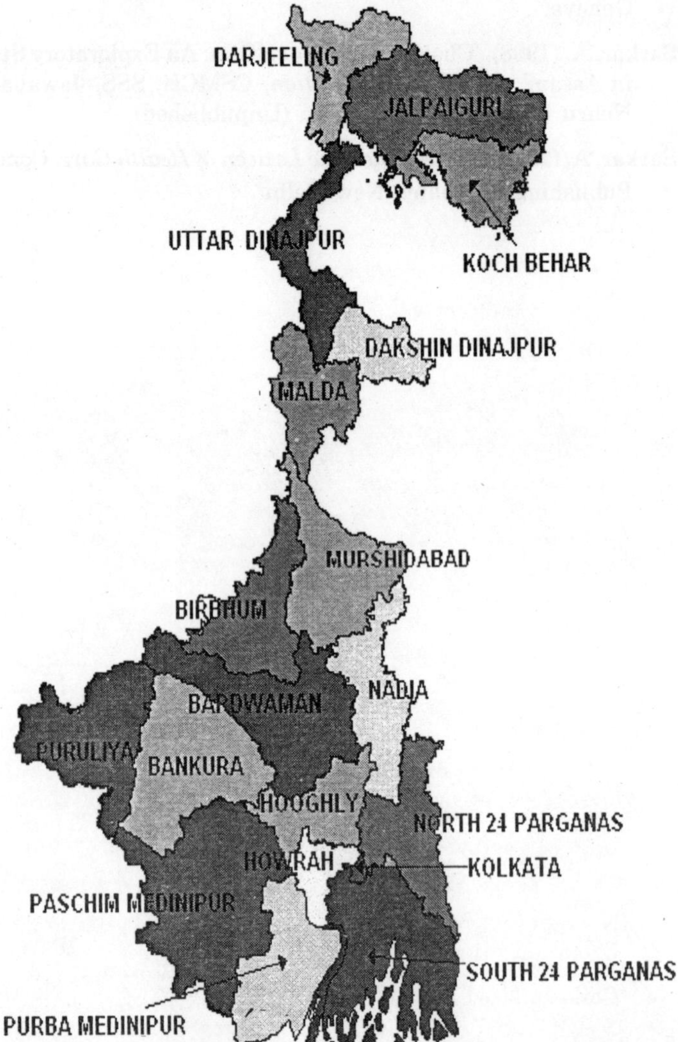

APPENDIX-II

List of NGOs in HIV/AIDS Care in West Bengal (2006-07)

Sl. No.	*Name of NGO*	*Target Group*	*District*
	1	*2*	*3*
1.	Durbar Mahila Samannaya Committee	CSW	Kolkata
2.	Society for Human Devt. And Social Action	CSW, Truckers	Kolkata
3.	Society for Community Intervention & Research	IDU	Kolkata
4.	Manas Bangla	MSM	Kolkata
5.	The Calcutta Samaritans	CSW	Kolkata
6.	Human Development Research Institute	ML. Truckers	Kolkata
7.	Bhoruka Public Welfare Trust	Truckers	Kolkata
8.	School of Human Genetics & Population Health	CSW	Kolkata
9.	Kolkata Socio-Cultural Research Institute	CSW	Kolkata
10.	City Level Plan Of Action for Street Children	Street Children	Kolkata
11.	Seth Bagan Mahila Sangha	CSW	North 24 Parganas
12.	Naihati Profile	CSW, Truckers	North 24 Parganas
13.	Narayantala Mass Communication Society	CSW	North 24 Parganas
14.	Child In Need Institute	CSW	North 24 Parganas

(Contd...)

1		*2*	*3*
15.	Chittaranjan Welfare & Research Institute	CSW	North 24 Parganas
16.	Indian Institute of Training & Development	CSW	North 24 Parganas
17.	Alokendu Bodh Niketan (Residential)	CSW	Howrah
18.	Samaj Kalyan Brato Sangha	IDU	Howrah
19.	Liberal Association for Movement of People	CSW	Hoogly
20.	SRISTY for Human Development	Truckers	Hoogly
21.	Disha Jana Kalyan Kendra	CSW	Burdwan
22.	Saheed Shibsankar Seva Samity	Truckers	Burdwan
23.	Vivekananda Education Society	CSW	Purba Medinipur
24.	Haldia Vigyan Parishad	Truckers	Purba Medinipur
25.	Gandhi Peace Foundation	CSW	Purulia
26.	Natunhat Development Society	CSW	Purulia
27.	Elmhirst Institute of Community Studies	CSW	Birbhum
28.	St. John Ambulance	Truckers	Birbhum
29.	Women Interlink Foundation	CSW	Nadia
30.	Suprova Panchashila Mahila Udyog Samity	CSW, Truckers	Murshidabad
31.	Nari Mukti Mahila Samity	Truckers	Dakshin Dinajpur

(Contd...)

1		*2*	*3*
32.	Gana Unnayan Parishad	Truckers	Jalpaiguri
33.	IPARW	ML	Jalpaiguri
34.	All India Transport Association	Truckers	Jalpaiguri
35.	Jalpaiguri HRIDAY	CSW	Jalpaiguri
36.	New Bharati Club	Truckers	Coochbehar
37.	West Bengal Voluntary Health Association	CSW	Darjeeling
38.	Naxalbari Integrated Development Society	IDU	Darjeeling
39.	DMSC North Bengal	CSW	Darjeeling
40.	Youth Mass Development Society	Truckers	Darjeeling (DGHC)
41.	Manas Bangla (Mittjyu)	MSM	Darjeeling (DGHC)
42.	FOSEP	CSW	Darjeeling (DGHC)
43.	Hill Social Welfare Society	IDU	Darjeeling (DGHC)
44.	Friends of Trees Forum	ML	Darjeeling (DGHC)
45.	Gorkha Dukh Nibaran Sangha	ML	Darjeeling (DGHC)
46.	Anugyalaya	ML	Darjeeling (DGHC)
47.	Indian Red Cross Society	IDU	Darjeeling (DGHC)
48.	BNP+	PLWHA (DIC)	Multi-District

(Contd...)

1	2	3
49. KNP+	PLWHA (DIC)	Multi-District
50. Sangobaddho	PLWHA (DIC)	Jalpaiguri
51. Sankar Foundation	PLWHA (DIC)	Darjeeling (DGHC)
52. Gandhi Mission Trust	PLWHA (CCC)	Paschim Medinipur
53. Calcutta Diecesan Trust	PLWHA (CCC)	Kolkata
54. Jesu Ashram	PLWHA (CCC)	Darjeeling (DGHC)
55. FXB India	WPI	Howrah
56. WISE	WPI	All Districts
57. Ved Vigyan Mahavidya Pith	WPI	Purba Medinipur
58. Sree Ma Mahila Samity	SHG	Multi-District
59. SPADE	SHG	Multi-District
60. SLARTC	PLWHA	All Districts

Bibliography

Articles

Aldaba, Fernando T. and Josefa P. Petilla (1997), "Governance and HIV: Government - Civil Society Interface: An Aspect of Governance Critical to an Effective Response", *HIV POLICY.ORG*. http://www.hivpolicy.org/bib/HPP000204.htm

Amin, G.A. (1999), "Globalisation, Consumption Pattern and Human Development in Egypt", Working Paper No. 9929, *SSRN*. http://papers.ssrn.com/sol3/papers.cfm?abstract_id=217075

Anand, K. et al. (1999), "Impact of HIV/AIDS on the national economy of India", *Health Policy*, 47(3), 195-205.

Asthana S, Oostvogels R. (1996), "Community participation in HIV prevention: Problems and prospects for community-based strategies among female sex workers in Madras", *Social Science Medicine*, 1996 Jul; 43(2): 133-48.

Barnett, T. (2002), "HIV/AIDS and Globalization: What is the epidemic telling us about economics, morality and pragmatism?", *AIDS Economics*, July 2002, IAEN. http://www.policyproject.com/pubs/other/SOTAecon.pdf#page=18

Baru, R. (1998), "Structural Adjustment and Health: Changing Role of NGOs." *Paper Presented at International Seminar on Global Governance and Social Policy*, Baltic Sea Centre: Kellokeski.

Baviskar, B.S. (2001), "NGOs and Civil Society in India", *Sociological Bulletin*, March 2001, 50 (1).

Bhatt, Anil (1995), "Voluntary Action in India: Role, Trends and Challenges", *Economic and Political Weekly*, 30(15) April.

Bhusan, V., M. Chandy, P.G.Babu, D. Denison, A. Srivastava, N.K. Saraswati and T.J.John (1994), "Transfusion Associated HIV Infection in Patients with Hematologic Disorders in Southern India", *Indian Journal of Medical Research*, 99:57-70.

Brodhead, T. and J.O'Mally (1989), "NGO and Third World Development: Opportunities and Constraints." *paper presented at the WHO's Global Programme on AIDS Management Committee Meeting*, 6-8.

Chillag K. et al (2000), "Factors affecting the delivery of HIV/AIDS prevention programs by community-based organizations", *AIDS Education and Prevention: An Interdisciplinary Journal*, Vol. 14, Issue-3.

Coovadia, H. M. and J. Hadingham (2005), "HIV/AIDS: global trends, global funds and delivery bottlenecks", BioMed Central. http://www.globalizationandhealth.com/content/1/1/13

Dabhi, J. (2005), "NGOs Response to Violence against The Marginalised and Discriminated Communities", *Social Action*, 55(1).

De, M., D. Banerjee, S.Chandra and D.K. Bhattacharya (1990), "HBV and HIV seropositivity in Multi-Transfused Hemophiliacs and Thalassaemics in Eastern India", *IJMR*, 91: 63-66.

Delion Jean, Gurung Damber, Reerink Ietje H, Schapink Dick and van Poelje, Rob. (2000), "Strategy to involve rural workers in the fight against HIV/AIDS through community mobilisation programs (Draft)", AIDS Campaign Team for Africa (ACT- Africa): World Bank Rural HIV/AIDS Initiatives (RAIDS).
http://www.worldbank.org/aids-econ/papers/rural.pdf

Duggal, R. (1988), "NGOs, Government and Private Sector in Health", *Economic and Political Weekly*, March 26, pp. 633-636.

Duggal, R., et al. (1995), "Health Expenditures across States- Part I and II", *Economic and Political Weekly*, (30)35-36.

Economist, (1999), "Citizen's Groups: The Nongovernmental Order, Will NGOs Democratize or Merely Disrupt Global Governance?", *The Economist*, December 11, 1999; Boli, J. & Thomas, G. M. (1999).

Elliot, C. (1987), "Some Aspects of Relations Between the North and South in the NGO Sector", *World Development*, 15 (supplement).

Fowler, A. (1992), "Building Partnerships between Northern and Southern Development NGOs: Issues for the Nineties", *Development Journal of SID*. I.

Garain, S. (1993), "Towards a measure of Organisational Effectiveness for Non-Governmental Organisations", *The Indian Journal of Social Work*, Vol. LV, No.2, pp. 251-270.

Garain, S. (1994), "Government – NGO Interace in India: An Overview", *The Indian Journal of Social Work,* Vol. LV, No.3, pp. 337-345

Garrett, L. (2007), "The Challenge of Global Health", *Foreign Affairs*, January/February 2007. (http://www.foreignaffairs.org/2007/1.html)

George, P and Marlowe, S. (2005), "Structural Social Work in Action: Experiences from Rural India", *Journal of Progressive Human Services*, 16(1).

Gomez, Jauregui (2004), "Feasibility of Government partnerships with NGOs in the Reproductive health field in Mexico", *Reproductive Health Matters*, 12(24), pp. 42– 55.

Gupta, V.S. (2003), "Contribution of NGOs in implementing population policy", *Yojana*, 47(7), pp. 6–9.

Indian Express (2001), "This HIV Positive Women Got the Virus from Her own Blood, Awaits Destiny", *Indian Express,* 3rd June 2001, Pune.

Jha, P. et al. (2002), "Improving the health of global poor", *Science*, 295(5562), 2036-39.

Kloos Helmut, Tadesse Wuhib, Damen Haile Mariam and Bernt Lindtjorn, "Community-based organizations in HIV/AIDS prevention, patient care and control in Ethiopia", *Ethiopian Journal of Health Development*, 2003; 17(Spl. Issue No):3-31.

Kumar, R.M., S.A. Udaman and A. Khurranna (1995), "A Prospective Study of Mother-to-Infant HIV Transmission in Tribal Women from India", *Acquired Immuno Deficiency Syndrome Human Retroviral*, 9: 238-242.

Larson, H.J. and J.P. Narain (2001), "Beyond 2000: Responding to HIV/AIDS in the New Millennium", *SEA/AIDS/122*, WHO/SEARO: New Delhi.

McCarty, A. (2001), 'Globalisation and Human Development.' *International Trade*, Econ WPA. http://ideas.repec.org/p/wpa/wuwpit/0110001.html.

McKay, J.P. and Others (1991), *A History of Western Society*, 4th ed. Houghton Mifflin, pp. 106-07.

Mathew, G. (1999), "Decentralised Institution – Government and Voluntary sector", *Economic and Political Weekly*, Feb.27, p. 529.

Mercer, M.A., L. Liskin and S.J. Scott (1991), "The role of non-government organization in the global response to AIDS", *AIDS Care*, 3(3): 265-270.

Mercer, Alec, Mobarak Hossain Khan, Muhammad Daulatuzzaman and Joanna Reid (2004), "Effectiveness of an NGO primary health care programme in rural Bangladesh: Evidence form the management information system", *Health Policy and Planning*, 19(4), pp. 187–98.

Merson, M. (2005), "HIV/AIDS: A Truly Global Response Needed For a Global Scourge" *Yale Global*, 20 November 2005, NEW HAVEN.

Morna, C.L. and PANOS (1991), "South African NGOs Seize the Initiative", *World AIDS*, 12:5-9.

Moreau, M. (1990), "Empowerment Through Advocacy and Consciousness-Raising: Implications of a Structural Approach to Social Work", *Journal of Sociology and Social Welfare*, 17(2).

Mugisha, Frank, Harriet Birungi and Ian Askew (2005), "Are reproductive health NGOs in Uganda able to engage in the health SWAp?", *International Journal of Health Planning and Management*, 20(3), pp. 227–38.

NACO (2007), "Behind the Numbers", *NACO News*, Vol.-III, Issue-3.

O'Gorman, Patrick & Paul Hardacre (2004), "Documentation of Best Practices and Needs Assessment of Service Providers in South Asian Association for Regional Cooperation (SAARC) Countries", http://www.hivpolicy.org/bib/HPP000723.htm

Osmani, S. R. (2005), "Globalisation and the Human Rights Approach to Development" – *paper presented at a High Level Seminar on the Right to Development on the occasion of the Sixtieth Session of the Commission on Human Rights,* the Office of the High Commissioner on Human Rights in Geneva, 9-10 February, 2004.

Paul, Dinesh and Shanta Gopalakrishnan (2003), "Impact of training on knowledge regarding modes of transmission and prevention of sexually transmitted infections including HIV/ AIDS of functionaries of non-governmental organizations", *Indian Journal of Community Medicine*, 28(4), pp. 161–64.

Phoolcharoen, Wiput (1998), 'HIV/AIDS Prevention in Thailand: Success and Challenges', *Science*, 280(5371), 1873-74.

Putzel, James (2004), "Governance and AIDS in Africa: Assessing the International Community's Multisectoral Approach" Paper presented at the annual meeting of the American Political Science Association, Hilton Chicago and the Palmer House Hilton, Chicago.

Rajasekhar, D. (2000), "NGOs in India: Opportunities and Challenges", *Journal of Rural Development,* Vol. 19(2), pp. 249-275.

Raj, P. (2002), *Globalisation and Human Rights*, PUCL Bulletin, July 2000.
http://www.pucl.org/index.htm

Rao, K.S., R.D. Pilli and B.R.Rao (1991), "Awareness of AIDS/ HIV among Voluntary Organisations in Andhra Pradesh", *Indian Journal of Sexual Transmission of Disease,* 1006(17): 19-21.

Reuters (2001), "Indian Firm Offers AIDS Cocktail for $ 1 a day", *Reuters,* February 9, 2001.

Roy, C.M. and Cain R. (2001), "The involvement of people living with HIV/AIDS in community-based Organizations: contributions and constraints", *AIDS Care*, Vol. 13, No. 4, pp. 421-432

Salamon, L. M. (1994), "The Rise of the Nonprofit Sector" *Foreign Affairs, 73*, 109-116.

Salunka, S.R. et al. (1998), "HIV/AIDS in India: A Country Responds to a Challenge", *AIDS*, 12 (Suppl. B): S27-S31.

Sarkar, A. (2001), "Development through NGOs in Barak Valley: A Critical Analysis", *Social Action*, Vol. 51, Jan-March, pp. 61-73.

Seckinelgin, H. (2005), "A Global Disease and Its Governance: HIV/AIDS in Sub-Saharan Africa and the Agency of NGOs.", *Global Governance*, Boulder: Jul-Sep 2005, Vol. 11, Issue 3.

Sen, S. et al (1993), "AIDS in Multi-Transfused Children with Thalassemia" *Indian Paediatry*, 30: 455-60.

Sengupta, B. et al (1992), "Serosurveillance of Transmissible Hepatitis B and C Virus in Asymptomatic HIV Infection in Haemophilics", *IJMR*, 96: 256-58.

Sheth, D.L. and Harsh Shethi (1991), "The NGO Sector in India: Historical Context and Current Discourse", *Voluntas*, 2(2).

Singh, Y.N. et al (1991), "HIV Infection in Asian Indian Patients with Haemophilia and those who had Multiple Transfusions", *IJMR*, 93: 12-14.

Srivastava, S.P. (1999), "Nature of Voluntary Action in India Today: A Critique", *Social Action*, January-March, 1999, pp. 1-14.

Stover J, et al. (2006), "The Global Impact of Scaling Up HIV/AIDS Prevention Programs in Low- and Middle-Income Countries", *Science,* 10 March 2006: Vol. 311. no. 5766, pp. 1474 – 1476.

Tellis, W. (1997), "Introduction to Case Study", *The Qualitative Report*, 3(2).

The International HIV/AIDS Alliance (2002), "Participation and empowerment in HIV/AIDS programming". http://www.hivpolicy.org/bib/HPP000597[1].htm

Tikku, Nirmal (2004), "NGOs in three north Indian states: Evaluation of NGOs working in the areas of nutritional and health status of women and children", *Social Change: Issues and Perspectives*, 34(3), pp. 34–52.

Unnikrishna, S.S., K. Abhayambika, R. Verghese, M. Leghori & Sarojini (1993), "Clinical presentation of AIDS – a Kerala experience", *Journal of Associate Physicians of India*, 41 (1): 38-40.

Varma, Manish (2001), "Reproductive and sexual health of adolescents: An NGO experience", *Health for the Millions*, 27(3), pp. 42–44.

Vishnu and H. Sudarshan (2003), "Public sector-voluntary organisation partnership for primary healthcare services: The experience of Karuna Trust and Vivekananda Foundation", *Health for the Millions*, 29(4 & 5), pp. 52–57.

WBIDC (2006), "Promotion of West Bengal as an Investment Destination". http://www.wbidc.com/index.htm

WEBINDIA123.COM (2000), "Indian States and Union Territories". http://www.webindia123.com/states/index.htm

Washington Post (2008), "Politics and Policy- President Bush Signs PEPFAR Reauthorization Bill", *Washington Post*, 31 July 2008. http://proquest.umi.com/pqdweb?index=1&did=884766741

Williams, B. and Campbell, C. (1999), "Community mobilization as an HIV prevention strategy: challenges and obstacles (South Africa)", *Sexual Health Exchange*, 1999 ;(2):4-6. http://www.popline.org/docs/1315/147138.html

Books

Allan, J. (2003), 'Theorising Crotical Social Work'. In June Allan, Bob Pease and Linda Briskman (eds.) *Critical Social Work – An Introduction to Theories and Practices*, Rawat Publications: New Delhi.

Alston, M. and Bowles, W. (2003), *Research for Social Workers– An Introduction to Methods*, Rawat Publications: Delhi.

Ariss, R.M. (1997), *Against Death – The Practice of Living with AIDS*, Gordon & Breach Publishers: Amsterdam.

Bagasao, T.M.P. (1998), 'Moving forward through community response: Lessons learned from HIV prevention in Asia and the Pacific'. In S. Gruskin, J. Mann and D. Tarantola (eds.) *Health and Human Rights*, Harvard School of Public Health: Boston, pp. 8-19.

Barnett, A. and Whiteside (2002), *AIDS in the Twenty-First Century: Disease and Globalization*, Palgrave-Macmillan: New York.

Barquet, N. and Domingo, P. (1997), "Smallpox: The Triumph over the Most Terrible of the Ministers of Death," in *Annals of Internal Medicine*, October 15, 1997, pp 636-38.

Baru, R. (1998), *Private Health Care in India: Social Characteristics and Trends*, Sage: New Delhi, pp 74-80.

Berg, B.L. (1995), *Qualitative Research Methods for the Social Sciences*, Allyn and Bacon: Boston.

Berman, P. and Dave, P. (1994), 'Experiences in paying for Health Care in India's Voluntary Sector'. In S. Pachauri (ed.) *Reaching India's Poor – Non-Governmental Approaches to Community Health*, Sage: New Delhi.

Berridge, V. and P. Strong (eds.) (1993), *AIDS and Contemporary History*, Cambridge University Press: UK.

Bhagwati, J. (2004), *In Defense of Globalisation*, Oxford University Press: New York.

Bloom, D. and Godwin, P. (eds.) (1997), *The Economics of HIV and AIDS – The Case of South and South East Asia*, Oxford University Press: New York.

Bor, R. and J. Elford (1994), *The Family and HIV*, Cassel: New York.

Bose, P.K. (ed.) (2006), *Health and Society in Bengal: A Selection from late 19th Century Bengali Periodicals*, Sage: New Delhi.

Brown, H. C. (1996), 'The Knowledge Base of Social Work'. In Antony, A. Vass (ed.) *New Directions in Social Work – Social Work Competences, Core Knowledge, Values and Skills*, Sage Publications: New Delhi.

Brown L.D. et al. (2000), 'Globalization, NGOs and Multi-Sectoral Relations'. In J. S. Nye and J. D. Donahue (eds.) *Governance in a Globalizing World*, Brookings Institution Press: Washington D. C.

Chandra, S. (2001), *Non-Government Organisations: Structure, Relevance and Function*, Kanishka: New Delhi.

Chandra, P. (2005), *NGOs in India: Role, Guidelines and Performance Appraisal*, Akansha Publishing House: New Delhi.

Charles, M. et al. (1993), 'The economic impact of AIDS on Thailand'. In D.E. Bloom and J.V. Lyons (eds.) *Economic Implication of AIDS in Asia*, pp. 7-34, UNDP: New Delhi.

Chatterjee and Sehgal (2004), 'HIV/AIDS Awareness and Control: The Role of Non-Governmental Organisations in the Country'. In S. Panda, A. Chatterjee and A. S. Abdul-Quader (eds) *Living with AIDS Virus: The Epidemic and the Response in India*, Sage: Delhi.

D'Adesky, AC (2004), *Moving Mountains: The Race to Treat Global AIDS*, Verso: London.

Dantwala, Sethi & Visaria (1995), *Social Change through Voluntary Action*, Sage: New Delhi.

D'Cruz, P. (2004), *Family Care in HIV/AIDS: Exploring Lived Experience*, Sage: New Delhi.

DeJong, Jocelyn (2002), *A Question of Scale: Expanding NGO Impact in HIV/AIDS*, ITDG Publishing: London, UK.

Denzin, N.K. and Lincoln, Y.S. (eds.) (1994), *Handbook of Qualitative Research*, Sage Publications: Thousand Oaks, CA.

Dharmarajan, S. (2001), *NGOs As Prime Movers – Sectoral Action for Social Development*, Kanishka: New Delhi.

Diamond, Jared (1998), *Guns, Germs and Steel: A short history of everybody for the last 13,000 years*, Vintage House: London.

Dicken, P. (1998), *Global Shift: Transforming the World Economy*, Paul Chapman: London, p.93.

DiClemente, Ralph J. (2000), 'Looking Forward: Future Directions for HIV Prevention Research'. In Peterson and DiClemente (eds.) *Handbook of HIV Prevention*, Kluwer Academic/Plenum Publishers: New York.

Dixit, A.P. (2005), *Global HIV/AIDS Trends*, Vista: New Delhi.

Duggal, R., Gupta, M. and Jesani, A. (1986), *NGOs in Rural Health Care*, FRCH: Mumbai.

Dutta, Suresh. (ed.), (1998), *AIDS Prevention and Control*, Anmol Publications: Delhi.

Encyclopedia of Britannica (2003), *AIDS* in Encyclopedia of Britannica Online, 12 April 2003. http://search.cb.com/eb/article?en=4225

Fisher, Julie. (1993), *The Road From Rio: Sustainable Development and the Nongovernmental Movement in the Third World*, Praeger Publications: Westport.

Fisher, Julie. (2003), *Non Governments: NGOs and the Political Development of the Third World*, Rawat: New Delhi.

Fowler, A. (1997), *Striking a Balance: A Guide to Enhancing the Effectiveness of Non-Governmental Organisations in International Development*, Earthscan: London, pp. 43-68.

Friedman, T. (1999), *The Lexus and the Oliver Tree: Understanding Globalisation*, Farrar Straus Giroux, pp. 7-8.

Gangrade, K.D. (1987), 'Development of Voluntary Action' in *Encyclopaedia of Social Work*, Ministry of Welfare, Government of India, New Delhi.

George, V & Robert M Page (eds.) (2004), *Global Social Problems*, Polity Press: Cambridge.

Gershman, J. and Irwin, A. (2000), 'Getting a Grip on the Global Economy'. In Jim Yong Kim, J.V. Millen, A. Irwin and J. Gershman (eds.) *Dying for Growth: Global Inequality and the Health of the Poor*, Common Courage Press: Maine.

Ghosh, S. (1994), 'Health Delivery Strategies: Lessons from the NGO Experience'. In S. Pacauri (ed.) *Reaching India's Poor-Non-governmental Approaches to Community Health*, Sage: New Delhi.

Giddens, A. (1984), *The Constitution of Society: An Outline of the Theory of Structuration*, Polity Press: Cambridge, p. 9.

Goode, William. J., Hatt, Paul. K. (1981), *Methods of Social Research*, McGraw Hill Book: Singapore.

Gordenker, L and Weiss, T.G. (1996), 'Pluralizing Global Governance: Analytical Approaches and Dimensions'. In Gordenker and Weiss (eds.) *The UN and Global Governance*, Lynne Rienner: Boulder, p. 17.

Green, A. and Matthias, A. (1997), *Non-government Organisations and Health in Developing Countries*, MacMillan Press: London.

Grindle, Merilee S. (2000), 'Ready or Not: The Developing World and Globalization'. In J. S. Nye and John D. Donahue (eds.) *Governance in a Globalizing World*, Brookings Institution Press: Washington.

Gupta, R.K. (2007), *Changing Role of Voluntary Organisation*, Sumit Enterprises: New Delhi.

Hajnal, P.I. (ed.) (2002), *Civil Society in the Information Age*, Ashgate: Burlington.

Harris, P.G. & P.D. Siplon (eds.) (2008), *The Global Politics of AIDS*, Viva Books: New Delhi.

Haslegrave, M. (1988), 'Resource guide to NGOs concerned with AIDS in Africa based in UK'. In *AIDS in Africa: The Social and Policy Impact*, Meller Press: Lewiston, New York.

Held, D. and others (1999), *Global Transformations: Politics, Economics and Culture*, Stanford University Press: Stanford, pp. 21-22.

Huddart, J. & J.V. Lyons (eds.) (1992), *NGO Responses to HIV/ AIDS in Asia: Case Studies*, UNDP: New Delhi.

Irwin A, J. Millen and D. Fallows (2003), *Global AIDS: Myths and Facts- Tools for Fighting the AIDS Pandemic*, South End Press: Cambridge, MA.

Jain, R.B. (1997), 'NGOs in India: Their Role, Influence and Problems'. In Noorjahan Bava (ed.) *Non-Governmental Organizations in Development: Theory and Practice*, Kanishka Publishers: New Delhi.

Jayal, N.G. (2007), 'The Role of Civil Society'. In S. Ganguly, L. Diamond & M. Plattner (eds.) *The State of India's Democracy*, John Hopkins University Press: Baltimore.

Kapoor, A.K. & Singh, D. (1997), *Rural Development through NGOs*, Rawat: New Delhi.

Kar, Samit (2001), *West Bengal – Beyond the Millennium,* Directed Initiative: Kolkata.

Katana, Milly (2001), 'NAP+, The People's Own Voice'. In *Voices from Africa* No. 10, UN-NGLS: NY.

Kennedy, Paul, D. Messner and Franz Nuscheler (eds.) (2002), *Global Trends and Global Governance*, Pluto Press: London.

Keohane, R.O. and Nye, J.S. (2000), *Power and Interdependence: World Politics in Transition,* 3rd ed., Addision-Wesley.

Kitching, G (2001), *Seeking Social Justice Through Globalization: Escaping a National Perspective*, The Pennsylvania State University Press: Pennsylvania.

Korten, David (1990), *Getting to the 21st Century: Voluntary Action and the Global Agenda*, Kumarian Press: West Hartford, CT.

Lawani, B.T. (1999), *Non-Government Organisations in Development*, Rawat: New Delhi.

Lawni, B. T. and Subhedar, I. (2006), *Social Work Perspectives*, Om Publications: Delhi.

Lee, K. (2003), *Globalization and Health: An Introduction*, Palgrave Macmillan: New York.

Malayalam Manorama (2002), *Manorama Year Book (Bengali Version) 2002,* Kottayam.

Malayalam Manorama (2008), *Manorama Year Book (Bengali Version) 2008,* Kottayam.

M. Payne (2007), *What is Professional Social Work*, Rawat Publications: Delhi.

Marshall, C. and Rossman, G. B. (2006), *Designing Qualitative Research,* Sage Publications: New Delhi.

Mayoux, L. (2006), 'Quantitative, Qualitative or Participatory? Which Methods, for What and When?'. In Vandana Desai and Robert Potter (eds.) *Doing Development Research*, Sage Publications: New Delhi.

M'Boa Leiliane, Aristide Kacou, Mariette Wandandi, Samuel Lijalem Hassan, Victor Kamanga, Dora Ofobrukweta, Regina Clement Akpan, Anne Fiedler and Esther Guzha (2001), 'NGO and Community Responses to HIV/AIDS'. In *Voices from Africa* No. 10, UN-NGLS: NY.

McNeill, W.H. (1977), *Plagues and Peoples,* Basil Blackwell: Oxford.

Mehta, S. and S.K. Sodhi (2004), *Understanding AIDS – Myths, Efforts and Achievements,* A.P.H. Publishing Corporation: Delhi.

Mercer, C. (2006), 'Working with Partners: NGOs and CBOs'. In Vandana Desai and Robert Potter (eds.) *Doing Development Research,* Sage Publications, New Delhi.

Mishra, S. (2000), *Voluntary Action in Health and Population – The Dynamics of Social Transition,* Sage: New Delhi.

Moreau, M.J., et al. (1993), *Empowerment II: Snapshots of the Structural Approach in Action,* Carleton University: Ottawa.

Moses Chingono (2001), 'AIDS Education and Prevention in Zimbabwe's Transport sector'. In *Voices from Africa* No. 10, UN-NGLS: NY.

Mullaly, B. (1997), *Structural Social Work Practice: Ideology, Theory, and Practice,* Oxford University Press: Toronto.

Nadkarni, V., Rego, A. & Vasundhara, D. (2003), 'HIV/AIDS in India: An Annotated Bibliography of Selected Studies (1990-2000)' in *The Gender and Reproductive Health Research Initiative Mapping- A Decade of Reproductive Health Research in India,* CREA: New Delhi.

Narain, J.P. (ed.) (2004), *AIDS in Asia: The Challenge Ahead,* Sage: New Delhi.

Nath, Lalit M. (2004), *HIV/AIDS in India: Some Issues,* VHAI: New Delhi.

Nye, J.S. (1990), *Bound to Lead: The Changing Nature of American Power,* Basic Books: NY, pp. 31-32.

Nye, J.S. and J. D. Donahue (eds.) (2000), *Governance in a Globalizing World,* Brookings Institution Press: Washington D.C.

Osmani, S. R. (2005), 'An Essay on the Human Rights Approach to Development'. In A. Sengupta (ed.) *Reflections on the Right to Development,* Sage Publications: New Delhi.

Pachauri, S. (1994), *Reaching India's Poor – Non-Governmental Approaches to Community Health*, Sage: New Delhi.

Panda, S., A. Chatterjee & A.S.Abdul-Quader (eds.) (2002), *Living with the AIDS Virus: The Epidemic and the Response in India*, Sage: New Delhi.

Patnaik, P. (1999), 'The Political Economy of Structural Adjustment: A Note'. In Mohan Rao (ed.) *Disinvesting in Health: The World Bank's Prescriptions for Health*, Sage: New Delhi.

Pawar, S.N., et al. (eds.) (2004), *NGOs and Development: The Indian Scenario*, Rawat Publications: New Delhi.

Payne, M. (1997), *Modern Social Work Theory*, Lyceum Books Inc: Chicago.

Perlas, Nicanor (2000), *Shaping Globalisation: Civil Society, Cultural Power and Threefolding*, Center for Alternative Development Initiatives (CADI) & Globenet3: New York.

Poku, Nana K., A. Whiteside & B. Sandkjaer (eds.) (2007), *AIDS and Governance*, Ashgate: Burlington.

Pruthi, R.K. (2006), *NGOs in the New Millennium*, SAAD Publications: Delhi.

Raghunath, D. & C. Durga Rao (eds.) (2007), *Research Issues in HIV/AIDS*, Tata-McGraw-Hill: Mumbai.

Rajasekhar, D. (ed.) (1999), *Decentralized Government and NGOs: Issues, Strategies and Ways Forward*, Concept Publishing Company: New Delhi.

Ramachandran, P. (2002), *Survey Research and Statistics for Health Workers: A Primer*, TISS: Mumbai.

Rao, D.B. (2000), *HIV/AIDS – Issues and Challenges*, DPH: New Delhi.

SAATHII (2003), *SAATHII Red Ribbon Pages: A Directory of HIV/AIDS Services in India*, SAATHII: India.

Salamon, Lester M. (1995), *The International Guide to Non-profit law*, Wiley: New York.

Sarkar, A. (2005), *NGOs – The New Lexicon of Health Care*, Concept Publishing Company: New Delhi.

Satpathy, R.C. (2003), 'AIDS Control: Indian Perspective'. In Satpathy, R.C. (ed.) *Encyclopedia of AIDS*, Vol.-3, pp 247-284.

Sawadogo, Marie Rose (2001), 'Private and Community-based HIV/AIDS Approaches in Burkina Faso'. In *Voices from Africa* No. 10, UN-NGLS: NY.

Schoepf, Schoepf, and Millen (1992), 'Theoretical Therapies, Remote Remedies'. In Steven Feierman and John M. Janzen (eds.) *The Social Basis of Health and Healing in Africa*, University of California Press: California.

Sethi, G. (1999), 'Government Response to HIV/AIDS'. In S. Pachauri (ed.) *Implementing a Reproductive Health Agenda in India: A Beginning*, Population Council: New Delhi.

Shaukat, M. and Panakadan, S. (2004), 'HIV/AIDS in India: Problems and Response'. In J.P.Narain (ed.) *AIDS in ASIA – The Challenges Ahead*, Sage Publications: New Delhi, pp. 158-170.

Sheth, D.L. and Sethi, H. (1996), 'The NGO Sector in India: Historical Context and Current Discourse, *Development Policy and Administration*, Sage: New Delhi, pp 281-301.

Sinha, S. (1995), *AIDS Awareness*, Anmol Publications: New Delhi.

Smith, J., Chatfield, C., & Pagnucco, R. (eds.) (1997), *Transnational Social Movements and Global Politics: Solidarity beyond the State*, Syracuse University Press: New York.

Smith, R.A. (ed.) (2002), *Encyclopedia of AIDS*, Pentagon Press: Delhi.

Stake, R.E. (1995), *The Art of Case Study Research*, Sage Publications: New Delhi.

Sur, A.K. (1992), *History and Culture of Bengal*, Best Books: Kolkata.

Tandon, R. (1994), 'Where are the people? Community Participation in Health'. In Pacauri (ed.) *Reaching India's Poor – Non-Governmental Approaches to Community Health*, Sage: New Delhi.

The Times (1995), *Atlas of World History* (4th Edition), Lomdarda, Milan.

Thomas, G. (1995), *AIDS and Family Education*, Rawat: New Delhi.

Thomas, G., N. P. Sinha & Thomas, K.J. (1997), *AIDS, Social Work and Law*, Rawat: New Delhi.

Thomas, G. (1997), *Prevention of AIDS – in Search of Answers*, SHIPRA Publications: Delhi.

UNESCO (2001), 'Field Work: Building Local Response' in *A Cultural Approach to HIV/AIDS Prevention and Care.*

http://unesdoc.unesco.org/images/0012/001255/125586e.pdf

UN Population Division (2001), *World Population Prospects: The 2000 Revision,* UN Population Division: New York.

Verma, R.K., Asha. A. Bhende & P. Mane (1999), 'NGO Response to HIV/AIDS: A Focus on Women'. In S. Pachauri (ed.) *Implementing a Reproductive Health Agenda in India: A Beginning,* Population Council: New Delhi.

Veeraraghavan, V. and S. Sungh (1999), *HIV & AIDS – An Interdisciplinary Approach*, Mosaic Books: New Delhi.

Voluntary Health Association of India (2001), *Community Action on HIV for Indian NGOs*, VHAI: New Delhi.

Went, R. (2000), *Globalization: Neoliberal Challenge, Radical Response*, Pluto Press: London.

Weiss, Lawrence D. (1997), *Private Medicine and Public Health: Profit, Politics, and Prejudice in the American Health Care Enterprise*, Westview Press: Boulder.

Wiarda, H.J. (2003), *CIVIL SOCIETY-The American Model and Third Word Development*, Westview Press: Boulder.

Williams Brian, Eleanor Gouws, Janet Frohlich, Catherine Campbell and Catherine MacPhail (2001), 'Lessons From the Front: NGOs and the Fight Against HIV/AIDS in South Africa'. In *Voices from Africa* No. 10, UN-NGLS: NY.

Reports

Bhoruka Public Welfare Trust (2006), *Annual Report 2005-2006*, BPWT, Kolkata.

Bhoruka Public Welfare Trust (2007), *Annual Report 2006-2007*, BPWT, Kolkata.

Clark, J. (2003), "Globalisation and Rural Development: Limits and Possibilities" in *Asian NGO Leadership Amidst Globalisation: A Documentation of the Asian Rural NGO Leaders'* Dialogue, October 27-31, 2003, Cyberjeya, Malaysia, Asia DHRRA: Quezon.

David Wilkinson and team (2000), *An Evaluation of the Ministry of Health/NGO Home care Programme for People with HIV/AIDS in Cambodia.* www.aidsallaince.org

Dommen, C. (2001), Background Note of the Workshop on "*The impact of globalisation on the full enjoyment of economic, social and cultural rights and the right to development*" held at Kuala Lumpur, Malaysia, 8-10 May 2001.

Durbar Mahila Samannaya Committee (2007), *Annual Report 2006-2007*, DMSC: Kolkata.

Durbar Mahila Samannaya Committee (2007), *Fifteen Years of Sex Workers' Struggle for a Better World*, DMSC: Kolkata.

Durbar Mahila Samannaya Committee 1997), *The "Fallen" Learn to Rise: The Social Impact of STD-HIV Intervention Programme*, DMSC: Kolkata.

GFATM (2003), *Report of Global Fund to Fight AIDS, T.B. and Malaria, 2003.* www.globalfundatm.org

GFATM (2007), Global Fund to Fight AIDS, T.B. and Malaria, *Press Release*, 27th September 2007. www.theglobalfund.org

Government of India (1981), *Sixth Five-Year Plan*, Planning Commission: New Delhi.

Government of India (1985), *Seventh Five-Year Plan*, Planning Commission: New Delhi.

Government of India (1992), *Eighth Five-Year Plan*, Planning Commission: New Delhi.

Government of India (2001), *India 2001- A Reference Annual*, Ministry of Information and Broadcasting: New Delhi.

Government of India (2001), *Census of India 2001.*

Government of India (2005), *National Rural Health Mission (2007-2012) - Mission Document*, New Delhi.

Human Development Research Institute (2007), *Annual Report 2006-2007*, HDRI, Kolkata.

Horizons (2002), *Greater involvement of PLHA in NGO service delivery: findings form a four-country study.*

http://popcouncil.org/horizons/ressum/plhabf/plhabf_impact.html

ILO (2003), *Socio-Economic Impact of HIV/AIDS on people living with HIV/AIDS and their Families*, ILO Regional Office, New Delhi.

Manas Bangla (2007), *Annual Report 2006-2007*, Manas Bangla, Kolkata.

NACO (1999a), *The Scheme for Prevention and Control of AIDS (Phase-II)*, pp. 2-12, Ministry of Health and Family Welfare, Govt. of India: New Delhi.

NACO (1995), *AIDS Education in School: A Training Package*, Ministry of Health and Family Welfare, Govt. of India: New Delhi.

NACO (1999b), *The Status of HIV/AIDS*, Ministry of Health and Family Welfare, Govt. of India: New Delhi.

NACO (2001a), *National Baseline General Population Behavioural Survey*, pp 52-54, Ministry of Health and Family Welfare, New Delhi.

NACO (2001b), *The Current Status and Trends of HIV/AIDS Epidemic in India*, pp. 1-18, Ministry of Health and Family Welfare, Govt. of India: New Delhi.

NACO (2003), *TI Evaluation Report, Vol. 1& 2*, prepared by Sexual Health Resource Centre, New Delhi.

NACO (2005), *HIV/AIDS Updates*, NACO, New Delhi. www.nacoonline.org

NACO/HSS (2006), *HIV Sentinel Surveillance Report,* NACO, New Delhi.

NACO/BSS (2006), *Behavioural Surveillance Survey Report*, NACO, New Delhi.

NACO (2007), *UNGASS Country Progress report: India*, NACO, New Delhi.

Office of the Registrar General (2001), *Census of India 2001*, Directorate of Census Operations, West Bengal, 2001. http://www.wbcensus.gov.in

Sankarnarayanan, G. & Muraleedharan, V.R. (2003), *AIDS, Youth and NGOs in Tamil Nadu: An Overview*, Foundation for Sustainable Development (India), Indian Institute of Technology, Madras; Chennai.

Society for Community Intervention and Research (2006), *Annual Report 2005-2006*, SCIR, Kolkata.

Society for Community Intervention and Research (2007), *Annual Report 2006-2007*, SCIR, Kolkata.

Society for Positive Atmosphere and Related Support to HIV/AIDS (2007), *Status Report 2007*, SPARSHA, Kolkata.

Tata Energy Research Institute (2002), *TERI Energy Data Directory and Year Book 2000-2001*, New Delhi.

Tata Energy Research Institute (2002), *TERI Energy Data Directory and Year Book 2005-2006*, New Delhi.

UNAIDS/WHO (2002), *AIDS Epidemic Update*, December 2002, Geneva. http://www.unaids.org

UNAIDS (2002), *Report on the Global HIV/AIDS Epidemic*, Geneva. http://www.unaids.org

UNAIDS (2004), *Report on the Global HIV/AIDS epidemic-July 2004*, Geneva. http://

www.globalizationandhealth.com

UNAIDS (2005), "*A scaled-up response to AIDS in Asia and the Pacific*".

http://www.hivpolicy.org/bib/HPP000473.htm

UNAIDS (2007), *Financial Resources Required to Achieve Universal Access to HIV Prevention, Treatment, Care and Support*.

http://data.unaids.org/pub/Report/2008/20080801_jc1509_universal_access_en.pdf

UNAIDS (2008), *Report on the Global AIDS Epidemic 2008*, Geneva. http://www.unaids.org

UNDP (1992), *Human Development Report, 1992*, Oxford University Press: New York.

UNDP (1997), *Human Development Report, 1997*. Oxford University Press: New York.

WBSAP&CS (2007), *Annual Report 2006-07*. http://www.wbhealth.gov.in

WBSAP&CS (2006), *Sentinel Surveillance Survey: West Bengal*, West Bengal State AIDS Prevention & Control Society, Kolkata.

WHO (1997), *AIDS: No time for complacency*, WHO Regional Office for South-East Asia: New Delhi. www.who.int/HIV_AIDS/first.html

WHO (2000), *WHO Policy Perspectives on Medicines, Globalisation, Trips and Access to Pharmaceuticals, 2000*, WHO: Geneva.

WHO (2001), *Report of the Commission in Macroeconomics and Health*, Jeffry Sachs (ed.), WHO: Geneva.

WHO (2003), *Global Health Sector Strategy for HIV/AIDS 2003-2007: Providing a Framework for Partnership and Action.* www.who.int/hiv/en

WHO (2003), *HIV/AIDS in Asia and The Pacific Region*, WHO/SEARO: New Delhi. www.who.int/HIV_AIDS/first.html

WHO/SEARO (2001), *Beyond 2000: Responding to HIV/AIDS in the new Millennium*, Heidi, J., Larson & J.P. Narain, WHO/SEARO: New Delhi.

WHO/SEARO (2003), *HIV/AIDS Programme Report*, WHO/SEARO, New Delhi. www.who.int/HIV_AIDS/first.html

World Bank (1987), *Operational Manual Statement: Collaboration with NGOs*, No. 5(30), p. 1.

World Bank (2000), *World Development Report 1999/2000: Entering the 21st Century*. Oxford University Press, New York.

WTO (2001), WTO/WHO Secretariat's Workshop on *Affordable Drugs*, 2001. www.wto.org/english/tratop_e/trips_e/tn_hosbjor_e.htm

Unpublished Documents

Baru, R. (1987), 'Factors Influencing Variations in Health Services – A Study of Selected Districts of Andhra Pradesh', M.Phil. Dissertation, Centre for Social Medicine and Community Health, School of Social Sciences, Jawaharlal Nehru University, New Delhi.

Bhattacharjee, S. (1996), 'NGO Approaches to Health and Development in India: Strategies and Sustainability', M.A. Dissertation, Prins Leopold Instuut Voor Tropische Geneeskunde: Belgium.

Pattanaik, S. (1988), 'Voluntarism and Development – A Social Science Focus on Health', M.Phil. Dissertation, Centre for Social Medicine and Community Health, School of Social Science, JNU, New Delhi.

Index

■■■